COOL IT

The Skeptical Environmentalist's Guide
to Global Warming

Bjørn Lomborg

To the Future

Copyright © 2007 Bjørn Lomborg

First published in 2007 by:

Marshall Cavendish Limited
Fifth Floor
32–38 Saffron Hill
London EC1N 8FH
United Kingdom
T: +44 (0)20 7421 8120
F: +44 (0)20 7421 8121
E: sales@marshallcavendish.co.uk
Online bookstore: www.marshallcavendish.co.uk

and

Cyan Communications Limited
Fifth Floor
32–38 Saffron Hill
London EC1N 8FH
United Kingdom
T: +44 (0)20 7421 8145
F: +44 (0)20 7421 8146
E: sales@cyanbooks.com
www.cyanbooks.com

The right of Bjørn Lomborg to be identified as the author
of this work has been asserted by him in accordance with the
Copyright, Designs and Patents Act 1988.

A CIP record for this book is available from the British Library

ISBN 978-0-462-09912-5

Typeset by Phoenix Photosetting, Chatham, Kent

Printed and bound in Great Britain by
Mackays of Chatham Limited, Chatham, Kent

CONTENTS

LIST OF FIGURES

LIST OF TABLES

PREFACE

Global warming has been portrayed recently as the greatest crisis in the history of civilization. As of this writing, stories on it occupy the front pages of *Time* and *Newsweek* and are featured prominently in countless media around the world. In the face of this level of unmitigated despair, it is perhaps surprising – and will by many be seen as inappropriate – to write a book that is basically optimistic about humanity's prospects.

That humanity has caused a substantial rise in atmospheric CO_2 levels over the past centuries, thereby contributing to global warming, is beyond debate. What is debatable, however, is whether hysteria and headlong spending on extravagant CO_2-cutting programs at an unprecedented price is the only possible response. Such a course is especially debatable in a world where billions of people live in poverty, where millions die of curable diseases, and where these lives could be saved, societies strengthened, and environments improved at a fraction of the cost.

Global warming is a complex subject. No one – not Al Gore, not the world's leading scientists, and least of all myself – claims to have all the knowledge and all the solutions. But we have to act on the best available data from both the natural and the social sciences. The title of this book has two meanings: the first and obvious one is that we have to set our minds and resources toward the most effective way to tackle long-term global warming. But the second refers to the current nature of the debate. At present, anyone who does not support the most radical solutions to global warming is deemed an outcast and is called irresponsible and is seen as possibly an evil puppet of the oil lobby. It is my contention that this is not the best way to frame a debate on so crucial an issue. I believe most participants in the debate have good and honorable intentions – we all want to work toward a better world. But to do so, we need to cool the rhetoric, allowing us to have a measured discussion about the best ways forward. Being smart about our future is the reason we have done so well in the past. We should not abandon our smarts now.

If we manage to stay cool, we will likely leave the twenty-first century with societies much stronger, without rampant death, suffering, and loss, and with nations much richer, with unimaginable opportunity in a cleaner, healthy environment.

ACKNOWLEDGMENTS

It has been a great privilege to be inspired by and to discuss, debate and challenge the issues around global warming with the many people I have met and whose work I have read over the years. There is no way I can thank all of them – opponents as well as proponents.

I do, however, want to extend a strong thank you to all the scientists in the field, from climate to economics, from universities and research institutes, who actually measure and model the world in so many different ways, and assemble and publish the bits and pieces of the information that are presented in this book. Without them we could have no sensible debate.

I also want to thank the many climate scientists and social scientists who have read part or all of this book, given me valuable inspiration, and clarified my thinking in numerous places. For various reasons, many did not want to be thanked. And of course, the customary caveat holds – only I am responsible for this book.

I do want to say thank you to Henrik Meyer for giving me smart and continuous feedback; to Ulrik Larsen for improving many of my metaphors; to Egil Boisen for great input and for suggesting the title *Cool It*; to Richard Tol for making many of the economic arguments work better; to Roger Pielke for many suggestions for this book throughout the time I've know him; to David Young for sharpening my arguments; to Chris Harrison for reminding me of all of the other angles; and to my mentor Jørgen Poulsen for constantly reminding me of the bigger picture. Also thanks to my great colleagues at the Copenhagen Consensus Center: Tommy Petersen, Clemen Rasmussen, Elsebeth Søndergaard, Sonja Thomsen, Tobias Bang and Maria Jakobsen.

I have been blessed with many great people at Cyan, and I want to extend my special thanks to Pom Somkabcharti who has taken the book through the entire, torturous process from manuscript to finished book. Also a great thanks to my copy-editor, Frances Brown, who actually made me write good English. And finally a grateful thanks to the talented publicity staff at Cyan, including Martin Liu, Chris Newson and Janey Burton. Also thanks to Jeff Scott, who first pushed me to write the book, and thanks to my agent, John Brockman, and his entire staff for believing in the book from day one.

This is a long and dedicated book, and I am delighted that Cyan has published it. However, if we are to make our democracies count, finding the best generational mission, it is important that the information gets spread far and wide, and for this a shorter, more quickly digestable book may be useful. Thus, I am also publishing a shorter version of *Cool It,* containing a text-based summary, with Knopf in the US. While every effort naturally has been made to ensure that all the information in the book is correct, errors will undoubtedly have crept in. I'll endeavor to post any mistakes on my website, *www.lomborg.com.*

Global warming is one of many problems facing us in the twenty-first century. I hope that this book can make us better able to fix our priorities and help the future do the best it can.

Bjørn Lomborg
Copenhagen, May 2007

POLAR BEARS: CANARIES IN
THE CAGE?

The debate encapsulated: polar bears going extinct

Countless politicians hail global warming as the preeminent issue of our day. The EU calls it "one of the most threatening issues that we are facing today."[1] Prime Minister Tony Blair sees it as "the single most important issue,"[2] a sentiment that is shared by the Conservative party[3] and two-thirds of British MPs.[4] The German Chancellor Merkel has vowed to make climate change the top priority within both the G-8 and the European Union in 2007,[5] and Italy's Romano Prodi sees climate change as the real threat to global peace.[6] While President George Bush has been reluctant to reduce America's carbon emissions it is clear that the leading presidential contenders such as John McCain and Hillary Clinton express much more concern.[7] Several coalitions of states have set up regional climate change initiatives,[8] and in California the Republican Governor Schwarzenegger has helped push through climate legislation, saying that global warming should be a top priority for the state.[9] And of course Al Gore has presented this message urgently in his lectures, as well as in the book and movie *An Inconvenient Truth*.[10]

In March 2007, while I waited to give evidence to a United States congressional hearing on climate change, I watched Gore put his case to the politicians. It was obvious to me that Gore is sincerely worried about the world's future. And he's not alone in worrying. A raft of books are telling us how we reached the "Boiling Point" and will experience a "Climate Crash," and some are even telling us we will be the "Last Generation" because "nature will take her revenge for climate change."[11] Pundits aiming to surpass each other even suggest that draconian cuts in individual economic and political freedom would be justified in order to avoid global warming causing a medieval-like impoverished and collapsed society just 40 years hence.[12]

Likewise, the media pounds us with the messages of ever worsening climate. The UK newspaper *The Independent* told us in 2006 how it was all over: the entire front page tells us how global warming has now crossed the tipping point, and how it will now be impossible to avoid "some of global warming's worst predicted effects, from destruction of ecosystems to increased hunger and water shortages for billions of people."[13] In 2006 *Time* magazine did a special report on global warming with the entire cover spelling out the scare story with repetitive austerity: "Be worried. Be *very* worried."[14] The magazine tells us the climate is crashing, both affecting us globally by playing havoc with the biosphere and affecting us individually through such health effects as heat strokes, asthma and infectious diseases. Beside the letters on the cover is a lone polar bear on a melting ice floe searching in vain for the next piece of ice to jump to. *Time* tells us that due to global warming "bears are starting to turn up drowned" and that at some point they will become extinct.[15]

We will address many of these overarching concerns later on. But it is instructive just to look at the story with the polar bears, simply because it in many ways encapsulates the problems with many of the other scares – once you take a look at the supporting data the narrative falls apart.

Al Gore shows a similar picture to *Time*'s and tells us "a new scientific study shows that, for the first time, polar bears have been drowning in significant numbers."[16] The World Wildlife Fund actually warned that polar bears might stop reproducing by 2012 and thus become functionally extinct in less than a decade.[17] In their pithy statement, "polar bears will be consigned to history, something that our grandchildren can only read about in books."[18] The UK *Independent* tells us, temperature increases "mean polar bears are wiped out in their Arctic homeland. The only place they can be seen is in a zoo."[19]

Over the past years this story has cropped up many times, based first on a World Wildlife Fund report in 2002 and later on the Arctic Climate Impact

Assessment from 2004.[20] Both relied extensively on research published in 2001 by the Polar Bear Specialist Group of the World Conservation Union.[21] (Very surprisingly, the World Conservation Union has the acronym IUCN – it is the organization charged with keeping track of the world's endangered species.)

Yet, what this group told us was that of the 20 distinct populations of polar bears – some 25,000 bears in all – one or possibly two were declining in Baffin Bay, more than half were known to be stable, and two subpopulations were actually *increasing* around the Beaufort Sea.[22] Moreover, it is reported that the global polar bear population has *increased* dramatically over the past decades from about 5,000 members in the 1960s, through regulating hunting.[23] Contrary to what you might expect and not something that was pointed out in any of the stories, the two populations in decline come from areas where it has actually been getting colder over the past 50 years, whereas the two increasing populations reside in areas where it is getting warmer.[24] Likewise, Al Gore's comment on drowning bears suggests an ongoing process getting ever worse. Actually it was a single sighting of four dead bears the day after "an abrupt windstorm" in one of the *increasing* bear populations.[25]

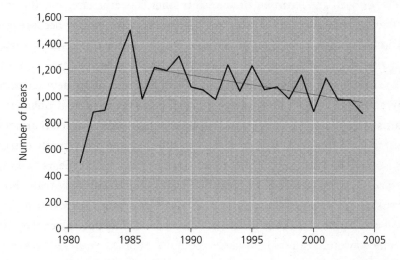

Figure 1 *Number of bears in Western Hudson Bay polar bear population 1981–2004, with decline from 1987 to 2004 depicted.*[26]

In 2006 the polar bear was listed as *vulnerable* by the IUCN, which again made the media run stories of the polar bear's impending demise.[27] However, it has been listed as *threatened* or *vulnerable* almost since the inception of the endangered lists more than 40 years ago, yet the population has increased dramatically.[28] The best-studied polar bear population lives on the western coast of Hudson Bay. It has gotten much press that it declined 17% from 1,200 in 1987 to fewer than 950 in 2004.[29] Not mentioned, though, is that the population research covers the entire 1980s. Here, the population had soared from just 500 in 1981, thus eradicating any claim of a decline.[30] Moreover, nowhere in the news coverage is it mentioned that 300–500 bears are shot each year, with 49 bears shot on average on the West coast of Hudson Bay.[31] Even if we take the story of decline at face value it means we have lost about 15 bears each year, whereas we have lost 49 bears each year to hunting.

In 2006 a polar bear biologist from the Canadian government summed up the discrepancy between data and PR: "it is just silly to predict the demise of polar bears in 25 years based on media-assisted hysteria."[32] With Canada home to two-thirds of the world's polar bears, global warming will affect them, but "really, there is no need to panic. Of the 13 populations of polar bears in Canada, 11 are stable or increasing in number. They are not going extinct, or even appear to be affected at present."

The polar bear's story holds three points. First, we hear vastly exaggerated and emotional claims that are simply not founded in data. Yes, it is likely that disappearing ice will make it harder for polar bears to continue their traditional foraging pattern, and that they more often will take up a lifestyle similar to that of brown bears, from which they evolved.[33] They may eventually decline though dramatic declines seem unlikely. But over the past 40 years the population has increased dramatically and the populations are now stable. The ones going down are in areas getting *colder*. Yet, we are told that global warming will make polar bears extinct, possibly within ten years, and that future kids will have to read about them in story books.

Second, if we care about the environment, presumably polar bears are not our only concern. While we only hear about the troubled species we also need to know that many species will do better with climate change. In general, the Arctic Climate Impact Assessment project predicts that the Arctic will experience *increasing* species richness and higher productivity.[34] It will have less polar desert and more forest.[35] The project finds that higher temperatures mean more nesting birds and more butterflies.[36] This doesn't make up for the polar bears – just as polar bears do not negate increasing nesting birds and butterflies – but we need to hear both parts of the story.

The third point is that our worry points the wrong way. We are being told that the plight of the polar bear shows "the need for stricter curbs on greenhouse gas emissions linked to global warming."[37] Even if we accept the flawed idea of starting to count bears in Hudson Bay at close to the maximum in 1987, such that we lose 15 bears each year, what can we do? If we try helping them by cutting greenhouse gasses, we can at the very best avoid 15 bears dying. We will later see that realistic options mean that we can do very much less good than that, probably only around 0.06 bears per year.[38] But 49 bears from the same population are getting shot each year, and this we could easily do something about. Thus, if we care for stable populations of polar bears, dealing first with the 49 shot polar bears might be both a smarter and a more viable strategy (and the one endorsed by the IUCN).[39] Yet it is not the one we end up hearing. In the debate on the climate, we often don't hear the proposals that will do the most good, but only the ones that involve cutting greenhouse gas emissions. This is fine if our goal is just to cut those gasses, but presumably our dominant goal is to improve human and environmental quality. Sometimes greenhouse gas cuts might be the better way to obtain this, but often it won't be. We have to keep asking ourselves if we first want to help 49 bears swiftly and easily or 0.06 bear, with high costs and slowly.

The argument in a nutshell

The argument in this book is simple.

Global warming is real and man-made. It will have a serious impact on humans and the environment toward the end of this century. Yet, it will have none of the catastrophic, end-of-civilization characteristics that are so often portrayed in the press.

Statements about the **strong, ominous and immediate consequences of global warming are often wildly exaggerated,** and this is unlikely to make for good policy.

We need smarter solutions for global warming. Dealing with global warming faces the dual problem that the climate system is a very slow one to change and that significant cuts are fairly costly. Thus, even large and very expensive CO_2 cuts made now will only make a rather small and insignificant impact far into the future. Dealing with climate change is a century-long process that will need to span generations, continents and parties. Thus, we must stop thinking about quick and expensive solutions but rather focus on low-cost, long-term research and development.

Many other issues are much more important than global warming. Today, climate change has become one of our civilization's primary concerns, and proposals to deal with it such as the Kyoto Protocol have become *causes célèbres*. However, in this book I will argue that we are wrong in making climate change our primary focus. We need to get our perspective back. There are many other and more pressing problems in the world where we can do much more good, for people who need it much more, ultimately with a much higher chance of success.

Navigating this argument will require a longer journey. We have become so accustomed to the standard story: climate change is not only real but will lead to unimaginable catastrophes while doing something about it is not only cheap but morally right, and anyone against this line of reasoning must have evil intentions. And while global warming has grabbed headlines and front pages it has relegated many of the world's other problems – that we can do so much more about – to a small mention in the C-section or caused them entirely to drop from the paper and from our minds.

Thus, we will go through the climate models and see how our use of fossil fuels is affecting the climate. But we will also see how the climate has been ever changing in our past and how it will continue to change in our future. I will talk about how we best address the problems of a climate that inevitably will change due to both natural and human causes.

But we also need to take a close look at the claims that are made on the impact of warming both today and into the future. We hear that "climate change is happening now" but this is only true in the most pedantic interpretation of that statement and certainly not with the ominous undercurrents that it is typically delivered with. As for the future weather, we often encounter scare stories that could come right out of Hollywood movies: how parts of Antarctica might slip into the ocean and raise sea levels dramatically, how we are headed for much more violent hurricanes like Katrina, how the Gulf Stream might shut down and throw Europe into the freezer, or any number of end-of-the-world scenarios. None of these scenarios carries much weight.

Yet, if there is a risk, shouldn't we act and do something? That of course depends on how much we can do and at what price. The scientific models show us that Kyoto will do very little good even a hundred years from now. The economic models show us that much of what we do under Kyoto is fairly expensive. It does not mean that there is no way of tackling the problem but it means we have to start thinking smarter and search for more efficient solutions. We will get back to what that means.

Many would say that even if there is only a small risk and we cannot do very much only at high cost we should still try. But we need to keep recalling that there are many other important problems beside climate change. Problems that we know much better, solutions that will be much cheaper, effects that would be much better understood, policies that will be much more robust.

Crucially, we need to remind ourselves that our ultimate goal is not to reduce greenhouse gasses or global warming per se but to improve the quality of life and the environment. Possibly, reducing global warming is the best way to make these quality improvements but clearly it is a question we need to ask. And as we go through the data we will see that it is quite plausibly one of the least helpful ways of serving humanity or its environment.

If this indeed turns out to be true, it poses some hard and soul-searching questions to the way we carry the environmental debate today. How did the climate change debate end up closing itself to questioning, comparing inconvenient questions with Holocaust denial? How did scare stories that are entirely separate from the scientific debate become commonplace and accepted?

I hope that this book can help us better understand global warming, be smarter about its solutions, but also regain our perpective on where most of our attention ought to be.

2

IT IS GETTING HOTTER:
THE SHORT STORY

Global warming has plenty of effects, like rising sea levels, impacts on hurricanes and agriculture, melting of glaciers, etc. We will look at these and many more in Chapter 3. But let us just start with the basics. Here we will look at just one factor – temperature.

As we call it global warming, temperature is perhaps the obvious place to start. In the words of one scholar, "heat stress is probably the most obvious thing people think of when the idea of global warming comes up."[40] Many academics argue that this is indeed the most important aspect, since heat waves are the number one killers in modern societies.[41] In Europe, the heat wave in 2003 cost 35,000 lives, whereas even hurricane Katrina in 2005 cost "only" about 1,500 lives.[42]

So let us here ask the crucial questions: what happens when temperatures increase? And what can we do?

Global warming: the basics

The reason why we're concerned about global warming is the so-called greenhouse effect. The fundamental principle is really quite simple and entirely uncontroversial.[43] Several types of gasses can reflect or trap heat, most importantly water vapour and carbon dioxide (CO_2).[44] These greenhouse gasses trap some of the heat emitted by the Earth, rather like a blanket wrapped around the globe. The basic greenhouse effect is good – if the atmosphere did not contain greenhouse gasses the average temperature on the Earth would be approximately 33°C (59°F) colder and it is unlikely that life as we know it would be able to exist.[45]

The problem is that man has increased especially the quantity of CO_2 in the atmosphere. About 80% of the extra CO_2 comes from burning oil, coal and gas whereas the other 20% comes from deforestation and other land changes in the tropics.[46] About 55% of the released CO_2 is absorbed again by the oceans, by northern forest regrowth, and generally by increased plant growth (plants use CO_2 as fertilizer),[47] but the rest is added to the atmosphere, such that the concentration of CO_2 has increased by 36% from pre-industrial times to the present day.[48] Simultaneously, natural processes slowly take CO_2 permanently out of the atmosphere.[49] (See the development of the CO_2 emissions in Figure 53, p. 170.)

You can think of CO_2 concentrations as the water level in a water container and CO_2 emissions as the water we each year pour into the container. Every year we pour in water the water level goes up, just as we every year emit CO_2 and the concentration goes up. However, since 55% of the CO_2 is absorbed by oceans, etc. we actually spill half the water outside the container. Moreover, because of the natural processes that slowly take CO_2 permanently out of the atmosphere, the container is slightly leaky, so that when we stop pouring in water every year, it will eventually return to a lower level.

The logic is that if greenhouse gasses hold on to the heat, then more greenhouse gasses like CO_2 will cause a further temperature increase. This is the man-made greenhouse effect and the reason behind global warming. All this is also fairly uncontroversial.

Without a major policy change, we will continue to burn more fossil fuel over the century.[50] In no small way this will be due to the gluttonous appetite for coal and oil from rapidly industrializing China and India. Whereas the developing world now is responsible for about 40% of the annual carbon emissions, by the end of the century it will more likely be 75%.[51]

In short, it is likely that over the century we will substantially increase CO_2 in the atmosphere, and cause the planet to warm. Let us look at what will happen when we turn up the heat.

Global warming: increasing temperatures

When talking about future climate, we obviously cannot observe the effect. Instead researchers make predictions about crucial factors, such as how much oil and coal each nation will use over the coming century. Then they put the CO_2 emissions into a model that can tell us what will happen to the temperature. Sometimes this model is hugely complex and run by a supercomputer, simulating both the Earth's atmosphere and the oceans chopped into more than a 100,000 building blocks, possibly also including sea ice, land and biological interactions.[52] These models are absolutely necessary for regional simulations. Other times the model is a much simpler, basic physical model, that just gives us the important information on global temperature increase.

In Figure 2, we have a simple, standard prediction for the coming hundred years from the medium scenario of the 2007 UN report (the Intergovernmental Panel on Climate Change, the IPCC). Here we are told that over the century global mean temperatures will increase about 2.6°C. But nobody lives at the global average. In reality, global warming will first of all make land warm faster than water (much easier to warm up a couple of meters of earth than to warm three kilometres of ocean depth). Moreover, global warming works such that it increases the *cold* temperatures much more than warm temperatures. So it increases night and winter temperatures much more than day and summer temperatures. Likewise it increases temperatures in temperate and arctic regions much more than over tropical areas.

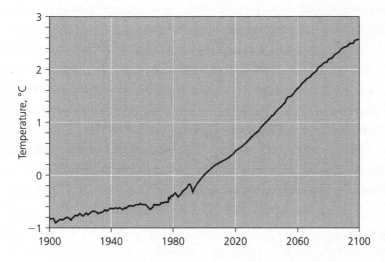

Figure 2 *Expected temperature increase from 2000 to 2100 in the business-as-usual scenario (with simulation of temperature increase from 1900 to 2000).*[53]

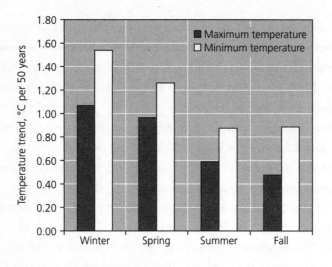

Figure 3 *Changes in maximum and minimum land temperatures in the northern hemisphere 1950–2004 across seasons.*[54]

We have actually already experienced this warming pattern in the twentieth century. Globally, minimum (night) temperatures have increased much more than maximum (day) temperatures.[55] When you look at Figure 3, you can see that over the past 50 years, day temperatures on the northern hemisphere have increased just 0.8°C whereas night temperatures have increased more than 1.1°C. This tendency has also been observed individually for the US, China, England, and northern and central Europe.[56] At the same time, more warming has taken place during the winter than during the summer – days have increased just 0.6°C in the summer but more than a full degree in winter.[57] Finally, winter temperatures have been warming the most in colder locations – actually, more than three-quarters of the winter warming in the northern hemisphere has been confined to the very cold high-pressure systems of Siberia and northwestern North America.[58]

Not surprisingly, this has meant that the US, northern and central Europe, China, Australia and New Zealand have experienced fewer frost days.[59] However, since most of the warming has happened to cold temperatures, only Australia and New Zealand have had their maximum temperature go up.[60] For the US, the maximum temperatures show no trend and for China the maximum has even declined.[61] For the Central England Temperature series, the longest temperature record in the world, going back to 1659, there has been a clear reduction in the number of cold days, but no increase in the number of hot days.[62]

But what will happen over the coming century, with temperatures rising 2.6°C? The standard story is that this will be a very unpleasant world. Whenever there is a heat wave, journalists will write the story of how this may be a glimpse of much worse things to come.[63] As one environmentalist points out, "If you don't like the current heat wave event, you're going to like it even less in the future."[64] Jacqueline McGlade, executive director of the European Environment Agency, tells us that people in northern and southern Europe, where the climate effect is expected to be greatest, will become "climate refugees," moving to the center of the continent.[65] And scientists even begin to question whether humans will be able to survive in this hotter world. Famously, the UK chief scientist, Sir David King, envisions that an ice-free "Antarctica is likely to be the world's only habitable continent by the end of this century if global warming remains unchecked."[66]

Nearly everyone discussing the future impacts of global warming use the 2003 heat wave in Europe as their prime example. In Al Gore's words: "We have already begun to see the kind of heat waves that scientists say will become much more common if global warming is not addressed. In the summer of 2003 Europe was hit by a massive heatwave that killed 35,000 people."[67]

And yes, we will see more heat waves. But talking only about heat waves means we leave out something even more important.

Heat deaths – way of the future?

The IPCC finds that the trends we have seen over the twentieth century will continue. Thus, with a global increase of 2.6°C, temperatures will increase more over land, more in the winter and most over the high northern latitudes, especially in Siberia, Canada and the Arctic.[68] In the winter time, temperatures might increase 5°C in Siberia compared to 2–3°C in Africa.[69] Likewise, there will be an increase in heat waves and a decrease in cold spells. Because of global warming's tendency to warm cold temperatures more, night temperatures will increase more than day temperatures over almost all of the planet.[70] Finally, there will be a marked decrease in frost days almost everywhere in the mid and high latitudes, which will lead to a comparable increase in the growing season length.[71]

With models it is estimated that heat events that we would only see every 20 years will become much more frequent – by the end of the century we will have such events happening every three years.[72] For cities like Chicago, home to a devastating heat wave in 1995, and Paris, they today have some five heat waves every three years. In a hundred years time, this will have increased 25–30%, to six heat waves every three years, and they will last longer.[73] This backs up the idea that we could be seeing many more heat deaths.

But cold spells will decrease just as much as heat waves increase – and they will decrease faster. In looking at so-called extreme cold-air outbreaks, the IPCC finds that these events will decline by about 85% in the northern hemisphere, and most of the reduction will already have taken place within the first 50 years.[74] Thus, in areas where there is one cold spell every three years, by the end of the century, such cold spells will only happen once every 20 years. This means fewer cold deaths.

Obviously, this puts the claim that there will be more heat deaths in perspective. Very often, we only hear about the heat deaths but not the cold deaths – and sometimes this is even repeated in the official literature, as in the US 2005 Climate Change and Human Health Impacts report, where heat is mentioned 54 times and cold just once.[75] We need to know just how many more heat deaths we can expect compared to how many fewer cold deaths.

For almost every society all over the world, there is an "optimal"or best temperature where deaths are the lowest.[76] On either side of this temperature – when it gets either colder or warmer – death rates will increase. However, *where* the optimal temperature lies is a different issue, as you can tell in Table 1. If you live in the Finnish capital Helsinki, your best temperature is about 15°C whereas in Athens you do best at 24°C. But the important point to notice is that the best temperature is often close to the mean summer temperature, so that you will only sometimes go above that temperature but very often below. In Helsinki, your best temperature of 15°C will only be exceeded on 18 days a year, whereas you will go below it a full 312 days of the year.[77] So although 248 extra people will die from it being too hot, some 1,379 people will die from it being too cold.[78]

Table 1 Annual heat and cold deaths per million aged 65–74 for various cold and warm regions in Europe.[79]

	South Finland	Netherlands	London	Baden-Württemberg	North Italy	Athens
Mean summer temperature	14.5	16.1	16.9	17.7	20.7	24.1
Optimum temperature (± 1.5°C)	14.8	18.8	20.8	20.5	18.3	24.2
Number of days warmer than optimum	46	18	5	22	89	63
Number of days colder than optimum	275	312	330	308	230	251
Annual heat deaths	248	53	40	108	325	445
Annual cold deaths	1,379	1,345	3,129	1,936	1,238	2,533

Now it may not be so surprising that cold kills in Finland, but the same holds true in Athens. Although the summer temperature here averages 24°C, so does the best temperature. So even though absolute temperatures are, of course, much higher in Athens than in Helsinki, temperatures still only run higher than the optimum temperature on 63 days a year, whereas 251 days are below the best temperature. Again, the death toll from excess heat is 445 people whereas the death toll from excess cold is 2,533. Although the above study of a large number of European cities is the most consistent large-scale study, we have similar results from Beirut, France, Japan, Shanghai and São Paulo.[80] The best temperature in São Paulo is 20°C, and for each 1°C increase researchers find a 2.6% increase in mortality, but for every 1°C decrease there is a 5.6% increase in mortality.

This tells us two things. First, that we are very adaptable creatures. We live well at both 15°C and 24°C (or at Shanghai's or Beirut's 27°C). We can adapt to both cold and heat. Such an adaptation to global warming will not be unproblematic, because we have already invested heavily in housing and infrastructure to handle the temperature of previous times. But that is why the second point is so important. It seems reasonable from the data that, within reasonable limits, global warming might actually be good for death rates.

Death in Europe

The heat wave in Europe in early August 2003 was exceptional in many ways. In France, the worst-hit country, it broke all records from the last 50 years, with maximum temperatures above 35°C and minimum temperatures at 20°C in Bordeaux, Lyons, Marseilles and Paris over 9–15 days.[81] With more than 3,500 dead in Paris, France suffered nearly 15,000 dead from the heat wave.[82] With 7,000 dead in Germany, 8,000 in Spain and Italy, and 2,000 in the UK, the total death toll ran to more than 35,000.[83] Obviously, this event has become a psychologically powerful metaphor for the frightening vision of a warmer future and our immediate need to prevent it.

The title of an – otherwise cool and balanced – academic paper says it all: "The 2003 Heat Wave in France: Dangerous Climate Change Here and Now."[84] The green group Earth Policy Institute, which first collected the total death toll, tells us that as "awareness of the scale of this tragedy spreads, it is likely to generate pressure to reduce carbon emissions. For many of the millions who suffered through these record heat waves and the relatives of the tens of thousands who died, cutting carbon emissions is becoming a pressing personal issue."[85]

In the public's mind the heat wave has been taken as a sure indicator of global warming. Several academic papers have also posited that this event was so exceptional that it could only be accounted for by way of climate change.[86] However, a recent paper has actually checked this and found that although the circumstances were unusual, equal or more unusual warm anomalies have occurred regularly since 1979.[87]

Moreover, while 35,000 dead is a terrifyingly large number, all deaths should in principle be treated with equal concern. Yet, this clearly does not seem to happen. Notice how 2,000 people died in the UK, and this produced a public outcry that is still heard. However, just recently the BBC ran a very quiet story about cold deaths.[88] It tells us that cold deaths in England and Wales for the past years have hovered around 25,000 each winter, and a small increase in 2004/5 now seems to have disappeared. It also casually mentions that the two winters of 1998–2000 saw about 47,000 cold deaths each year.[89] It goes on to discuss how the government should make more winter fuel available and how the majority of deaths are caused by strokes and heart attacks.

The fact that a single heat death episode of 35,000 from many countries can get everyone up in arms whereas the number of cold deaths at 25,000–50,000 each and every year in just a single country passes almost unnoticed indicates a lack of proportion. Of course, we want to help avoid another 2,000 dying from heat in the UK. But presumably we would want at least as much to avoid many more dying from cold.

Earth Policy Institute tells us "though heat waves rarely are given adequate attention, they claim more lives each year than floods, tornadoes, and hurricanes combined. Heat waves are a silent killer, mostly affecting the elderly, the very young, or the chronically ill."[90] It is true they are bigger killers than floods, tornadoes and hurricanes. Curiously, it is also true that

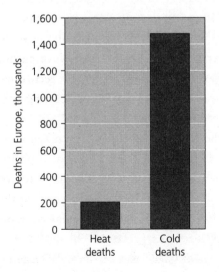

Figure 4 *Estimated heat and cold deaths in Europe per year.*[91]

most heat deaths are silent. Whereas we heard much about the 35,000 deaths, the estimates from Table 1 indicate that every year more than 200,000 people die from excess heat in Europe,[92] i.e. six times more die silent heat deaths. We will look at these deaths below.

But much more so, cold deaths are the silent deaths, and in much greater numbers. It is reasonable to estimate that each year about 1.5 million people die from excess cold in Europe.[93] This is more than seven times the total number of heat deaths.[94] Just in this millennium, Europe has lost more than 10 million people to the cold, 300 times the iconic 35,000 heat deaths from 2003. That we so easily forget these deaths and so easily embrace the exclusive worry about global warming tells us of a breakdown in our sense of proportion.

How will we cope with more heat?

When we talk about the future of heat and cold deaths where the world might have warmed some 2.6°C as in Figure 3, what matters is not first and foremost the absolute numbers but the *change* in those numbers. Of course, when cold deaths are seven times higher than heat deaths in Europe, it seems likely that while a higher temperature will increase a relatively small heat death number, it will be outweighed by a bigger decrease of a much bigger cold death number.

That is also what the analysis indicates. Let us for the moment assume – very unrealistically – that we will not adapt to the future heat. Still, for the European study the researches conclude that at least for 2°C, "Our data suggest that any increases in mortality due to increased temperatures would be outweighed by much larger short term declines in cold related mortalities."[95] For Britain it is estimated that a 2°C increase will mean 2,000 more heat deaths but 20,000 fewer cold deaths.[96]

Indeed, a paper trying to incorporate all studies on this issue (a so-called meta-study) and apply the results to a broad variety of settings both developed and developing around the world found that "global warming may cause a decrease in mortality rates, especially of cardiovascular diseases."[97]

But of course it seems very unrealistic and conservative to assume that we will not adapt throughout the twenty-first century. Several recent studies have looked at adaptation for up to 28 of the biggest, geographically diverse cities in the US.[98] In Figure 5 you see the development for Philadelphia over the past 40 years. Look at the curve for the 1960s. As the temperature gets higher, what you see is that deaths drop from 42 at –5°C down to 35 around 25°C. This is the effect of less cold. But then the effect of the heat kicks in, and the curve rises again, so that in the high 30s deaths are back up at 42. This is how the relation between temperature and death looks in most places of the world – although for Helsinki the turning point would be much lower, and for Beirut higher.

However, the astounding fact is that, as the decades progress, not only have deaths decreased overall, but especially the sensitivity to heat has declined dramatically. Whereas a temperature increase from 25 to the high 30s would have caused seven extra deaths each day in the 1960s, this effect had virtually vanished in the 1990s. The main reason for the lower general death rates is probably improved medical care and access to medical facilities. One of the main reasons for the lower heat susceptibility is likely to be increased access to air-conditioning. While it is still hard to pin down the exact effect of air-conditioning, studies estimate a reduction in heat mortality from 21% to 98%.[99]

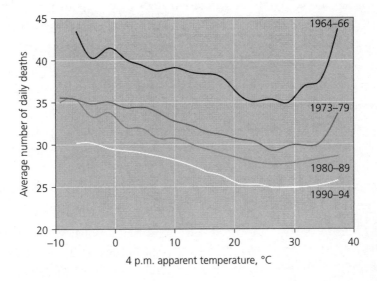

Figure 5 *Average number of deaths per day at apparent temperature for different decades (1964–66, 1973–79, 1980–89, 1990–94) for Philadelphia.*[100]

These studies seem to indicate that over time and with sufficient resources we actually learn to adapt to higher temperatures and consequently that we will experience fewer heat deaths even when temperatures rise.

But actually we have already experienced temperature rises on the scale of what we're expecting over the coming century – in many of the major cities around the world.

Heat cities

Today about half of the world's population lives in cities, and the UN estimates that 60% will live in cities by 2030.[101] As 74% of people live in cities in the developed world already, and that number will hit 80% before 2030, it seems reasonable to assume that by the end of the century the developing world will do likewise. Thus, when our 2.6°C temperature increase takes place the large majority of humanity will live in cities.

Cities are remarkable in this context, because they have already experienced large temperature increases and are thus ways for us to peek into the future and get a sense of how bad 2.6°C will be.

Why? Because bricks, concrete and asphalt, which dominate cities, absorb much more heat than vegetation does in the countryside. This is called the urban heat island.[102] The British meteorologist Luke Howard originally discovered the effect in the early 1800s in London, but as cities grow and replace ever more vegetation with high-rises and tarmac, we have seen the effects documented in cities around the world – from Tel Aviv, Baltimore and Phoenix to Guadalajara in Mexico, Barrow in Alaska, Shanghai, Seoul, Milan, Vienna and Stockholm.[103]

In Figure 6 we see the population for Tucson, Arizona, over the past century. The southwestern United States have seen some of the fastest-growing cities in the US, and Tucson has experienced a doubling of the population over the past three decades to about three-quarters of a million people. This has also led to dramatic growth in developed urban and suburban land area. The population increase matches well the temperature increase we see for Tucson, with an almost steady temperature in the first part of last century but a marked acceleration in the second part. Research indicates that since 1969 Tucson has seen a 2.6°C increase just from the

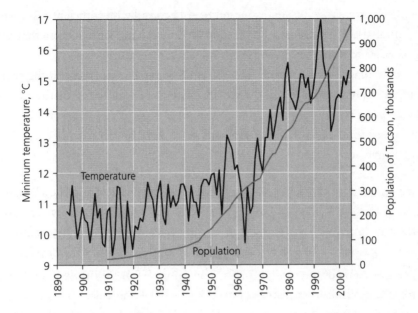

Figure 6 *Population of Tucson, Arizona, and the mean annual minimum temperature.*[104]

urban heat island.[105] And since there has also been a temperature increase in the general area, presumably from both global warming and natural variability, the average minimum temperature over the past 40 years for Tucson has increased more than 6°C.

Likewise, we have seen an increase in the urban heat island over Athens in the past 50 years. Here maximum temperatures have increased by about 2°C.[106] In downtown Los Angeles, maximum temperatures over the past century have increased by some 2.5°C and minimum temperatures by some 4°C.[107] New York has a similar night-time urban heat island of 4°C.[108]

Recently, we have been able to use satellite measurements of the direct temperatures over the entire surface of a city. When researchers looked at Houston, they realized it was a fast-growing city. From 1990 to 2000 it grew by 300,000 residents – a full one-fifth increase. Yet when they looked at the change in temperature as measured from the sky, they found an amazing result. Over a short 12 years, the night-time surface temperature increased by about 0.8°C.[109] Over a hundred-year period that would translate into almost 7°C temperature increase.

And indeed, for huge cities these are the kinds of temperature differences that are being found around the world. Asian cities are today the most rapidly growing regions of the world. Sixteen of the world's 24 mega cities (cities with more than 10 million people) will be in Asia by the year 2015.[110] Not surprisingly, this is also where we find some of the largest urban heat islands. The daytime temperature difference between the tropical cities of Bangkok and Manila and their countrysides is 7–8°C.[111] The same temperature differences are found for temperate cities like Seoul and Shanghai. If we go to the mega city of Beijing, researches have found that temperatures diverge some 10°C in the daytime and 5.5°C at night. And Tokyo with its 20 million inhabitants sees some of the most dramatic consequences of the urban heat island. While the daytime temperature of the area surrounding Tokyo in August was 28.5°C, the downtown was measured at 40+°C.[112] And this high temperature is not just affecting a small inner core of the city – the high-temperature area covers some 8,000 km^2 or the equivalent of 140 times the area of Manhattan.[113] Nights in August Tokyo only provide a slight solace, as the temperature drops to 19°C in rural areas but remains at 26.5°C in the city.

At the place where the urban heat island was first discovered, London is now also seeing a strong warming. Since the 1950s, the number of nights with intense urban heat has increased by four days each decade.[114] Today temperatures are 4–6°C higher, and during the August 2003 heat wave reached 9°C.[115] These worldwide urban temperature increases tell us at least two things.

First, many of these urban temperature increases over the past half or full century are of the same order or bigger than the 2.6°C that we expect to see over the coming full century.[116] It is likely that for many cities the temperature increases mainly from the urban heat island of the twentieth century are of a bigger scale than the temperature increases from global warming in the twenty-first century.[117] Yet the increases have not brought the cities tumbling down.

Over the past hundred years, metropolises have had to adapt to temperatures that rose faster and higher than what we will expect in this century. Their inhabitants both were poorer and had less technological ability to adapt. Yet, the higher temperatures did not produce widespread and frequent heat waves killing sizable numbers of inhabitants

This does *not* mean that the urban heat island may not have been bad for some or possibly even most cities. Although deaths have in general been declining (as we saw for Philadelphia above), they might have declined even faster without it. But it means that the doomsday predictions are sorely mistaken when they focus solely on ever more heat deaths without taking into account fewer cold deaths, and that adaptation will possibly strongly mitigate the temperature effects. If our forefathers were able to do so, it seems reasonable to assume that, being much richer and having vastly more technical prowess, we will be able to repeat their feat.

This also does *not* deny that with global warming the impact on cities will be considerably worse, because they will be hit by a double whammy – temperature increases both from CO_2 and from still-increasing urban heat islands.[118]

But this leads straight to the second point. Unlike our forefathers, who did very little or nothing about the urban heat island, we are in a good position to tackle many of its effects. Presumably our goal is to prevent part of the problems of increasing temperatures over the coming century. It is curious that we focus so much of our attention on cutting CO_2, when it is likely that we could do much more and at much lower cost to cut temperatures by addressing the urban heat island.

Studies show that very simple solutions can make a great difference. One of the two main reasons cities are hotter is that they are drier. Cities lack moist green spaces and have large, impermeable surfaces with drainage, quickly leading any water away. Thus, the sun's energy goes into heating the atmosphere instead of into the cooling evaporation of water.[119] If we plant trees and provide vegetation and water features in the urban environment, this will – apart from making a more beautiful city – dramatically cool the surroundings. For instance, air around the River Thames or within urban parks is on average 0.6°C cooler than neighbouring built-up areas.[120] If we significantly and pervasively increase moisture, models show that at noon on the third day of a fine weather spell temperatures can be decreased by as much as 8°C.[121]

The other main reason that cities are hotter is that they have a lot of black asphalt and dark, heat-absorbing structures. Although it may seem almost comically straight-forward, one of the main solutions is very simple

– paint the tarmac and buildings white.[122] Increase the general reflectivity and natural shading from buildings and you can avoid a great deal of the heat build-up. In theoretical models, changing the entire city's reflectivity could lower the heat by 10°C.[123]

Real-world political suggestions focus on "cool communities," reroofing and re-paving in lighter colors as well as planting trees. It is estimated that such a program for Los Angeles – involving planting 11 million trees, reroofing most of the 5 million homes, and painting a quarter of the roads – would have a one-time cost of about $1 billion.[124] However, it would have *annual* added benefits of lowering air-conditioning costs by about $170 million, and providing $360 million in smog-reduction benefits. Plus the added benefits of a greener LA. And perhaps most impressive, it would lower LA temperatures by about 3°C – or about the temperature increase envisioned for the rest of this century.

Cutting carbon to do good – maybe

But even though temperature rises may not be as devastating as you thought and even if there are other, cheap ways to deal with much of the temperature increase, is it not also obvious that we want to cut CO_2 emissions?

Well, it may not be as obvious as it seems. It really depends on how much good we can do, and at what cost. Let us look at what we can do.

At the moment the only real political initiative calling for carbon cuts is the so-called Kyoto Protocol, signed in Japan in 1997 under UN auspices.[125] It has been championed by many environmentalists, including Al Gore, who as vice president directed the US negotiations.[126] Here it was decided that the industrial nations should reduce their overall emissions of CO_2 in the period 2008–12 such that they would be 5.2% below their emissions in 1990.[127]

While 5.2% may not sound like much, it is relative to the level in 1990. Since emissions would otherwise have increased with growing economies, the Kyoto commitment actually means that OECD countries would have to cut their emissions compared to their "natural" emissions in 2010 by 28%.[128] For the entire industrialized world, the emission cuts would be 19.6%.[129]

Of course, many events have challenged Kyoto since 1997, most noticeably its rejection by the Bush administration in 2001. But let us first look at what the effects would have been, had Kyoto actually worked out.

The results of Kyoto depend, of course, on many choices that will be made in the future. If nobody were to make any restrictions after the first commitment period ending in 2012, it seems reasonable to expect that it would have made very little difference. But to evaluate Kyoto let us, as is customary, look at what would happen if the industrialized countries were to stick to their emission commitments from Kyoto throughout the century. Again, this baseline is not as toothless as it may sound – since CO_2 emissions from the OECD countries would otherwise have continuously increased, keeping the Kyoto promise and staying 5.2% below 1990 levels will really mean making deeper and deeper cuts, such that in 2050 the entire OECD must have cut its "natural" emissions by more than 50%.[130]

Given the centrality of Kyoto in the public discourse, especially in Europe, and how it is often being seen as one of the defining measures of discord between the US and the rest of the world,[131] it surprises most people to see how little Kyoto would actually change the future. Figure 7 shows us

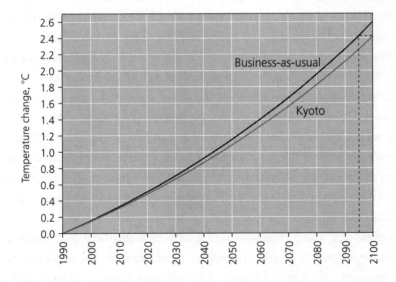

Figure 7 *The expected increase in temperature with business-as-usual and with the Kyoto restrictions extended forever. Broken line shows that the temperature for the business-as-usual scenario in 2095 is the same as the Kyoto temperature in 2100 (2.42 °C).*[132]

that temperature, instead of rising by 2.6°C by the end of the century, would reach a slightly lower 2.42°C, a drop of about 0.18°C.[133] It is worth emphasizing that this result is scientifically entirely uncontroversial, and that the data in Figure 7 are derived from work by one of IPCC's foremost modelers.

Perhaps more informative is to look at the temperature that we would have hit in 2095 – invoking Kyoto would mean that this temperature would first be reached in 2100. To put it more clearly, doing Kyoto forever essntially means postponing global warming for about five years by the end of the century.

This is why the *Washington Post* calls Kyoto a "mostly symbolic treaty."[134] *Science* magazine tells us that "climate scientists say that it will be miraculous indeed if the Kyoto pact … even temporarily slows the accumulation of warming gases in the atmosphere."[135] Jerry Mahlman of Princeton University added that "it might take another 30 Kyotos over the next century" to control warming.[136] Even its staunchest backers admit that Kyoto is only a small first step,[137] and politicians routinely tell us we need to become much more ambitious.[138]

To date, 165 countries have ratified Kyoto. But it has also been a rocky ride. First, the US rejected the treaty in 2001. This matters, since the US is the world's single biggest emitter, responsible for 21% of total emissions.[139] If we take out the US commitment in Figure 7, the temperature effect of Kyoto would be even smaller – a reduction of about 0.12°C over the coming century, or the equivalent of postponing warming for three years.[140]

With the US out, Australia also announced that it would reject the Kyoto Protocol (though at 1.5% of world emission this had less impact).[141] At the same time, a number of countries fought hard and succeeded in softening the treaty, allowing them to count extra forest growth (which will soak up CO_2) as a carbon reduction.[142]

Several other countries have had a hard time fulfilling their goals, none more than Canada, which was supposed to cut its emissions by 6%, but has seen them rise by 27%.[143] Conflicting messages about whether Canada is still in or has abandoned its Kyoto commitment have been resurfacing regularly, but most observers agree it will be extraordinarily difficult for Canada to cut its emissions sufficiently in just a few years' time.[144] Countries like Austria, Belgium, Denmark, Ireland, Italy, Portugal and Spain are off track to meet their Kyoto requirements – Spain is off by 27%.[145] Fortunately, other EU members overachieving their targets, such as Sweden, Finland and the UK, will probably make up for these countries.

Perhaps the single most important feature of the Kyoto Protocol is that it strongly favors Russia and the other former Eastern Bloc countries, the so-called transition economies. The collapse of the Soviet Union in 1991 led to a dramatic economic decline among all the transition economies and a concomitant decline in CO_2 emissions. Over the 1990s Russia's emissions dropped by one third.[146] But because the Kyoto Protocol has a base year of 1990, and the transition economies promised to make little or no reductions, they essentially have huge CO_2 allowances they do not use. Despite a healthy economic recovery, Russia is not significantly increasing its emissions, and so it is today still 32% below its allowance.[147] This excess allowance, so-called "hot air" is crucial in determining the actual effect of Kyoto.

Thus, even though the OECD countries have promised to cut their emissions by 28% from what they would otherwise have been, Russia and the other former Soviet Union members could at the same time expand their emissions by 45%.[148] A key part of the Kyoto Protocol is that Russia's allowances could be traded against the West's excess. In the original text, it is clearly stated that such trading should only be "supplemental to domestic actions"[149] but in reality it seems less and less likely that such a strict interpretation will hold.[150]

It is clear that Kyoto is not very stringent. Factoring in the immense allowances for transition economies, the original treaty asked for a 12% effective cut-back.[151] With the US out, the total restrictions actually vanished, allowing a total CO_2 *increase* of 0.7%.[152] Through the softening of the treaty by allowing forests, the total allowed increase has gone up to 3.8%.[153]

So what will happen with Kyoto? It depends on how much hot-air trading will go on. This again hinges on how much the West will allow itself to buy and how much Russia might want to drive prices up. Most analyses expect that the outcome will be very tiny, around a 1% reduction from what would otherwise have happened.[154] Even Tony Blair has accepted that Kyoto will reduce emissions by 2% or less.[155] In the words of one team of economists, "Kyoto is not much different from business as usual. The residual costs for OECD countries complying with the Kyoto Protocol are rather small and may reasonably be interpreted as governments' willingness to appease voters who want to see some climate policy action but are not willing to pay much."[156]

If no other treaty replaces Kyoto after 2012, it turns out that the total effect of the Kyoto reductions will have been postponing the rise in global temperature a bit less than seven days in year 2100.[157]

This leads to two obvious questions. First, why is the effect of cutting emissions so little? The answer is that the emissions from the developed world matter less and less, as China, India and other developing countries dramatically grow their economies. China is set to overtake the US as the biggest carbon emitter before 2010 and will probably double its emissions by 2030.[158] Yet, neither China nor India seems likely to accept real limits anytime soon, basically because they put poverty reductions before climate policies. (The lack of participation by China and India was one of the main reasons for the US rejection of Kyoto.[159])

As Lu Xuedu, deputy director at China's Office of Global Environmental Affairs, pointed out: "You cannot tell people who are struggling to earn enough to eat that they need to reduce their emissions."[160] Likewise Subodh K. Sharma, adviser at the Indian Ministry of Environment and Forests, agrees: "We do not want to make any commitment. India is on a growth path, and per capita consumption is still low. India is going to demand strengthening of the commitment by the developed countries."[161]

Both China and India are essentially telling us that there are other and bigger priorities, like food and development. This is a point we will get back to.

Second, we still need an answer to our question at the beginning. Even if we only reduce the temperature a little, is that not better than nothing? Well, that depends. If you look at Britain, where it was estimated that about 2,000 more would die from heat and 20,000 fewer would die from cold, cutting carbon emissions and cutting temperature rises in this particular case would actually mean more dead in Britain. Does this hold elsewhere? We will get back to that. But it is clear that whether it is a good idea to reduce temperature definitely depends on how much it will cost to reduce it. As China and India point out to us, there are other important priorities apart from temperature reduction, and possibly a poor person in China would rather have more food than slightly lower temperatures over the century. So let's look at the cost of Kyoto and other carbon cuts.

Cost of cutting carbon

The Stanford Energy Modeling Forum has assembled the most and best of studies of the cost of the original Kyoto. Here they had a large number of macroeconomic models estimating the cost of cutting emissions under different assumptions, as seen in Figure 8. The most important was whether or not hot air could be traded. Obviously, if there was no trade, the US and Europe would have to find their own cuts, meaning more and more costly cuts. The cost was found to be about $390 billion each year for the duration of the treaty. With trade of hot air, Russia's allowances could be used and more efficient cuts could be made, and the total cost would be about $180 billion annually. For theoretical purposes, the study also asked what would be the cost if Kyoto would still hold just for the developed world, but reductions could be made all over the world. This is not possible, since it would require India and China to commit themselves to emission targets, but Figure 8 shows that there would be significant gains to such a policy, at half the price of the $180 billion per year.

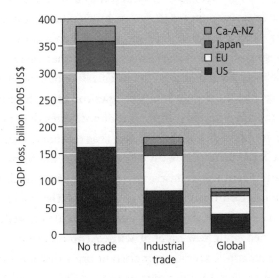

Figure 8 *Average cost of Kyoto in 2010 if everyone participates with no trade of carbon emissions, trade among industrialized nations and world trade.*[162]

By far the most realistic scenario would have been the industrial trade at $180 billion per year. While it would definitely not bankrupt the industrialized world, it is still a significant amount – about 0.5% of GDP. Also worth noticing is how the US in all three scenarios would have had to pay relatively more than Europe (about the same in absolute terms, but Europe is bigger), which also helps explain why the US would pull out.

Of course, with the US out, the cost is lower and the effect dramatically lower. The cost depends largely on whether or not the energy sector expects there to be a future Kyoto (in which case they will start to prepare, even in the US) and whether Russia will hold on to its permits for the next round (making permits scarce and expensive). Models estimate costs as low as $5–10 billion and as high as close to the $180 billion from the full Kyoto.[163]

Often, people ask: what do these prices mean? Why does it even have to be costly to cut CO_2? Who pays and how? These are good questions, and this is something economists have worked on for a long time. There are many different ways that cutting carbon can be costly.

Oil by itself is the most important and most valuable commodity of international trade.[164] At more than $1,500 billion a year, it alone accounts for more than 3% of global GDP.[165] With gas and coal, fossil fuels make up more than $2.5 trillion dollars or 5.5% of global GDP. Consequently there is big money to be made by saving energy, and incremental smart ideas in myriad companies and organizations every year shave off about 1% of our energy use each year.[166] Actually, as far back as we have statistics, we have learnt to produce ever more goods with the same amount of energy. Whereas the US in 1800 produced only 1 present-day dollar for a unit of energy, today it produces almost 5 dollars.[167]

Although a large part of the energy efficiency increase takes place in industry and organizations, we also experience the effect as consumers. The average US car has improved its mileage by 67% since 1973.[168] Likewise, home heating in Europe and the US has improved by 24–43%.[169] Many appliances have become much more efficient – the dishwasher, the washing machine and the air conditioner have cut about 50% of their energy use over the past decades.[170] Part of this improvement has been due to increasing energy prices in the 1970s and 1980s, and part of it due to government efficiency standards, but a large portion is simply due to the accumulation of little, smart innovations.[171] In total, the efficiency increase is almost 1% per year.[172]

This by itself should lead us to believe that we would use less and less energy. But while the car's engine gets more efficient, we get a car with air-conditioning. While our washing machine uses less energy, we also buy a dishwasher. We heat each room more efficiently, but have ever more space.[173] While we produce each dollar worth of goods ever more efficiently, we produce even more worth. Ingenuity still works and people constantly find ways to cut energy use – if they didn't our energy consumption would increase 75% more over the next 50 years[174] – but our total energy consumption increases, and so do our carbon emissions.[175]

Thus, if we want to cut emissions by more than what comes from natural ingenuity, we need to motivate people to emit less. Here, economists advocate using a tax on carbon. While nobody likes taxes (maybe apart from the finance minister), they send a powerful signal to avoid or at least reduce carbon emissions. If you have to pay more, you will probably cut back on some of your energy consumption – maybe you will switch off the air conditioner in the car, or possibly even bike.

More important is what happens to industry, power plants and heating facilities where the majority of the emissions lie. Coal is cheap but emits lots of CO_2, whereas gas is more expensive but emits less, and renewables, such as biomass or solar energy, are even more expensive but emit no CO_2. With a carbon tax, businesses will tend toward cleaner but more expensive energy sources, or processes that are more complicated but use less fuel.

This explains why cutting carbon will have real cost. It is not the tax in itself – after all, the money from taxes will be used for public good, perhaps even for allowing other taxes to be cut. But the fact that businesses will have to use more expensive fuels or find more expensive work-arounds means that the same products and services will now be more expensive – a cost that will ultimately be borne by us, as consumers. Now, there is nothing inherently wrong about this – since CO_2 actually does harm, you could argue that the prices before the tax didn't reflect this harm. Or to put it differently, the extra cost we pay should be compared to the environmental benefit that we receive in less global warming. This perspective is worth contemplating.

CUTTING EMISSIONS AND MAKING MONEY

It is often claimed that we can cut emissions and actually *make* money. For instance, in your own home, you could lower the heat and put on a sweater or unplug some of your gizmos when they are not being used. In a recent global warming awareness week in the UK, Tony Blair pledged to turn down his thermostat while Sir David Attenborough promised to unplug his mobile charger.[176] Isn't this costless or even advantageous – after all, cutting your heating or electricity bill means money in your pocket?

Economists are typically wary of such claims.[177] Why, they ask, would you not have done so, if it really was already in your own interest to do so? Why would Sir David have to wait till the awareness week to pledge to unplug his mobile charger if it had been an advantage for him to do so all along? This is reminiscent of Japan's Environment Ministry, trying to catch up to the Kyoto greenhouse gas targets by turning off the heat in February 2006:[178]

The ministry's "Warm Biz" campaign urges Japan's bureaucracy and businesses to bundle up with sweaters and scarves to cut down on energy use. "It's actually not that cold. We're all keeping warm from the heat of our computers," ministry spokesman Masanori Shishido said, but admitted he has taken to wearing thermal underwear.[179]

Likewise we are often told about a range of energy efficiency home improvements that we rarely do but which would actually save us money – again the economists wonder why we haven't already done them if they are this beneficial. For instance, engineers and manufactures claim that insulating your house will reduce the energy bill by 22–53%. An academic study found by analyzing monthly energy bills that the advertised savings were vastly overstated, thus explaining many house owners' reluctance.[180] In the UK, a well-known environmental architect campaigns to get people to add a near-silent micro windmill to the gable end of their houses. At a cost of £1,000 and a promise of saving up to 50% of household electricity demand it seems like a good deal.[181] However, an independent analysis found that it would typically only produce about 5% of household electricity – one-tenth the promised amount.

Likewise it is often pointed out that companies like Shell, BP and DuPont have reduced their emissions dramatically and made money at the same time.[182] DuPont is often headlined because it reduced its greenhouse gasses dramatically by 65% from 1990 to 2003 while it has saved $2 billion – more than any other company.[183] However the comparison is not particularly apt. The emission reductions are not in CO_2 but largely through exotic greenhouse gasses like HFC-23 (which is 12,000 times more damaging than CO_2). Since HFC-23 is a by-product in refrigeration production, it is much easier to reduce dramatically than CO_2.[184] Moreover, DuPont actually estimates that this reduction cost it about $50 million.[185]

Analytically separate, DuPont set a goal to reduce energy consumption. This involved a large amount of labor,[186] but eventually ended up netting the company $2 billion over the period. In at least in one case study of a German DuPont plant, a large part of the benefit stems from a generous German subsidy.[187]

Economists would point to the fact that cutting greenhouse gasses for DuPont actually cost money, because doing so was harder than not doing so. To cut HFCs, DuPont had to use engineers to analyze production lines, buy new equipment and change production facilities. All in all, the greenhouse gas reduction still may have been cheap, but it was not free.

As for the $2 billion saved in energy, good for DuPont. Clearly, if this policy was the best use of resources for DuPont no additional policy incentive was needed.[188] So again, if companies can actually make the most of their money from cutting carbon emissions, they will obviously do so, but consequently these emissions would never actually occur. Thus, when we see carbon emissions from companies growing, it must be because it was not their best use of resources to cut these last tons.

Costs and benefits – the value of a ton of CO₂

Scientists, lobbyists and politicians will all tell you that we should do all good things – not just with climate change but for all the world's woes. Of course, we don't.

Likewise, it is often pointed out that "we have the technology" to fix much of global warming.[189] Which is true. But we also have the technology to go to the moon, yet we don't go very often, simply because it is very expensive.

But if we don't fix everything about all problems, we have to think about priorities – ask where we should start to deal with the problems. It is obvious that we should do something about CO$_2$ emission and equally obvious that we shouldn't cut all of it – essentially bringing our society to a halt.

One way to think about this question is to ask about one of the next tons of CO$_2$ we are about to put into the atmosphere.[190] How much harm will that ton do? And how cheaply can we avoid it?

Over the next year, two soccer moms will drive their kids back and forth to school and emit a ton of CO$_2$;[191] 125 people are going to leave their cell phone chargers in the plug 24/7 (though presumably not David Attenborough) and over the year cause the utilities to emit an extra ton of CO$_2$.[192] Three people will have hot showers for four minutes each day and add an extra ton of CO$_2$ to the atmosphere.[193] In addition, many industrial and commercial processes that most of us don't even know exist will add their tons as well.

The question then is, which ton should we cut first? That is a hard one. Maybe the soccer moms should walk? Maybe we should get the 125 guys to unplug their chargers, but how do we organize that? This is the magical part about a carbon tax – we don't actually have to find out who should cut their emissions first. Instead, the people who have the least to lose will step up first.

If we place a tax of 1 dollar on a ton of CO$_2$, gasoline will go up about 1 cent for a gallon (or 0.25 cents per liter).[194] Each of the soccer moms will have to pay 50 cents more each year from driving their kids to school. The electricity bill will go up about 60 cents per 1,000 kWh. The 125 guys will collectively pay 1 dollar for their cell chargers or a little less than a cent extra each. And to shower, you will have to pay 33 cents extra. Now, we don't know who will change their behavior slightly – or even if any of them will. But we know that there are some people who will. Chances are that they will come from the industry (because a cent per gallon when you use lots gets your attention sooner).

In Figure 9 we see how a $1 tax on CO_2 next year will lead to an overall drop in emissions of a bit more than 2%. Remember, this is over and above the 1% efficiency improvement that every year comes from smarter ways to use energy (the "free" reduction). So we can cut emissions. We actually have a very simple and efficient knob to turn emissions down. The temptation is to say: "Why don't we turn the knob all the way up – with $30 we can cut almost 40%?"

But cutting emissions also has costs. As we saw above, industries will have to switch to more expensive fuels or more expensive procedures. Taking a shorter shower also has a cost, although in a more indirect sense. If your cost of a hot shower is ¢10 a minute, judging your finances and your preferences, you might have settled on a daily four-minute shower. If a carbon tax increases this cost, you might end up deciding that you will only do three minutes instead of four. We will have gotten a CO_2 reduction, but you will also be less pleased – you will have forgone a minute under the shower that you previously judged to be worth ¢10.

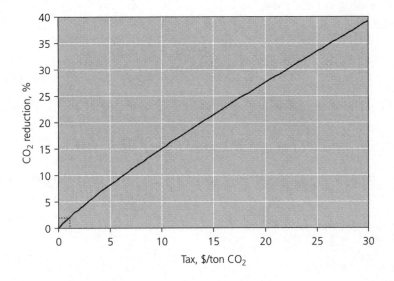

Figure 9 *Tax on CO_2 and how much CO_2 emissions it will cut globally: $1 tax cuts about 2% (dotted line), $10 cuts 15%.*[195]

In a global macroeconomic model, the total present-day cost for a permanent $1 CO_2 tax is estimated at more than $11 billion.[196] So we might want to think twice about cranking up the knob to $30, which will cost almost $7,000 billion.[197]

Essentially, the cost of turning the knob should somehow be weighed against the benefits of less global warming. There are two ways of thinking about this, leading to a somewhat similar result.

In one way we could think about CO_2 as pollution. Pollution is a negative by-product of many activities. The activity itself is valuable to us, but the pollution causes problems for others. The difficulty is that we don't take these problems into account when making decisions about our process – after all, they are not *our* problems. But if we had to pay for the damage, then they suddenly *would* become our problems. This is the idea behind the "polluter pays" principle.

If we have to pay the price of the problem we cause, it will not necessarily mean that we will stop everything we do – after all, the activity is also valuable – but we will be forced to weigh it against the damage it will cause, and we will only make things that will do more good than harm.

This means that we must figure out the price of CO_2 – how much damage does the next ton of CO_2 that you send into the atmosphere do? Naturally, this is a daunting question, which has no definitive answers. But over the past ten years some of the world's top natural scientists and economists have come up with a broad range of assessments that yield a fair amount of insight.

In the biggest review article of all the literature's 103 estimates, the climate economist Richard Tol finds two important points.[198] First, the really scary, high estimates typically have been neither subjected to peer review nor published. In his words: "studies with better methods yield lower estimates with smaller uncertainties." Second, he finds that, with reasonable assumptions, the cost is very unlikely to be higher than $14 per ton of CO_2 and likely to be much smaller.[199] When I specifically asked him for his best guess, he wasn't too enthusiastic about shedding his cautiousness – as is invariably the case with true researchers – but gave his best estimate of $2 per ton of CO_2.[200]

This means that the damage we will cause by putting out one more ton of CO_2 is most likely to be $2 and very unlikely to be higher than $14.

Consequently, we would do best by putting a \$2 tax on CO_2 to reflect this damage – to make sure that we properly take into account the damage we cause from using fossil fuels. If we don't have a carbon tax, we end up thinking that we can pollute with CO_2 for free, even though each ton does \$2 worth of damage. But likewise, we shouldn't over-tax CO_2. If we tax it at \$85, as proposed in one radical report,[201] we would forgo opportunities that would produce \$84 of benefits. However, with \$2 of real damage, society would lose out on \$82 of net benefits. This is no trivial loss – all the myriad lost opportunities of socially beneficial projects between \$2 and \$85 add up to a total one-time economic cost of more than \$38,000 billion.[202] This is more than three times the annual US GDP.[203]

So getting the tax right matters. If we put it too low, we emit too much CO_2; if we put it too high, we end up much poorer without doing enough good. So a crucial question is the cost of cutting CO_2 under Kyoto. For the UK, the marginal cost is estimated at \$23 per ton of CO_2[204] – between two and eleven times too high compared with the likely cost of climate change.

Doing Kyoto turns out to be too expensive compared to the good it does. We end up spending fairly large amounts of resources (up to \$23 per ton of CO_2 averted), but do only little good (about \$2). Maybe we could have done more good for the world with those \$23 elsewhere? The answer turns out to be yes.

Costs and benefits of climate action

Most of us don't usually buy a ton of CO_2 and thus it is a bit hard to find an intuition as to whether \$2 or \$23 is cheap or expensive. Moreover, if we were only going to cut a couple of tons, the cost probably wouldn't matter one way or the other. But as we are talking about cutting millions and even billions of tons, maybe it would make more sense to talk in total costs and total benefits. This would have the added advantage of making it much more comparable to our other choices. As participants in a democratic debate we routinely do make (collective) choices to spend billions of dollars, euros and pounds on many public policies, including education, health, roads and foreign aid.

The models that estimate the total costs and benefits of global warming have been around since the early 1990s, starting with the so-called Dynamic

Integrated Climate–Economy (DICE) model by economist William Nordhaus from Yale University.[205] This model has undergone extensive development and enlargement since, now incorporating 13 economic regions in the Regional Integrated Climate–Economy (RICE) model.[206] DICE and RICE have inspired all the other modelers, and according to the IPCC they have all produced more or less the same results.[207] What is unique about these models is that they include both a climate system and an economic system, with costs to the economic system stemming from both climate changes and greenhouse gas emission restrictions.

These integrated models try to incorporate the costs of all the different impacts from climate change, ranging through agriculture, forestry, fisheries, energy, water supply, infrastructure, hurricane damage, drought damage, coast protection, land loss (caused by a rise in sea level, e.g. as in Holland), loss of wetlands, forest loss, loss of species, loss of human life, pollution and migration.[208] Costs are expressed as the sum of two quantities: the costs of adaptation (building dams, changing to other crops, etc.) and the costs we must incur from the remaining non-adapted consequences (not all land is saved by building dams, production may fall despite the introduction of new crops, etc.).[209]

The models also incorporate the fact that cutting more CO_2 quicker gets ever more expensive, as we saw in Figure 9, and calculate for any carbon cut the total cost to society.

So we have a model that can take any CO_2 policy and show us *both* the economic cost of CO_2 cuts *and* the benefits (the avoided damage) from lower temperatures on agriculture, wetlands, human life, etc. This means that we can see both the costs and the benefits of the Kyoto Protocol and of more stringent regulations, as well as ask what would be the best global warming strategy.

For the full Kyoto with the US participating, Figure 10 shows on the left side the total cost over the coming century to be more than $5 trillion.[210] There is also an environmental benefit from slightly lower temperatures toward the end of the century – about 0.16°C.[211] The total benefit for the world is almost $2 trillion. Yet in total, this shows that the Kyoto Protocol is a bad deal: for every dollar spent, it only does the world about 34 cents worth of good.

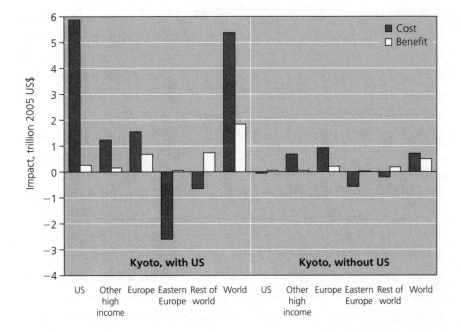

Figure 10 *Total cost and benefit of Kyoto, left with the US, right without the US, both assuming full trade of permits between industrial participants. Other High Income is primarily Canada, Japan and Australia. (Negative cost, e.g. for eastern Europe, incl. Russia, means benefit – because they sell carbon credits.)*[212]

There are also several important features which help explain the current political situation. The US would have paid a disproportionately large share, more than the total cost of Kyoto at almost \$6 trillion, whereas it would have received much less benefit than, for example, Europe. Compared to the rest of the world, the US is a net loser, whereas the rest of the world on balance benefits. This would probably in large part explain why the US has been the least engaged party. The same pattern repeats itself for Canada and Australia, with large costs and small benefits.

Conversely, Europe has the best deal of the rich world, paying \$1.5 trillion but getting almost half back in benefits. It is still not a good deal, but certainly goes a long way to explain why Europe has been the most prominent backer for Kyoto.

Russia and the other transition economies would have benefited greatly from Kyoto, because they could have sold their emission permits at a high price, to the tune of almost $3 trillion. Of course, when the time had come for western countries to pay up, it seems politically unlikely that the public in either Europe or the US would have accepted annual transfers of more than $50 billion for what is essentially hot air.[213]

Finally, with a net benefit of $1.4 trillion, the rest of the world is somewhat better off, with a little less than half accruing to the lowest-income countries. This benefit, however, has to be seen in the context of the rich world forking out almost $9 trillion. For every dollar spent, the rich countries do about 16 cents of good in the developing world.

With the US out of Kyoto, we can see on the right side of Figure 10 that there is not much left. Essentially, Europe, Japan and New Zealand pay $1.5 trillion, most of which will buy hot air, and a little that will buy an extremely tiny temperature change of 0.04°C by 2100.[214]

It is perhaps worth noticing that all of the costs and benefits above assume that policies are implemented globally and efficiently – that the smartest policies are used and coordinated globally, given the required reductions. Thus, should the rich countries avoid trading hot air with Russia, the costs could escalate to almost double, with virtually no extra benefit.[215] And should policy makers decide on CO_2 reductions that are more expensive than necessary, the total cost has essentially no upper limit. In the UK, the Kyoto CO_2 tax ought to be about $5 after the US has left.[216] However, the UK also requires electricity generators to supply 10% of their electricity from certified renewable sources under the so-called "Renewables Obligation." Currently, that cost is estimated at $169, or more than 30 times too expensive.[217] And remember that the Kyoto tax is probably too high compared with the damage cost of about $2. Thus, for every dollar spent on the renewables obligation, the UK gets 3 cents back on their Kyoto promise, and does about 1 cent worth of good.

When confronted with the point that doing Kyoto is an extraordinarily expensive way of doing very little good far into the future, many react by saying we should do much more. But as Figure 11 tells us, doing more than Kyoto is not a better deal – it is actually likely to cost ever more to do ever less extra good. And it is still worth remembering that the cost figures require politicians to choose the very smartest tools available.

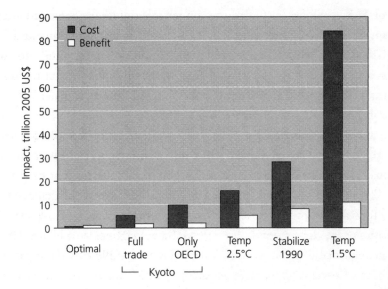

Figure 11 *Costs and benefits for several climate change initiatives. The optimal strategy is the economically efficient strategy. Kyoto is represented by full trade (trading hot air with Russia) and Only OECD (where only the rich world trades). Stabilize at 1990 is a global extension of Kyoto. The remaining two options show costs and benefits as stabilizing at 2.5°C and 1.5°C.*[218]

This result also makes good intuitive sense. If we do a little, it is easy – surely anything you do could be improved relatively cheaply to emit a little less CO_2. The metaphor is that we pick the low-hanging fruit first, which is easily accessible. However, as we try to cut more and more, it will get ever more expensive – we have to reach high into the tree for the remaining, scarce fruit. (This is also evident in Figure 9.) Also, the first cuts we make mean we cut the highest, most scary part of the temperature increases. However, as we cut ever deeper, we will start to cut into more usual temperatures. So while the cost increases with more cuts, the benefit decreases.

This is evident when we move from Kyoto to some of the more ambitious policies contemplated.[219] Stabilizing the temperature increase to 2.5°C does more good – it reduces temperature by 0.48°C – but at a rather high cost of $15.8 trillion. Actually, the models also give us a cost of the total damage from global warming (i.e. how much better off we would be if global warming wasn't happening), which is about $14.5 trillion. Thus, from stabilizing at 2.5°C we actually end up paying more for a partial solution than the cost of the entire problem. That is a bad deal.

Stabilizing all countries' emissions at 1990 level is almost a Kyoto for the entire world, and something that has been suggested, for example, by the EU. Here the cost rockets to almost $30 trillion with only $8 trillion worth of benefits. Barring a very different distribution of permits, such a move would lock all countries into their position in 1990, and this would make it very costly for the developing world to grow. Obtaining benefits of little more than $2 trillion, the lowest-income countries would have to pay almost $10 trillion. The world would spend a dollar doing just 29 cents worth of good, and the least developed countries would get just 24 cents for each dollar spent.

The most ambitious plan is limiting temperature rise by 1.5°C. This is essentially the stated preference of the EU, which in a council decision in 1996 decided that temperatures should rise no more than 2°C above pre-industrial level, i.e. no more than 1.2°C from today.[220] The EU has reconfirmed this decision almost every year since 1996. As the model shows, it is possible to achieve such very low temperature increase, but only at the formidable cost of $84 trillion. For every dollar spent, it will do 13 cents of good.[221]

Actually, the only reduction that does more good than it costs is the one labeled optimal. This initiative sets a global carbon tax that balances with the future environmental benefits from carbon abatement.[222] It starts off with a carbon tax around $2/tCO$_2$ today, rising to about $27 at the end of the century, reflecting how damages rise with more CO$_2$ in the atmosphere.[223] The total impact is rather small – it only reduces temperature by 0.1°C by the end of the century. Uniquely, it costs about $600 billion but does twice that in benefits, meaning for each dollar it does 2 dollars of social good.[224]

This result is surprising and runs counter to most of the climate change debate. We try to cut CO$_2$ through Kyoto, but in reality it is a poor use of resources. Many, including the EU, think we need to go much further, but the results in Figure 11 show us that this is likely to be an even poorer use of resources. In general, this emphasizes that we need to be very careful in our willingness to act on global warming. Going much beyond the small, optimal initiative is economically unjustified. And this conclusion does not just come from the output from a single model.

All major, peer-reviewed economic models agree that even when more catastrophic consequences have been taken into consideration "it is striking that the optimal policy involves little emissions reduction below uncontrolled rates until the middle of the next century at the earliest."[225] Equally, another study concluded that "the message of this admittedly simple model seems to be that it matters little whether carbon emissions are cut or not, only that protocols to stabilize emissions or concentrations are avoided."[226] An overview concluded that the first insight gained from these models was that "all appear to demonstrate that large near-term abatement is not justified."[227] Another that "To date, cost-benefit analyses have advised emission reductions that are substantially more modest than what is on the political agenda."[228] The conclusion of a very critical essay inadvertently sums it up: "The economic literature on climate change implies that there is no urgent need for serious climate policy."[229] A central conclusion from a meeting of all economic modelers was: "Current assessments determine that the 'optimal' policy calls for a relatively modest level of control of CO_2."[230]

In the latest review from 2006 the previous research is summarized: "These studies recommend that greenhouse gas emissions be reduced below business-as-usual forecasts, but the reductions suggested have been modest."[231]

Why is this such a robust result? If we look at costs and benefits over time in Figure 12 we see the reason. Essentially, the cost comes up-front, whereas the benefit comes much further down the line. For the first 170 years the costs are greater than the benefits. Even when the benefits catch up in the late twenty-second century, there is still a payback time before the total benefits outweigh the total costs around 2250. Thus, as one academic paper points out, "the costs associated with an emissions stabilization program are relatively large for current generations and continue to increase over the next 100 years. The first generation to actually benefit from the stabilization program is born early during the 24th century."[232]

The shapes of these two curves are relatively invariant from model to model due to the fundamentals of the climate system – that benefits from change only come very slowly and that costs are significant and up-front. Our revealed preferences show that we are generally unwilling to make large

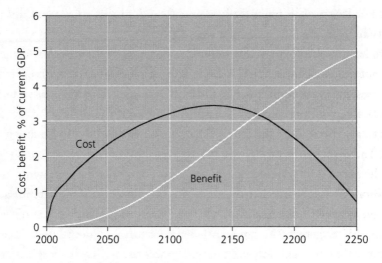

Figure 12 *Costs and benefits over time of stabilizing at 1990 CO$_2$ levels.*[233]

and increasing sacrifices over the coming centuries to create benefits for much richer generations many centuries away. Thus, for large-scale reductions in CO$_2$, total costs invariably outweigh benefits.

What we need are smarter ways to deal with climate change, which is something we will come back to.

Effects of a hotter world

It is time to answer the fundamental questions we started out with. What will happen in a warmer world? And what can we do?

We have looked at some of the main temperature related effects of a warmer world. We will have more heat deaths but also fewer cold deaths. As we get richer we become better able to cope with heat – as our data showed for Philadelphia, get better access to medical treatment, and air-conditioning can almost eradicate excess heat deaths.

We have also looked at what changes might occur over the next hundred years' warming – and for humans it will probably look a lot like the changes that happened in the cities over the last century, where temperatures rose by many degrees without dire consequences. Moreover, with cheap technologies we can cool temperatures in cities, where 80% of humanity will be by

2100. For LA, we can paint the asphalt and plant millions of trees and cool the city by 3°C.

We have looked extensively at what we can do about global warming. It turns out that we can do fairly little at fairly high costs. The Kyoto Protocol in its present form might postpone temperature increases by almost a week in 2100. Even with the US on board and all industrialized countries sticking to the treaty throughout the century, temperatures will be postponed just five years. The costs on the other hand are significant. For the emasculated Kyoto it will be about $700 billion. For the full Kyoto it would have been more than $5 trillion. At less than $2 trillion, the benefits do not nearly match that.

If we go even further ahead, the costs escalate far beyond the benefits, with the EU target of 2°C temperature increase costing more than $80 trillion, more than five times the total impact of global warming. Here we would do some 13 cents worth of good for each dollar we spend. Not a good deal.

But we need to look at the entire world to finally give an answer to our question of cold and heat deaths. The answer is depicted in Figure 13, the

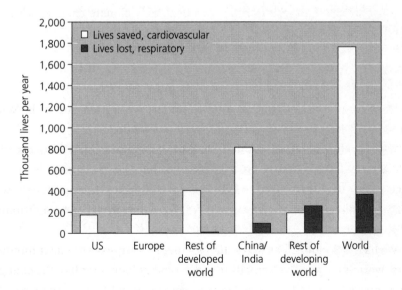

Figure 13 *Projected extra deaths and lives saved due to temperature increases from global warming in the year 2050.*[234]

first complete survey for the world, published in 2006. What it shows us very clearly is that climate change will not cause massive disruptions or huge death tolls. Actually, for the world in general, the direct impact of climate change in 2050 will mean *fewer dead*, and not by a small amount.[235] In total, 1.4 million people will be saved each year, as a result of more than 1.7 million fewer deaths from cardiovascular diseases but only 365,000 more deaths from respiratory disorders.

It is important to note that most of the lives saved are those of old people, whereas many of the lives lost in the third world are those of children. Thus, if we look at the number of life-years saved, the picture is still the same for all developed countries and China and India, but not so for the rest of the developing world, where the number of life-years lost would outweigh the number of life-years saved by 10 to 1. However, most of the debate, as we will also see below, counts the dead, and moreover most people would probably find it hard to justify trading off a large number of old people per child saved. (Notice that other effects on deaths would be increases in infectious diseases like malaria. We will look at these later, but we can already reveal that this will not substantially change the picture.)

The reaction of both my editor and several of my friends on reading this chapter was telling – and perhaps also similar to your reaction. "Yes, but what happens after 2050 – when do warming deaths outweigh cold deaths?" It is a good question, and one that the survey actually answers. The result doesn't just hold true in 2050. In the central estimates of the model, *lives saved will continue to outweigh deaths from cardiovascular and respiratory diseases at least until the year 2200*, though gradually at lower levels.[236] That is a strong and important result. But just as important is that you (well, certainly my friends and my editor) instinctively felt the need to ask about whether this held true in, say, 2100. If I had told you – as we will discuss on pages 130–41 – that malaria will increase by 2050, would you have felt the same need to ask "yes, but what happens after 2050?" Probably not, because we are so used to thinking that climate change will result in something bad. Yet, remember to ask that specific question when we get there – because it turns out that malaria will probably be gone by 2100.

For both the US and Europe, the annual saved deaths are almost exclusively those from cardiovascular diseases, a total of almost 200,000 fewer deaths in each region. This number is made up from both more cardiovascular heat deaths and many fewer cardiovascular cold deaths – about 1 to 5.[237] This trend also holds true for the rest of the developed world, with Russia and the other eastern European states alone saving almost 300,000 lives.

Perhaps more surprising, this trend is also very visible for China and India, which will experience almost 100,000 more respiratory deaths but more than 800,000 fewer cardiovascular deaths. The only region where deaths will outweigh lives saved is the rest of the developing world, especially Africa. Here almost 200,000 deaths will be avoided but more than 250,000 will die.

Now we can also answer what we can and should do. Many commentators point out how global warming will hit the developing world hardest. As we see with heat deaths, this is true. But most commentators would go on to suggest that we should cut carbon emissions, possibly dramatically, to help the third world. This, however, turns out to be very questionable advice.

If we got everyone on board for Kyoto, including the US, we would see temperatures reduced in 2050 by about 0.07°C, or a postponement of temperature increases by less than three years.[238] This would mean that the developing world would experience slightly less warming by 2050. Outside of China and India, it would experience about 6% fewer deaths from respiratory disorders, or save more than 15,000 lives that would otherwise have been lost. This seems to confirm that CO_2 reductions are the way to go.

But first, we have to remember that the world would pay about $180 billion annually for Kyoto for 50 years before this benefit would occur. Roughly that means paying almost $100 million for each life saved,[239] which is much more than we pay to save lives in the developed world, and certainly vastly more expensive than what a life can be saved for in the developing world, which is estimated at less than $2,000.[240]

Second, this entirely disregards the fact that fewer will be saved from cold deaths in the developing world – more than 11,000. So, in reality, we have only saved slightly fewer than 4,000 (now at the price of $300 million per person).

Third, we cannot just change the thermostat where temperature impact is overall negative. We also end up changing it in all the other places, in the US,

Europe, Russia, China and India. Here the effect of Kyoto on lives lost directly from temperature impacts would mean an increase in deaths of about 88,000. Thus, to save 4,000 people annually in the developing world, we end up sacrificing more than a trillion dollars and 80,000 people annually.

Global warming is not the only issue

This does *not* mean that we should do nothing and just embrace global warming. We have looked at just one aspect – direct impacts from temperature. There are other issues with global warming, which we will return to shortly, that mean the general and long-term impact will be predominantly negative.

But it tells us three things, loud and clear. First, our understanding of global warming as shaped by the media and the environmental pundits is severely biased. We are being told by scientist James Lovelock that with the coming climate change devastation, it is every nation for itself, that the 35,000 dead in Europe in 2003 was just the prelude to a new Stone Age, "as if we were committed to live through the mythical tale of Wagner's *Der Ring des Nibelungen* and see our Valhalla melt in torrid heat."[241] He proclaimed in 2006 in the UK *Independent*, "before this century is over billions of us will die and the few breeding pairs of people that survive will be in the Arctic where the climate remains tolerable."[242] This is far beyond the pale of our understanding of climate change, yet Lovelock is being applauded by people like Sir Crispin Tickell and Al Gore.[243] However, not getting the facts right potentially means we make staggeringly bad policy judgements.

Second, when we talk about global warming, we seem obsessed with regulating just one parameter, namely cutting CO_2.[244] But while turning the CO_2 knob may be part of the solution, surely our primary concern ought to be to advance human and environmental well-being the most, where many other knobs are in play. While cutting CO_2 will save some people from dying of heat it will simultaneously cause more people to die from cold. This highlights how reducing CO_2 as a solution means indiscriminately eliminating both negative but also positive effects of global warming. We ought at least to consider adaptive strategies as alternatives that would allow us to hold on to the positive effects of climate change while reducing or eliminating its damages.[245]

Third, global warming is not the only issue we need to tackle. This especially holds true for the third world. In Figure 14 we see the World Health Organization's estimates of what kills us. WHO finds that climate change kills about 150,000 people in the developing world now, but as we will see in the section on malaria below, they forgot to include cold deaths, so this estimate is vastly overstated.

Nevertheless, it is obvious that there are many other and more pressing issues for the third world, such as almost 4 million dying from malnutrition (underweight), 3 million from HIV/AIDS (unsafe sex), 2.5 million from indoor and outdoor air pollution, more than 2 million from lack of micronutrients (iron, zinc and vitamin A) and almost 2 million from lack of clean drinking water.

Even if global warming exacerbates some or many of these problems (as we will consider below), it is important to point out that the total magnitude of the problems is likely to far exceed the contribution from climate change.

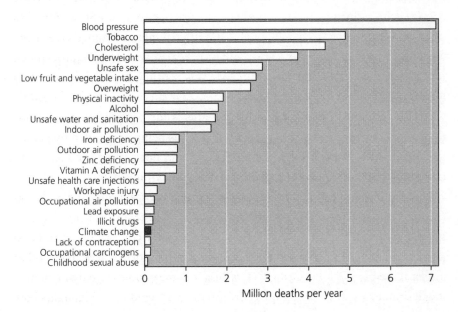

Figure 14 *Number of deaths attributable to different risk factors in 2000 from the World Health Organization, all in all about 40 million deaths (about 70% of total). Climate change (which is far too large because it does not include avoided cold deaths) makes up 0.3% of total deaths.*[246]

Thus, policies to reduce the total problems will have much more leverage than policies that only try to address the global warming part of the issues.[247] Again, we have to ask if there are better ways to help than by cutting CO_2.

Surya P. Sethi, the principal energy policy adviser to the Indian government, noted at the UN climate meeting in Nairobi in 2006 how India still has many development challenges:[248] 50% have no access to electricity; cooking is the largest use of energy for 75% of households; and 70% of cooking is done using traditional biomass, wood and dung (which causes indoor air pollution, killing more than 1.5 million people each year, Figure 14). In addition, 35% of India's people live on less than $1 per day and 80% live on less than $2 per day. He pointed out that lack of access to modern energy supplies correlates with high infant mortality, low life expectancies, high gender inequality, and low literacy rates. India's economy must grow at 8% per year for the next 25 years in order to lift the bottom 40% of its people to a decent standard of living.

Sethi then produced his punch line. India could cut projected CO_2 emissions between 2012 and 2017 by 550 million tons at an additional cost of $25 billion for more energy efficient technologies. This is in total what India has spent over the past five years for social and poverty reduction goals. "I do not have the funds for both. My choice is to improve the lot of India's poor or reduce CO_2 emissions so the developed world can breathe easier."

If we go with that thought, we have to ask ourselves what we want to do first. In the so-called Copenhagen Consensus process, we asked this general question to some of the smartest economists in the world: where would you spend extra resources to do good first?[249] Experts put forward their best solutions from climate change and communicable diseases, through conflicts, education, financial instability, governance and corruption, malnutrition and hunger, and population growth, to sanitation and water, and subsidies and trade barriers. But they didn't just say their proposals would do good – they said how much good they would do and how much they would cost.

A panel of top-level economists, including four Nobel Laureates, then made the first explicit global priority list ever, shown in Table 2. It divided the world's opportunities into very good, good, and fair, according to how much more good they would do for each dollar spent, and bad opportunities where each dollar would do less than a dollar worth of good.

Table 2 Global priority list for spending extra resources, from Copenhagen Consensus 2004.[250]

		Challenge	Opportunity
Very good opportunities	1	Diseases	Control of HIV/AIDS
	2	Malnutrition	Providing micronutrients
	3	Subsidies and trade	Trade liberalization
	4	Diseases	Control of malaria
Good opportunities	5	Malnutrition	Development of new agricultural technologies
	6	Sanitation and water	Small-scale water technology for livelihoods
	7	Sanitation and water	Community-managed water supply and sanitation
	8	Sanitation and water	Research on water productivity in food production
	9	Government	Lowering the cost of starting a new business
Fair opportunities	10	Migration	Lowering barriers to migration for skilled workers
	11	Malnutrition	Improving infant and child nutrition
	12	Malnutrition	Reducing the prevalence of low birth weight
	13	Diseases	Scaled-up basic health services
Bad opportunities	14	Migration	Guest worker programs for the unskilled
	15	Climate	Optimal carbon tax ($25–$300)
	16	Climate	The Kyoto Protocol
	17	Climate	Value-at-risk carbon tax ($100–$450)

Some of the top priorities also correspond to some of the top risk factors in Figure 14.[251] Preventing HIV/AIDS turns out to be the very best investment humanity can make – for each dollar it spends saving lives it will do about 40 dollars worth of social good. For $27 billion, we can save 28 million lives over the coming years.[252]

Malnutrition kills almost 2.4 million people each year. Perhaps even more dramatically, it affects more than half the world's population, by damaging eyesight, lowering IQ, reducing development and restricting human productivity. Investing $12 billion could probably halve the incidence and death rate, with each dollar doing more than $30 worth of social good.[253]

Ending first world agricultural subsidies and ensuring free trade would make almost everyone much better off. Models suggest that benefits of up to $2,400 billion annually would be achievable, with half of that benefit accruing to the third world. In achieving this, it would be necessary to bribe first world farmers, but the benefits of each dollar used would do more than $15 dollars worth of social good.

Finally, malaria kills more than a million each year. It infects about 2 billion people each year (many several times) and causes widespread debilitation. Yet, an investment of $13 billion could cut incidence by half, protect 90% of newborns, and cut deaths of under-fives by 72%.[254] For each dollar spent we would do at least $10 worth of social good.

At the other end of the spectrum, the Nobels placed climate change opportunities, including Kyoto, at the bottom under the heading "bad opportunities," underlining what we saw above, namely that, for each dollar spent, we would end up doing much less than a dollar worth of good for the world.

But the Copenhagen Consensus did not just ask top economists. We asked 80 young college students from all over the world, with 70% from developing countries, with equal gender representation, and from the arts, sciences and social sciences. After five days independently inquiring of the experts in all the areas, they came to a surprisingly similar result to the Nobels. They placed malnutrition and communicable diseases on top; climate change next to last.[255]

The major Danish paper *Politiken* (a Danish, slightly left-leaning *Guardian* or *New York Times*) organized an expert panel (including environmental experts) in Uganda to make their own priority list. It was surprisingly similar, with free trade and communicable diseases at the top, climate change at the bottom.[256] One conservation grassroots member, Happy James Tumwebaze, tells us even though climate change does affect life in Kampala, it is not his top priority. "If I were to use a dollar helping people in the developing world, I would try to combat poverty and hunger. Global warming only intensifies the problems we already have."[257]

In 2006 we asked a wide range of UN ambassadors to make their priority list after two days of intensive debates. Besides the three biggest countries China, India and the US, countries as diverse as Angola, Australia and Azerbaijan participated, along with Canada, Chile, Egypt, Iraq, Mexico, Nigeria, Poland, South Korea, Somalia, Tanzania, Vietnam, Zimbabwe and many others. They came out with a quite similar list, placing communicable diseases, clean drinking water and malnutrition at the top, with climate change toward the bottom.[258]

This should make us pause and reflect. None of these forums has said that climate change is not real or not important. But they ask us to consider whether we would do better by addressing the real and pressing needs of

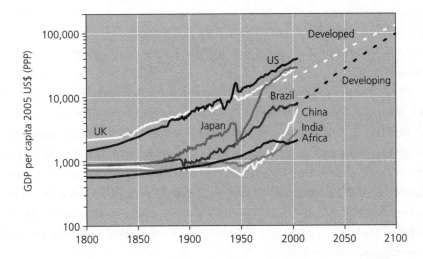

Figure 15 *Income per person for different nations and regions 1800–2003 and IPCC best predictions for 1990–2100, in 2005 dollars. Notice vertical scale is logarithmic.*[259]

current generations that we can solve so easily at low cost, before we try to tackle the long-term problem of climate change where we can do so little at high cost.

They also point out that in addressing these immediate problems we do more than just fix the problems of today. Imagine dramatically reducing HIV/AIDS and malaria. Picture a time when more than half the world's population doesn't succumb to development deficiencies from malnutrition. Envision agricultural subsidies scrapped, such that the third world can sell their products in first world markets. This will not just give an immediate boost, but will leave communities strengthened and economies growing faster, meaning much stronger and richer societies by 2100. It will enable these societies to deal much better with future problems – be they natural or from global warming. Investing in today also means a better tomorrow.

Actually, if we look at the income development per person over the past two centuries, it is clear that almost everyone has become much better off, as you can see in Figure 15. Since 1900, Africans have had the slowest growth, ending up "only" 2.5 times better off today. Japan, on the other hand, has had an amazing development, making each Japanese 18 times richer today. India has only grown 3.5 times, the UK is some 5 times richer, the US 7 times, Brazil and China more than 8 times. The development for India and China is even more impressive given that their growth really only started after 1950.

While people in the rich world perhaps sometimes just tend to scoff at such numbers, because increased richness "just means we can buy an extra DVD-player," it neglects that increased income in the developing world means that you can feed your children better, treat them from easily curable diseases and afford an education for them. Studies overwhelmingly show that higher incomes mean that you are better fed, healthier and ultimately will live longer.[260] You can afford better housing, clean drinking water and longer education.[261] You will afford simple cookers and kerosene heating, avoiding dirty and polluting dung.[262] Just for India, kerosene would avoid half a million deaths each year.[263]

In the developed world we have sometimes forgotten that, only a hundred years ago, we experienced many of the same problems. In 1900, each year one in a hundred people would die from an infectious disease in the US.[264] More than one in every ten American children died within their first life-year.[265] In the land of the free, only 15% had flush toilets, 3% electrical light, and refrigerators were still twenty years in the future.[266] Still today, being richer means that you can afford better health care, better education and better housing, ultimately meaning you will live longer.[267] Money does make you happier, mainly because it gives you the ability to control your circumstances, because you can weather outside shocks, such as unemployment and illness.[268]

Look at what the UN expects will happen over the rest of the century. People in both the developed and developing countries will become richer. In the industrialized world, people will see their incomes grow six-fold, as we saw during the last century. Income in the developing countries is expected to soar 12-fold.

This is important when talking about climate change. In 2100, when many of warming's problems will take place in earnest, the average person in the developing world is expected to make about $100,000 (in present value) each year in the UN's most likely scenario. Even the very worst scenario envisions the average person to be earning over $20,000.[269] Even in this very unlikely case, the average person in the third world will be richer than a present-day Portuguese or Greek or richer than most west Europeans in 1980.[270] Much more likely, he or she will be richer than today's average American, Dane or Australian. This richness will of course enable these countries to better weather outside shocks, whether these come from climate change or the many other challenges the future undoubtedly will deal us.

And this is the final part of the reason that Nobels, youngsters, UN ambassadors and Ugandan experts all place disease and malnutrition so high and climate so relatively low. When we try to help the developing world by cutting our carbon emissions, we are trying to help people far into the future, where they will be much richer. We are not helping a poor Bangladeshi in 2100 but much more likely a rather rich Dutchman.

The question then becomes whether we wouldn't do better by helping a poor Bangladeshi today, who needs the help so much more, and whom we can help much more for the dollars we spend. And helping present-day

Bangladeshis to become less sick, better fed and better able to participate in the global marketplace will not just do obvious good, but also enable them to better their society, grow their economy, and leave a richer and more robust Bangladesh to the future generations.

Our generational mission

Yet it is clear that many people in the developed world still devote extra-ordinary attention to climate change. In Figure 16 we see how people from Japan, Spain, France, Great Britain and Germany are very worried about climate change. In one recent survey in Australia, environmental concern came in as absolutely the most important priority for the leaders of the world, before eliminating poverty, or dealing with terrorism, human rights and HIV/AIDS.[271] Likewise, in another survey, the US, China, South Korea and Australia all found improving the global environment a more important

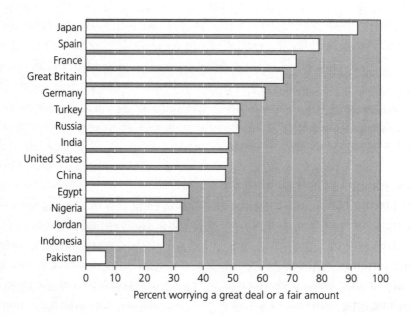

Percent worrying a great deal or a fair amount

Figure 16 *Worry about global warming in different countries, April/May 2006. Percentage of people who have both heard of global warming and worry about it a great deal or a fair amount.*[272]

foreign policy goal than combating world hunger.[273] South Korea actually put it right at the top of its list of the 16 main global threats.[274]

We have to ask ourselves why we are so singularly focused on climate change, when there are many other areas where the need is also great and we could do so much more with our effort.

Al Gore gives us two reasons to focus predominantly on climate change. First, it is a planetary emergency. "At stake is the survival of our civilization and the habitability of the Earth."[275] Yet, this turns out to be far from the truth. As we saw above, this is not what the science is telling us for the temperature rise over the coming century. We are not going to "see our Valhalla melt in torrid heat." If anything, the science actually tells us that *fewer* people will die with moderately more heat. Of course, Al Gore could have other scary stories up his sleeve (he does), and in the following chapters we will look at how they hold up (not very well).

Al Gore's second reason is probably more telling and closer to the truth. He tells us how global warming can give *meaning* to our lives.

> The climate crisis also offers us the chance to experience what very few generations in history have had the privilege of knowing: *a generational mission*; the exhilaration of a compelling *moral purpose*; a shared and unifying *cause*; the thrill of being forced by circumstances to put aside the pettiness and conflict that so often stifle the restless human need for transcendence; *the opportunity to rise* ... When we rise, we will experience an epiphany as we discover that this crisis is not really about politics at all. It is a moral and spiritual challenge.[276]

He explains to us how global warming can give us a moral certainty like the one Lincoln had fighting slavery or Roosevelt fascism, Wilson battling for the rights of women or Johnson for the rights of minorities.[277]

Even without questioning the historical rewrite necessitated by imagining certainty in those periods of strong uncertainty, it seems unrealistic to expect that climate change will give us such singularity of purpose. If anything, the ten-year drawn-out battles around the relatively minor restrictions of Kyoto show us that anything costing individual nations trillions of dollars will be strongly contested and lead to strife rather than serenity.

DOING IT ALL

When forced to prioritize between climate, HIV, free trade, malaria and malnutrition, many try to wiggle out and claim that "we should do it all." This is an attractive proposition. It appears magnanimous and all-inclusive. It is also wrong.

When families debate the relative merits of spending their savings on a vacation, a college fund or a new kitchen, few would applaud the solution "let's do it all" because it disregards the budget constraint.

In a political setting, "doing it all" may be a more frequently heard remark, but it is equally unpersuasive, because the underlying constraint remains. And really, if we can do it all, why haven't we already?

Historically, it seems that instead of doing it all, we have done ever less of anything. American CO_2 emissions increased under Gore as they did under Bush, Bush Sr. and Reagan.[278] America's aid budget continued to shrink under Gore, as it had ever since the mid-1960s.[279]

And not only is money limited, so is attention. There is only one front page, only a few top news stories. If we say everything should be a top priority, but continuously have climate change on the front cover, while malnutrition becomes a paragraph on page A27 or drops off the charts entirely, we should not be surprised when the lack of attention turns into lack of funds.[280]

As another way out of the conundrum, it is often pointed out that world military expenditures run to more than $1 trillion – we should spend less on destruction, and with all the extra money we wouldn't have to prioritize between all good issues.[281] While money spent by the first world on global warming, malnutrition or HIV is money that is spent to do good mainly for everyone, it seems unlikely that military spending falls into the same category. But even if we convinced the military to part with, say, $100 billion, we still couldn't do it all. We could go further down the list of great things to do in Table 2, but we would still have to prioritize.

Bottom line, we all have to do best things first. If we spend more time tackling one challenge, we don't have as much time for another. At whatever level of donations, more money spent on one of the top challenges, will mean less money for the other challenges. When Richard Branson from Virgin in September 2006 pledged $3 billion to alleviate global warming, that was $3 billion, which couldn't be spent on malaria.[282] Thus, although it is frightfully opportune to say "let's do it all" we really have to confront the challenge of prioritizing.

Although apocryphal, the story goes that when queen Marie Antoinette in eighteenth-century France heard the peasantry had no bread to eat, she said, "let them eat cake."[283] I sometimes imagine that a kind economist could have pointed out to her that giving the people bread instead might be more cost-efficient. A hundred sovereigns would perhaps feed 1,000 with cake but 10,000 with bread. If the economist hadn't lost his head at this point, she would probably have answered, "well, then give them both." But of course, bread to half still doesn't make cake better for the rest.

But perhaps more importantly, should we go for the exhilaration of a generational mission, just simply because it makes us feel good? Should it not actually be because we are doing the best our generation can do? And this, of course, brings us right back to asking whether there are greater opportunities for us to tackle first.

Gore immediately points out that there are many other generational missions:

> The understanding we will gain [from tackling climate change] will give us the moral capacity to take on other related challenges that are also desperately in need of being redefined as moral imperatives with practical solutions: HIV/AIDS and other pandemics that are ravaging so many; global poverty; the ongoing redistribution of wealth globally from the poor to the wealthy; the ongoing genocide in Darfur; the ongoing famine in Niger and elsewhere; chronic civil wars; the destruction of ocean fisheries; families that don't function; communities that don't commune; the erosion of democracy in America; and the refeudalization of the public forum.[284]

As the list goes on, it actually and somewhat ironically becomes clear that this list in itself is in need of prioritization. Gore essentially tells us we should do all things from climate change to fixing democracy. And it would be beautiful if we could do so. But until now, we haven't done any of these very well. Perhaps it would be wise to start thinking about which we should do first. (Clearly, Gore does so himself. He engages us primarily on climate change, not HIV, famine or genocide.)

Gore tells us that we need to hear the voices of the future, speaking to us now. We have to imagine them asking: "What were you thinking? Didn't you care about our future?"[285] He is absolutely right. We have to answer to future generations and ask ourselves which generational mission we want to embark on. Do we want to have taken on Kyoto, moved further down that path, spent trillions of dollars and done a little good for rich people in a hundred years? Do we seriously believe such a choice can convince the future that we cared?

Or do we want to focus first on fixing the major problems of today, give billions of poor people a new beginning and a better life that will strongly reinforce their future?

Do we just want to feel good, or do we actually want to do good?

Better strategies

This does not mean we should do nothing at all about climate change. It means we need to be much smarter. We need to abandon expensive and inefficient strategies like Kyoto and search for new opportunities.

Of course, part of us still wants to say "let's do it all." And I agree. In an ideal world we would deal with all the world's woes. We should win the war against hunger, end conflicts, stop communicable diseases, provide clean drinking water, step up education and halt climate change. But we don't. And so we have to start to face reality.

When we realize that there are many problems in the world – like HIV, malnutrition, free trade, malaria, clean drinking water, etc. – where we can do immense amounts of good, it seems obvious to me that we must focus our attention and our big expenditure there first.

But it does not mean we shouldn't start thinking about how we can cheaply tackle climate change in the long run. The big problem about cutting carbon emissions Kyoto style is that it costs a lot now, and does very little for the future. Moreover, if we paid the bill for cutting emissions down to 1990 level this year, we will have to pay just as much (or even a little more) next year to cut it to the same level. That is a bad deal. And it also means that, for the next hundred years, we will have to negotiate ever more excruciatingly costly treaties between 192 countries, many of them poor countries like China and India, hungry for more power. That is going to be hard. Or looking just at Kyoto, maybe more like impossible.

The trick probably lies in understanding that what matters is not whether we cut a little now, but whether we eventually cut a lot. So maybe we should try going a different way.

Right now we could get all the world's energy from solar cells taking up very little (and otherwise useless) space. The equivalent of 2.6% of the area of the Sahara.[286] Why don't we? Because it would be horrendously costly. But solar energy has come down in price by about 50% per decade over the past 30 years. Even at a much slower pace, it will probably become competitive before mid-century for many uses, and before the end of the century for most uses. If we invested more in research and development (R&D) this development would probably go faster. Likely, such an investment would do much more good than Kyoto ever could, and be much cheaper.

And of course, solar power is but one – if very promising – opportunity. We have wind power, that is already competitive in some places, for example Denmark. We have carbon capture, fusion and fission, energy efficiency, biomass and biodiesel. It is hard to tell which will work best, but maybe we shouldn't. Maybe we should let nations search out these opportunities for the long-term benefit of the world.

My proposal for tackling global warming in the long run is that all nations commit themselves to spending 0.05% of GDP in R&D of non-carbon emitting energy technologies.[287] This approach would cost about $25 billion per year, seven times cheaper than Kyoto and many more times cheaper than a Kyoto II. It would involve all nations, with richer nations naturally paying the larger share. It would let each country focus on its own future vision of energy needs, whether that means concentrating on renewable sources, nuclear energy, fusion, carbon storage, conservation or searching for new and more exotic opportunities.

Such a massive global research effort would also have potentially huge innovation spin-offs (a bit like NASA's going to the moon also gave us computers and velcro). Because the costs are low and there will be many immediate innovation benefits, countries do not have to be ever more strongly cajoled into ever more restrictive agreements. They will partake because it involves them in a strong, science-based endeavor. They will partake because it is a smart thing to do.

And most importantly, it will likely do much more against global warming.

3

GLOBAL WARMING:
OUR MANY WORRIES

In chapter 2 we looked at what happens when temperatures increase. But that is only one of many concerns with global warming. We now need to turn to all the other issues that are raised, and often exaggerated, in making us see where we should go next. But first, let us look at the climate in the past.

Long history: CO_2 and temperature

It is often pointed out that our CO_2 emissions and temperatures are headed far outside the scope of the "normal." This is true in one sense, but certainly not in another. In Figure 17 let us look at data that has been made very famous by Al Gore.

It shows us the last 650,000 years of temperature and CO_2. We only know this because we have drilled very far into the permanent ice sheet in Antarctica and examined all the layers. Each year's snow has been preserved by the next, almost like the rings of a tree, and each layer has trapped little bubbles of air from that time. We can then count the years down to the bottom, and when we carefully analyze the composition of air in each layer we can tell the CO_2 content and also deduce the temperature in that period.

The bottom part of Figure 17 shows the temperature with today over on the right. The present temperature is fixed at 0°C for reference, but this is Antarctica, so the real temperature is about minus 55°C.[288] If we go back in time, we see how we came out of the last ice age some 10,000–20,000 years ago, and how it lasted for 90,000 years. The last interglacial was a short one of perhaps 15,000 years, then dropping back into cold mode. The past four interglacials show the same general pattern of short hot periods and long cold periods in a 100,000 year cycle. Further back, it gets a little more confusing as the world was tumbling out of a 41,000 year cycle and into the 100,000 year cycle. The cycles are driven by subtle changes in Earth's orbit around the sun.[289]

Al Gore uses this graph to make several points. First, he asks us to consider how closely CO_2 and temperature match up and invites us to believe that CO_2 is the factor forcing temperature.[290] Yes, it is impressive how CO_2 and temperature go hand-in-hand. And yes, it is very likely that in our world additional CO_2 from fossil fuels will drive up temperatures. But this was not the case over the past 650,000 years when there were no power plants or cars.

Careful analysis shows that over the past 650,000 years CO_2 lags temperature: *first* temperature rises, *then* CO_2 rises; and likewise temperature *first* drops, *then* CO_2 drops. This is no small time-frame; estimates show lags of anywhere from 200 to 6,000

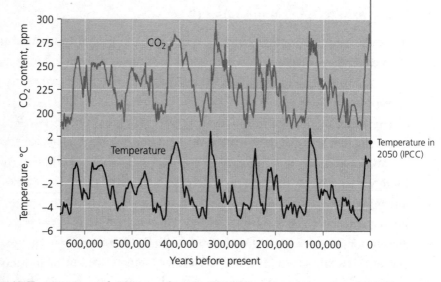

Figure 17 *Temperature and CO_2 over the past 650,000 years at Antarctica, showing eight glacials and seven interglacials. Notice how the last four interglacials had higher temperatures than ours. Added is the CO_2 concentration in 2005, and what it will likely be in 2050 (both from Al Gore and IPCC).[291] CO_2 is measured in ppm (parts per million).*

years, with most around 600 to 2,000 years.[292] In parts of the graph you can actually see it yourself. The most visible part is probably where the last inter-glacial begins its sudden decline into the ice age, around 118,000 years ago (over 10,000 years it drops from +1°C to −3°C), but high CO_2 concentrations linger for another 6,000 years.[293]

It is still not entirely clear why CO_2 rises and falls with temperature, but one reason seems to be that the changing wind patterns of cold and warm worlds hold back or empty out CO_2 from the deep oceans. In cold climates, the Westerly winds are closer to the equator, allowing respired CO_2 to accu-mulate in the deep ocean. In warm climates, these winds move poleward and flush respired CO_2 out of the deep ocean.[294] Likewise, ice ages may dramat-ically increase algae production because breaking-off icebergs provide the algae with essential nutrients such as iron.[295] When algae die, some of their bodies sink to the bottom and lock away their absorbed CO_2, thus lowering the CO_2 content in the air.

So this graph is a particularly poor way to showcase the importance of CO_2.

Gore's second point is that CO_2 and temperature levels are way outside "normal" and headed toward catastrophic levels. In the lowest dot above the graph you see the CO_2 level in 2005 and can see that Gore is absolutely right. The fact that we use fossil fuels and emit carbon means that the level of CO_2 is beyond anything we have seen for the past 650,000 years. Of course, with human civilization dominating the planet an outstanding array of parameters are outside the scope of prehistoric experience.

We have never had as much of the surface area of the planet growing food; we have never had as much electromagnetic exposure from radio, TV and microwave radiation; and even the night side of the planet has never been lighter, with ubiquitous electric lighting. The biosphere has never been more closely connected, with the organisms in ships' ballast water going from one end of the world to the other in weeks and people flying from continent to continent in hours. Levels of almost any constituent have changed because of man: we can see the signature of Roman and Greek mines and smelters in the Greenland ice cores of 2,000 years ago.[296] Humans now move rocks and sed-iments for agriculture and construction more than ten times faster than nature's erosion.[297] Likewise, some of the most important indicators of human welfare have moved far outside the norm. From an average life expectancy of 20–30 years from prehistory through Roman times, humans now live to be more than 67 years old on average.[298] Prosperity, violence and democracy are also far from their historical norm.[299] Clearly, just by saying indicators are outside of the "norm" does not make them catastrophic.

As we will see below, CO_2 levels are not outside the norm if we take a longer viewpoint. It is also worth realizing that our present temperatures and the temperatures up till 2050 are not outside the norm – actually our interglacial is *colder* than the last four interglacials.[300] It is estimated that the last interglacial in Greenland was at least 5°C warmer than at present.[301]

Gore's third point is how much worse things will get. He points out how CO_2 levels will increase much more by 2050, as you can see in Figure 17, although he ends up exaggerating a fair amount.[302] In his perhaps most memorable stunt, Gore shows a fine-tuned flair for showmanship when he ascends a mechanical lift at the edge of a gigantic version of Figure 17 and rides it all the way up to show how far outside the 2050-point will be. Obviously, with the tight connection between CO_2 and temperature in the past it is an easy leap to expect that the temperature will follow up the mechanical lift. Actually, Gore makes us more than expect. As he explains, the difference between top and bottom of the temperature graph is an ice age. That short distance represents the difference, in Chicago, between a nice day and a mile of ice over your head. "Imagine," he then asks us pointing at the temperature graph, "what three times that much on the warm side would mean."[303]

Of course, it is entirely misleading to suggest that the expected CO_2 increase will mean three times the warming we saw going from ice age to now – about 15°C in total. Actually, we do know how much warming we can expect to see in 2050 from the UN climate panel – namely about 1.59°C or almost ten times less, as we also saw in Figure 2.[304]

This does *not* mean that global warming will not happen or that it will not predominantly have negative impacts. But it is important to get the facts right – exaggeration will not help us select the right priorities.

In the larger picture, both temperature and CO_2 are definitely not outside the norm, while their connection increasingly breaks down.

In Figure 18 we see the temperature over the past 67 million years – the end of the age of dinosaurs to the left and today at the far right at 0°C.[305]

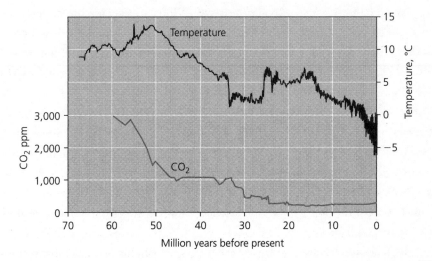

Figure 18 *Deep sea temperature over the past 67 million years, with today at 0°C.*[306] *CO_2 over the past 60 million years.*[307]

Here we also see how the world struggled for several million years with recurring ice ages and interglacials – the crammed wiggling between 0°C and minus 5°C at the far right is essentially the temperature swings we saw above in Al Gore's figure from Antarctica (Figure 17). Before three million years ago, the world was consistently much warmer than today. Thus, in the bigger geological context, the temperature today is cold.

Likewise Figure 18 shows us how CO_2 has dropped dramatically over the past 60 million years, and that for the first 30 million years it was much higher than any CO_2 concentration we worry about today. Finally, looking at the connection between temperature and CO_2, it is clear why Al Gore chose not to show this slide. Yes, the world was much warmer 60 million years ago with much higher CO_2 content. But the connection seems fairly weak. While CO_2 declined rapidly around 60–50 million years ago, temperatures increased. While CO_2 remains flat for the last 20 million years, world temperatures drop 10°C into recurrent ice ages.[308]

Looking much further back, through the past 500 million years (the age of multicellular life, the most recent 10% of Earth's history), we have poorer data, but the outline is one characterized generally by even higher temperatures, very high levels of CO_2 and even less connection between the two.

Apart from a major glaciation around 300 million years ago, temperatures were as high or even much higher than the high temperatures in Figure 18.[309] Likewise, models and data suggest that CO_2 content was at least 1,000 ppm and often much, much higher.[310] Recent reviews of the connection between CO_2 and temperature over this time-span have found that that there is little connection. One set of researchers found a "poor correlation" and that unless there is something wrong with our fundamental data "CO_2 is not likely to be the principal climate driver."[311] One of the main CO_2 modelers likewise analyzed the long-term connection between temperature and CO_2. Apart from our current cool and low-CO_2 world, "no correspondence between CO_2 and climate is evident in the remainder of the record."[312]

To reiterate, none of this means that temperatures will not increase in the future as we pump out more CO_2. This is what we saw early on, in Figure 2. But it means that we should talk about their effect as our best models show them, not suggest from past climates that future temperatures are out of this world (they're not), that CO_2 levels are entirely beyond the norm (they're not), or that the 50 year future will be three times the last ice age on the warm side (which is simply ludicrous).

Recent history: CO_2, temperature and glaciers

Let us try to look similarly at our past millennium. Much ink has been used (and many foul words uttered) over the reconstruction of a temperature measure for the past thousand years. A team of researchers lead by Michael Mann found in 1998–99 that temperatures had been almost constant since the year 1000 until 1900, when temperatures increased dramatically.[313] The graph was dubbed the hockey stick, because the 900-year constant temperature resembles the long shaft lying horizontally, with the short blade shooting up in the past hundred years.[314]

It was a potent graph to showcase how unusual the recent temperature increase has been, and it was featured several times in the 2001 IPCC report, including prominently on page 3 in the *Summary for Policymakers*.[315] It was the basis for claiming, "the 1990s have been the warmest decade and 1998 the warmest year of the millennium."[316] However, it also turned out that there were serious problems with the methods.

Since we have only used thermometers systematically and globally over the past century and a half (the world's longest record in central England only goes back to 1659[317]) we have to look for other ways of measuring temperature, like the analysis of oxygen from Antarctic ice cores. For places outside the cold Arctic, we can try to estimate temperature from looking at tree rings (because trees grow wider rings in warm weather), corals (measuring growth rings or trace elements), lake and ocean sediments, boreholes, etc.

Mann used just tree rings from 22 or more different places around the world and through a complicated process combined them to get a hockey stick. However, it turned out that even if he had thrown out the tree ring data and just put in any odd, random data series, the process tends to churn out a hockey stick.[318] So maybe we don't see the rising blade of end-of-the-millennium temperatures but only the pre-ordained outcome of a computer glitch.

Moreover, it seems that even if one is careful about avoiding this automatic hockey stick, combining tree rings over many centuries is fraught with difficulty. If the temperature changes over 500 years, but you only have series of overlapping 100 year tree rings, stitching them together will tend to subdue the long-term temperature trend. Again, studies show that if you put temperature data with strong minima and maxima into the Mann process, you will tend to get a very flat, uneventful result.[319] Possibly, the long, stable shaft of the hockey stick was an outcome of the computer program, too.

Most research has confirmed that the Mann graph in itself is somewhat flawed in its very simple message: for the past 900 years climate virtually didn't change, but since mankind started churning out CO_2, temperatures have gone sky-high.[320] But although the temperature over the past centuries has varied more, one of Mann's central points still stands: we can start seeing the man-made warming toward the present, standing out from the natural variability in Figure 19.[321] This is the only long-term temperature series that is not based just on tree rings but on a number of other indicators, like boreholes from Greenland, seashells from Chesapeake Bay and stalagmites from Norway.[322]

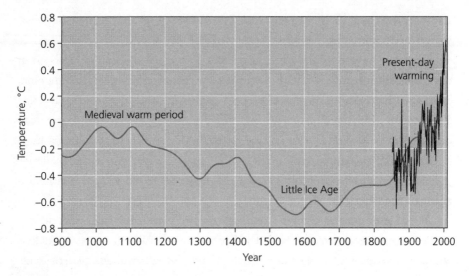

Figure 19 *Northern hemisphere temperature from 900 to 2006, based on a variety of indirect measurements for 900 to 1925, and thermometer records for 1850 to 2006.*[323]

Figure 19 shows us how in the early part of last millennium there was a relatively warmer period known as the "Medieval Warm Period."[324] This was the period when the warmer climate and reduced sea-ice made possible the colonization of the otherwise inhospitable Greenland and Vinland (Newfoundland) by the Vikings.[325] In Alaska, the mean temperature was 2–3°C warmer in the eleventh century than today.[326] Likewise, the Japanese cherry blossom returned to early blooming in the twelfth century and the snow line in the Rocky Mountains was about 300 meters higher than today.[327]

The middle of the last millennium also saw a marked cooling, named the "Little Ice Age." Evidence from a wide range of sources shows colder continents where glaciers advanced rapidly in Greenland, Iceland, Scandinavia and the Alps.[328] The arctic pack ice extended so far south that there are six records of Eskimos landing their kayaks in Scotland.[329] Many European springs and summers were outstandingly cold and wet, and crop practices changed throughout Europe to adapt to a shortened and less reliable growing season, causing recurrent famines.[330] The harsh winters were captured by the Flemish artist Pieter Bruegel (1525–69), who initiated a new genre by completing at least seven winter landscapes in two years.[331] Possibly the worst winter in France in 1693 is estimated to have killed several million people – about 10% of the population.[332] Likewise in China, warm weather crops, such as oranges, were abandoned in the Kiangsi Province, and in North America the early European settlers reported exceptionally severe winters, with Lake Superior iced over till June in 1608.[333]

It is perhaps worth noticing that while many events during the Little Ice Age are seen and reported as negative, this does not seem to be the case with most of the Medieval Warm Period.

It is clear that part of the temperature increase since then has simply been the emergence from the Little Ice Age. It is also clear, though, that we are now seeing a warming signal beyond that, indicating man-made global warming.

Both of these warming signals, the extended warming since the Little Ice Age, have caused glaciers to recede. Many activists have seized on pictures of these retreating glaciers as symbols of global warming – Al Gore fills 18 pages of his book with before-and-after pictures of glaciers.[334]

But several facts impede this rather simple message. First, glaciers have been greatly advancing and receding since the last ice age. In Switzerland, there have been 12 such advances and retreats over the past 10,000 years.[335] One of the best studied glaciers in Norway – my namesake Bjørnbreen – was entirely absent for 3,000 years over two periods, about 7,000 years ago, and over the last 10,000 years it has been reborn six times.[336] In fact, most glaciers in the northern hemisphere were small or absent from 9,000 to 6,000 years ago.[337] While glaciers since the last ice age have waxed and waned, overall they seem to have been growing bigger and bigger each time, until reaching their absolute maximum at the end of the Little Ice Age.[338] It is estimated that, around 1750, glaciers were more widespread on Earth than at any time since the ice ages 12,000 years ago.[339] When Bjørnbreen peaked around 1800, it was actually twice as large as any of its five previous incarnations.[340]

So it is not surprising that as we're leaving the Little Ice Age we are seeing glaciers dwindling. We are comparing them with their absolute maximum over the past ten millennia. The best-documented overview of glaciers shows that glaciers have been receding continuously since 1800.[341]

The perfect glacier icon, the snow-clad Mount Kilimanjaro, has been receding at least since 1880.[342] When Hemingway published his *Snows of Kilimanjaro* in 1936, the mountain had already lost more than half its glacier surface area in 56 years.[343] This is more than it has lost in the 70 years since. Actually, the central theme from the inception of published research on Kilimanjaro in 1891 has been the drastic recession of its glaciers.[344]

Moreover Kilimanjaro has not lost its ice to increasing temperatures (they have remained rather stable below freezing), but because of a shift around 1880 toward drier climates.[345] Thus, Kilimanjaro is not a good poster icon for global warming. In the latest satellite study, it is concluded "results suggest glaciers on Kilimanjaro are merely remnants of a past climate rather than sensitive indicators of 20th century climate change."[346]

Yet, we are often told that we need to reduce CO_2 emissions to avoid the receding glaciers. Greenpeace tells us – televised with Kilimanjaro in the background – that the mountain's entire ice field might be lost by 2015 due to climate change.[347] "This is the price we pay if climate change is allowed to go unchecked."[348] But of course, with Kilimanjaro we would be able to do exactly nothing, since it is losing ice because of a drier climate. Even if we granted that its demise was partially related to global warming, nothing we could do would have even the slightest impact before 2015.

Again, with our goal presumably being to improve the state of humanity and the environment, we have to ask both what we can do and whether cutting CO_2 is the best way forward. When Greenpeace informs us "Mount Kilimanjaro's fast-melting glaciers symbolise the fact that climate change may be felt first and hardest by the environment and people of Africa"[349] it is mixing two messages. No, Kilimanjaro is not a good symbol of climate change, but yes, climate change will definitely hit harder in the developing world. While pictures of the beautiful glaciers from Kilimanjaro along with admonishing concerns over CO_2 undoubtedly work well with the western media and opinion makers, they hardly address the real problems of the Tanzanian farmers on the slopes. Surveys show they have very different concerns, like lack of capital to buy seeds, fertilizers and pesticides, and pests and animal diseases, while they also have to contend with costly education, high HIV infection rates, malaria and low-quality health services.[350] We have to dare to ask whether we help them best by cutting CO_2, which would make no difference to the glaciers, or through HIV-policies, that would be cheaper and faster, and have much greater effect.

Yet, there is a real concern when it comes to glaciers that feed rivers. Al Gore points to the Himalayan glaciers on the Tibetan Plateau. They are the biggest ice mass outside of Antarctica and Greenland and they are the source of rivers that reach 40% of the world's population.[351] A stable glacier is not a continuous source of water into rivers (if it was, it would quickly vanish), but it acts as a "water tower," accumulating water as ice in the winter, then releasing it in the summer.[352] In this way, melting glaciers provide as much as 70% of the summer flow in the Ganges and 50–60% of the flow in other major rivers.[353]

The concern is that if glaciers entirely disappear, the overall amount of water available over a year would probably remain the same (with roughly the same amount of precipitation), but it would be distributed very differently, possibly leading to severe summer droughts.[354] To a large extent this can be remedied by improved water storage, but of course that would have large extra costs. Thus, Gore tells us that "within the next half-century ... 40% of the world's people may well face a very serious drinking water shortage, unless the world acts boldly and quickly to mitigate global warming."[355]

However, there are two important points to be made. First, with glacial melting, rivers actually *increase* their water content, especially in the summer, providing *more* water to many of the poorest people in the world.[356] Glaciers in the Himalayas have been declining significantly since the end of the Little Ice Age and caused increasing water availability throughout the last centuries, possibly contributing to higher agricultural productivity.[357] Of course, with continuous melting, eventually the glaciers will run dry, but the simulations IPCC refers to do not see a complete reduction of glaciers by mid-century but rather a 60% reduction.[358] Thus, essentially global warming on glaciers means that a large part of the world can use more water for more than 50 years before they have to invest in extra water storage. These 50+ years can give societies the breathing space to tackle many of their more immediate concerns and grow their economies so that they can better afford to build water storage facilities.

Now, you may be cringing and saying that "we should conserve the pristine glaciers." And of course, in the best of all worlds where there were no competing demands, that would be great. But in a world of many other issues, might it be worth considering that developing countries would be interested in using some of their finite natural resources like glaciers to grow richer? Certainly we did so in the developed world, when we cut down much of our forests and grew rich.[359] Moreover, it is perhaps worth contemplating the alternative. In the Karakoram and Hindu Kush mountains of the Upper Indus Basin, summer temperatures have been bucking the global warming trend and cooled about 1°C since 1961.[360] The consequence has been a reassuring thickening and expansion of the Karakoram glaciers but – predictably – the summer runoff in the rivers Hunza and Shyok has decreased about 20%.[361] This is important, as they provide more than 25% of the inflow to the Tarbela Dam, which controls one of the world's largest integrated irrigation networks. So which would we rather have? More water available or less?

This leads to the second point and a commentary on Gore's statement of urgency. What *can* we actually do? We could implement Kyoto at very high cost, but make virtually no impact on the Himalayan climate by 2050. Glaciers have been receding for several centuries, accumulation rates have dropped since 1840 due to a change in the trade winds, and even bold and quick CO_2 cuts will change this very little. But apart from all the other issues (malnutrition, diseases, etc.) where we could do much more good, we could also do much more good by investing in better water infrastructure, such that India and China can better utilize the extra water now, and prepare for when the rivers revert to "normal" water flow but with more in the winter, less in the summer.

Gore is right that lack of water from glaciers will eventually become a problem, but forgets to point out that it is a boon now. And essentially he advocates that we turn the big, hard knob of CO_2 cuts, which will do little at high costs, while we have to ask whether there are other, nimbler and more efficient knobs to turn first, where we can do much more good.

Rising sea levels

Apart from the obvious connection to temperature, one of the most doom-laden impacts from global warming is seen as rising sea levels. It is perhaps not surprising, since from time immemorial most cultures have had legends of catastrophic floods, which covered the entire earth and left few animals and plants to survive.[362] In western societies its most famous version is the story of Noah saving what he can in his Ark. When Al Gore visited the Oprah Winfrey show in December 2006, she pointedly and repeatedly asked if he felt like Noah.[363]

Many commentators powerfully exploit this doom of flooding, like Bill McKibben saying of global warming and our responsibility that "we are engaging in a reckless drive-by drowning of much of the rest of the planet and much of the rest of creation."[364]

But what has actually happened and what is likely to happen with sea levels? During the last glacial, much of the world's water was locked up in ice, so when it melted from 20,000 to 6,000 years ago the sea levels rose some 120 meters.[365] We don't have many data since then, but sea levels have remained fairly stable since then – probably with swings of less than tens of centimeters per century.[366] In Roman times, sea levels were about 13 cm lower than now.[367]

When sea levels rise, it is not due to sea ice melting, because it is already displacing its own weight – if you put ice cubes in a glass of water, the water line will not change when they melt.[368] Thus, contrary to common statements, the Arctic melting will not change sea levels, as it is already floating.

Instead sea levels rise because of two factors. First, when water gets warmer, like everything else it expands. Second, runoff from land-based glaciers adds to the global water volume. Over the past 40 years, glaciers have contributed about 60% and water expansion 40%.[369]

So how much has the water level increased over the past centuries? You would think this would be a simple question – take the measurements of any old port, for example one of the longest series of records in the world, from 1774 in Stockholm, and chart them.[370] However, here sea levels over this period have actually *decreased*. This is because Sweden during the last ice age had a mile of ice above it, and now that the ice is gone, the land (and the gauge attached to it) is still slowly rising, currently about 5 mm each year.[371] Of course, in measuring the sea level, this has to be corrected for.

Moreover, you would imagine that measuring the sea level should be the same all over the planet – after all it ought to level out after a while, just like in a bathtub. But in the global weather system things never get to level out – persistent winds will change the levels, and changes in the wind will likewise change sea level rise. For instance El Niño, with its persistent westerly warm winds across the Pacific, will push back more water toward Asia and Australia and make it warmer and expand. Consequently, in the past decade sea levels there have been rising by 5–15 mm each year whereas the West coasts of North and South America have seen declining sea levels.[372]

Nonetheless, when using the more than 1,800 tide gauge stations around the world, we get the longest data series for sea levels, as shown in Figure 20.[373] Here we see how the sea level was declining in the first part of the 1800s. This was probably due to the volcanic eruption of Tambora in Indonesia in 1815, which had global climate consequences.[374] As a result 1816 became known in Europe and the US as "the year without a summer" because the immense amount of ash blown into the stratosphere cooled the planet, drastically cutting the growing season and resulting in failed harvests and widespread famines.[375]

Since then, sea levels have risen by about 1.8 mm per year, or 18 cm over the past hundred years.[376] However, this has been a stop–go motion over the

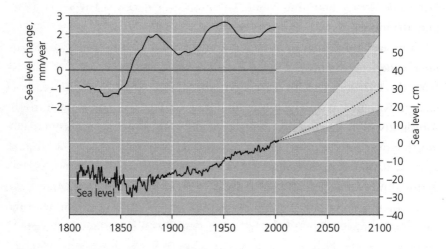

Figure 20 *Sea level rise from 1807 to 2002 and IPCC projection till 2100. Upper left is the sea level change per year.*[377]

past 150 years, as you can see in the top left corner of Figure 20. In the later part of the 1800s, sea levels rose by almost 2 mm per year, but in the first part of the 1900s the rate fell below 1 mm. Fifty years ago it was at 2.5 mm and after a lull in the seventies it is back at around 2.4 mm per year.

In its 2007 report, the UN estimates that sea levels will rise about 29 cm over the rest of the century.[378] While this is not a trivial amount, it is also important to realize that it is certainly not outside the historical experience. Since 1860 we have experienced a sea level rise of about 29 cm, yet this has clearly not caused major disruptions. It is also important to realize that the new prediction is *lower* than the previous IPCC estimates. The new span is 18–59 cm (midpoint 38.5 cm), down from 9–88 cm in 2001 (midpoint 48.5 cm).[379] This continues a declining trend from the nineties (where the first IPCC expected 67 cm), and the eighties, where the US EPA projected several meters.[380]

Often, the risk of sea level rise is strongly dramatized in the public discourse. A cover story of *U.S. News & World Report* famously predicted how "global warming could cause droughts, disease, and political upheaval" and other "nasty effects, from pestilence and famine to wars and refugee movement."[381] We will return to these concerns later, but their primary projection for sea level rise ran: "By midcentury, the chic Art Deco hotels that now line Miami's South Beach could stand waterlogged and abandoned."

Yet, sea level change in 2050 will be no more than the change we already *have* experienced since 1940 or less than the change the Art Deco hotels from the 1920s and 1930s have stood through.[382] Moreover, with sea level changes occurring slowly throughout the century, economically rational foresight will make sure that protection will be afforded to property that is worth more than the protection costs, and settlements will be avoided where costs will outweigh benefits.[383] The IPCC cite the *total* cost for the US national protection and property abandonment for a 1 meter sea level rise (more than thrice what is expected in 2100) at about $5–6 billion over the century.[384] Considering that the adequate protection costs for Miami would be just a tiny fraction of this cost spread over the century, given that the property value for Miami Beach in 2006 was close to $23 billion,[385] and that the Art Deco Historic District is the second largest tourist magnet in Florida after Disney, contributing over $11 billion annually to the economy,[386] 12 cm will simply not leave Miami Beach hotels waterlogged and abandoned.

But this of course, is exactly the opposite of what we often hear from global warming advocates. Al Gore has perhaps made their point most forcefully in his book and film. In a very moving film clip he shows us how large parts of Florida, including all of Miami, will be inundated by 20 feet of water.[387] He goes on to show us equally strong clips of San Francisco Bay being flooded, the Netherlands being wiped off the map, Beijing and then Shanghai being submerged, Bangladesh being made uninhabitable for 60 million people, and even how New York and its World Trade Center Memorial will be deluged.

How is it possible that one of today's strongest voices on climate change can say something so dramatically different from the best science, as we see from the IPCC in Figure 20. The IPCC estimates a foot, Gore tops them 20 times. Well, technically, Al Gore is not contradicting the UN, because he simply says: "If Greenland melted or broke up and slipped into the sea – or if half of Greenland and half of Antarctica melted or broke up and slipped into the sea, sea levels worldwide would increase by between 18 and 20 feet."[388] He is simply positing a hypothesis, and then in full graphic and gory detail showing us what – hypothetically – would happen to Miami, San Francisco, Amsterdam, Beijing, Shanghai, Dhaka and then New York.[389]

Gore is correct in identifying Antarctica and Greenland as the most important players if he is to manage to support his hypothetical 20 feet. The UN estimates that over the century by far the largest contribution to sea level rise will be warmer water expanding – this alone will constitute 23 of the 29 cm by 2100.[390] Melting glaciers and ice caps will contribute a bit more than 8 cm over the century.[391] Likewise, Greenland is expected to contribute 3.5 cm by itself.[392] This adds up to 34.5 cm over the coming century. However, as the world warms, Antarctica will not noticeably start melting (it is still way too cold), but because global warming also generally produces more precipitation, Antarctica will actually be accumulating ice, *reducing* sea levels by 5.5 cm.[393] Thus, the overall estimate of 29 cm or one foot.

So where could Gore hope to find his 19 missing feet? All climate models are in fair agreement on the larger part of the expanding water, so it is unlikely that he will find it there.[394] Likewise he cannot hope to find it in the melting glaciers, although he showed us so many of them receding. Even if all glaciers and ice caps entirely disappeared, it would still only contribute somewhere between 15–37 cm or maximally a foot.[395] However, if Greenland melted, that would contribute 7.3 meters, or 24 feet. If Antarctica entirely slipped into the ocean, it would contribute a whopping 56.6 meters or 186 feet.[396]

But will they? The available analyses tell us a *very* different story (which of course is also why they don't support the Gore stance). Let us look at them individually, since Greenland and Antarctica are very different. Whereas the Antarctic is surrounded by ice shelves and is located in a region where little or no surface melting occurs, Greenland is situated in a region where temperatures are high enough to cause widespread summer melting.[397]

Greenland is, as IPCC pointed out, overall losing mass. The longest studies from the early 1990s till 2002 show that it has been thinning around the edges, but accumulating mass in the high interior, leading to an approximately stable state (actually slightly gaining mass).[398] These studies have all been done with satellite altimeters – essentially measuring how high Greenland is.

However, very recent measurements over the period 2002–5 have used a new technique measuring the Earth's gravity field, and linking the changes in the gravity field to increases or decreases of ice on Greenland. These studies show that ice loss is increasing and that Greenland is overall losing mass, with some estimates up at 0.7 mm sea level rise per year.[399] However, this estimate is only for two years. Moreover, the winter of 2002–3, which preceded the mass-loss acceleration, was a year of unexpectedly high snowfall in southeast Greenland, and 2005, which immediately followed it, was a year of record melt.[400] Thus, it is difficult to say if this is a true long-term trend or whether it is due to an interannual variation in accumulation or melting.[401] By early 2007, two of the major glaciers in Greenland were seen reverting to much lower ice mass loss.[402] Likewise the latest overview shows Greenland contributing less than 0.3 mm per year.[403]

However, even if we grant Gore the 0.7 mm result – which, as we shall see, is an absolutely extreme outlier – this would still mean that his 20 feet of sea level increase would take a thousand years.[404] Moreover, there are strong reasons to believe that this high level of melt-off would not be sustainable for longer periods, simply because there would be less to melt.[405]

So why does IPCC believe that Greenland melt will be much, much lower? Well, for starters, all models show much less long-term melting. In an overview of the main models, Greenland's contribution over the coming century is between a sea level increase of 4 cm and a decrease of 1 mm.[406]

Much of Al Gore's intellectual background for these claims comes from climatologist Jim Hansen. Hansen in many ways started the modern concern about global warming at a Congressional hearing with Al Gore in 1988 during a sweltering US drought. Here he said that there was strong evidence for the greenhouse effect and it was time to stop waffling.[407] Al Gore helped name Hansen as one of the most influential people in *Time* magazine in 2006.[408] Hansen reviewed Gore's book very favorably in *New York Review of Books*, and pointed out how Gore's gut instinct about the Earth teetering on the brink has essentially proven true.[409]

Hansen has gone publicly on the record – as the only prominent climatologist – to say that with the business-as-usual scenario we will see a collapse of Greenland and part of the Antarctic, causing a sea level rise of 80 feet, with more than 20 feet per century.[410] However, Hansen's supporting argument is an editorial in *Climatic Change*, where he suggests that the top models are not adequate, and gives some suggestions as to why this may be the case. Yet, his own central reference on the matter claims that Greenland will contribute to a sea level increase of 0.6–6.6 cm till 2100.[411] Notice how this is right in line with IPCC's central estimate of 3.5 cm.

He closes his argument – very honestly – saying: "In the case at hand, I realize that I am no glaciologist and could be wrong about the ice sheets. Perhaps, as IPCC (2001) and more recent global models suggest, the ice sheets are quite stable and may even grow with doubling of CO_2. I hope those authors are right. But I doubt it."[412]

If we look at Figure 21 we see the results of all models that clearly show both Greenland and Antarctica making small contributions over the century. Moreover, Antarctica is generally the larger, negative contributor, as IPCC predicts. Actually, IPCC estimates that the very worst additional increase to be expected from Greenland could be 20 cm over the century, but this is only possible in a model where CO_2 rises between two and four times higher than

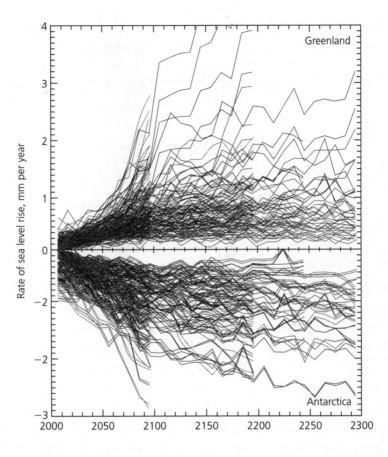

Figure 21 *All the model estimates over the coming 300 years of Greenland sea level increase (all positive) and Antarctica sea level increase (all negative and generally bigger).*[413] *Notice that the Al Gore/Hansen prediction for Greenland would be about 120 mm in 2100, that is about 45 times higher than the highest here.*

expected by 2100.[414] Thus, there is very little support for the assumption of the 20 feet from Gore and Hansen.

It is actually thought provoking to realize that the Hansen/Gore claim of 20 feet over the next century translates into an expectation of 120 mm of sea level change per year by 2100.[415] On Figure 21 that would be 40 times higher than the *absolutely highest* model estimate and an astounding 174 times

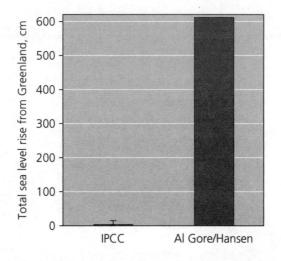

Figure 22 *The estimate of Al Gore/Hansen of twenty-first-century sea level rise due to Greenland melt. The IPCC estimate is 3.5 cm, and uncertainty is indicated by the lowest (1 cm) and highest (15 cm) estimates from all available models, as show in Figure 21. Al Gore and Hansen expect 609 cm, or 174 times more.*

higher that the average.[416] This is demonstrated in Figure 22, where you can see the dramatic difference between Gore and the scientists at IPCC. It would have beautiful theatrical value to show this graph on a big screen, and use a mechanical lift to rise 174 times above the reasonable value, to show Al Gore's estimate.

Gore might – as many others have done – point to the fact that even the IPCC expects that, with sufficient warming, Greenland will disappear.[417] However, this requires a rather, but not unrealistically, high temperature increase globally of 3.1°C, which will first happen sometime around 2100. Moreover, for Greenland to start disappearing, it is necessary to sustain this high temperature for many, many centuries, which seems unrealistic, given we are already in the twenty-second century, due to developments of CO_2 alternatives.[418] And even in this worst-case scenario, and assuming much higher concentration of CO_2 than anyone expects by the end the century, the models suggest that Greenland instead of contributing 3.5 cm will not flood the world with Gore's 20 feet, but maximally contribute 55 cm in the following centuries and decline thereafter.[419]

In 2006 we finally got the longest temperature data series for Greenland, and in Figure 23 we see why we may be hearing much more about melting, because temperatures have indeed increased dramatically in the 1990s. Yet, as you can tell, it seems that Greenland has bypassed the general warming tendency since 1940 and instead cooled until the 1990s (not something we have heard a whole lot about). Thus, some researches have suggested that the temperature increases we see both in the 1930s and now are more linked to a change in the so-called North Atlantic Oscillation (NAO, which we will hear more about in the chapter on hurricanes).[420] This would both explain the different temperature development in Greenland, and also show us why the temperature increases we see now look as similar as the ones in the 1920s and 1930s. Studies show that the temperature increases happened even faster back then.[421] Moreover, despite the strong temperature increase, the warmest year in Greenland was 1941 and the two warmest decades were the 1930s and 1940s.[422]

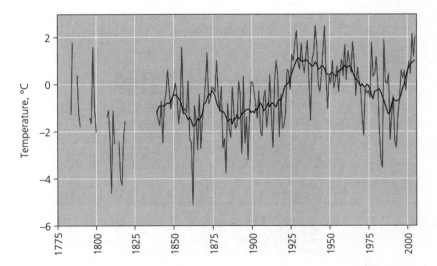

Figure 23 *Greenland annual temperature from 1785 to 2005.*[423] *It is likely that the low temperatures in the early 1800s were due to the Tambora eruption.*

For Antarctica, the story is even more reassuring. The gigantic ice sheet began accumulating some 35 million years ago (as we can also see as the drop in temperature in Figure 18) and has been a permanent fixture in the globe's environment ever since.[424] The ice sheet is on average 2 km (6500 feet) thick and rises in many places to more than 3 km.[425] During the last ice age, especially the West Antarctic ice sheet was much larger, and in the present interglacial Antarctica has been adjusting to the warmer temperatures by net loss of ice.[426]

Surprisingly to many, precipitation is so low that most of the continent is a desert (making it the world's largest desert). However, temperatures are cold enough (about –34°C) that almost nothing melts or evaporates and thus the snow tends to accumulate.

However, much of the world's attention on Antarctica has focused on just a very small part, the Antarctic Peninsula, which stretches to within 600 miles of South America. Al Gore focuses exclusively on this 4% of Antarctica.[427] If you look at Figure 24 you can perhaps tell why. The vast part of Antarctica has cooled.[428] The Amundsen–Scott base at the South Pole has seen temperature decline since the beginning of measurements in 1957.[429] However, the small Antarctic Peninsula has warmed dramatically. Measurements show that it has warmed more than 2°C since the 1960s, at several times the rate of global warming.[430]

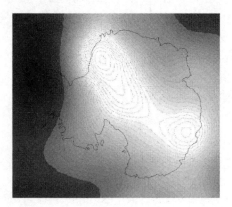

Figure 24 *Temperature change from 1969 to 2002 in Antarctica.*[431] *Dark is getting warmer, light is getting colder, strong contrast line is no temperature change. If you were Al Gore, where would you focus?*

Here Gore shows us how the ice is rapidly melting and how an entire ice shelf (the less-than-poetically named Larsen-B ice shelf) dissolved within 35 days in early 2002.[432] The significance of this break-up relies on us believing that Larsen-B has been intact from time immemorial, and now as the warming is breaking it up it will portend dramatically higher sea levels.[433] But both are wrong.

Studies show that in the middle of our present interglacial, the Larsen area saw "widespread ice shelf breakup."[434] It is likely that the Larsen area was open water from perhaps 6,000 to 2,000 years ago.[435] Instead, the maximal ice shelf dates only from the Little Ice Age a couple of hundred years ago, much of which is what has subsequently collapsed.

Moreover, the break-up of the ice shelf did not cause a sea level rise, because it was already floating.[436] While it probably led to ice shelves flowing more quickly into the sea and glaciers are definitely retreating, the story left out one important fact.[437] Precipitation on the Antarctic Peninsula is large and increasing, probably due to climate change, and this likely outweighs the melting.[438] That is, despite the spectacular pictures that Al Gore can show us of Larsen-B, the Antarctic Peninsula is probably causing an overall *lowering* of sea levels.

This, of course, is the story of the much bigger continent writ large. While most of Antarctica is too cold to see ice beginning to melt, more heat means more precipitation and consequently an increase in ice, or a *decrease* in sea levels in all models.[439] While studies are uncertain of whether Antarctica is accumulating or shedding ice right now, all models predict ever more accumulation over the century.[440]

Summing up, this does not mean we will not experience sea level rise due to global warming. However it will not be 20 feet or more, but – entirely in line with the IPCC – about 29 cm over the century, or about the same as what we have experienced over the past 150 years.

So what will be the consequences of this sea level increase? Often we are presented with a view of society passively accepting the ever-rising seas.[441] In the UK 2006 Stern Review, one such example was given: "A Government study calculated that in the UK the average annual costs of flood damage to homes, businesses and infrastructure could increase from around 0.1% of GDP currently to 0.2–0.4% of GDP if global temperatures rise by 3 to

PENGUINS IN DANGER?

Al Gore also shows us how the rising temperatures in the Antarctic Peninsula have dramatically affected the emperor penguins, who starred in the 2005 documentary *March of the Penguins*.[442] This colony of penguins, just 500 meters from the pioneering French research station Dumont d'Urville, has been constantly monitored since 1952. It was constant at around 6,000 breeding pairs until the 1970s, when it dropped abruptly to about 3,000 pairs, and has remained stable since.[443] This could possibly be linked to climate change, although the abrupt one-time decline makes it less likely.[444] However, it is but one single and rather small colony of about 40 colonies around Antarctica, and only the best studied because of its situation.[445] Some of the largest colonies each contain more than 20,000 pairs, and several of them may be increasing.[446] The IUCN estimates that there are almost 200,000 pairs and that the population is stable, placing it in the category "least concern."[447] Moreover, the other main Antarctic penguin, the Adélie penguin, has in the same region seen an increase of more than 40% over the past 20 years, underscoring the problem in simply blaming global warming and not telling the full story.[448]

4°C."[449] However, these alarming figures only hold true if one assumes that the UK will take no additional measures – essentially doing absolutely nothing and allowing itself to get flooded, perhaps time and again. The UK estimates that the cost of flooding is about £800 million today, but could increase to £27 billion in 2080.[450] In contrast, the UK government's own assumptions take into account a modest increase in flood prevention (about par with economic growth), finding that the cost of flooding will actually sharply *decline* from 0.1% of GDP to 0.02% in spite of climate change.[451]

Often in the debate on flooding, such alarming but essentially misleading figures are presented.[452] However, as above, it seems reasonable to expect that these alarming figures will never come to pass and that rational countries will choose strategies that will actually reduce costs while sea levels increase.

This also holds true globally, as we shall see. However, for us to talk about what will happen in the future, we first need to get acquainted with the four scenarios from the IPCC. The climate panel distinguishes the future in two ways.[453] One way looks at whether the future will be most concerned with and focused on *economic* or *environmental* development. The two scenarios that focus on the economic development are denoted *A* whereas the other two scenarios concerned about environmental sustainability are denoted *B*. The other way describes the degree of cohesion – whether the world has coalesced into one *global* community or has fractured into *regions*. The global scenarios get the number *1* whereas the regional scenarios get the number *2*. The "standard" scenario is the economically and globally focused A1, which is commonly seen as the most likely future, if we don't change our ways. The most prominent contender is the still globally focused but much more environmentally aware B1, which many in the IPCC system seem to prefer.[454]

Now, look at Figure 25, which tells us that today about 10 million people get flooded each year becasue of coastal flooding (and about 200 million are in the danger zone of getting flooded). Even if there were no global warming, this number would increase due to more people being placed in harm's way, both because populations will increase and because coastal areas seem to be more attractive. This is evident in the US, where the total population has quadrupled over the past century but the Florida coastal population has increased more than fifty-fold.[455]

Moreover, many countries and cities are also subsiding – basically sinking. Venice is perhaps most famous, but its sinking has many different causes. A more clear-cut example is Santa Clara in California, where near-continuous water usage from 1920 to the 1970s lowered the water table by 50 meters and caused the valley floor to subside by 4 meters before water extraction was strongly regulated.[456] Shanghai likewise subsided more than 2.5 meters in the first part of last century before water extraction was regulated. Finally, land changes since the ice age mean that some parts, like Scandinavia, are rising after getting rid of the ice sheets, whereas others are

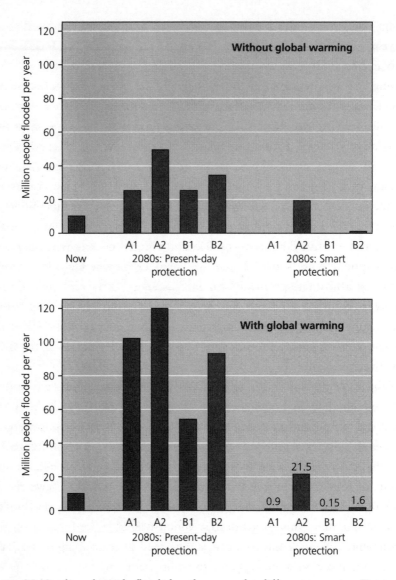

Figure 25 *Number of people flooded each year under different scenarios. Top panel without global warming, today and in the 2080s with today's protection and smart protection. Bottom panel with global warming.*[457]

sinking. London and all of south-east England is subsiding by about 3 mm each year – more than the global sea level rise.[458]

So in the 2080s, if we don't do anything and even without global warming, we will see a sharp increase in the numbers of people flooded to 25–49 million annually (and the numbers in the danger zone reaching 400–800 million). As above, it seems rather unlikely that we would not take relatively cheap action through barriers (like the London Barrier), dikes and levees, coastal protection and – rarely – giving up land. Through such processes we would end up with many fewer people flooded. For A1 and B1 we would have essentially no people flooded, whereas in A2 there would remain a substantial 19 million people flooded, and even in B2 there would be a million flooded. Why? Because in the regional worlds of A2 and B2, people are less rich and consequently can afford less protection.

This is an important point. Choices of fundamental approaches to the world (global or regional? economy or environment?) often will have economic consequences leading to different outcomes on environmental issues. Even in the B2 world, where our primary concern is the environment, we might end up having more people flooded, simply because we forgot to worry enough about economic development.

With global warming, rising sea levels and constant protection, many more people will get flooded, as we can see in the lower part of Figure 25. Given that A1 will be much more interested in money, it will use massive amounts of fossil fuels to power the economy, leading to a sea level rise in the 2080s of 34 cm[459] and causing about 100 million people to get flooded each year. Compare this to gentle B1, which will be more focused on the environment, use much less fossil fuels, and lead to just 22 cm of sea level rise, causing about 54 million people to be flooded.

But again, it seems unlikely that societies will not be smart about coastal protection. If they choose these strategies, at fairly low cost, they will see many fewer people flooded each year. In A1, we will have about 0.9 million flooded each year and in B1 fewer than 0.2 million. Again, A2 and B2, despite lower sea levels, end up with high numbers of people flooded, due to their low incomes. So, clearly, choosing an environmentally concerned B2 will give less environmental benefit than the not-so-concerned A1.

Notice what Figure 25 tells us. Even though global warming will cause sea levels to rise significantly, it will most likely lead to many fewer people being flooded each year, because of higher incomes allowing much more flood protection. For A1, we will see a reduction from 10 million being flooded today to fewer than a million in the 2080s. Essentially, the economic wealth increase over the coming century makes it possible to reduce the potential impact from about 100 million to less than a million – a reduction of more than 100 times. With an environmental approach to climate change we can do much less. With the B1 we can reduce the number of flood victims by much less – from 0.9 to 0.15 million or about six times.[460]

Of course, it would be a natural reaction to say "let's do both" and opt for B1. But this disregards the fact that sea level rise is not the only problem and there are many other challenges in the world that need attention. Here it is important to realize that A1 is a much richer world than B1. The IPCC estimates that a person in world A1 will on average make $72,700 in the 2080s, whereas a person in world B1 will make $50,600.[461]

Moreover, the models producing Figure 25 only roughly take into account the richness of the world – essentially they do not allow for richer worlds to buy even higher degrees of protection. Thus, it is likely that an A1 world would essentially arrange for protection for the last 0.9 million simply because it could afford to.[462] This we can also see in additional economic analyses of flooding.

It is estimated that almost all nations in the world will establish almost maximal coastal protection almost everywhere, simply because it turns out that doing so is fairly cheap. This was also what we saw when we talked about the historical downtown of Miami. For more than 180 of the world's 192 nations, coastal protection will cost less than 0.1% GDP and will afford 100% protection.[463]

Even some of the vulnerable nations that are often used as poster images for the scares of global warming will remain almost entirely protected. The most affected nation will be Micronesia, a federation of 607 small islands with a total land area of only four times Washington DC, stretching some 2,900 km across the Pacific east of the Philippines.[464] If nothing were done, Micronesia would lose some 21% of its area by the end of the century.[465] However, with protection, its 100,000 inhabitants will lose just some 0.18% of their land area (or a little less than the West Potomac Park in DC) if sea levels rise by 34 cm under A1.[466] However, if we choose the B1 world, even though we will have a much lower sea level rise of 22 cm, the Micronesians will also be less well off, such that they will end up losing a larger land area of 0.6% or more than three times as much. With B2 and A2 they will lose as much as 1.8% and 2.9%. Yet, notice that even in the most extreme event, the most exposed nation retains over 97% of its area, and more likely more than 99.8%.

For Tulavu, with 12,000 inhabitants and a land area of less than 10% of Washington DC, land loss from sea level rise in the A1 world will be 0.03% or less than 2 acres, about one tenth of the White House Rose Garden.[467] Again, in a B1 world this loss will be tripled. For the Maldives, the loss without protection would amount to 77%, but with protection the loss would be 0.0015% or about an acre, with higher loss from a B1 world.[468]

For Vietnam the loss would be about 0.02% of land area, and in Bangladesh, the loss would – perhaps surprisingly – be virtually nil at 0.000034%. Again, had we chosen B2 losses in both countries would have amounted to more than 0.25%.

Why are these losses so much lower than what one usually hears? This is due to the simple point of costs and benefits facing each nation. Micronesia would lose 21% of its land at a cost of 12% of its GDP; however for 7.4% of GDP it can save almost all, making protection the better deal. For all other nations, the deal is much better and consequently the protection even higher. The 77% land loss for the Maldives is worth more than their entire GDP (122%) – whereas protection will cost about 0.04% of GDP, making almost every square meter worth saving.[469] While Vietnam would lose some 15% of its land without protection and suffer an 8% GDP loss, its protection costs are about 0.04% of GDP, too.

Another way to put this is to note that as sea levels have risen since 1850, we have allowed ourselves to lose very little land, exactly because the value of the land was much higher than the cost of protecting it. Obviously, with richer nations and scarcer land this relationship will hold throughout the coming century.

Yet a multitude of opinion makers tell us that the consequences will be disastrous and we need to change our ways. Tony Blair tells us that "sea levels are rising and are forecast to rise another 88 cm by 2100, threatening 100 million people globally who currently live below this level."[470] Consequently we must implement Kyoto.

Yet, if we look at Figure 26 we realize – as with temperature – that carbon cuts will make fairly little difference in sea level rise. If everyone, including the US and Australia, implemented Kyoto and stuck to the agreement it would postpone sea level rises by about four years in 2100 at significant cost. It would leave the world poorer but not much better at dealing with the problems.

Likewise Greenpeace tells us implausibly that the Maldives will be submerged, and "if current warming trends continue, cities like London, Bangkok and New York will end up below sea level – displacing millions and causing massive economic damage."[471] The solution is rapid CO_2 reductions, and it "is our only hope to avoid disastrous sea level rise."

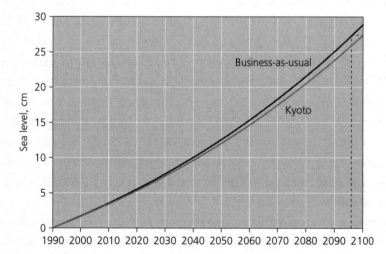

Figure 26 *Sea level rise over the coming century with and without Kyoto.*[472] *Notice how the sea level rises in 2096 will be postponed four years by Kyoto.*

As we have seen above, such a solution again fails to take into account what can be done and at what cost. If we aim for a B1 world, which is on the edge of what is possible, we will reduce sea level rises to 22 cm, but at the same time we will reduce individual wealth by 30% in 2100. This will have direct consequences because poorer people in 2100 will be able to fend off sea level rises less well and that will lead to *more* dry land being lost to the sea in all regions, including Micronesia, Tuvalu, the Maldives, Vietnam and Bangladesh. Even poorer solutions like A2 or B2 will lead to 60–75% wealth reductions and (sometimes even dramatically) less coastal protection. Moreover, the shrill messages of the Maldives being submerged clash with the actual estimates of 0.0015% dry land loss.

We have reached an important point in our discussion on climate change. If our goal is to improve the welfare of people and the environment, and not just reduce carbon emissions, we have to openly inquire how best to do so. Doing too little about climate change is definitely wrong, but, apparently, so is doing too much. Clearly, sea level rise is an important issue and it will have consequences throughout the century and beyond. It will have real costs and in an ideal world we would like to wish it away. However, if we do too much to avoid sea level rise, we will end up with lower levels but also less wealth that in turn will make us less able to deal with the sea rising. We should definitely not do nothing about global warming, but doing much and quickly may actually leave the world overall worse off.

While cute quotes of "drive-by drowning" sound good, images of low-lying Pacific islands look suggestive on TV, and films of an inundated Florida with Al Gore's voice-over look scary, this information is not correct and is likely leading us to make poor or even counter-productive decisions. We are not going to see Florida inundated – sea levels will rise by 29 cm over the coming century, not Al Gore's claimed 20 feet. Sea levels will rise as much over the next hundred years as they did in the past 150 years, which was a problem but one we managed.

If we choose to focus on a world where we and especially the developing world gets richer, we are likely to see vanishingly little land lost. It is only if our fear makes us go down the paths of much less rich future worlds that our actions – although well intentioned – may cause more loss of land, and lower human welfare.

Extreme weather, extreme hype

Stronger and more frequent hurricanes have become one of the standard exhibits of the global warming worries. The National Resources Defense Council tells us that "global warming doesn't create hurricanes, but it does make them stronger and more dangerous."[473] Friends of the Earth proclaims "Hurricanes in Florida. Storms in the UK. Extreme weather events are predicted to become more frequent because of climate change."[474] Greenpeace tells us "there is strong evidence that extreme weather events – such as hurricanes – are increasing (and becoming more severe and frequent) because of climate change."[475]

All show and tell us of the horrors of hurricanes, especially in developing countries. Friends of the Earth commented on Hurricane Mitch, which ripped though Nicaragua and killed 10,000 people in floods and mud slides, with a lengthy quote of a survivor beginning: "We found many bodies without heads, and severed limbs scattered."[476] They even began their press release with a quote of *Lacrimosa* from the requiem mass pointing a moral finger: "There will be tears on that day, when from the dust shall arise, guilty man to be judged."

The solution offered is invariably CO_2 cuts and Kyoto.

With the strong 2005 hurricane season and the devastation of New Orleans by Katrina, this message has reverberated even more powerfully. Al Gore spends 26 pages on showing pictures of the suffering from New Orleans and names every single hurricane in 2005. Carl Pope, executive director for the Sierra Club, confides in us: "Katrina showed that when the climate changes, it's catastrophic. It's not just about it getting warmer. It's about climate becoming chaotic, weather becoming extreme."[477] Internally, he suggested "that our strategy should seek to ride the waves of existing public urgency, rather than waiting for information and education to create a new current of concern about global warming itself." Specifically the Sierra Club should "ride the wave of public concern created over extreme weather by Katrina and Rita."[478]

Robert F. Kennedy, when looking at the New Orleans tragedy, blamed it on the US "derailing the Kyoto Protocol" and said that "now we are all learning what it's like to reap the whirlwind of fossil fuel dependence."[479]

Just a day after Katrina wrecked Louisiana, Ross Gelbspan told us that its "real name is global warming."[480] The German environment minister Jürgen Trittin stated that Katrina was retribution to the US for not dealing with global warming and that its damage might make the US come to its senses and implement Kyoto.[481] In his words: "There is only one conclusion to be drawn: Greenhouse gas emissions must be radically reduced."[482]

Yet these standard statements have much resemblance to the stories of the polar bears. They are vastly overstated and they point our worries the wrong way.

So has global warming caused stronger and more frequent hurricanes, and what will happen in the future? Let us here use the latest consensus statement from the UN World Meteorological Organization (parent organization for the IPCC), which is more recent and more specific but generally in agreement with the 2007 IPCC report.[483] It makes three strong and specific points.

1. Though there is evidence both for and against the existence of a detectable anthropogenic [human-caused] signal in the tropical cyclone climate record, to date no firm conclusion can be made on this point.[484]

They basically tell us that the strong statements of humans causing more and stronger hurricanes (or tropical cyclones as researchers call them) are simply not well supported. We just don't know as yet. When Al Gore tells us that there is a "scientific consensus that global warming is making hurricanes more powerful and more destructive" it is incorrect.[485]

2. No individual tropical cyclone can be directly attributed to climate change.

The strong statements on Hurricane Katrina are simply not supportable. We will get back to their third point, but let us first look at the evidence that has led many to make these judgements.

Most of this recent debate comes from the publication of two papers in 2005. The first was written by Kerry Emanuel from MIT, and it shows us how the total power of all hurricanes in the North Atlantic and the West Pacific has almost doubled over the past 50 years.[486] The second was written by a team led by Peter Webster from Georgia Institute of Technology and

Greg Holland from NCAR, which showed that the past 30 years have seen an almost doubling of the most severe hurricanes – the so-called category 4 and 5 hurricanes.[487] Although both authors were careful not to explicitly attribute these rises to global warming, it still seems like pretty clear-cut evidence of stronger and more damaging hurricanes in a warming world. Predictably, that was also how the press saw the case, with "Global warming causing stronger hurricanes" as the headline in USA Today.[488]

So why are both Emanuel and Holland signed up along with 123 other hurricane experts to the consensus statement? For three reasons.

First, it turns out that it is really hard to get good data on hurricanes going back very far. Only recently have we had good satellite tracking (before 1970 none, in 1975 just two satellites, and now eight technologically superior ones) – preliminary analysis indicates that we have probably missed at least 70 category 4 and 5 hurricanes in the eastern hemisphere just in the years 1978–90.[489] In a period of 13 years we didn't realize that 70 or more hurricanes were of the very worst kind. Likewise and incredibly, our data on hurricane power have missed the hurricane that caused the world's worst hurricane disaster, killing 500,000 people in Bangladesh in 1970. Going further back, only in the North Atlantic have we had regular weather aircraft reconnoitering since the 1940s, and this basin only covers 11% of global hurricanes.[490] Although aircraft cannot monitor as well and completely as satellites, they are still much better than what most of the world has had to make do with, which is essentially expecting ships to call in hurricanes or wait for them to get noticed when they hit populated land. Yet, many hurricanes stay at sea – only 25% of all hurricanes formed in the North Atlantic eventually hit the US.[491]

Second, if hurricanes didn't change much from decade to decade, we would be fine with analyzing the last 30 years and seeing if there is an increase. The problem is that everyone acknowledges that hurricanes move in cycles. For instance, in the Atlantic there seems to be a 50–60 year cycle called the Atlantic multidecadal mode, with many hurricanes in the 1930–60 period, a lull from 1970 to 1994, and currently again an increase in hurricane activity.[492] So obviously, if we only see an increase from 1970 onwards as in Webster, we might simply be seeing the transition from a lull to an active period. Likewise, Emanuel's work, which stretches further back, requires extensive downward adjustment of the active period data for 1940–60 – if not, the result disappears.[493]

Third, the trends that Webster and Emanuel find are much too strong compared to what theory predicts – some five to eight times stronger.[494] Some could find this to mean that outcomes will be even worse than we expected. But with the above serious problems of data that likely explain at least part of the strong findings of Webster and Emanuel, it seems more plausible that theory indicates a less strong connection. Thus, most expect a moderate increase in hurricane windspeed of 3–5% per °C with global warming.[495]

Let us just see a single example of the issues. On the right hand side of Figure 27 you see Webster's graph for how the number of intense hurricanes has almost doubled since 1970. These are the data used for arguing that the number of intense hurricanes is strongly increasing.

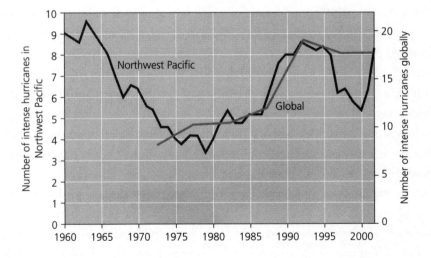

Figure 27 *Annual number of intense (category 4 and 5) hurricanes globally in five-year averages from 1970 to 2004 and number of intense hurricanes (category 4 and 5) in the Northwest Pacific from 1960 to 2004, five-year moving average.*[496] *Notice, Northwest Pacific hurricanes make up almost half of the global number of hurricanes.*

However, in the same figure you see the numbers of intense hurricanes in the Northwest Pacific, which is the single biggest hatchery of intense hurricanes, making up almost half of Webster's total data set. These numbers go much further back, to 1960. Webster deliberately excluded these data because they may be inaccurate due to lack of routine satellite observations. Yet it seems likely that, if the older data are inaccurately reported, they would be *underreported* because some of the intense hurricanes never made landfall and remained undetected before the satellite era.[497] Critics have also claimed that the early wind speed estimates are too high (which should make the numbers in the 1960s lower) or too low (which would make them higher).[498] Nonetheless, they are the best we have.

What the data from the Northwest Pacific tell us is that, yes, looking from 1970 onwards, we might think the number of intense hurricanes had doubled through to the 1990s, but actually that is only because we don't look further back. If we bring in the 1960s, we realize that there were just as many or possibly even more intense hurricanes back then, and that the 1970s was simply the lull between the high activity periods.

What the WMO consensus statement tells us is that we just don't know whether one or the other is the right interpretation right now. Moreover, most of the participants expect it to be a decade before we can tell who is right.[499]

However, this brings us to the third and perhaps most important WMO consensus point. We don't really care about hurricanes as such – what we care about is their damage. Do they end up killing people and cause widespread disruption? And with global warming, will they kill and disrupt even more? The answer is – perhaps surprisingly – that the whole hurricane debate is somewhat tangential to this important question.

3. The recent increase in societal impact from tropical cyclones has largely been caused by rising concentrations of population and infrastructure in coastal regions.[500]

While the theoretical debate whether hurricanes are increasing or not increasing is unlikely to have a clear-cut outcome any time soon, most observers end up pointing out how *damage* from hurricanes is rising dramatically and quickly. Al Gore ends his discussion on hurricanes by presenting the historically increasing hurricane and flooding costs, telling us it is the "unmistakable economic impact of global warming."[501] He tells us that by 2040, weather related disasters could cost as much as $1 trillion "driven by climate change."[502] The numbers are correct. But in attributing them to global warming he is wrong.

Figure 28 clearly show us that the global cost of climate related disasters has increased relentlessly over the past half century, and it seems to provide ample underpinning for Gore's "unmistakable economic impact of global warming." Yet, just comparing costs over long periods of time does not make sense without taking into account the change in population patterns and demography as well as economic prosperity. Worldwide, we are two-and-a-half times as many people today as in 1950, each is more than thrice as rich, most probably have more than tripled their physical wealth, and many have migrated to low-lying and coastal, risk-prone areas.[503]

Thus, there are many more people, residing in much more vulnerable areas, with many more assets to lose. In the US today, the two coastal south

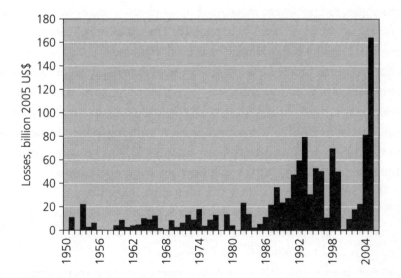

Figure 28 *Global economic losses from great weather related disasters, 1950–2006.*[504] *Notice that 2006 had no great weather disasters, not something that has been generally reported.*

Florida counties, Dade and Broward, are home to more people than the number of people who lived in 1930 in *all* 109 coastal counties stretching from Texas through Virginia, along the Gulf and Atlantic coasts.[505] Harris County in Texas has nearly tripled since 1960, and today its population is equal to the entire 1955 coastal county population from the Florida panhandle northward to South Carolina.[506]

A large part of the damage in Figure 28 comes from flooding, which is often also claimed to be connected with climate change (see next section). However, let us here look at the best long-term, clearly weather related loss records, namely hurricane damage in the US.

All the top of Figure 29 we see the damage costs rising through the century. It is the very same pattern – or possibly even more pronounced – as the one we saw for global weather damage. Essentially no costs before mid-century, and just three years close to the present standing out. Here Katrina makes up two-thirds of the 2005 season costs, Charley and Ivan make up most of 2004, and Hurricane Andrew is responsible for almost all of 1992. It looks like a slam-dunk for climate-makes-worse-hurricanes.

But a group of researchers began to wonder whether the reason why the early part of the century got off so much more cheaply was because there were fewer people and fewer assets to be harmed. Thus, they asked the hypothetical question: what would the damage have been, if all hurricanes throughout the last 105 years had hit the US as it is today, with today's number of people and wealth? The answer can be seen in the lower part of Figure 29. Suddenly, the picture changes dramatically. If the 1926 Great Miami hurricane had hit today it would have created the worst damage ever in US hurricane history. Hitting just north of where Hurricane Andrew hit in 1992, this category 4 hurricane would have plowed right into the Art Deco district and downtown Miami and cost $150 billion worth of damage, or almost twice the damage of Katrina.[507] As it hit in 1926, it did damage or destroy all downtown buildings, but as these were far fewer and much less valuable, the total damage was more than 200 times less at $0.7 billion present-day dollars.

The same story goes for the second-largest hurricane from 1900, hitting Galveston head on, inundating the whole of the city in 8–15 feet of water.[508] Had it hit today, it would have caused damage of about $100 billion, but in 1900 with fewer and simpler buildings, it "only" cost some $0.6 billion.[509]

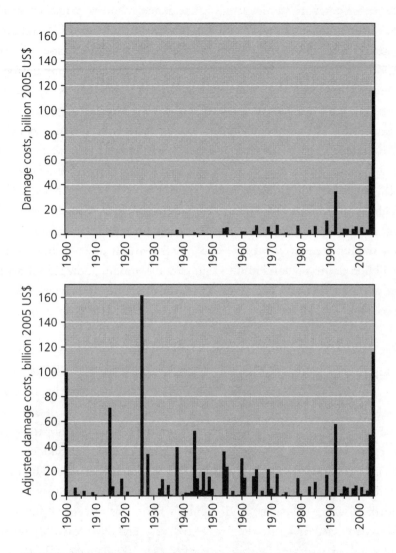

Figure 29 *US hurricane damage, 1900–2005. Top panel shows the actual economic cost in 2005 US$; lower panel shows the cost if the hurricanes had hit today. Damage for 1900–25 is underestimated and more uncertain due to poor data availability.*[510]

When we compare all hurricanes to the damage they would have wrought today, Katrina ranks third at $81 billion, followed by another 1915 Galveston hurricane at $68 billion, and then Hurricane Andrew at $56 billion.

Suddenly, there is no increase in damage over the century with warmer and newer hurricanes being much worse. What we're seeing is the effect of more people with more stuff closer to harm's way. This picture is reinforced by the fact that the damage from the earlier part of the 1900s is probably underestimated. First, given coastal development today it is unlikely that any hurricane could strike and cause no damage. But before 1940, 32 storms actually made landfall and left no government records of any damage. Thus, it is likely that the early damage is underreported.[511] Second, the 1926 Miami hurricane damage was a smaller proportion of the national economy than a similar event would be in 2005. Certainly, an event in the order of $100 billion or more would lead to significant shortages in the affected areas and result in inflationary pressures. Thus, the direct historical cost estimates are probably on the low side.

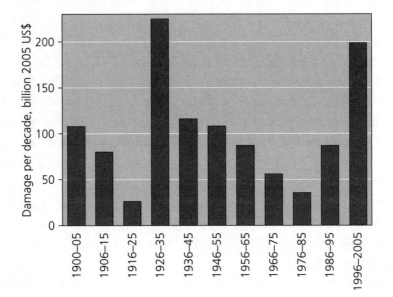

Figure 30 *US damage cost from hurricanes per decade 1900–2005 normalized to present day.*[512]

Thus, as the WMO consensus points out, we are seeing unprecedented levels of hurricane damage not as the "unmistakable economic impact of global warming" but instead as the unmistakable impact of more people and more wealth closer to the sea. If we look at the costs per decade, 1926–35 was the costliest decade, followed by the last decade, 1996–2005, and then 1936–45, 1946–55 and 1900–05. No scary pattern. Look at how 1976–85 was remarkably low – no wonder we have forgotten how hurricane damage can be much worse.

What this also tells us is that damage will continue to grow as long as more people with more stuff move closer to the sea. This is why it is likely that we will see much higher costs in the future. The Association of British Insurers finds that had Hurricane Andrew hit in 2002 rather than 1992, "the losses would have been double, due to increased coastal development and rising asset values."[513] According to one current insurance industry report, "catastrophe losses should be expected to double roughly every ten years because of increases in construction costs, increases in the number of structures and changes in their characteristics."[514]

It seems likely that such a decadal doubling of damage will continue, and this is the background for the $1 trillion damage Al Gore refers to. It comes from a scenario constructed for the UN Environment Program, where they projected a doubling of damage every 12 years, finding that it is very likely that by 2040 we will have a record damage of $1 trillion.[515] Thus, it is not a scenario linked to global warming but a projection of past trends – that "has largely been caused by rising concentrations of population and infrastructure in coastal regions," as WMO puts it. That is why it is incorrect when Al Gore claims the $1 trillion peak in 2040 will be "driven by climate change."[516]

But, one might object, does this incorrect claim matter, if Al Gore can manage to make us aware of the larger global warming danger and act before it is too late? Isn't this just academic hair-splitting without real world consequences? Well, no.

Because we still have to ask what it is we want. Presumably our goal is not to cut CO_2 emissions per se, but to do good for humans and the environment. We want to help the people who are potential victims of future Katrinas, Charleys and Andrews. But how can we best do that?

In Figure 31 we see the relative impact of climate changes and social changes on hurricane damage over the next half-century. It essentially tells us the efficiency of turning the big knob of climate versus the efficiency of turning the social policy knobs.

If society stays the same – no more people living close to the coast, no more costly and densely built neighborhoods – and climate warms, causing worst-case increase in hurricanes, the total effect will be less than a 10% increase in hurricane damage. To put it differently, if we could stop the climatic factors right now, we would avoid 10% more damage in 50 years' time. On the other hand, if climate stays the same – no more warming – but more people build more and more expensive buildings closer to the sea, as they have done in the past, we will see an almost 500% increase in hurricane damage. To put it differently again, if we could curb societal factors right now, we could prevent 500% more damage in 50 years' time.

So if we want to make a difference, which knob should we choose first – the one reducing damage by less than 10% or the one reducing damage by almost 500%? The difference in efficiency between the climate knob and the societal knob is more than 50 times. This seems to suggest that policies

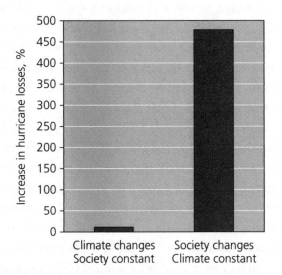

Figure 31 *The relative importance of climate changes and social changes in hurricane damages, 2000–50.*[517]

addressing societal factors rather than climate policies will do the most good first. But of course, we have to ask *how much* can we reasonably turn the knobs?

With the climate knob, it is clear that just turning it toward Kyoto has been exceedingly difficult. If we managed to get everyone, including the US and Australia, to participate in Kyoto and continue to adhere to its ever more binding reductions all the way to 2050, it would essentially mean a slightly lower temperature by 2050, thus a slightly lower hurricane damage increase of about half a percent.[518]

What about the societal knob? We may be a bit hazy on how we could even go about turning the societal knob, simply because we hear very little about it. Clearly we could try to stop people from moving to the sea or prevent them from building nicer houses, but that would be somewhat unrealistic and unwanted. But there are many other possibilities. We could better map vulnerability – some US communities have never been evaluated for flood risk. This would ease evacuation plans, community education and relief distribution.[519] We could regulate vulnerable land, including zoning, regulation, taxing and public acquisition of land at risk. We could avoid state subsidized, low-cost insurance that encourages people to settle in high-risk areas. We could improve building codes to improve the ability of structures to withstand high winds, and enforce existing codes better. We could maintain and upgrade the protective infrastructure such as dikes and levees. We could invest in improved forecasts, better warning systems and more efficient evacuations. We could reduce environmental degradation, where loss of vegetation reduces the soil's ability to absorb water and destabilizes hill slopes, leading to dangerous landslides. Likewise we could protect wetlands and beaches that act as natural seawalls against hurricanes.

Let us just look at a single, simple example. After Hurricane Katrina, one insurance company found that the 500 locations that had been damaged but had implemented all the hurricane-loss prevention methods experienced only one-eighth the losses of those which had not done so.[520] At a cost of $2.5 million, these building owners had avoided $500 million in losses. Often, simple structural measures can yield big benefits, for example bracing and securing roof trusses and walls using straps, clips or adhesives to minimize hurricane damage.[521]

With almost 90% total damage reductions from simple procedures, let us conservatively assume that we could at least cut loss increases in half through cheap and simple policy measures. This would, over the coming half-century, mean a hurricane damage reduction of 250 percentage points.

Thus, in a world with increasing hurricane damage from both global warming and societal factors, Kyoto could probably reduce the total increased damage by about 0.5% and simple preventive measures could reduce that same damage by about 50% – or a hundred times better. Moreover, Kyoto runs into trillions of dollars of cost, whereas the protective measures would be several orders of magnitude lower. Thus, if we care about helping potential victims of future Katrinas and Andrews, it appears unquestionable to suggest that we should focus on societal factors first.

Of course, there will always be the incentive to say "should we not do both?" – but as long as we don't do all there is to do with societal policies, doing climate policies will be a very poor use of resources to deal with future hurricane impacts. There might be other good reasons to carry out climate policies, as we will explore below, but hurricanes are not one of them.

In a nutshell, Katrina really does carry home the message. What caused the tragedy in New Orleans was not the hurricane itself – it was not a killer category 5 but a regular category 3 hurricane that had been predicted for years.[522] Models and exercises had repeatedly shown that New Orleans was not ready for a direct hit.[523] In the words of one expert, it "was a disaster waiting to happen" and, unlike previous hits, New Orleans had just run out of luck.

As one climatologist pointed out, "it is probable that this hurricane would have occurred irrespective of any recent increase in greenhouse gasses."[524] On the other hand it was clear that the catastrophe happened because of bad planning, poorly maintained levees and environmental degradation of the city's bolstering wetlands. So, had you been in charge in the 1990s of helping potential victims of future Andrews, you should not first have worked to cut greenhouse gasses, but should have invested heavily in better planning, better levees and healthier wetlands. And that lesson remains as we try to prevent the losses from future Katrinas.

It is perhaps sobering to realize that while the industrialized world (and the big insurance companies) worries about increasing financial costs and crossing the $1 trillion damage threshold, hurricanes cost less in the third world, but cause many more deaths.[525] Yet here also the message stays the same. Unlike investments in CO_2 cuts, we know effective action is possible to reduce disaster losses even in the face of poverty and dense population.[526] During the 2004 hurricane season, Haiti and the Dominican Republic, both on the island of Hispaniola, provided a powerful lesson. As Julia Taft of the UN Development Program explained: "In the Dominican Republic, which has invested in hurricane shelters and emergency evacuation networks, the death toll was fewer than ten, as compared to an estimated two thousand in Haiti. Haitians were a hundred times more likely to die in an equivalent storm than Dominicans."

At the end we have to ask ourselves whether we want to do a little good or a lot of good first. Together with a number of other prominent scientists, Emanuel and Webster – who at the start of this chapter suggested there might be a connection between global warming and increasing hurricanes – put out a strong statement on the US hurricane priorities:

As the Atlantic hurricane season gets underway, the possible influence of climate change on hurricane activity is receiving renewed attention. While the debate on this issue is of considerable scientific and societal interest and concern, it should in no event detract from the main hurricane problem facing the United States: the ever-growing concentration of population and wealth in vulnerable coastal regions. These demographic trends are setting us up for rapidly increasing human and economic losses from hurricane disasters, especially in this era of heightened activity. Scores of scientists and engineers had warned of the threat to New Orleans long before climate change was seriously considered, and a Katrina-like storm or worse was (and is) inevitable even in a stable climate ...

We call upon leaders of government and industry to undertake a comprehensive evaluation of building practices, and insurance, land use, and disaster relief policies that currently serve to promote an ever-increasing vulnerability to hurricanes.[527]

These scientists don't ask for CO_2 cuts, but for smart, societal policies that will make a big difference. In the words of two of the top specialists in hurricane losses:

Those who justify the need for greenhouse gas reductions by exploiting the mounting human and economic toll of natural disasters worldwide are either ill-informed or dishonest ... Prescribing emissions reductions to forestall the future effects of disasters is like telling someone who is sedentary, obese, and alcoholic that the best way to improve his health is to wear a seat belt.[528]

Flooding rivers

The story of river flooding is much the same as the concerns we saw with hurricanes. Unusually severe floods in the 1990s and the early 2000s, from St. Louis in the US to Poland, Germany, France, Switzerland, Spain and the UK in Europe, have garnered renewed attention to the problem of flooding.[529]

Very often an explicit link is made to climate change. After the severe flooding of Prague and Dresden in 2002, both British Prime Minister Blair, French President Chirac and German Chancellor Schroeder used the flood as a prime example of global warming and why we must commit to Kyoto.[530] According to Schroeder this flood shows us "climate change is no longer a sceptical prognosis, but a bitter reality. This challenge demands decisive action from us," which he understood as a requirement for "all states to ratify the Kyoto Protocol."[531]

And yes, it is true that global warming eventually will increase precipitation, especially heavy rains.[532] Models also show that this will lead to more flooding.[533] There is also some evidence that increased rain is already occurring, although the IPCC has still not been able to link it to global warming.[534] Thus, it would seem that Schroeder might have a point.

But there are two problems with Schroeder's argument. First, the increasing rain does not seem to be translated into increasing flooding in rivers. This holds true in a global sample of almost 200 rivers, where 27 did indeed show increasingly high flows, but even more (31) rivers were decreasing and the large majority showed no trend.[535] This also holds true for the smaller number of very long-term series we have for world rivers.[536] Why is this?

When studying US rivers we can see increasing precipitation causing increasing stream flow, but if we check *when* the increase happens, it turns out that it happens mostly during the fall, when there is generally lower flow and little risk of flooding, whereas it happens rarely in spring and with high flows.[537] Likewise, in Europe, a study of the two major rivers, the Oder and the Elbe (which flooded Prague and Dresden in 2002) showed that over past centuries summer floods show no trend and winter floods have actually *decreased*.[538]

This is well correlated with the historic evidence that shows much greater flood risks in the colder climates of the Little Ice Age.[539] With much snow and a late thaw, ice jams typically blocked a swollen river, producing high water levels, followed by floods and dike bursts.[540] This pattern was the main cause of flooding on the lower Rhine during the Little Ice Age, with almost all dike bursts in the Netherlands the result of ice jams. These floods have decreased sharply in the twentieth century, due to warming.[541] Likewise, an analysis of the River Werra in Germany shows that the highest flood risk was in the 1700s.[542] For the River Vltava in the Czech Republic, floods have decreased over the past century.[543]

We seem to have a very selective memory of floods, thinking that our age is special. And in a sense it is, but perhaps not in the way we think. In general, loss of life and injuries due to flooding have been declining in Europe, with large-scale loss of life in episodes preceding the nineteenth century, with the twentieth-century death toll significantly lower and deaths in the 1990s again even lower.[544] Flooding has been pervasive throughout our history. All but two of the 56 major floods that affected Florence since 1177 occurred before 1844.[545]

What does set our period apart is that *economic losses* have been rising sharply in recent years, constituting some 25% of all economic losses from natural disasters over the last 55 years.[546] However, just as with hurricanes, this tendency seems to be much more related to other factors than climate change, and this is the second problem with Chancellor Schroeder's point.

No matter what the climate future holds, flood impacts may continue to get worse. As the US Congressional Office of Technology Assessment has pointed out, "vulnerability to flood damages is likely to continue to grow" mainly because populations in flood-prone areas continue to increase, putting more property and greater numbers of people at risk, while flood-moderating wetlands continue to be destroyed.[547]

This is in no small way due to the widespread use of levees. The US has about 40,000 km (25,000 miles) of levees – enough to encircle the world at the equator. The problem is that, with levees, people take fewer precautions ("we're safe behind the levee"), and they encourage more people with more expensive structures to settle behind them. This would be fine, if flood risk is reduced to zero, but, as the National Academy of Science points out, "it is short-sighted and foolish to regard even the most reliable levee system as fail-safe."[548] Thus, losses are likely to be much higher when the levee system inevitably fails.

In the US levees are constructed to ensure that there is less than 1% chance of a flood in any given year. Very misleadingly, this is called a 100-year protection (1% each year should seem like 100% over 100 years), but if you do the math the real risk is much higher, at 26% risk of flooding in just 30 years.[549]

Moreover, levees themselves tend to increase flooding.[550] Imagine a river 1,000 meters wide.[551] Now assume that it is pinched to 500 meters by a levee. In order for the river to pass at the same flow, it must rise to a higher elevation at the pinch point and upstream. Likewise, levees can increase downstream flood levels by reducing the floodplain's ability to store water. In a place that historically would have been flooded, a levee protecting the land also denies the river water storage, essentially passing the flood more quickly and more massively downstream. Thus, whenever a levee is constructed, it means water levels will increase upstream and downstream, leading others to increase their levees, resulting in an unpleasant leapfrog levee game of avoiding having the lowest levee.

This increasing flooding has been systematically documented for the Lower Missouri River. Flows that were fully contained within the Missouri channel in the early twentieth century now create floods, and extreme high flows today are 3.7 meters *higher* than they would have been in the 1930s.[552] The same result is found for the Elbe, where at Dresden extreme high flows raise the river height 1.2 meters more than they would have done in 1860.[553]

As with hurricanes, we have a situation where by far the larger part of the increasing damage comes from societal rather than climate factors. Unlike for hurricanes, however, we do not have the same numerical precision on the relative importance, simply because flooding is highly dependent on the specifics of each catchment. Yet, we can still see the same connection as with hurricanes when we look at Figure 32.

In the top panel of Figure 32 we see flood damage cost for the US since 1929. It is highly variable, with the damage in 1993 of the great Mississippi flood in St. Louis standing out. Yet, it clearly shows that costs are escalating.

That picture, however, clearly also includes more people with more

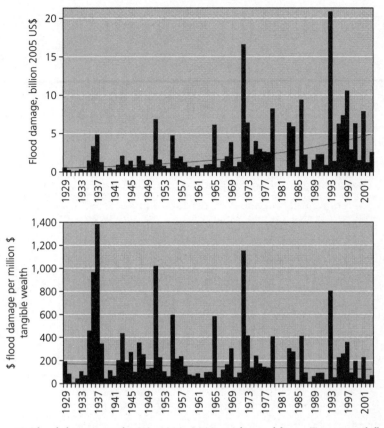

Figure 32 *Flood damage in the US, 1929–2003, with trend lines. Top is total flood damage in present-day dollars. Bottom is flood damage per million dollars of tangible wealth. Missing data for 1980–82.*[554]

wealth living in or near floodplains. One way to redress this would be to look at how much of the nation's goods gets damaged each year in floods.[555] The bottom panel shows how in 1929 approximately $200 of each $1 million worth of goods got damaged. Again, the trend is highly variable, but clearly downwards, so that in 2003 only $70 dollars of each $1 million was lost. This indicates that as society has more tangible wealth, yes, more will get damaged in floods, but it will actually be a smaller and smaller proportion. Overall, floods are getting not more but rather *less* damaging.

This does not mean we should not strive to make floods even less damaging. But – as with hurricanes – we have to ask ourselves where we can do most good first.

Although we still cannot see a global warming signal in the US rivers or some of the large European rivers, it is likely that, as we get further into the century, increasing heavy precipitation will make floods relatively worse. But if we do focus mostly on dealing with this issue and do Kyoto, we will still only be able to postpone warming and increasing flood damage some five years by the end of the century.

The only large-scale study of the comparative climate and social effects on flooding comes from the UK government *Foresight* studies. Here it is shown that a complete change from high-carbon A1 to B1 with more than a halving of temperature increases can reduce damage from fluvial and coastal flooding by 25%.[556] Thus with Kyoto we might be able to achieve a 3% reduction in damage.[557]

If, on the other hand, we focus on dealing with the concrete flooding issues, we have many opportunities to reverse the rising damage trend, stabilize it and perhaps even make it decline. Most flood analysts point out that the ideal strategy for reducing losses would be to limit or even reduce people and wealth on floodplains.[558] However, this would probably be both politically hard and practically impossible. Yet a reasonable policy would focus on the two issues identified above.

We would inform people better about the flood risks, leading to fewer overconfident placements, and encourage more precautions. This would also entail no public subsidies to settlements in floodplains – unlike what is currently happening around St. Louis.[559] We would have more stringent public planning, as is the case in places like Denver and Boulder, Colorado; Austin, Texas; Phoenix, Arizona; and Charlotte, North Carolina, where limited encroachment and guided development decrease flooding.

We would use levees more sparingly and allow some floodplains to do just that – be flooded sometimes, and thereby provide buffers for the remaining areas. We would return some areas back to wetlands, which would both decrease flooding and improve environmental quality. This is beginning to be the approach in Europe, where the Netherlands adopted the "Room for the Rhine" policy in 1997, allowing more places to flood occasionally.[560]

The costs for such policies would be some orders of magnitude lower than Kyoto's trillions of dollars, and they would work much more quickly.

The UK *Foresight* studies show that the sensible, increased flood management comes at minimal cost and achieves a reduction of damages of more than 91%.[561]

It is worth realizing the difference in efficiency between Kyoto and flood management. Using the UK example, for about 0.01% of GDP you get a benefit from damage reduction of 0.12% of GDP – a benefit-to-cost ratio of 11. From Kyoto, at the cost of 0.5% of GDP, you get a benefit of 0.00009% of GDP.[562] Or expressing it in financial terms, for each dollar spent on Kyoto, that dollar spent on flood management would do more than 1,300 times more good for flooding risk.

Flooding is not getting out of hand; the costs are declining compared to total wealth. It is not predominantly a signal of global warming and increasing heavy rains. But financial consequences of flooding are strongly increasing, because of increased population and wealth behind levees that occasionally fail and also increase flooding elsewhere.

We come back to Chancellor Schroeder urging us to help the future flood victims in Dresden by focusing on Kyoto. This would involve large sums of money, and would do virtually no good in the short run, postponing problems toward the end of the century by five years. Essentially it is a promise to the citizens of Dresden that their increasing flood costs will increase slightly more slowly.

On the other hand, societal policies such as better information, more stringent building policies, fewer subsidies, flood areas and more wetlands would be able to stabilize or even reduce losses at much lower cost and much sooner. It seems reasonable to ask if doing that shouldn't be our first priority.

TORNADOES, HAIL, LIGHTNING, ETC.

There are obviously many other climate risks besides hurricanes and flooding, such as storms, tornadoes, hail, and lightning. In the US, hurricanes and floods make up more than 70% of the economic damage and are increasing, which is why they are the most referred to in the climate discussions.[563] However, lightning and tornadoes have killed many more people, so perhaps we should also take a brief look at these incidences.

Al Gore shows in his book a double page with an ominous tornado ripping through the land, and states that "in 2004, the all-time record for tornadoes in the United States was broken."[564] Although intimating that this is yet another sign of the "planetary emergency of global warming," he neglects to tell us that this record only took place in the weakest tornado category, and it is likely caused by better detection.[565]

Tornadoes are classified by the Fujita scale from F0 to F5.[566] F0 is the weakest, causing "minimal damage" to chimneys, TV antennas, trees and windows.[567] F5 causes "incredible damage": homes are leveled, with all debris removed; schools and motels have walls and roofs gone; top stories are demolished.

The registered number of the weakest tornadoes has been increasing since the 1950s. This is probably because of more people in the countryside, expanded weather spotter networks, and recently the increased availability of cell phones.[568] As one climatologist describes tornado spotting: "In the past, some would spin out in a farm field and never be seen by anyone but the farmer. But it's pretty hard for a tornado to escape notice anymore . . . there are fewer and fewer of these slipping through the cracks."[569] In the early 1990s the number of registered tornadoes increased dramatically because of the installation of Doppler Radar networks picking up lots of "minimal damage" tornadoes nobody had seen before.[570] This is the likely background for Gore's claim of a record number of tornadoes in 2004. NOAA describes such an argument as "a misleading appearance of an increasing trend in tornado frequency."[571]

If we instead look at the trend in the number of serious tornadoes, it is more likely that these would have been reported even during the decades before Doppler Radar use.[572] In Figure 33 we see the number of tornadoes at F3 strength and above (from severe to

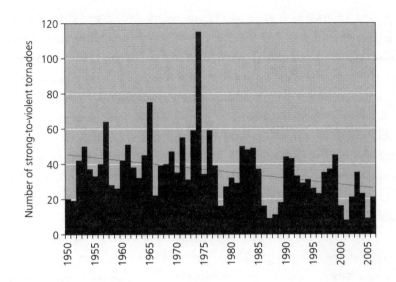

Figure 33 *Number of strong to violent (F3–F5) tornadoes in the US, 1950–2005, with trend.*[573]

incredible damage). These tornadoes cause almost 90% of all deaths, but the same trend is seen for F2 and above tornadoes.[574]

Essentially, we see that serious tornadoes have *declined substantially* over the past half-century. This is in direct opposition to the Al Gore claim and it is an important additional piece of information for the discussion on global warming.

Moreover, the US has not experienced an "incredible damage" F5 tornado in seven years, the longest F5-free period in US tornado history.[575] It also turns out that the economic tornado loss has been declining since 1950, and when adjusted for tangible wealth this conclusion is strengthened.[576]

When looking at hail, we likewise see a decline in the average number of days of hail in the US.[577] This is also reflected in a decreasing trend in economic losses from hail.[578]

Finally, if we look at lightning, the main cost is lives lost, and surprisingly lightning used to be the biggest weather disaster killer in the US. However, as we see in Figure 34, deaths from lightning have declined rapidly. In 1940, almost three people in a million would die each year, whereas today about one in ten million dies.[579] The relatively large number of deaths is due to the fact that lightning is ubiquitous – in Texas lightning strikes more than 1.5 million times each year.[580] A similar drop in lightning deaths has taken place in the UK, and death rates are about half those of the US.[581] A large part of the reason behind the decline comes from the fact that we are outdoors less, and live less in the countryside.[582] Although global warming is expected to increase lightning, trends have not been reliably established, and are clearly not showing up in US mortality.[583]

Likewise, we also see that deaths from both floods and hurricanes are now lower than they were in the 1940s. And to conclude on Al Gore's problematic statement on tornadoes, deaths from tornadoes – like tornadoes and cost of tornadoes – have been consistently declining over the past 65 years.

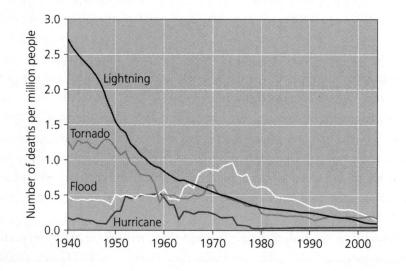

Figure 34 *Death from lightning, tornadoes, floods and hurricanes in the US, 1940–2004.*[584]

A new ice age over Europe?

The concern about global warming stopping the Gulf Stream is probably – at least as of now – the only issue that has had its own Hollywood disaster movie and a Pentagon worst-case scenario. Yet it is also one of the least well founded fears.

The Gulf Stream and its associated currents flow from the Gulf of Mexico up along the US coast to Newfoundland, where they break up, with most currents flowing toward the Canary Islands, but the ones we will focus on continue toward the UK and Europe and toward the Norwegian Sea.[585] As water evaporates from the warm current it becomes ever more salty, dense and cold, until it sinks in the seas between Norway and Newfoundland, and returns along the bottom of the ocean, completing the so-called North Atlantic thermohaline circulation, or more simply the "Atlantic conveyor."

Al Gore tells us the standard story of how the Gulf Stream keeps Europe warmer – with Paris and London much warmer than Montreal or Fargo, which are close to the same latitude.[586] However, according to Gore, climate scientists are now realizing that the Gulf Stream is "surprisingly fragile."[587] About 10,000 years ago, when the last glacial ice sheets in North America melted, a giant pool of fresh water built up around the area of the Great Lakes. One day, Gore tells us, the ice dam broke; an unprecedented amount of fresh water flooded the North Atlantic and disrupted the sinking salty water from the Atlantic conveyor. In essence, the Gulf Stream shut down and Europe, left without its heat, went back into an ice age for another 1,000 years.[588] Now, climate scientists are worried it could happen again. Of course, there is no glacial ice sheet and giant fresh-water pool around today, but in his movie Gore looks at the North Atlantic map and coyly asks if there is "another big chunk of ice near there" and, observing Greenland, says "oh, yeah."[589]

Actually, at the end of the last ice age there were three major reversals, where temperatures dropped (curiously, none of them was at Gore's 10,000 years, but at about 12,500, 11,500 and 8,200 years ago).[590] For the last and largest event, more than 100,000 km^3 of water flooded into the North

Atlantic in less than a year and probably significantly slowed the Gulf Stream for 400 years.[591]

Yet, the relevance of this story crucially depends on it being in the same order of magnitude, and there clearly is a problem with the size of the fresh water influx. Over the coming century, the IPCC expects Greenland to dump some 126 km^3 of water per year (the 3.5 cm over the coming century that we talked about in p. 78) – almost a thousand times less than what happened in the story Gore tells us.[592]

Gore quotes only one expert, Dr. Ruth Curry from Woods Hole Research Center: "The possibility of such extreme events precludes ruling out that disruption of the North Atlantic Ocean Conveyor in the 21st century could occur as a result of greenhouse warming."[593] What she says is that, since it can happen, we can't rule it out – which is a truism. Yet, perhaps a clearer description of her point would have come from *Nature* where "she agrees that the circulation will not be unduly affected this century."[594]

A team of modelers looked at what would happen if Greenland melted at triple the rate expected by the IPPC, or as they put it the "upper limit on possible melting rates."[595] Although they see a reduction in the Gulf Stream, they find "its overall characteristic is not changed" and that "abrupt climate change initiated by Greenland ice sheet melting is not a realistic scenario for the 21st century."[596]

Yet, this has definitely not stopped the worry. The original concern of a Gulf Stream breakdown originated with geochemist Wallace Broecker in the 1980s, who put the theory forward one week before the world met in Japan to agree to the Kyoto Protocol.[597] It was popularized in 1998 by William Calvin with his article entitled "The great climate flip flop," which graced the cover of *The Atlantic* – as a neurophysiologist, Calvin had been interested in whether rapid climate change had been a decisive factor in human evolution.[598] Here he told us how an abrupt cooling could be triggered by global warming, with chilly consequences. "Europe's climate could become more like Siberia. Because such a cooling would occur too quickly for us to make readjustments in agricultural productivity and supply, it would be a potentially civilization-shattering affair, likely to cause an unprecedented population crash."[599]

This line of thought was picked up by a think-tank at the Pentagon, and worked into a global scenario in 2003. In 2004 *Fortune* magazine revealed "the Pentagon's Weather Nightmare," a story which flashed around the world with headlines like "Now the Pentagon tells Bush: climate change will destroy us."[600] The study sketches a "plausible" scenario, talking explicitly about a repeat of the 8,200 years ago Gulf Stream collapse.[601] It envisions a tripling in temperature increases, and bigger hurricanes and storms, which by 2007 make The Hague in the Netherlands uninhabitable.[602] By 2010 the Gulf Stream collapses, and by 2020 "Europe's climate is more like Siberia's."[603] Scandinavia, Germany and Holland begin migrating toward Spain and Italy in 2012, and by 2030 "nearly 100% of the European population moves to a different country."[604] As abrupt cooling reduces productivity, "aggressive wars are likely to be fought over food, water, and energy."[605] By 2030, nuclear war seems to be a likely outcome.[606]

It is not hard to see how this became the inspiration for the Hollywood blockbuster *The Day After Tomorrow*.[607] The movie is an excuse for breathtaking special effects as Manhattan is buried in 30-story snowdrifts and Asia is hit by killer grapefruit-sized hail. The British Queen's helicopter is frozen in mid-flight and Los Angeles is hit by 250 mph multiple tornadoes. Amidst it all, a fearless paleoclimatologist played by Denis Quaid straps on his snow shoes to trek from Washington DC to New York to rescue his son. The bad guy is the Vice President, who bears a striking resemblance to real-life Vice President Dick Cheney. The Cheney doppelganger arrogantly dismisses the Kyoto Protocol – it's too expensive – and rejects concern about climate change as fear mongering. The scriptwriters save him from death to subject him to a "mea culpa" public address at the movie's climax: "We thought that we could affect the Earth's delicate systems without suffering the consequences. We were wrong ... I was wrong." This State of the Nation address is broadcast live on the Weather Channel.

Yet, the problem with these scary forecasts is that they expect too much. Even if we ignore the fact that Greenland will not supply the disruptive amount of fresh water, a shut-down of the Gulf Stream will not mean Europe becomes Siberia. In the event 8,200 years ago, some remote places did experience large temperature drops, with Greenland seeing a drop of 7.4°C.[608]

But most of northern Europe saw temperatures 0.5–3°C lower, with little effect in southern Europe.[609] For all of Europe, the difference was probably 1.5°C. For comparison, the average temperature difference between Siberia and Europe is almost 13°C.[610]

In a comparison of all models a research team estimated the consequences of an event beyond the most extreme expectations of the Greenland ice sheet. Instead of the 3.5 cm expected for the coming century, they used 86 cm – an increase of almost 25 times.[611] This is the equivalent of directing the discharge from the Amazon River right into the North Atlantic. Predictably, the Gulf Stream weakened by 30%. Yet the result of this dramatic experiment was a cooling over western Europe of just 0.5–1°C.[612]

Even if we shut down the Gulf Stream entirely, the result is far below the one advertised by Gore, the Pentagon and Hollywood. In a forced shutdown, one group of modelers find a cooling of the UK by 3–5°C in the first decade, but 20 years later the cooling is already reduced to 2–3°C as the Gulf Stream is beginning to spin up by itself.[613] Temperature drops are smaller in the rest of Europe.

In the comparison between all models, the researchers even tried increasing the melt of Greenland a further ten-fold to 860 cm over the century – even more than the apocalyptic vision of Gore. This would be the equivalent of placing the mouths of all rivers in the world in the North Atlantic. They found that it would lead to a near-collapse of the Gulf Stream; yet even in this incredibly extreme scenario lasting a century the temperatures still dropped much less than the 13°C to Siberia – some 7°C over northern Europe and about 4°C on average across Europe.[614]

The reason why even a complete shut-down of the Gulf Stream fails to deliver spectacular cooling is because Al Gore and many others have bought into the standard – but incorrect – understanding that the Gulf Stream is what keeps western European winters some 15–20°C higher than eastern North America.[615] It is true that the Gulf Stream provides some extra heat to Europe – on the order of 2–3°C, as we also saw above.[616] Yet, as it rises from the Mexican Gulf the Gulf Stream actually warms both sides of the North Atlantic, also contributing some 2–3°C warming to the East Coast of North America. Thus, this is not the reason why Europe is much warmer in the wintertime. Two other factors cause that.

First, in the mid-latitudes the predominant wind direction due to the Earth's rotation is westerly. Because an ocean loses heat much slower, this means that it will be warmer than land in the wintertime and consequently warm up any land to the east of it. Thus, Europe benefits from the warm westerly winds, whereas the US East Coast just gets cold winds from the center of the continent. (Notice how the West Coast of North America similarly enjoy warmer weather, with Vancouver much warmer than the Newfoundland on the same latitude.)

Second, the Rocky Mountains force the Westerly winds southwards, where they pick up heat before they head back north, hitting Europe with mild subtropical air. When the Westerly winds veer southward over the Rockies, this simultaneously pulls the arctic air southward and right into the East Coast.

Given that these much larger temperature impacts have nothing to do with the melting of Greenland, the MIT ocean physicist Carl Wunsch pointed out in *Nature* that the ice age scares are much overblown. In fact, "the only way to produce an ocean circulation without a Gulf Stream is either to turn off the wind system, or to stop the Earth's rotation, or both."[617]

Yet, we still worry. For a very potent exhibit of this worry, we can look at the meeting Tony Blair had set up in Exeter in early 2005 in preparation for his G-8 summit later that year, where he would put climate change at the top of the agenda. Here, all the best and brightest within climate research and policy were to meet and focus on "Avoiding Dangerous Climate Change," as the meeting was called.[618]

Two papers discussed the stability of the Gulf Stream. The first paper used a simple model of the North Atlantic Ocean.[619] This model was the original background for worrying about the breakdown of the Gulf Stream and was formulated in 1961.[620] It reduces the immense complexity of the North Atlantic to just two boxes – a polar box and an equatorial box, where water flows back and forth. The trick is that with suitable choices of set-up, this box model of the Gulf Stream can easily break down. This of course was part of the original interest in the model – that it shows us a simple set-up that might be indicative of some of the crucial features of the real Gulf Stream.[621]

If you will allow a short but educational regression: this is the same reasoning that lies behind creating genetic variants of mice grown to develop cancer cells to allow for easy study. For instance, all TRAMP transgenetic mice develop prostate cancer in just 12 weeks, but in studies where these mice are fed the equivalent of 18 cups of green tea each day, only 20% develop cancer.[622] Now, this doesn't mean that humans will develop 100% prostate cancer without green tea or that 18 cups of green tea each day will reduce your risk by 80%. But it is an interesting finding, which suggests that, all things being equal, more green tea possibly means less risk of prostate cancer, although we still have no idea what the reduced risk might be. (Actually, the FDA found recently that the effect is highly unlikely to be different from zero.[623])

Likewise this box model shows us that with more Greenland melting, there is a higher risk of a shut-down of the Gulf Stream, which is probably true. However, the authors go on and apply this model directly to reality. They set up the model such that it sometimes collapses, sometimes does not, and then – lo and behold – report that it collapses about 50% of the time.[624]

They then go on to show that with carbon taxes we can reduce the risk. Again, this is undoubtedly true, but the question – just like with green tea – is how much. They claim that a $27 CO_2 tax can reduce the risk by 28% in 2100. They tell us how a $100 tax is just ¢50 on the gallon, but neglect to tell us how this tax will have to grow to about $6/gallon in 2100, causing an economic loss of $36 trillion and essentially shutting down the fossil fuel economy by 2060.[625] But the real problem is whether this is just the green tea example above. In the model the risk reduction is 28%, but this requires the real risk to be about 50% and the model to be reasonable. If the risk is much lower – say, close to zero – the risk reduction will likely be much closer to zero.

Yet, predictably, the result in the UK's *Guardian* newspaper was "Hotter world may freeze Britain: fifty-fifty chance that warm Gulf Stream may be halted."[626]

However, it is interesting to realize that, at the conference, there were two presentations on the stability of the Gulf Stream, resulting in two papers, as we mentioned above. The journalist from the *Guardian* sat through both, and even referred to the other in passing. But while the headline grabbing first paper used one simple two-box model to talk about the Atlantic Ocean, the other paper did a review of the major comprehensive computer models.[627] The authors pointed out that the shut-off mode essentially comes from the simple box-models and thus asked if this instability exists in the "most comprehensive climate models used to make climate projections (GCMs)." Although they definitely pointed out the need for more research, their basic conclusion was straightforward and very different. They projected that the Gulf Stream would slow down, somewhere between 0% and 50%. We will discuss that in just a bit. But then they told us: "No GCMs have shown a complete shutdown, or a net cooling over land areas. Hence a shutdown during the 21st century must be regarded as unlikely."[628]

Thus, the risk of a shut-down was estimated at 50% by a two-box model. But when we used the most advanced models in the world, models that have been extensively evaluated against observation of the Gulf Stream and a large number of other physical facts, the risk of a shut-down was estimated at zero percent. Yet, somehow this information was clearly not as newsworthy, and the meeting left most people under the impression that the Gulf Stream was in severe danger.

But isn't it still bad that the Gulf Stream may slow down 0–50%? Again, this depends on your perspective. If our goal is intrinsically to keep the Gulf Stream the same then, yes, it is bad (as would be any other change, positive or negative and of any size). But if – more plausibly – our goal is to improve human and environmental quality, it might actually be an *advantage*.[629] If the Gulf Stream weakens over the coming century, it will be while temperatures in general increase due to global warming. So if the Gulf Stream weakens and *decreases* temperatures, it will be against a background of *increasing* temperatures. All the advanced models show that the net outcome is still warming over all land areas, such that the weakening of the Gulf Stream simply means *less* warming over Europe – presumably the goal of all climate policy today.

The latest Gulf Stream scare came in late 2005, leading right up to the annual climate meeting in Montreal. Over the past 47 years, scientists have measured the Gulf Stream just five times with a ship sailing across the latitude 25N from Africa to the Bahamas.[630] Their last measurement was in 2004, and suddenly researchers found that while the Gulf Stream north remained steady, more of the stream turned back toward the Canary Islands and less headed toward the far north before plunging to the deep and turning south. All in all, the researchers estimated that the Gulf Stream had slowed some 30%. Admittedly, this estimate was "uncomfortably close to the uncertainties"[631] as the researchers put it – essentially the uncertainty of the 30% was almost 30 percentage points – but the story still reverberated round the world and made headlines for the Montreal meeting.

National Geographic told us "'Mini ice age' may be coming soon."[632] The UK *Times* told us how "Britain faces big freeze as Gulf Stream loses strength" and the *Sydney Morning Herald* even saw a way to make this a global issue in "Scientists forecast global cold snap," throwing in a reference to *The Day after Tomorrow*.[633] *New Scientist* chose it as one of their top stories from 2005, showing how "global warming may soon spiral out of control" and "plunge western Europe into freezing winters and threaten climate systems worldwide."[634]

A few people thought this concern might be a bit premature. If the Gulf Stream was really slowing down, we should have seen temperatures drop 1–2°C, yet no such change had been seen.[635] Carl Wunsch pointed out the obvious hype: "The story is appealing, but it is a very extreme interpretation of the data. It's like measuring temperatures in Hamburg on five random days and then concluding that the climate is getting warmer or colder."[636]

In order to get a better grip on the Gulf Stream, scientists moored 19 observation stations across the Atlantic in 2004, which have provided continuous data since then. In late 2006, at the first scientific meeting on the accumulated data, it became clear that there is no sign the Gulf Stream is slowing down. In *Science* magazine the headline ran "False alarm: Atlantic Conveyor Belt hasn't slowed down after all."[637] In *New Scientist* the headline was "No new ice age for western Europe."[638] Unfortunately, it seems no other major news outlets found this important to pass on to their readers.[639]

The Guardian in the UK did report from the scientific meeting, but only to tell us "scientists have uncovered more evidence for a dramatic weakening."[640] Their science editor went on to tell us how the ocean had apparently stopped for ten days and, with an allusion to *The Day after Tomorrow*, shows concern for what would have happened if it had lasted 30 or 60 days.

One of the participants, Professor Martin Visbeck, felt compelled to correct *The Guardian* and explained how the ten-day hiatus was presented as a side point, an "oddity" which could just be an artifact of the analysis with no "indication of something alarming."[641] Importantly, "more than 95% of the scientists at the workshop concluded that we have not seen any significant change of the Atlantic circulation to date." [642]

Science told us how the no-change message had "confirmed what many oceanographers suspected all along." *New Scientist* told us how the scary messages had "been dismissed by many climate scientists, who say their models show the current will keep going for at least another hundred years or so."[643] Yet, chances are, you read the scary story but didn't get the story set straight.

So, let us sum up. Al Gore and many others have told us that a melting Greenland might make the Gulf Stream shut down, throwing Europe into a new Little Ice Age à la Siberia. Yet, all the models indicate that Greenland will not provide nearly enough water for the Gulf Stream to be seriously challenged. Even if that happened, the models show that the expected effect on Europe would be much less than Siberian, because the main heat engine for Europe is the wind from the Rockies. Moreover, none of the most comprehensive models show that a shut-down will happen.

Thus, the IPCC in its 2007 report is very clear: "none of the current models simulates an abrupt reduction or shut-down."[644] If we take a look at the IPCC's own figure, it shows that models might have a 0–60% reduction over the coming century, but *none* shows a shut-down or rapid reduction.

Moreover, the IPCC tells us that *even if the Gulf Stream shuts down completely*

> Europe will still experience warming since radiative forcing overwhelms
> the cooling associated with the MOC [Gulf Stream] reduction. In conse-
> quence, catastrophic scenarios about the beginning of an ice age triggered
> by a shut-down of the MOC are mere speculations, and no climate model
> has produced such an outcome. In fact, the processes leading to an ice age
> are sufficiently well understood and completely different from those
> discussed here, that we can confidently exclude this scenario.[645]

It makes you wonder why Gore, Pentagon futurists and Hollywood still sell us a very different picture.

More illness: malaria in Vermont?

For the Climate Conference in Milan 2003, the World Health Organization published a book that estimated increased temperatures since the 1970s to have caused 150,000 deaths in 2000.[646] Green organizations, political parties and pundits have incessantly repeated this figure.[647] Not surprisingly, a headline of "Climate change death toll put at 150,000" works well.[648]

Yet, let us take a peak below the hood of this number. The World Health Organization regularly assesses why about 60 million of us die each year, from high blood pressure, tobacco, lack of food, etc., as we saw in Figure 14. For the 2002 edition, and under the directorship of Gro Harlem Brundtland, it was decided to see how many deaths could be ascribed to climate change.

The result was a 300-page multi-author book with a large number of interesting papers, but the actual ascription took place in just one chapter.[649] Here, they set out to estimate the effects of cold and heat, malnutrition, diarrhea, malaria and floods. The analysis was redone in 2005 and came out with substantively the same results.[650]

Floods turn out to be minimal and, as we saw above, probably also more related to societal changes. Malaria and malnutrition we will look at in this and the next chapter. But a curious thing happened with cold and heat deaths. In the 2003 analysis, they spend three pages estimating and apparently calculating – though never showing – cold and heat deaths.[651] But when they get to aggregate the numbers, they simply leave out cold and heat deaths, leading to the total death toll of 153,000.[652] In the 2005 update, although they mention both cold and heat deaths and attempt an estimate of heat deaths, they equally leave it out of the total.[653] Their result can be seen in the left part of Figure 35.

Now, if it was because cold and heat deaths were minor issues, this may have been understandable, but as we saw in pp. 15–18, this does not seem to be the case. Actually, if we make a rough estimate of the lives lost and saved by the temperature increase since the 1970s of 0.36°C, it gives about 620,000 avoided cold deaths and 130,000 extra heat deaths.[654] This, of course, dramatically influences the total outcome, meaning instead of 150,000 dying of global warming, there are actually almost 200,000 more people surviving each year. Again, it is important to stress that there are several caveats and that this does not mean we should just embrace global

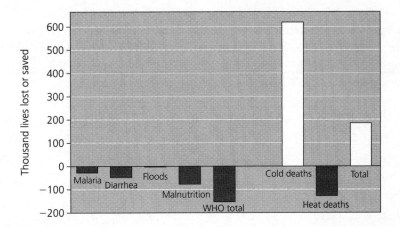

Figure 35 *WHO estimates for today's annual climate deaths from malaria, diarrhea, floods and malnutrition, with lives lost as negative.*[655] *WHO left out cold deaths and heat deaths, here roughly estimated with the grand total to the right.*[656]

warming. First, we need to remember that there is more to global warming than deaths from temperature and disease. Second, because many of the diseases kill young people, whereas cold deaths generally afflict old people, there is a larger loss of life-years.

Nevertheless, this number of 150,000 deaths from climate change has had a tremendous leverage and unfortunately it has been based on only doing part of the sums. Had all the relevant data been included, it would more likely have shown the very opposite picture.

We see the same trends in many other areas of disease and global warming. Al Gore tells us how increasing temperatures are going to mean more germs and viruses. He shows us pictures of viruses like SARS and avian flu and attempts to connect them with global warming,[657] although there really is no connection. In a recent review, it was found:

> It is especially during the last ten years that very dangerous viruses for
> mankind have repeatedly developed in Asia, with the occurrence of
> Alkhurma hemorrhagic fever in Saudi Arabia (1995), avian flu (H5N1) in
> Hong-Kong (1997), Nipah virus encephalitis in Malaysia (1998), and,
> above all, the SARS pandemic fever from Southern China (2002). The

evolution of these viral diseases was probably not directly affected by climate change. In fact, their emergential success may be better explained by the development of large industry poultry flocks increasing the risks of epizootics, dietary habits, economic and demographic constraints, and negligence in the surveillance and reporting of the first cases.[658]

Telling us to focus on climate change instead of dealing effectively with ever larger poultry flocks in close connection with many people, instead of upping our surveillance, means missing a crucial opportunity to deal with SARS and avian flu. It is a bit like pointing the wrong way when the fire engine stops for directions.

Likewise, Gore tells us that global warming underlies the increase in drug-resistant tuberculosis, without any supporting arguments.[659] Clearly the main causes for increasing tuberculosis are HIV infections, rapid urbanization, poor sanitation and – for instance in the ex-Soviet nations – a breakdown of health infrastructure.[660] Drug resistance has been with tuberculosis since modern treatment began 50 years ago, but is an increasing problem due to lack of patient compliance, improperly administered drug therapies and lack of available second-line drugs.[661] One tuberculosis doctor tells this story of Magdalena:

> When Magdalena was 15 years old she was diagnosed with smear-positive pulmonary tuberculosis (TB). She lived with her mother, a stepfather and 13 siblings in a very humble dwelling in an Andean country. Her stepfather would often beat her because she was unable to perform her assigned domestic chores. As a result, she would flee and abandon her treatment. She was prescribed several regimens which she took erratically. Three years later she was still smear-positive; the chest X-ray showed multiple cavities in both apices and drug susceptibility testing confirmed resistance to isoniacid (H), rifampicin (R), ethambutol (E) and streptomycin (S). The following year she became pregnant and died of respiratory insufficiency 6 months later.[662]

Magdalena suffered from highly resistant tuberculosis and she could not be treated adequately for lack of medication. Telling us to focus on Kyoto seems unreasonable, when what Magdalena needed, and what the 8 million annual tuberculosis victims need, is better sanitation, better health care and better drugs.[663]

Clearly SARS, avian flu or drug-resistant tuberculosis is not caused in any meaningful sense of the word by global warming. This does not mean that all is well, but it means that we need to examine these often heard statements that climate will necessarily worsen all infectious diseases.

One example is the West Nile virus, which probably arrived in New York on a plane with a stowaway infected mosquito.[664] Its original strength was clearly helped along by New York climate conditions such as a warm and dry summer.[665] Yet, when Gore shows us that it spread from the original infestation in New York in 1999 to the West Coast by 2003, he is unwittingly showing us that climate had very little influence in the establishment of West Nile virus, as it traveled through the remarkably varied climates of North America from New York to cold Manitoba or to warm Texas in the same time-frame. If anything, it actually spread faster in the North, traveling from Wisconsin to Washington State in just one year, whereas Louisiana to California took two years.[666] Thus, the infestation was not about climate but was because the birds of the American continent were open to colonization of the West Nile virus, just as the yellow fever reached New World primates 350 years ago.[667]

Again, if we want to deal with the real problem of West Nile virus and possible new viruses, we should be concerned about disinfecting aircraft and controlling mosquito populations in the US, not Kyoto.[668]

By far the most important discussion on increased health lies with malaria, with half a billion infections annually and more than one million dead.[669] (For comparison, West Nile virus infects about 3,000 people annually in the US, and 146 died in 2006, which is about half as many as the 300 Americans who die each year drowning in their own bathtubs.[670])

Clearly a lot of voices have worried about increasing malaria from global warming. In Leonardo DiCaprio's March 2000 interview with Bill Clinton from the White House, the President told us climate change will have "public health consequences. We're already seeing in Africa, for example, malaria being found at higher and higher altitudes where it used to be too cool for the mosquitoes."[671] British Prime Minster Tony Blair tells us climate change will have stark consequences for us and our planet, and points to rising malaria as one of the main examples.[672] The UN Secretary-General tells us "a warmer world is one in which infectious diseases such as malaria and yellow fever will spread further and faster."[673]

The scare is raised that malaria could even come to the shores of developed countries. The famous cover story from *U.S. News & World Report*, which predicted water-logged Art Deco hotels in Miami, also expected that "global warming could cause droughts, disease, and political upheaval" and "a cascade of nasty effects, from pestilence and famine to wars and refugee movement."[674] Specifically, they tell us that in the future "malaria could be a public health threat in Vermont." This is in line with the UK chief medical officer who in 2002 predicted, "by 2050 the climate of the UK may be such that indigenous malaria could become re-established."[675] The *Guardian* announced in early 2007, "Climate change brings malaria back to Italy."[676]

Like most stories, there is at core some truth to the claim that malaria will increase with temperature, but many of the public statements made on the connection between global warming and malaria have ventured far outside the reasonable.

Malaria is caused by the malaria parasite, of which the most common and deadliest is *Plasmodium falciparum*.[677] Mosquitoes spread the infection, first picking up the parasite when biting malaria-infected humans, and then transferring it when bitting other uninfected humans. There are more than 400 species of mosquitoes, but by far the major transmitter is the mosquito *Anopheles gambiae*.[678] About 90% of all malaria deaths occur in Sub-Saharan Africa, where the most deadly parasite and the most resilient mosquito reside.[679]

For the malaria parasite to develop in the mosquito, it requires that temperatures are not lower than 16°C, whereas the mosquito itself will die above 40°C.[680] This is the background for the idea that increasing temperatures could cause malaria to spread – as the world warms, more places will be at least 16°C warm. Essentially, it is easy to run a model and tell us how many more people will live within areas that will go from below 16°C to above 16°C over the coming century. Models show that there will be about 300 million more people within these areas, and that they therefore would be "at risk of malaria" by the 2080s.[681]

However, this emphatically does not mean that 300 million more will be infected by malaria, as we will see below, only that this is the extreme upper limit. Actually, the same models find that in 2007 slightly more than 5.5 billion people are at risk of malaria – i.e. 84% of the world's population.[682]

This is more than ten times the 500 million people infected each year, and clearly shows that many other factors besides climate determine whether or not malaria will be an actual risk.[683]

Perhaps the most important factor is better appreciated when we start realizing that malaria was endemic in most of the developed world just 50–100 years ago. When I first started reading about malaria in England in the Little Ice Age, the last Dutch malaria epidemic in 1943–46, or 30% of the population in Tennessee River valley affected by malaria in 1933, I found it hard to believe that I hadn't heard about this.[684] But there is abundant evidence – from eight references to malaria in Shakespeare to carefully reconstructed malaria death rates from 43 counties in England and Wales from 1840 to 1910.[685] Rather, it shows how quickly we forget and how quickly we lose sense of context.

Malaria was indeed endemic in much of Europe throughout the Little Ice Age. In a recent review, it was pointed out how "a considerable volume of documentary evidence shows that P. vivax [malaria] was endemic among the human populations of many wetland areas in England, the Netherlands, and other parts of northern Europe from at least the 16th to 19th centuries AD. Even in as cold a country as Finland there was an outbreak as recently as the Second World War."[686]

In the saltmarshes of eastern England there was a sulfurous stench, which many believed caused malaria – Shakespeare's "unwholesome fens," hence the Italian term "mala aria" (bad air).[687] In the hardest hit areas of Essex and Kent, virtually all vicars chose to live elsewhere, and understandably so.[688] Death rates were generally much higher. The excess infant death rates in the marsh areas of Essex were twice those of the rest of England, with the absolute death rate above today's developing world.[689]

Malaria was found in many places across the continent. In Russia, there were recurring epidemics throughout the northeastern part of Russia in the 1800s: Kiev had epidemics in the 1850s, 1860s and 1870s with malaria supposedly accounting for 80% of the illness recorded.[690] Malaria was even seen in Siberia in the 1800s and was prevalent as far north as the Arctic Circle into the 1950s. In 1905–6 the annual number of infections was over 3 million, with many areas having 5–16% of the population ill each year.[691] In 1924, the Soviet authorities estimated that there were more than 5.5 million cases annually, and independent sources put this at 13 million.[692]

In 1923, the League of Nations created a Malaria Commission, which visited a number of countries in Europe suffering from malaria, and produced rather bleak reports for the opportunities to address malaria.[693] The League of Nations estimated in the 1930s that Europe, with some 200,000 cases annually, had as many cases of malaria as Africa (though Africa's number was probably way too small) and that the USSR still had more than 2 million cases each year.[694] In Moscow 20% of the population was infected each year in the 1940s.[695]

As far north as Finland, malaria was endemic throughout the 1800s.[696] Malaria was still endemic in Poland and in the countries bordering the Black Sea and the eastern Mediterranean until after World War II. This was when Italy seriously attacked their malaria problem, but only in 1970 could WHO declare Italy malaria free.[697]

As Europe came out of the Little Ice Age and temperatures rose, malaria infections dropped off, and in the second half of the twentieth century Europe became malaria free. What happened? In the 1600s the only cure – quinine from the bark of the quina-quina tree – was discovered in the New World and brought to Europe, where hundreds of Europe's royalty bought the expensive cure, including King Louis XIV for 2,000 guineas.[698] Because of the quina-quina tree's slow growth, and limited success in planting it elsewhere, the Spanish succeeded in keeping a virtual monopoly on quinine for several hundred years.[699] This meant low supplies and high prices that kept most commoners from enjoying its benefits before the middle of the 1800s.

At the same time, in the UK, marshlands were increasingly being drained, which reduced the breeding grounds for the mosquitoes, and an increasing number of livestock probably diverted biting from humans toward cattle, pigs and horses.[700] Improved housing also reduced transmission; better nutrition reduced mortality, and increased incomes meant better health care and affordable quinine.[701]

By the end of the Second World War DDT was introduced, and it effectively eradicated malaria through indoor house spaying and control of mosquito breeding grounds.[702] At the same time, synthetic treatments like chloroquine made cheap and effective drugs available.

Malaria in the US was similarly pervasive. Up until the 1940s, malaria was endemic in 36 states, including Washington, Oregon, Idaho, Montana, North Dakota, Minnesota, Wisconsin, Iowa, Illinois, Michigan, Indiana, Ohio, New York, Pennsylvania and New Jersey.[703] Dr. Currie, writing in 1811, began his book *A View of the Diseases Most Prevalent in the U.S.A.* by describing malaria: "A fever of an intermitting or remitting type or form is an endemic of America, and more or less epidemic every year during the autumnal season in all low and moist situations in every part of the continent."[704]

In California the Permanent Secretary of the California State Board of Health noted in 1875 "that malarial fevers and consumption constitute the most prevalent forms of disease."[705] Experts estimated that for the nineteenth and first part of the twentieth century "malaria has caused more ill health and loss of life in Florida than all other insect-borne diseases combined."[706] In 1920, almost 2% of the US population had malaria each year, and by the mid-1930s the US still experienced more than 400,000 cases each year.[707]

Only after the Second World War were Centers for Disease Control established, with their first major task being to combat malaria. (This is also why CDC headquarters lie in Atlanta, because most of the malaria disease was found in the Southeast.)[708] Between 1947 and 1949 over 4.5 million American homes were sprayed and in 1951 malaria was considered eradicated. Again, a long list of factors caused the final eradication, including public health improvements, better nutrition, more people in cities (where mosquitoes have less foothold), better access to medication, large-scale draining, and finally the mosquito-control programs along with home sprays.[709]

Perhaps tellingly, an analysis of malaria in Mississippi from 1944 showed how malaria deaths had been declining from 1,500 in 1916 to fewer than 400 in 1937.[710] Since the number of dead still fluctuated from year to year, the analysis tried to see if it could be caused by rainfall or temperature. No connection. However, because Mississippi so greatly depended on just one product – cotton – there was a strong variability in most people's income, depending on strong or weak cotton prices. Thus, when we look at the number of dead versus Mississippi income we see a strong inverse relation – when incomes were high, malaria deaths were low and vice versa.

When you think about it, it makes good sense. When you have high income, you are better fed, you keep your home in better repair, especially with regard to screening, and if you get sick, you can better afford medical services and buy quinine. During low income years, you have less food, less stamina, your house falls into disrepair and you don't get proper medical attention. Actually, with the data from Mississippi we can see that in high-income years, there are many more malaria cases for each death – meaning that people could afford treatment – whereas in low-income years, people would forgo treatment and would more often die.

What malaria in Europe and the US shows us is that we eliminated malaria while the world warmed over the past century and a half. While temperature does impact on malaria, it is clearly not destiny. What probably matters much more is a wide array of factors, from nutrition and health care, through draining and mosquito eradication, to income and availability of quinine or newer treatments.

This is also why the expectations of malaria returning to Europe or the US seem unfounded. In a recent European study, they find that malaria risk will increase 15% in the UK due to climate change. However, since there is an effective national health system in place this essentially means 15% more of zero malaria. Thus, with the UK evidence they conclude – contrary to the UK chief medical officer who merely speculated – "In Britain, a 15% rise in risk might have been important in the 19th century, but such a rise is now highly unlikely to lead to the reestablishment of indigenous malaria." Similar conclusions have been reached in studies of Italy – the reason the *Guardian* could claim otherwise is only because more immigrants bring in more malaria.[711] Likewise for the US, an – otherwise very pessimistic – summary of health risks found that reestablishment of malaria due to a warming climate "seems unlikely" as long as the current infrastructure and health care systems are maintained.[712] We will not have malaria in Vermont.

Today, many of the same problems play themselves out in Sub-Saharan Africa. A belt runs through the middle of the continent where temperatures and precipitation make excellent conditions for malaria.[713] Much of the region has weak, poor and often corrupt governments that find it hard to implement, enforce and pay for large-scale draining and spraying. Moreover, concerns from western governments, NGOs and local populations make it hard to utilize DDT, which is still the most cost-effective insecticide against mosquitoes and, properly used, has negligible environmental impact.[714] Populations are also characterized by poor health, with, for example, malnutrition and HIV interlinking with malaria to worsen all three.[715] At the same time, poverty makes it harder to obtain preventive measures and effective drugs.

Over the past 20 years we have seen malaria death rates rising in Sub-Saharan Africa whereas the general death rate has been declining.[716] At the same time, temperatures have on average been increasing, which has made it an easy and general assertion to claim that global warming is the culprit.[717] There has been a substantial literature trying to ascertain the veracity of this claim, and on the whole it is clear that at best temperature is only one of many important factors.[718] In the recent World Bank review, they find that the main cause of increasing death rates is not increasing temperatures or increasing poverty, but the fact that chloroquine – the mainstay of treatment over the past 50 years – is increasingly failing, because the malaria parasite is becoming resistant.[719] There are new and effective combination treatments based on artemisinin available, but unfortunately, they are about ten times more expensive than the old chloroquine.[720]

So what should we do? This depends on how much global warming really matters to malaria. One way to get an upper limit on the importance of global warming is to look at the projections of populations at risk. These are the models that show an extra almost 300 million people will be living in areas that could harbor malaria in the 2080s because increasing temperatures expand the area where the parasite can multiply.[721]

Again, it is important to point out that this is an absolute upper limit for several reasons. First, much of the increase happens in Europe and the US, where strong health care systems and infrastructure mean that malaria will not reestablish itself. Second, the analysis does not take into account better technology and higher incomes.[722] Of course, when developing countries go from an average per person of $5,000 today to $100,000 in 2100 it seems unrealistic to assume that this will not mean more protection and less malaria.[723] Finally, the models also disregard that increasing urbanization will decrease malaria.[724] Contrary to what many believe, moving to the city typically means both fewer mosquitoes (because of less swampland they can breed on) and better health care.[725]

This is also reflected in a careful analysis where researchers tried to see whether more people at risk would *actually* lead to more malaria. Their findings "showed remarkably few changes, even under the most extreme scenarios."[726]

Nevertheless, let us try to see the worst-case scenario for what climate will do to malaria. The same models that tell us 300 million more will be at risk from global warming also tell us what will happen *without* climate change. Here, they project an increase from 4.4 billion in 1990 to 8.8 billion people at risk in 2085.[727] The total population at risk will thus be 9.1 billion out of a population of 10.7 billion.

But notice the proportions: 8.8 billion will be at risk from malaria in 2085 due to social factors, whereas 0.3 billion will be at risk due to global warming. Thus, even if we could entirely stop global warming today (which we can't) we would only change malaria risk in 2085 by 3.2%.[728] More realistically, with the Kyoto Protocol, including the US and Australia, and committing everyone to constant emissions throughout the rest of the century, we would reduce malaria risk by 0.2% in 80 years.[729] As the model team tells us: with a stringent climate policy "there is little clear effect even by the 2080s."[730]

Compare this to current expectations that we can cut malaria incidence to about half by 2015 for about $3 billion annually – or 2% of the cost of Kyoto.[731] This was the number 4 priority in the Copenhagen Consensus. Because we can do this within a decade whereas climate policy will take half a century or more, the difference in actual people helped is even more dramatic. Till 2085 Kyoto will avoid about 70 million people from getting infected by malaria (or about 0.1% of all malaria infections). Compare that to a simple and cheap halving of malaria incidence by 2015, which will avoid more than 28 billion people suffering from malaria.[732] This policy will do about 400 times more good, as is illustrated in Figure 36.[733]

We do, however, have one global estimate on *actual* malaria deaths from climate change by 2050.[734] This study also looks at a number of other diseases, namely dengue fever and diarrhea (both of which will also increase

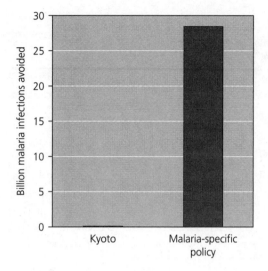

Figure 36 *The number of people saved from malaria infection until 2085, by a full Kyoto policy and a policy to establish the Millennium Goal of halving malaria by 2015.*[735]

with temperature) and schistosomiasis (a debilitating parasite disease, which will diminish with temperature). However, only malaria and diarrhea will be of major significance, and, as it turns out, diarrhea will cause far more deaths (though malaria is much more commonly discussed and documented in the literature, which is why we have focused on it here). In all, diarrhea will cause almost 500,000 extra deaths by 2050, and malaria some 65,000 extra deaths.

However, when we compare the full picture in Figure 37 we see that the number of dead from both heat deaths and diseases (malaria, diarrhea, schistosomiasis, dengue fever) still do not outweigh the deaths saved from cold deaths. Lives lost to malaria in the developed world will be zero, and respiratory and diarrhea deaths are in the order of a few thousands. It is perhaps interesting to note that, for all the developing countries, the number of lives saved actually outweighs the number of lives lost, because the benefit to China and India is greater than the cost to the remaining developing countries.

While malaria deaths will increase over the coming half-century, it is

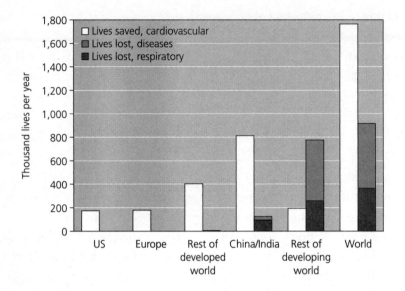

Figure 37 *The total number of lives saved and lost to disease (malaria, diarrhea, schistosomiasis, dengue fever), cold and heat for regions and the world in 2050.*[736]

important to point out that this trend will not continue, simply because increasing income effectively will eliminate it. If we look at malaria-stricken countries it is not surprising that the poor bear the brunt of the malaria burden. In Zambia, in the poorest fifth of children more than 70% are infected, whereas in the richest fifth less than 30% are.[737] Likewise, poor households across 22 different countries are less likely to have mosquito nets and much less likely to have insecticide-treated nets than rich households.[738] Rural children – who are often also poorer – are less likely to use nets and less likely to get treatment.[739] And rich children in general get more treatment from malaria.[740]

In many ways, this is no different from conditions in Mississippi in the 1930s – if you were poor, you would have a substantially higher risk of getting malaria, not getting treatment and dying. But people no longer die from malaria in Mississippi, simply because the state and the surrounding society are now rich enough to afford to avoid it. Personal income in Mississippi in 1930 was $202, or in today's money $1,974 – compare this to today's income of $24,925.[741] Over the past 70 years, Mississippi has got more than 12 times richer, and this is the same increase we expect from developing countries over this century.

In Sub-Saharan Africa per person income is still lower than Mississippi in the 1930s at just $745.[742] Studies show that when countries get about $3,100 per person income, their personal wealth will allow them to buy more protection and treatment while at the same time societies will be able to provide sufficient general health care, and environmental management such as house spraying and mosquito eradication.[743] Thus, even with very pessimistic assumptions about Africa's growth rate, it seems likely that Africa will cross the $3,100 threshold around 2080. With all other regions passing the threshold sooner, this will essentially mean that malaria will be eradicated late in this century (and even sooner with a successful and cheap vaccine).

This means that the numbers we got from Figure 36 are reasonably the total numbers. Through simple malaria policies we can prevent more than 28 billion infections before malaria gets eradicated or just 70 million through Kyoto, *if we only look at the climate impact.*

However, there are also *economic* impacts. If we implement Kyoto, this has costs for the rich countries, as we discussed above. Such costs will also permeate to the poorer countries because there will be less growth in international trade. This will slightly slow the poor countries' growth rate, meaning individual countries will attain the $3,100 threshold slightly later. This has consequences for malaria deaths. Whereas Kyoto was meant to have *reduced* the number of malaria deaths, model estimates show that it is likely that a full Kyoto would *increase* malaria deaths by 2%, simply because the financial impacts would be much bigger than the slight climate ameliorations.[744]

Supposedly our goal is to diminish malaria and other infectious diseases. What we have seen above is that malaria is a disease related strongly to economic development and weakly to changing climate. Malaria was endemic in most of Europe and the US just a century ago. Yet, coming out of the Little Ice Age, these societies fought and won the battle over malaria, simply because of increasing wealth and good social policy. If we try to help developing countries deal with malaria, we can focus on easy paths that will cut infections by more than 28 billion. We can also choose the much more expensive path of Kyoto and do little good, cutting 70 million infections and quite plausibly causing *more* infections through decreased economic growth.

The problem is that often the climate argument is virtually the only one offered. A recent Associated Press story spends 774 words on telling us how climate is making malaria worse in Kenya, with 12 words toward the end tersely telling us "Preventive programs, such as distribution of mosquito nets, can halt malaria's spread."[745] Many malaria articles talk about nothing but climate.[746] The story of climate being the main driver of malaria seems irresistible. The Associated Press story ends by repeating an often-told story of Nairobi that has found its peak with Al Gore.

Gore tells us how "mosquitoes are profoundly affected by global warming. There are cities that were originally located just above the mosquito line, which used to mark the altitude above which mosquitoes would not venture. Nairobi (Kenya), and Harare (Zimbabwe), are two such cities. Now, with global warming, the mosquitoes are climbing to higher altitudes."[747]

However charming this story seems, it is simply wrong. Nairobi was founded for a railway not for health reasons.[748] The town's first medical officer wrote that even for the early ivory and slave caravans, Nairobi "had always been regarded as an unhealthy locality swarming with mosquitoes." In 1904, a committee of doctors "petitioned that the entire municipality be relocated, simply because it was a spawning ground of disease."[749] Actually, if we look at the incidence of malaria in Nairobi since 1930, we see that there was a major outbreak of malaria while temperatures were some of the lowest measured in Nairobi. Nairobi is today considered free of malaria.[750]

However, in other parts of Kenya, malaria is really occurring, but this is not a new and unprecedented phenomena. In a report on Kenyan malaria in the twentieth century for WHO, the authors find that the disease pattern in Kenya in the 1990s was similar to the 1940s, and that is should rather be named a *re-emerging* problem.[751] In what can only be described as strong language for a WHO report, the authors note than many have linked the new epidemics to climate change and they note "a tendency to link all phenomena to popular scientific themes and this may also be true of malaria epidemics in Africa."[752] However, the real reason for the reemergence, the

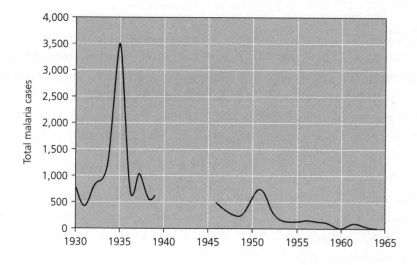

Figure 38 *Malaria cases in Nairobi, 1930–64. Nairobi is today considered malaria-free.*[753]

report finds, is not climate change but drug resistance, lack of control of mosquitoes and a range of policy problems.[754]

Stories end up having real-world effects and charming stories even more so. And if the stories are wrong, we are likely to do less good than we could otherwise have done.

More heat means more starvation?

Having enough food is perhaps one of the most basic and important issues for many people in the world. It is also the first of the UN's seven so-called Millennium Development Goals that the world set itself for 2015 – namely halving the proportion of people who suffer from hunger.[755]

Yet, many worry that climate change will dramatically undermine our future ability to feed ourselves. Stories of how global warming will "greatly increase the number of hungry people" and how we are facing "catastrophe" with "whole regions becoming unsuitable for producing food" abound.[756] While there is a grain of truth in these claims, they are vastly overplayed and again – if our concern truly lies with food security and the world's hungry – lead us to focus on the wrong solutions.

To put the issue in context, it is perhaps worth realizing that for a long time we have worried about future starvation. In one of the most influential books on hunger, Paul Ehrlich's *The Population Bomb* published in 1968, it was flatly stated: "The battle to feed humanity is over. In the course of the 1970s the world will experience starvation of tragic proportions – hundreds of millions of people will starve to death."[757]

This bleak view seems so obvious – more and more people should mean less food for each individual. It was first formulated in 1798 by Revd. Thomas Malthus, an English economist and demographer.[758] The argument was made remarkably popular in the 1970s by the best-seller *Limits to Growth* and entered the common understanding.[759] Yet, it is also wrong.

Since 1961, world population has doubled, but food production has almost tripled, and, for the developing world, population has only slightly more than doubled but food production has quadrupled.[760] The result has been rapidly rising calories available, especially in the developing world, as is evident in Figure 39. At the same time, food prices have dropped by almost two-thirds.[761]

Likewise, the proportion of people starving has been steadily declining since 1950 from more than 50% of the world's population to 17% today, as you can see in Figure 40. Moreover, the longest UN scenarios expect this proportion to drop steadily toward 2.9% in 2050. This will still represent 290 million people undernourished at that time, but it is important to point out that they are not hungry because we cannot feed them, they are hungry because they do not have the money to create the demand for more agricultural production.

A few large-scale surveys have looked at the effect of climate change on agricultural production together with the global food trade system.[762] There are four crucial findings that they have in common.

First, all models envision a large increase in agricultural output – more than a doubling of cereal production over the coming century.[763] Thus we will be able to feed the world ever better, as also indicated in Figure 40. In the words of one modeling team: "Globally, land and crop resources, together with technological progress, appear to be sufficient to feed a world population of about 9 billion people (13 billion in A2) in 2080."[764]

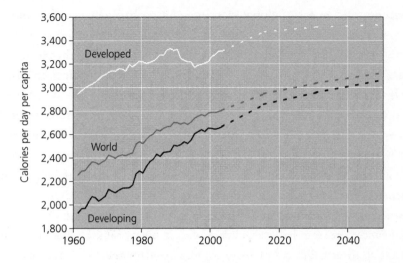

Figure 39 *Daily intake of calories per person in the industrial and developing countries and world, 1961–2003, with UN's prediction till 2050.*[765]

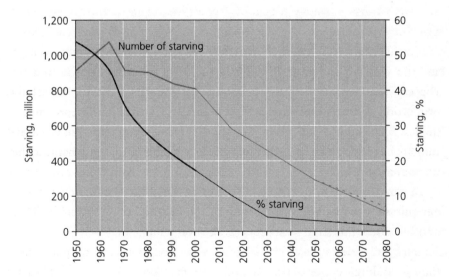

Figure 40 *Percent undernourished (black curve) and millions of undernourished 1950–2080, prediction from UN, 2000–50, prediction from climate models to 2080. The dotted lines indicate the worst climate effects till 2080 if no additional economic effort is made.*[766]

Second, the impact of global warming will probably be negative, but in total very modest. For the most pessimistic models and the most pessimistic climate impacts, the total reduction compared to a scenario without any climate change is 1.4%.[767] At a lower impact, the most optimistic model actually forecasts a net *increase* in agricultural production of 1.7%.[768]

To put these numbers in perspective, the average growth rate for agriculture over the past 30 years was 1.7%.[769] In other words, in the most negative scenario, the loss of 1.4% production over the coming century is less than one year of today's productivity increase.[770] In other words, the total loss from climate change in the twenty-first century is the equivalent of the world agricultural output doubling in, say, 2081 rather than 2080.

Likewise, this will have very little impact on the global economy. The total agricultural GDP will probably see changes from a 1.5% reduction to a 2.6% increase.[771] However, agriculture will constitute less than 1% of the Total GDP; thus the total economic impact will be miniscule, with at worst a 0.015% economic reduction.[772]

Third, while globally there will be very little change, regionally this is not true. Global warming in general has a negative impact on third world agriculture whereas it in general has a positive impact on first world farming. This is because temperature increases are good for farmers in high latitudes where more warmth will lead to longer growth seasons, multiple croppings and higher yields. For farmers in tropical countries – typically third world countries – higher temperatures will on the other hand mean lower agricultural productivity. For both places, however, CO_2 in itself counts as a positive factor, since it acts as a fertilizer, making crops grow better everywhere.[773]

In worst-case scenarios, this will mean a 7% yield decrease in the developing world with a 3% yield increase in the developed world.[774] For some hard-hit places this can mean relative yield reductions of 10–20% over the coming century, but it has to be seen in the context of total production even in the least developed countries rising by about 270%.[775]

Over the coming century, there will be a growing dependence of developing nations on food imports from developed countries. However, this is not primarily a global warming phenomenon, but a consequence of more people and less arable land in the developing world. Even without global warming, imports for the least developed countries would double over the century because of demographics.[776] Global warming causes this import rate to increase by 10–40%.[777]

We have to remember that, in 2080, developing country consumers are going to be much richer than they are today. One modeling team points out that future third world consumers "are largely separated from agricultural production processes, dwelling in cities and earning incomes in the non-agricultural sectors. As in today's developed countries, consumption levels depend largely on food prices and incomes rather than on changes in domestic agricultural production."

Fourth, global warming will likely mean more malnourished people. In the most likely scenario it means increasing the number of malnourished from 108 million in 2080 to 136 million, as can also be seen in Figure 39.[778] The other scenarios have impacts from warming ranging from 28 million more to 28 million less (meaning that CO_2 reductions would *increase* the number of malnourished).[779]

It is important to put these numbers in context. As we saw above, the world now has about 800 million malnourished. Over the coming century we will add at least 3 billion more people, yet it is likely that we will end up with *many fewer* hungry – around 136 million.

However, how many hungry the world will end up with depends much less on climate than on demographics and income.[780] The different IPCC scenarios show that while climate means somewhere between 30 million more or less, population and income mean somewhere between 90 to 1,065 million malnourished.

Once again, we have the situation where social policy choices matter much more than climate choices. If we choose a society where we stop climate change, at best we can reduce the number of malnourished by some 28 million (and if we are unlucky we could actually end up with *more* malnourished). If we choose a society with higher populations or with slower economic growth we could end up with 975 million more malnourished. It is clear that what matters is that we find the scenario that offers the low absolute number, which is correlated with high income (see Figure 41).

If this sounds like a recurrent point, it is correct. Even the modelers themselves point out that "What emerges from the [studies on malaria, hunger, water, etc.] is that these differences, flowing from different pathways

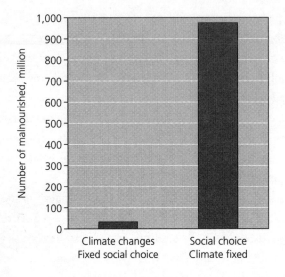

Figure 41 *For a given society, climate may mean 28 million more malnourished; for any climate, social choices of demographics and income may mean 975 million more malnourished.*

of development, are frequently more important than climate change itself in influencing the scale and distribution of global and regional impacts."[781]

Another way to see this is to realize that, in a rich world, the last 108 or 136 million hungry are results of a *political* priority, and one we could easily afford to reduce or eliminate.[782] As pointed out by the modeling team: "To put it very bluntly, for the wealthy societies – even the currently poor regions are assumed to reach economic levels exceeding in per capita terms current average OECD incomes – hunger is a marginal issue and remains so even with climate change."[783]

Thus, using climate policy to obtain a small reduction is simply not the best strategy. If we implemented Kyoto, this would reduce malnutrition by 2 million people in 2080 for about $180 billion annually.[784] However, if we really care about helping the hungry, we can do much better. We could focus on simple measures like investing in agriculture – improved soil health, water management and ag-tech research – and direct policies like school meals and nutrient fortification (like iodine in salt).[785] The UN estimates that we could reduce hunger by 229 million people by 2015 for about $10 billion annually.[786]

Again, it is worth pausing at these results. We can avoid 229 million people going hungry throughout this century for $10 billion annually. For the same amount of money spent on Kyoto, we can get one-eighteenth of the 2 million avoided toward the end of the century. If we look at the effect over the entire century, it is the equivalent of avoiding hunger for 39,000 people each year.[787] The difference between these two achievements is more than 5,000 to 1.[788] For each time our investment in climate saves one person from hunger, a similar investment in direct hunger policies could save more than 5,000 people, as you can see in Figure 42. This, of course, is why the Copenhagen Consensus results put malnutrition all the way up in second place (right after HIV), put the eradication of agricultural subsidies in third place and put agricultural research in fifth.

At the end of the day, it is important we face up to these facts. What should we do first? If we really care for the hungry of the world, should we not try to save 5,000 rather than one?

Such a question seems almost rhetorical in nature. Yet it is painfully obvious that the question often does not get asked and certainly never gets answered, when newspapers end up focusing on how climate change may

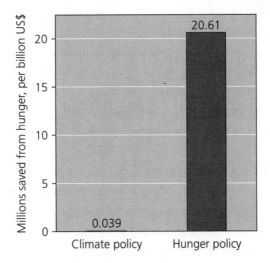

Figure 42 *Number of million people saved from hunger throughout the century per billion dollars spent, for climate and hunger policies.*

"greatly increase the number of hungry people." It makes us overly aware of one challenge but leaves us unable to see other and much better options elsewhere.

This quandary was perhaps never clearer than in 2004 when, quite remarkably, serious development organizations like Oxfam and Christian Aid, who are committed to "overcome poverty and suffering," began toying with climate change as one of the primary goals. They joined Greenpeace, WWF and Friends of the Earth in stating that without urgent and radical action on climate change the chances of achieving the millennium development hunger goal in 2015 would be seriously reduced.[789] First, it is outrageous to even suggest that any realistic climate policy could have any substantial effect on climate, let alone hunger, by 2015. Second, the statement marked the beginning of abandonment by many serious and sensible development organizations of aiming to achieve their primary goals through rational and efficient measures; instead they are increasingly going for popular and easily sellable but ultimately very ineffective measures, such as Kyoto.

The real problem, of course, is that the victims are not well-meaning firstworlders, but the 229 million anonymous people we could easily have helped.

Water shortages

Al Gore tells us how the devastating drought and hunger just below the Sahara (the so-called Sahel) is not caused by nature, corruption or mismanagement. Rather, the more we understand about global warming, "the more it looks as if we may be the real culprits."[790] In Gore's view, CO_2 caused a significant part of the troubles that the Sahel has been experiencing.

Likewise, UK commentator George Monbiot tells us how "The water boom is over" and how a dryer future with less fresh water and less food will mean "almost unimaginable future misery."[791]

Water is an important indicator for future well-being. It has also long been a worry in environmentalist circles, where the argument is that we're approaching a water crisis. The standard argument runs: Ever more people live on Earth and they use ever more water. Our water consumption has almost quadrupled since 1940. This cannot go on. In an environmental report from the UN, it is claimed that this global water shortage constitutes a "full-scale emergency," where "the world water cycle seems unlikely to be able to cope with the demands that will be made of it in the coming decades. Severe water shortages already hamper development in many parts of the world, and the situation is deteriorating."[792]

Such headlines are misleading. True, there may be *regional* and *logistic* problems with water. We need to get better at using it. But basically we have sufficient water.[793]

Water, of course, is the ultimate renewable resource – it rains down every year. Even if we only look at the rainwater that is available to us, we have about 12,500 km³, or about 5,300 liters/1,400 gallons *per person per day.*[794] For comparison, the average citizen in the EU uses about 566 liters of water per day. This is about 10% of the global level of available water and some 5% of the available EU water. An American, however, uses about three times as much water, or 1,442 liters every day.

If we look at global water use, we have indeed increased our water use from about 330 km³ to about 2,100 km³ over the past 100 years, as you can see in Figure 43. However, this still only constitutes about 17% of the available water. Moreover, it is important to realize that this increase has

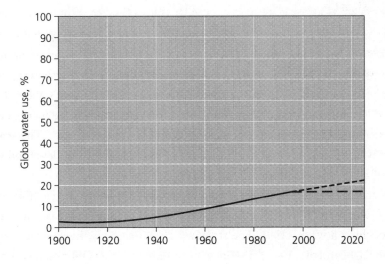

Figure 43 *Global use of available water, 1900–95; high and low prediction to 2025.*[795]

vastly improved human welfare both in direct water availability and in increasing food production dramatically.[796]

The obvious problem is that precipitation is not equally distributed over the globe. Some countries such as Iceland have about 1.5 million liters of water for each inhabitant every day, whereas Kuwait must make do with just 22 liters.[797] The physical human need is just about 2 liters of water a day, which clearly all nations can provide.[798] Typically, humans need about 100 liters per day for drinking, household needs and personal hygiene, which again almost all nations can provide.[799] (Kuwait can't, but at some cost they desalinate seawater, which underscores that most of the underlying problem is *poverty* rather than actual resource limits.[800])

The vast majority of water is used for industry and especially agriculture – in the developing world, more than 80% of the water goes to agriculture.[801] In many ways, importing food or industrial goods with high water contents can offset water demand in dry regions – so-called virtual water trade.[802] Since a ton of grain uses about 1,000 tons of water, this is in effect a very efficient way of importing water.[803] Israel imports about 87% of its grain consumption, Jordan 91%, Saudi Arabia 50%.[804]

With more wealth, many rich nations are also using their water resources better. Israel, with few water resources, achieves a high degree of efficiency in its agriculture, partly because it uses the very efficient drip irrigation system to green the desert, and partly because it recycles household wastewater for irrigation.[805]

It is estimated that many irrigation systems waste 60–80% of all water.[806] Following the example of Israel, drip irrigation in countries as diverse as India, Jordan, Spain and the US has consistently been shown to cut water use by 30–70% while increasing yields 20–90%.[807] Several studies have also indicated that industry, almost without additional costs, could save anywhere from 30 to 90% of its water consumption.[808] In many developing countries the big irrigation systems could be dramatically improved and total costs slashed if water was better priced.[809]

The UN summarizes in its 2006 world water report that lack of water "is primarily driven by an inefficient supply of services rather than by water shortages."[810] The global World Water Vision report from the World Water Council stated it even more clearly in its summary: "There is a water crisis today. But the crisis is not about having too little water to satisfy our needs. It is a crisis of managing water so badly that billions of people – and the environment – suffer badly."[811]

Thus, arguably the biggest water challenge in the world today is to get water to the 1 billion people who still don't have access, and sanitation to the 2.6 billion who still don't have access.[812] Yet, there is also reason for optimism. Over the past 37 years we have managed to give more than 3 billion more people access to sanitation and more than 4.5 billion access to clean drinking water. As can be seen in Figure 44, in 2007 88% of the developing world has clean drinking water and 62% sanitation.

The question, however, is whether global warming has already begun undermining this progress – as Gore suggests in the Sahel – and whether it will more generally undermine water access in the future.

The typical way to address this question is to use the so-called *water stress index*. This index tries to establish an approximate minimum level of water per capita to maintain an adequate quality of life in a moderately

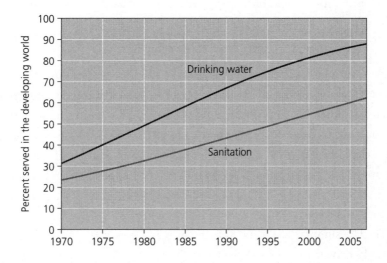

Figure 44 *The proportion of people with access to clean drinking water and sanitation in the developing world, 1970–2007.*[813]

developed country in an arid zone. This approach has been used by many organizations including the World Bank and in the standard literature on environmental science.[814]

Apart from the 100 liters per day for drinking, household needs and personal hygiene, it includes an additional 500–2,000 liters for agriculture, industry and energy production. Since water is often most needed in the dry season, the water stress level is then set even higher – if a country has less than 4,660 liters per person available it is expected to experience periodic or regular water stress. Should the accessible runoff drop to less than 2,740 liters the country is said to experience chronic water scarcity. Below 1,370 liters, the country experiences absolute water scarcity, outright shortages and acute scarcity.[815] As we pointed out above, these limits are obviously not rigorous, since technology (drip irrigation) and imports (virtual water) can dramatically lower the needs for water.

When looking forward to 2085, it is clear that more people are going to be water stressed.[816] However, this is simply a consequence of increasing population – more people will automatically drop below the water stress level as population increases, but this ignores that increased economic ability will probably more than compensate for the lower amount of water available.[817] After all, in an industrial society the vast majority will not be involved in water-intensive industries like farming, and thus these water-intensive industries can to a larger degree be placed where most water is available.[818]

However, our question is how climate change will affect water stress. This has been calculated on the basis of populations and available water in the 1,300 major watersheds around the world.[819] You can see the result in Figure 45. What this shows is that global warming actually *reduces* the number of people living in water stressed watersheds. Moreover, the warmest scenario A1 reduces the water stress more than the cooler B1.

Today, we have about 2 billion people in watersheds that are water stressed.[820] If we assume rapid global economic development with high income increases, moderate population growth and strong global warming (A1) we would see almost 3 billion people in water stressed areas in 2085, but because of global warming this will actually be lower than today, at less than 1.7 billion.

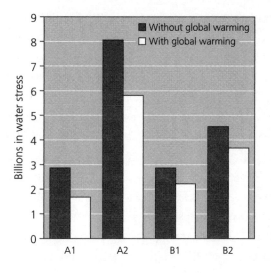

Figure 45 *Billions of people in water stressed watersheds in 2085 with and without global warming, for four different scenarios (see A1–B2 explained on p. 87).*[821]

This is because a warmer world also means more precipitation – in general, models predict about 5% more precipitation by 2100.[822] This does not mean that all regions will get equally more rain. Most of the planet will get wetter, such as southern and eastern Asia and parts of Africa, but some parts will get dryer, especially the Mediterranean area, central and south Africa, and the southern US. In Figure 46 we can see the regional outcome. It is clear that the vast majority of the people being less water stressed will live in south Asia and the northwest Pacific.

Take a look at Africa (the first five bars in Figure 46), which Al Gore focuses on. It is true that central Africa will get more water stressed with global warming. With the A1 scenario, central Africa will likely experience about 28 million more water stressed people. The same tendency is also true for southern and northern Africa, which will see 15 million more water stressed. But it also needs to be said that 23 million in western Africa will experience *less* water stress, and 44 million in eastern Africa likewise. In total, with warming we have an Africa where 24 million *fewer* will be water stressed. Only focusing on one area really doesn't give us the right information. Negative numbers mean more people in that region will become water stressed. In total 1,193 million will avoid becoming water stressed.

It is important to stress that the extra precipitation possibly will need to be stored for the dry season to be useful (as does the current precipitation).[823] However, the upshot is that when the discussion comes to water, global warming will actually make fewer people in the future become water stressed. Thus, if we choose to act against climate change, this may have other beneficial properties, but we have to remember that we will also have to deal with more people being water stressed.

It is clear that since fighting global warming actually increases the number of people vulnerable to water stress, this is not the best way to

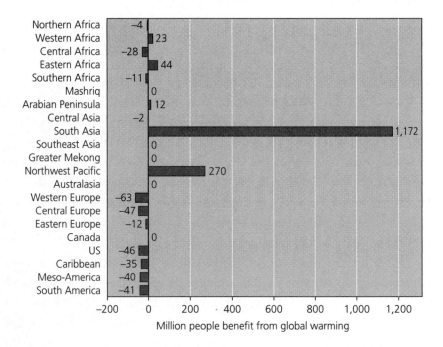

Figure 46 *Million people in different regions in 2085 who will avoid becoming water stressed due to global warming with A1, compared to no global warming.*[824]

reduce the number of people vulnerable to it. But there are other, very beneficial and inexpensive ways to improve access to water and sanitation, which
is still needed for 1 billion and 2.5 billion people respectively, as we saw
above. We could bring basic water and sanitation to all of these people for
an annual cost from 2007 to 2015 of about $10 billion, or the equivalent of
less than $4 billion forever.[825]

Thus, while Kyoto will at the very best mean zero change in the number
of people with access to clean drinking water and sanitation (but possibly
fewer with access), at $150 billion annually, we can help 3 billion people get
access for just $4 billion annually (Figure 47).[826] This will mean averting
almost a billion cases of diarrhea each year.[827] Perhaps surprisingly to many
in the first world, but crucially important to the 3 billion, access will save on
average 200 hours per person each year, walking to and waiting for water
and access to toilets, with a total monetary value of more than $200
billion.[828] Providing clean drinking water and sanitation was the sixth
priority on the Copenhagen Consensus list.

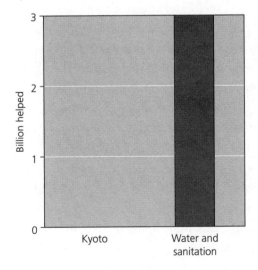

Figure 47 *The number of people helped by Kyoto (best case) and targeted water and
sanitation.*

But hasn't global warming done something bad with respect to water? What about Al Gore's claim that the Sahel, just below the Sahara, has suffered during its prolonged drought in the 1980s and 1990s and that "we helped manufacture the suffering in Africa."[829] It is absolutely correct that the Sahel has suffered, and that climate models when fed the surrounding sea temperatures can re-create the Sahel drought.[830] However, when two sets of researchers asked all the climate models whether they could actually re-create the Sahel drought, the resounding answer was no.[831] Of 19 models only 8 could re-create the drought and even the best could not even simulate its magnitude, beginning or duration.[832] Seven models even produced *excessive* rain. One research team concludes "the drought conditions were likely of natural origin."[833]

What we often fail to realize is that Africa is prone to long periods of drought. A 200-year study shows that dry periods similar to our time persisted during most of the first half of the 1800s.[834] Looking even further back, we see century-long drought episodes, the worst of which lasted 200 years around year 0.[835] According to the UN, history shows "droughts lasting decades to centuries are a recurrent feature" in Africa.[836]

But as Gore is wrong on this particular issue, it also points to a flaw in his larger reasoning. Even if global warming causes more water stress in one area (like central Africa), we have to remember that it simultaneously causes much less water stress elsewhere (like western and eastern Africa). Thus, when Gore proposes to stop global warming to alleviate water stress in one place, he inadvertently ends up advocating *more* water stress in other areas. This underscores the problem of turning the "big button" of CO_2, which potentially both has good impacts (alleviating drought some place, though not in the Sahel) but also has bad impacts (removing more available water elsewhere). Again, other policies directly aimed at dealing with the problems, e.g. the Sahel, whether they are caused by global warming or not, would likely do more good while allowing us to harvest the benefits of global warming (regionally more water availability).

And Monbiot's concerns about "unimaginable future misery"? Well, they are based on models for the coming century that show increasing drought.[837] The problem is that these models use indirect measures (like modeled stream flow and soil moisture simulations) that have also been used extensively to look at the last hundred years. But they don't fit the data. The models find "a very strong increase in the area of combined severe dry and wet conditions in Europe over the last three decades."[838] Yet the most recent study shows that Europe was driest in 1947 and wettest in 1915, and that there is no evidence for widespread and unusual drying in European regions over the last few decades.[839]

The longest data series on actual measured soil moisture in the world comes from the Ukraine. Although all climate models show that the Ukraine should have become dryer over the past 40 years, it has actually gotten much wetter.[840] Actually, this trend holds true for all the long measured soil moisture sites in the world (from 600 stations primarily in the US, Russia, China, Mongolia and India). Where the climate models expect more summer drying, we have seen increasing wetness.[841] This leads researchers to suggest that the current batch of climate models do not include the most important factors to address these issues.[842]

Thus, the central issue of water remains that global warming will mean more precipitation and more water availability for more people. The future water challenge is not primarily regulating global warming but ensuring that 3 billion people can get access to clean drinking water and sanitation. This would be remarkably inexpensive at $4 billion and make available an extra 200 hours per person, while avoiding almost a billion annual incidences of diarrhea.

Poor, but from global warming or bad policies?

One of the most frequently heard arguments for climate action is that global warming will harm the world's poor the most: as we have seen above, global warming will cause more heat deaths and malaria, cause problems from rising sea levels and depress food production in some regions. Because the developing world has less adaptive capacity, global warming will hit harder here.[843]

This has led many to argue that CO_2 reductions are the real "interests of the poor."[844] Since the developing world is the least responsible for global warming (as it emits the least CO_2) but is hit the hardest, this adds to the moral necessity of CO_2 reductions.[845]

However, as we have seen above, CO_2 reductions are often a very inefficient way to help the poor. Haiti has been hard hit by hurricanes, but potential CO_2 reductions will make very little difference far into the future. On the other hand, social and political changes like the ones made by Haiti's neighbor, the Dominican Republic, can reduce mortality a hundredfold.

Likewise, global warming will probably slightly increase malaria, but CO_2 reductions will do little good compared to direct investments in fighting malaria, which will do 20,000 times more good. And yes, food production will decrease in some places, but if our goal is to fight malnutrition, targeted policies can do more than 5,000 times better by investing directly in hunger prevention.

This dilemma is starkly clear in the discussion on future poverty. Here, the Stern Review from the UK government in late 2006 sums up the often-repeated view on development and global warming:

> For some of the poorest countries there is a real risk of being pushed into a downwards spiral of increasing vulnerability and poverty ... Developing countries would be affected especially adversely. This applies particularly to the poorest people within the large populations of both Sub-Saharan Africa, and South Asia. By 2100, in South Asia and sub-Saharan Africa, up to 145–220 million additional people could fall below the $2-a-day poverty line.[846]

The figure of 220 million extra poor has reverberated around the globe.[847] Yet, with economies expected to grow over the century, this finding of substantially more poor might seem a bit surprising.

Let us just briefly look at how poverty has progressed and will likely continue into the future. There are many measures of poverty, but probably the most broadly used is the proportion or number of people living at below $1-a-day, which is also the official measure of the World Bank.[848] This measure shows us how much of the developing world lives below (or more accurately consumes below) the purchasing power of about one US dollar per day. While consumption is not the only issue in defining poverty, it certainly makes a major difference and is the best indicator for a global or regional analysis.[849]

In Figure 48 we see how poverty has declined dramatically over the past 50 years from almost 50% in 1950 to less than 20% today and will likely reach about 10% in 2015. The same picture is evident for south Asia and Sub-Saharan Africa, though these regions are poorer and in essence have started at almost 50% poor 30 years later in 1980. Today the region has about 30% below $1-a-day, but a sustained economic growth will likely continue toward essentially eradicating poverty by 2080.

Against this background the Stern Review claim of 220 million more poor seems like a dramatic increase and a testimony to the severe impact of climate change. Yet, the calculation made two crucial decisions and chose to underplay the sense of proportion.

Stern chose to look at the A2 scenario, which is essentially a very high population growth with low economic growth scenario. Yet, it is generally agreed that A2 is too negative: "current opinion considers the population component of SRES A2 'out of the range', as its associated population growth rates seem now too high."[850] Consequently, choosing A2 works because it produces more poor, but it can only be considered an absolute worst-case scenario.[851]

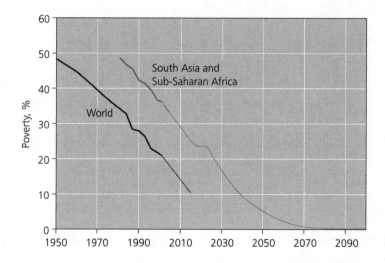

Figure 48 *The proportion of poor in the world, 1950–2015, and for south Asia and Sub-Saharan Africa, 1981–2100.*[852]

Moreover, Stern chose the $2-a-day limit for the world's very poorest, who are still struggling to get past $1. This choice of course increases the number of poor. Yet, the World Bank explicitly says that $2-a-day reflects "poverty lines more commonly used in lower-middle-income countries."[853]

Finally, Stern chose to assume that the world will warm extra much, compared to the baseline scenario.[854]

You can see the result in Figure 49. In the worst-case world, the population below $2-a-day keeps outpacing economic growth until the 2030s in south Asia and Sub-Saharan Africa where it maxes out at 1.9 billion people. After that it still only slowly starts declining, crossing 1.8 billion 30 years later and 800 million just before the end of the century. With a high degree of warming, it is likely that the slightly slower GDP growth will show up as a slower decline in the number of poor, as you can see in the thin white line in Figure 49. By 2100, global warming will cause the world to have 51 million more people below $2-a-day. If Stern – besides choosing the worst scenario, high poverty limit and high climate impact – also tweaks the risk of things going very wrong, he then gets the 220 million extra poor.[855]

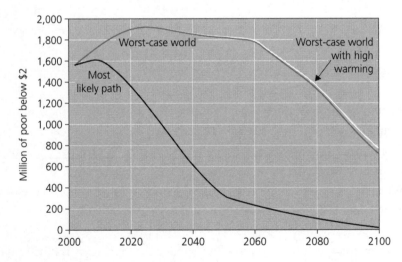

Figure 49 *Millions of poor in south Asia and Sub-Saharan Africa, 2002–2100, with Stern's worst-case scenario (A2) and the most likely development (A1). White line behind both graphs shows the most likely damage done by exceptionally warm global warming. (Line behind A1 can hardly be seen.)*[856]

But it is worth taking a step back and looking at the total impact. Even with the most extreme global warming impact, economic growth will diminish poverty by more than 220 million eight years later. Still extreme, the 51 million you see in Figure 49 will nevertheless be caught up by economic growth in less than two years.

Moreover, the Stern Review's strong statements about worst worst-case scenarios would undoubtedly have looked less strong had they shown the total development as we see in Figure 49. But nowhere in the Review or the background report are the absolute numbers of extra poor compared to the absolute total number of poor.

Perhaps even more important is to look at the other, more likely, policy option, namely going down a different – and more likely – development path, the A1. This will cause much more rapid reduction in poverty in south Asia and Sub-Saharan Africa. The A1 has both a lower population growth and higher GDP growth. The World Bank's expectation for poverty in south Asia and Sub-Saharan Africa is spot on A1 and 13 percentage points lower than Stern's, again indicating that Stern has picked the wrong scenario.[857]

The A1 expects to see the number of poor people quickly reduced (after 2010), dropping from 1.6 billion to 300 million just after 2050 and to just 19 million in 2100. Moreover, this future is also much more robust toward climate change – you virtually can't see the different climate line in Figure 49, which expects 3 million more poor in 2100, or the decline of less than a year.

Again, we are at a point where we have to realize that we have several opportunities to tackle the problems. If we really care about reducing the number of poor in the world, we have to ask if cutting carbon emissions is really the best way to achieve that goal.

When Stern only mentions the extreme number of extra poor that global warming might produce, he naturally makes us think – oh yeah, we have to do something about climate change. But when we look at Figure 49, we start realizing that maybe even if we could stop global warming, it is much more important that we focus on setting society down the path of A1 rather than A2. Stopping global warming entirely will prevent 8 million of 1,800 million people from being poor in 2050, yet choosing A1 instead will drop that number to 320 million – helping 1.5 billion people or almost 200 times more people.

And we cannot stop global warming entirely. If we manage to implement Kyoto fully in A2 (including the US, everyone sticking to their reductions until 2100), we will on average over the century see a reduction of 1 million poor people.[858] If we manage to move from A2 to A1, we will on average reduce the number of poor people by a billion – that is almost a thousand times better, as is illustrated in Figure 50.[859]

This once again underscores the recurrent theme of how we need to start thinking about which knobs we should turn first when dealing with the world's problems. This becomes obvious if we look at the cost of global warming in relation to the total world economy. Figure 51 shows the total cost of applying the various policies to total future consumption. For comparison, the total cost of global warming will cost us approximately 0.5% of our overall consumption ($14.5 trillion). Even our most extreme climate policy, the EU target of 2°C, will "only" cost 2.7% of our overall wealth ($84 trillion).

This total future consumption also underscores that *global warming is not anywhere near the most important problem in the world*. What matters

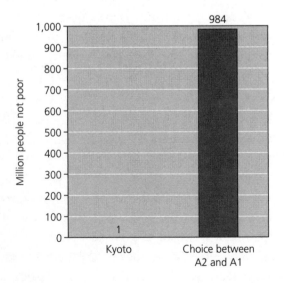

Figure 50 *The difference in reducing number of poor people through climate change policy choice and economic policy.*

is making the developing countries rich and allowing the citizens of developed countries even greater opportunities. In Figure 51 we see the total income over the coming century for the four main scenarios in the IPCC. If we choose a world focused on economic development within a global setting, the total income will be some $3,000 trillion. However, should we go down a path focusing on the environment, even if we stay within a global setting, humanity will lose more than $550 trillion or 18% of the total

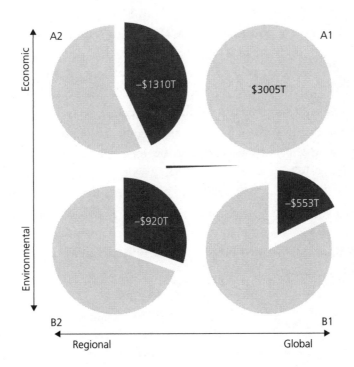

Figure 51 *The four main scenarios in IPCC, along the dimension Global–Regional and the dimension Economic–Environmental. The total worth of income over the century 2000–2100 is estimated at $3,005 trillion in A1, the global economically focused scenario.[860] The cost of focusing on the environment in a global setting is $553 trillion (B1), the cost of focusing on the economy but in a regionalized setting is $1,310 trillion (A2), and the cost of focusing on the environment in a regionalized economy is $920 trillion (B2). For comparison, the total cost of global warming is estimated at $14.5 trillion, or 0.5% of the A1 scenario (the slice in the middle). The world economy in 2006 was $48 trillion.[861] All amounts in 2005 US$.*

potential income. And should we choose a more regional approach to solving the problems of the twenty-first century, we would stand to lose $920–1,310 trillion or more than a quarter to almost half of the potential income. Moreover, the loss will mainly be to the detriment of the developing countries – switching from A1 to B1 would cost the developing world 40% of its total income.[862]

Again, this should be seen in the light of a total cost of global warming at about $14.5 trillion, or a cost of all the other environmental policies throughout the twenty-first century of about $60 trillion.[863] What this illustrates is that if we want to leave a planet with the most possibilities for our descendants, in both the developing and the developed world, it is imperative both that we focus primarily on the economy and not the environment and that we focus on solving our problems in a global and not a regionalized context. Basically, this puts the spotlight on securing economic growth, especially in the third world, while ensuring a global economy, both of which tasks the world has set itself within the framework of the World Trade Organization (WTO). If we succeed here, we could increase world income by $553–1,310 trillion, whereas even if we achieve the absolutely most efficient global warming policies, we can increase wealth by just $0.6 trillion (Figure 11, p. 41). To put it squarely, what matters to our and our children's future is primarily decided not within the IPCC framework but within the WTO framework.

4

THE POLITICS OF
GLOBAL WARMING

What can we do with the climate knob?

Al Gore is right, that the debate about climate change is a debate about our generational mission. Essentially, *in the next 40 years what do we want to have accomplished?*

Global warming is happening, the consequences are important and mostly negative. It will cause more heat deaths, sea level rise, possibly more intense hurricanes and more flooding; it will give rise to more malaria, starvation and poverty. From this list of ills, it is not surprising that a vast array of environmental organizations, pundits and politicians have concluded that we must act to fix global warming.

The problem with this analysis is that it overlooks a simple but important fact. Cutting CO_2 – even substantially – will not matter much for the list of problems. Actually, from polar bears to poverty, as we have seen throughout this book, we can do little with climate policies and a lot with other, social policies.

If we claim that our concern lies with people dying from climate effects, like the European summer heat wave in 2003, we have to ask ourselves why we are primarily thinking about implementing expensive CO_2 cuts. These will at best leave future communities warming slightly less fast, still causing ever more heat deaths. Moreover, as warming will indeed prevent even *more* cold deaths, we have to ask why we are thinking about an expensive policy that will actually leave *more* people dead from temperature (see Figure 13, p. 45).

Yet, other social policies could allow us both to capture the benefits of global warming through reduced cold deaths, and to deal with the lower but increasing heat deaths, through cool cities with water, parks and white surfaces, and better availability of air-conditioning and medical care. This would be orders of magnitude cheaper and would do much more good. Would we not prefer that to be our generational mission?

We care about low-lying islands and people being flooded from rising sea levels. Yet, we have to ask ourselves why we then primarily talk about limiting carbon emissions that will reduce sea level rise but also leave islanders less well off, ultimately leaving them with *more* lost dry land. As we saw in pp. 77–8, income matters much more than sea level rise in how well communities will be protected.

If we manage to cut emissions dramatically, following the UN's most optimistic scenario, we can reduce sea level rise from 34 cm to 22 cm over the coming century. But doing so will also cause humanity to be less well off in 2100, reducing the average individual's wealth by 30%. Micronesia, the nation which will lose most dry land, will lose 0.6% of its area – three times as much as in the higher-sea-level-but-richer world. Do we really want that to be our mission?

We profess our concern for increasing hurricane damage in, for instance, the US, and the terrible toll it exerts on third world countries. But why would we want to focus on CO_2 cuts when the experts still don't know if emissions are connected to stronger hurricanes, and even if they are, we could make only a very little difference of about 0.5%.

If we want to curtail hurricane damage, we could do much more through social policies like mapping vulnerability, better evacuation plans, community education and relief distribution, zoning, regulation, taxing and public acquisition of land at risk, dropping state subsidized insurance, improving and enforcing building codes, upgrading levees and reducing environmental degradation of wetlands and beaches that act as natural sea walls against hurricanes. These policies could reduce damage by more than 50% at a fraction of the climate policy cost.

If we want to reduce the many deaths in the third world, we likewise could employ cheap emergency policies of shelters and evacuation networks that can reduce death rates by 99%. Vulnerability is caused by poverty – the poor being forced to settle in shacks on steep unstable slopes and flood-prone areas where they bear the brunt of any climate extreme. Thus, in the long run, the solution is to make them healthier and richer. Besides the obvious good, this will make them much better able to deal with climate extremes, present or future.

As we have pointed out throughout this book, this pattern goes for all major issues connected to global warming. Let us just recap the ones where the published literature gives us the opportunity to establish a balance between how much good we can do with climate polices and with other policies.[864] Which should be our generational mission?

Malaria will slightly increase from global warming, but if we really care about malaria victims we have to ask why we would ever first contemplate helping very few very slowly through climate policies. If we do Kyoto, we can avoid 70 million people getting infected toward the end of the century. If we focus on targeted policies, mosquito nets, medicine and mosquito eradication, we could save 28,000 million from malaria – or more than 400 times better. When we also realize that doing so would be 50 times cheaper, we are faced with a stark choice: every time we save one person through climate policies, we could have saved 20,000 people with smarter, simpler malaria policies.

Likewise, global warming will probably decrease the speed with which poverty gets alleviated over the century. Yet, cutting carbon emissions is probably one of the least efficient ways to combat poverty, whereas picking a high-growth, global policy approach (like a successful Doha round, with open markets and eliminated subsidies) will do much more to achieve the poverty goal. For each person Kyoto could make less poor, simple economic policies could save almost 1,000 people from poverty.

When we consider water scarcity, global warming actually makes water more available. Thus, we found that climate change would have a net effect of improving access for 1.2 billion people, and since Kyoto would actually make matters *worse*, by making more water stressed people, again this gives positive support to alternative policy choices. As we've discussed, we could easily afford to provide water and sanitation to 3 billion people who today go without.[865]

When talking about flooding, yes, global warming makes flooding more likely but other policies are vastly superior in dealing with flooding, for example better information, no public subsidies for floodplain building, stricter planning, fewer levees, allowing floodplains to act as natural buffers and increasing wetlands. For every dollar saved with Kyoto we can save 1,300 dollars through smarter, social policies.

For each person we help avoid malnutrition through climate policy we can do much, much more. Through simple policies like investing in agriculture – improved soil health, water management and ag-tech research – and direct policies like school meals and nutrient fortification (like iodine in salt), we can instead save 5,000 people.

With all these choices, we have to ask the question over and over again. When choosing our generational mission, which policies should come first?

We have become fascinated by the "big knob" of climate change and been sold the idea that if we can just turn this one knob, we can ameliorate most other problems in the world. Yet, this is demonstrably false.

What we have to come to terms with is that even though CO_2 causes global warming, which is important, cutting CO_2 simply doesn't matter much for most of the world's important issues. From polar bears to poverty, we can do immensely better with other policies.

This does not mean doing nothing about global warming, as we also pointed out in chapter 2. It simply means realizing that early and massive carbon reductions will prove costly, hard and politically divisive and likely will end up making fairly little difference to the climate and virtually no difference to social impacts. Moreover, it may well take away our primary attention from the many other issues, where we can do much more good for the world and its environment.

Rather, we need to focus on smart, cheap and enticing strategies for improving energy sources toward the middle of the century, through research and development in low-CO_2 energy.

What we should do instead: increase in R&D

The fundamental problem with today's climate approach is that ever-stricter emission controls, as in Kyoto, and a possible tighter Kyoto II, are likely to be unworkable. It is perhaps worth dispelling the myth that Kyoto's troubles are only due to the rejection of the treaty by a recalcitrant Bush administration. First of all, there has consistently been a majority against an even weaker version of Kyoto in the US Senate. But perhaps more importantly, besides the US and its fellow non-ratifier Australia, many of the participants in Kyoto – including Canada, Japan, Spain, Portugal, Greece, Ireland, Italy, New Zealand, Finland, Norway, Denmark and Austria – are failing to meet the treaty's requirements for CO_2 reductions, and many have little or no prospect of meeting them before the treaty expires in 2012.[866] Had Bush simply joined the many nations that outwardly suggest compliance but actually show little intention to fulfill it, it would have become obvious that the treaty was never going to work.

Instead, Kyoto unfortunately has become the symbol of opposition to a unilateral US and thus has received political resuscitation without being questioned for its efficiency or achievability. And this is the real issue. That Kyoto at the same time is impossibly ambitious and yet environmentally inconsequential. That it attempts to change century-old energy patterns in 15 years, ending up costing a fortune and delivering almost nothing.

It is worth noting that the same problem besets the new EU pledge, the first real commitment since Kyoto in 1997. In March 2007 the EU promised that they would unilaterally cut emissions to 20% below 1990 levels by 2020.[867] This would mean a 25% cut of emissions from what they would otherwise have been in 2020.[868] Yet the effect on temperature would be smaller than Kyoto, as shown in Figure 52, postponing warming by the end of the century by about two years. The cost would be about $90 billion per year in 2020.[869] Thus, we see the same pattern from both the well-established Kyoto Protocol and the new EU minus-20% decision – that they have fairly small impact at fairly high cost.

If we look at the development of CO_2 emissions over the past half-century in Figure 53, they have – apart from short reversals with the oil crises and the Soviet breakdown – increased inexorably. If we set 1990 to 100, emissions were already at 109 in 1997, when the Kyoto Protocol was created. Kyoto asked industrial countries to restrict their emissions by 12% in 2010 from what they would otherwise have been – to 133 rather than 142.[870]

But even that rather modest target was a tough call. Changing national energy systems take a long time and has huge costs. Those countries that are on track toward meeting their targets were well on their way to doing so

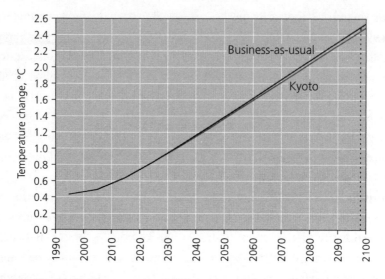

Figure 52 *The expected increase in temperature with business-as-usual and with the EU minus-20% restrictions extended forever. Broken line shows that the temperature for the business-as-usual scenario in 2098 is the same as the reduced temperature in 2100 (2.48°C).*[871]

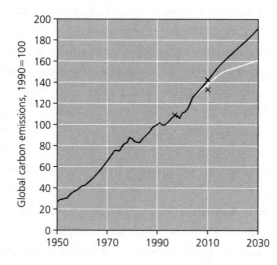

Figure 53 *Global carbon emissions, 1950–2030, with IEA standard and alternative scenarios from 2005.*[872] *X marks Kyoto start in 1997 and its three end-points in 2010 – the original intention at 133.3, and present goal at 142.2, and business-as-usual at 142.7.*

without Kyoto.[873] The twelve nations that have reduced emissions the most since 1990 are all former Eastern Bloc countries that have undergone radical economic restructuring. Germany, which has also managed considerable reductions, has done so largely because it absorbed a former Eastern Bloc country, and Great Britain's reductions are principally the consequence of actions by Margaret Thatcher in the 1980s to break the British coal union and move that nation's energy system away from coal and toward gas – for reasons that were predominantly political and economic, not environmental. In 1997 when Kyoto was negotiated, German and British emission levels were already both 9% below their 1990 level.[874]

But many other countries have had a much harder time reaching the targets, especially the US, Australia and Canada, which are all experiencing population growth rates of more than 10% per decade, naturally tending to increase national emissions. With the more relaxed agreements in Bonn and Marrakech, and the US dropping out, Kyoto essentially collapsed, allowing *more* emissions than were expected in business-as-usual.[875] Even though the EU has valiantly fought to make restrictions binding, there is not much left of an ambitious target. As you can see in Figure 53, it is now expected that Kyoto will lead to a slight reduction in emissions of about 0.4%, from 142.7 to 142.2. In Figure 53 you can't even tell the two X's apart.

Actually, Kyoto is not the first time we have made such commitments. At the Earth Summit in Rio in 1992, we promised to cut emissions back to 1990 levels by 2000.[876] Although we managed as a group, it was only due to the recession in the Eastern Bloc. For the OECD countries, we overshot our target in 2000 by more than 12%.[877]

These attempts clearly show that cutting emissions has been politically (and economically) very hard to carry through. We will get back to that.

Equally, look at the future. The International Energy Agency expects that emissions will continue to soar, not least from China, India and the other developing countries. The OECD will increase its emissions some 20% till 2030, whereas the developing countries will more than double their emissions.[878]

The IEA "alternative" scenario looks at what the world might look like if its leaders take "resolute action." Here emissions will increase more slowly, about 17% less than it would otherwise be in 2030. One might expect that would be because we would use much more renewable energy, but that is really the smallest part. Mostly, this would come from simply using less energy – becoming much more efficient. We would also use less polluting coal and more cleaner gas, with slightly more nuclear and biomass. The classic renewables, such as wind and solar, would still constitute a very small 2.4% in 2030 in the alternative scenario – up from 1.7% in the standard scenario.[879] The total proportion of renewables (water, biomass, wind and solar) is today 13%, and in 2030 it will likely have risen to just 14% — and with the great assumptions of the alternative scenario maybe even 16%.

Look at the development of our energy efficiency in Figure 54 – how much value we produce per ton of CO_2. This shows that we have progressively gotten better, producing more value in 2004 than we have ever done before. Yet, it also underscores that if we are to achieve even the standard

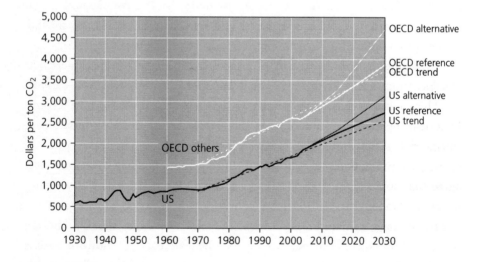

Figure 54 *Efficiency in production of value. How much can we produce per ton of CO_2? US production 1930–2030, the rest of OECD 1960–2030, in 2000 US$ and projection from 2005.*[880] *The IEA alternative scenario is the thin line. The dotted line is a trend line for 1970–2004.*

scenario, we will have to do much better in 2030. Our historical experience tends to support that we can and will do so. It is perhaps worth realizing that we cannot see any indication of the Kyoto Protocol increasing the efficiency in the rest of the OECD up until 2004.

But the alternative scenario also clearly asks for much bigger improvements than we have seen until now as is evident in Figure 54, and consequently, much greater investments.[881] If the past trivial reductions achieved by the Kyoto Protocol are anything to go by, it seems the alternative scenario is more than exuberantly optimistic. Moreover, in this scenario, the largest reduction – even relatively – is expected to happen in the developing world, where the willingness to pay will be even lower.[882]

This underscores the harsh truth, that in the short and medium term it will be very difficult and costly to change nations' energy structures and emissions. This is why a Kyoto II with more stringent CO_2 cuts and more participation, from both the US and developing countries, will be a very hard sell indeed. Most experts when polled also expect that a possible Kyoto II will be rather weak.[883]

There is an economic, a political and a technological problem with the Kyoto process of ever increasing CO_2 emission cuts. The fundamental *economic* problem with both Kyoto and its stricter follow-ups is that all macroeconomic models show that they are poor investments (see p. 43).

This, however, easily spills into the larger *political* problem of Kyoto. First, it will get progressively harder to convince people that they should pay substantial sums for rather negligible environmental improvements a century away. Second, as costs mount this will undercut the willingness to agree that some nations get away with free-riding, or – more likely – will mean that many nations will claim to adopt the restrictions but give up during the process without obvious penalties. Third, high emission restrictions and low achievements will erode the support for future treaties. Clearly, the failure of Kyoto to deliver any substantial restriction lowers the chance of successful follow-up.

Basically, the political problem of the Kyoto process is that it requires ever more nations to sit down and agree that they will each take actions that are immediately costly but that will benefit everyone else a little, far into the future. This means that the ever tougher and the necessary more inclusive deals get ever harder to conclude. That is a very fragile process.

Arguably, the *technological* problem with the Kyoto process has the greatest impact. In the long term, global warming will only be substantially reduced if we can make a transition to a non-fossil fuel economy. Many Kyoto advocates will claim that the Kyoto restrictions on emissions will spur new investments in research and development (R&D) that will enable us to move closer to such a transition. But this is backwards.[884] If we want technology we should ask for and invest in technology. When we ask for immediate carbon emission reductions as in Kyoto, we should not be surprised that the vast majority of the investments go toward that specific goal.

The overall effect of the Kyoto process seems rather to be to encourage nations to work within the status quo and play the system to meet short-term targets, rather than to reward long-term and high-risk investment aimed at encouraging technological change. In the words of an assessment of the UK: "The government gives priority to support for renewables R&D projects in technology areas that are likely to have the greatest impact, *in the short term*, in both domestic and export technology markets."[885] In the Kyoto treaty there is a complete absence of provisions to stimulate R&D.[886]

The lack of incentive in Kyoto becomes abundantly clear in the public R&D available for energy. In general, R&D has fallen sharply in real terms for most industrialized countries since the early 1980s.[887] While this is true for the big areas of R&D for fossil fuels and nuclear, it is also the case for the important areas of global warming – R&D on renewable energy and energy efficiency. As you can tell in Figure 55, R&D has dropped since the early 1980s and has been approximately stable over the past 15 years at about 0.006% of GDP in the major OECD countries participating in Kyoto. The Kyoto Protocol clearly has not generated substantial new investments in R&D. For comparison, the total public R&D for the OECD countries lies above 2%.

It is estimated that the vast majority of R&D investments are public and, moreover, there are very few assessments of private R&D.[888] One longer data series for the renewables in the US shows a low level and a similarly

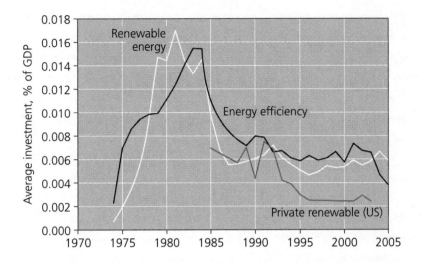

Figure 55 *Average share of GDP of public R&D in renewable energy and energy efficiency for most OECD countries participating in Kyoto, 1974–2005. Private renewable R&D for the US.*[889]

declining tendency as seen in Figure 55. For comparison, in 1980 the private energy R&D in the US was slightly bigger than R&D in drugs and medicines – today energy has dropped about 80% while the biotech industry has tripled.[890]

This demonstrates that although global warming needs strong R&D investments in non-carbon or low-carbon energy technologies, the Kyoto approach simply does not supply it.

At the end of the day, if cutting CO_2 costs by $20/ton the rich world might be willing to make some – if often symbolic – cuts at high price, but it is extremely unlikely that we will get China, India and the other developing countries on board. What we need to do to tackle climate change is to make this cost drop dramatically – if we could cut CO_2 to, say, $2/ton, it would be much more likely that we could get everyone on board with massive cuts.

This is why I suggest that a much more appropriate response to climate change would be a worldwide commitment to R&D for non-carbon emitting energy technologies. We should not head mindlessly toward a Kyoto II that would impose ever stricter standards, but do so at high economic costs, with low benefits and fragile political commitments, while not addressing the fundamental issue of finding new energy technologies that will carry us through the twenty-first century.

Instead we should commit ourselves to spending 0.05% of GDP in R&D of non-carbon emitting energy technologies. This approach would cost about $25 billion per year. It would increase funding to R&D about ten times,[891] yet it would be seven times cheaper than Kyoto and many more times cheaper than a Kyoto II. It could easily involve all nations, with richer nations automatically paying the larger share. It would let each country focus on its own future vision of energy needs, whether that means concentrating on renewable sources, nuclear energy, fusion, carbon storage, or conservation, or searching for new and more exotic opportunities.

This money should be spent on research all the way from exploratory to applied; pilot programs to test and demonstrate promising new technologies; public–private partnerships to incentivize private sector participation in high-risk ventures (just like those now used to get pharmaceutical companies to develop tropical disease vaccines); training programs to expand the number of scientists and engineers working on a wide variety of energy R&D projects; government procurement programs that can provide a predictable market for promising new technologies; prizes for the achievement of important technological thresholds; multilateral funds for collaborative international research; international research centers to help build a global innovation capacity (like the agricultural research institutes which lay at the heart of the agricultural Green Revolution in the 1970s); as well as policy incentives to encourage adoption of existing and new energy-efficient technologies, which in turn fosters incremental learning and innovation that often leads to rapidly improving performance and declining costs.[892]

We need this investment to be public. One of the main reasons that R&D for new energy is so relatively low is that the private return is typically only 20–30% but the public return around 50%.[893] Basically, private investors are not able to appropriate the full returns because the technological "spillover" in energy is large. If you make a fundamental, new discovery on how to produce more energy with less CO_2, you might make it to market first, but many others will follow, making great progress for society but not necessarily for the original investor. Here we need government investments for large social benefits.

Preliminary studies indicate that such a level of R&D would be sufficient to stabilize CO_2 concentrations at double the pre-industrial levels, essentially meaning that such an investment should be able to limit temperatures to about 2.5°C increase from today.[894]

Such a massive global research effort would also have potentially huge innovation spin-offs. The Apollo moon program, with a total price tag of about $200 billion, is perhaps the most well known for its spin-offs, ranging from computer miniaturization to CT and MRI scanners.[895]

Similarly, because the costs are much lower and there will be many immediate innovation benefits, the political fragility of the process disappears. The project will not be vulnerable to the occasional free-rider, simply because most governments will still pay fairly little and can appropriate a large share of the immediate benefits in patents and industry spin-offs. Countries will no longer have to be ever more strongly cajoled into ever more restrictive agreements. Rather, they will partake because it involves them in a low-cost, long-term, viable solution to global warming.

Thus, we need to abandon the Kyoto process with its focus on costly but ineffective and politically fragile cuts in CO_2. The original Kyoto, which runs until 2012, will achieve virtually no carbon cuts – it will mean just 0.4% lower emissions and have absolutely no climate impact. Even if a stronger Kyoto II could force through higher CO_2 cuts into the future, it would still only marginally influence the temperature.

And even if much higher cuts could be achieved, changes in temperature would do little to help the people who need it most. In the developed world, people affected by hurricanes and floods primarily need better (and better-enforced) building codes, protective infrastructure and natural wetlands. In the developing world, malaria-exposed populations primarily need mosquito nets and artemisinin drugs; the hungry and poor primarily need agricultural investments and an end to first world subsidies.

And even if the extended Kyoto process doesn't break down and actually delivers some parts of its promise, the tenuous, convoluted, constant political battle takes away our attention from the many better and more efficient issues, where we can do so much more. This is the real moral problem of the global warming argument – it means well, but by almost expropriating the public agenda, trying to address the hardest problem, with the highest price tag and the least chance of success, it leaves little space, attention and money for the much better solutions.

Instead of smart solutions we get scared witless

Global warming is being described in everyday media in ever more dire terms. The IPPR think-tank (which is strongly in favor of CO_2 cuts) in 2006 produced an analysis of the UK debate. It summarized the flavor thus:

> Climate change is most commonly constructed through the alarmist repertoire – as awesome, terrible, immense and beyond human control. This repertoire is seen everywhere and is used or drawn on from across the ideological spectrum, in broadsheets and tabloids, in popular magazines and in campaign literature from government initiatives and environmental groups. It is typified by an inflated or extreme lexicon, incorporating an urgent tone and cinematic codes. It employs a quasi-religious register of death and doom, and it uses language of acceleration and irreversibility.[896]

This kind of language makes any sensible policy dialogue about our global choices impossible. In public debates, the argument I hear most often is a variant of "if global warming is going to kill us all and lay waste to the world, this has to be our top priority – everything else you talk about, including HIV/AIDS, malnutrition, free trade, malaria, clean drinking water, may be noble but utterly unimportant compared to global warming." Of course, if the deadly description of global warming were correct, the inference of its primacy would also be correct, but as we have seen above, global warming is nothing of the sort. It is one – but only one – problem of many we will have to tackle through the twenty-first century.

Yet, these pervasive, apocalyptic descriptions of global warming persist, strongly aided by the media, as it thrives on bad news. "A good story is usually bad news," writes a textbook for journalists.[897] Although it is not easy to explain why, we all seem to be curious about and fascinated by bad news, and this sells newspapers. The tabloid papers are forced to focus more on sensation because they depend on their readers finding them exciting enough to buy them every day. A recent study showed how the use of the word "fear" has increased in American media, actually doubling in head-lines.[898] And climate sells particularly well. The IPPR points out how "alarmism might even become secretly thrilling – effectively a form of "climate porn.""[899]

Moreover, journalistic stories tend to focus on conflicts. A conflict has that gripping dramatic element familiar from fairy tales and other literature, a battle between good and evil, which the audience must follow to the bitter end to find out what happens. Journalists are actually taught how to tailor their stories to patterns from fairy tales.[900]

Closely related to the story of conflict is the question of guilt.[901] It is not uncommon for one of the involved parties to be given the blame for the conflict, which helps to give the news a more human touch. We have seen examples of this in the US, where efforts to do something about garbage dumps is given far higher priority compared to combating radioactive radon, even though combating radon would be far more effective. Why? Because a garbage dump provides "good pictures" and because garbage dumps are "somebody's fault."[902]

PAST BAD NEWS

A good past example of how everything gets blamed on global warming was the US encounter with the 1997/8 El Niño. Notice how we don't particularly worry about this any more (and the IPCC has steadily said that it is hard to link to global warming[903]). Yet in 1998 it had firmly captured our attention. Al Gore frequently told us how global warming is making El Niño worse.[904] Evenutally, almost any climate event got linked to El Niño: "as early 1998 progressed, it became difficult to find a weather-related story that did not mention El Niño's influence."[905] We were told how cities were "bracing for the climate event of the century."[906] We got informed of the "weird weather" and endless lists of problems:

Experts are saying that this El Niño is one of the most intense on record. San Francisco has had its wettest winter since 1867. Damage from storms and mud slides is expected to cost California more than $300 million, and has caused at least 10 deaths. In Florida, more than 300 homes were destroyed and more than three dozen people were killed by a series of powerful tornadoes. "This shows that El Niño is very dangerous for Florida" said Scott Spratt, a meteorologist for the National Weather Service.[907]

Actually, El Niño got blamed for anything from wrecking tourism,[908] causing more allergies,[909] melting the ski-slopes,[910] and yet dumping snow in Ohio, causing 22 deaths.[911] Perhaps the most surprising statement was Disney's accusation that El Niño had caused its shares to fall.[912] And even when El Niño did have a positive effect, this was powerfully ignored, as in *Time* magazine: "Large parts of the eastern and north-central U.S. continued to bask in the warmest winter in years, one that brought cherry blossoms to Washington in the first week of January. That might sound like the opposite of a disaster, but every weather anomaly has its dark side."[913] And then the journalists went on to tell us about the problems of warmer weather.

However, a researcher did the sums in *Bulletin of the American Meteorological Society*, counting up all the problems and all the benefits from El Niño.[914] And while all the bad occurrences of Californian storms, crop damage, government relief costs, and human and economic losses from tornadoes were true, they were only one side of the story. At the same time, higher winter temperatures meant about 850 fewer human cold deaths, much diminished heating costs, less spring flood damage, and savings in highway-based and airline transportation. Moreover, a well-documented connection between El Niño and fewer Atlantic hurricanes was well expressed in 1998 – the US actually experienced no major Atlantic hurricanes and thus avoided huge losses.

The total damages were estimated at $4 billion, whereas the total benefits were estimated at $19 billion. But given the wide media coverage of all the bad news, the fact that El Niño was overall beneficial for the US was not the impression left with the average reader or viewer.

Actually, exaggeration, conflict and blame are an old game in the climate debate. Perhaps, most chillingly, this was evident in the witch trials in medieval Europe. After the Inquisition's eradication of the actual heretics (like Cathars and Waldensians), most witches from the early 1400s onwards were accused of creating bad weather.[915] The Pope in 1484 recognized that witches "have blasted the produce of the Earth, the grapes of the vine, the fruits of the trees ... vineyards, orchards, meadows, pasture-lands, corn, wheat and all other cereals."[916] As Europe descended into the Little Ice Age, more and more areas experienced crop failure, high food prices and hunger, and witches became obvious scapegoats in weakly governed areas. As many as half a million individuals were executed between 1500 and 1700, and there was a strong correlation between low temperatures and high numbers of witchcraft trials across the European continent.[917] Even today, such climate link is still prevalent in Sub-Saharan Africa, where extreme rainfall (both droughts and floods) are strongly linked to the killings of "witches" – in just one district in Tanzania, more than 170 women are killed each year.[918]

Less violently, the wet summer of 1816, after the eruption of the volcano Tambora (see p. 76) was blamed by many in Europe on the new practice of using lightning conductors.[919] The authorities had to issue grave warnings concerning the violent and illegal acts against the conductors. Interestingly, the same conductors had some years earlier been blamed for widespread droughts. The wet summers of the 1910s and 1920s were blamed both on the extensive gunfire from World War I and on the initiation of short-wave Transatlantic radio.[920]

Over the past hundred years, much of the discussion sounds curiously like the one we have today. Try and read this excerpt on climate change from *Newsweek*:

> There are ominous signs that the Earth's weather patterns have begun to change dramatically and that these changes may portend a drastic decline in food production – with serious political implications for just about every nation on Earth. The drop in food output could begin quite soon, perhaps only 10 years from now.

> The evidence in support of these predictions has now begun to accumulate so massively that meteorologists are hard-pressed to keep up with it. In England, farmers have seen their growing season decline by about two

weeks since 1950, with a resultant overall loss in grain production estimated at up to 100,000 tons annually. During the same time, the average temperature around the equator has risen by a fraction of a degree – a fraction that in some areas can mean drought and desolation. Last April, in the most devastating outbreak of tornadoes ever recorded, 148 twisters killed more than 300 people and caused half a billion dollars' worth of damage in 13 U.S. states.

To scientists, these seemingly disparate incidents represent the advance signs of fundamental changes in the world's weather. Meteorologists disagree about the cause and extent of the trend, as well as over its specific impact on local weather conditions. But they are almost unanimous in the view that the trend will reduce agricultural productivity.[921]

While this sounds surprisingly similar to the greenhouse worries we hear today, it is actually a story from 1975 entitled "The Cooling World" – from a time when we all worried about global cooling. (Notice how, just like Al Gore, they also use the top number of killer tornadoes as evidence, see Figure 33, p. 115.)

In the early part of the 1900s, the world also worried about a new ice age. In 1912, the *Los Angeles Times* told us "Fifth ice age is on the way: human race will have to fight for its existence against cold."[922] In 1923 *Chicago Tribune* declared in a front page that "Scientist says Arctic ice will wipe out Canada" along with huge parts of Asia and Europe.[923]

However, the world was already warming then, and papers began picking up that point in the 1930s, asking if it might be related to CO_2.[924] In 1952, the *New York Times* reported "the world has been getting warmer in the last half century." In 1959 they pointed out that glaciers were melting in Alaska and the "ice in the Arctic ocean is about half as thick as it was in the late nineteenth century."[925] In 1969 the *New York Times* quoted a polar explorer that "the Arctic pack ice is thinning and that the ocean at the North Pole may become an open sea within a decade or two."[926]

However, by the 1940s, global mean temperatures began to fall, which by the 1970s led to claims that Earth once more was heading toward a new ice age. One popular book described the world: "Between 1880 and 1950 Earth's climate was the warmest it has been in five thousand years ... It was a time of optimism ... The optimism has shriveled in the first chill of the cooling. Since the 1940s winters have become subtly longer, rains less dependable, storms more frequent throughout the world."[927] Growing glaciers were now seen as a problem: "The rapid advance of some glaciers has threatened human settlements in Alaska, Iceland, Canada, China, and the Soviet Union."[928] It was estimated that the cooling had already killed hundreds of thousands in the developing world, and if proper measures were not taken, it would lead to "world famine, world chaos, and probably world war, and this could all come by the year 2000."[929]

Science Digest pointed out in 1973, "at this point, the world's climatologists are agreed on only two things: that we do not have the comfortable distance of tens of thousands of years to prepare for the next ice age, and that how carefully we monitor our atmospheric pollution will have direct bearing on the arrival and nature of this weather crisis. The sooner man confronts these facts, these scientists say, the safer he'll be. Once the freeze starts, it will be too late."[930]

Science News claimed that we may be approaching a full-blown ice age: "Again, this transition would involve only a small change in global temperature – two or three degrees – but the impact on civilization would be catastrophic."[931] Other commentators worried about "worsening droughts."[932] The *New York Times* ran a story headlined: "Scientists ponder why world's climate is changing; a major cooling widely considered to be inevitable."[933]

Of course, today there are much better arguments and more credible models underpinning our worry about global warming, and since our societies are adjusted to the present temperature, a major departure either way will entail costs.

But notice how the descriptions typically only talk about the impending problems and conspicuously leave out any positive consequences. If we worry about more malaria from warming today, a world believing in cooling should have appreciated the reduction of infected areas. Equally, if we worried about a shortening of growing seasons with a cooling world, we should be glad that global warming will lengthen the growing season.

Also notice how the descriptions tend toward hyperbole, telling us how we might lose Canada and vast parts of Europe and Asia to an advancing ice age or how "world famine, world chaos, and probably world war" could come by the year 2000. Many of these (incorrect) claims sound curiously like the (equally incorrect) Pentagon claims today of an impending ice age from a Gulf Stream shut-down where "Europe's climate is more like Siberia's" and nuclear war seems to be a likely outcome.[934]

This tendency to believe the worst about the future is undoubtedly due to a deep-seated human tendency to believe that things were better in the old days and that everything is going in the wrong direction. The Scottish philosopher David Hume wrote in 1754 that "the humour of blaming the present, and admiring the past, is strongly rooted in human nature, and has an influence even on persons endued with the profoundest judgement and most extensive learning."[935] Sal Baron wrote in his book about the history of the Jews that prophets who made optimistic predictions were automatically considered to be false prophets.[936] An Assyrian stone tablet, many thousands of years old, tells us of the obstinate feeling of decline: "Our earth is degenerate in these latter days; bribery and corruption are common; children no longer obey their parents; every man wants to write a book, and the end of the world is evidently approaching."[937]

But the age-old media focus on bad news about the natural world received a strong revival when, by the 1960s, environmentalism could also display conflict and allocate guilt. This is perhaps most evident in the founding of environmentalism by Rachel Carson. Named by *Time* magazine as one of the hundred most influential people of the twentieth century, she kick-started popular environmental awareness with her 1962 book *Silent Spring*.[938]

Here she told us how pesticides like DDT – the "elixirs of death" – were spoiling the Earth, potentially leaving us with a silent spring, devoid of singing birds. But perhaps more importantly, these chemicals could kill our children and us, especially through cancer. Carson put the cancer issue at the forefront of public attention. This focus, combined with a flurry of new cancer studies and a newly started EPA, struggling for bureaucratic independence, made cancer one of the main arenas for environmental regulation.[939] But equally important – this was somebody's fault. Although Carson didn't directly accuse the chemical industry, this was certainly how the book was understood.[940]

Importantly, Carson did point out the flip side of a crucial issue to which her generation was blind. Using pesticides didn't just accrue benefits in better and more abundant food, but also had costs in killing wildlife and humans. This requires us to make a trade-off.

Today we know that this trade-off lies with clear restrictions on some pesticides but certainly that well-regulated pesticide use has large benefits. It is estimated that the total cancer deaths from pesticides are very low, probably about 20 deaths annually in the US.[941] If pesticides were totally phased out, costs for the US would be at least $100 billion annually. Moreover, since the price of fruit and vegetables would increase the most (more than a doubling), consumption would probably decrease by at least 10%. Since a large consumption of fruit and vegetables is one of the best ways to avoid cancer, estimates show that a decrease of 10% would cause about 26,000 surplus cancer deaths in the US annually.[942] Thus, $100 billion and 26,000 deaths is not a good trade-off for saving 20 people.

Unfortunately, this trade-off was entirely drowned in the bad news of dying birds, and the conflict and blaming of the chemical industry. In the *New York Times* 1962 review, the headline told us "There's poison all around us now," telling us how "a continuation of present programs that use poisonous chemicals will soon exterminate much of our wild life and man as well," and the review goes on to blame the "government agencies that have encouraged poisoning campaigns ... unwilling to take blame for extensive programs that seem senseless."[943]

The absence of trade-offs and the focus on bad news and blame in the formulation of environmental policy has had important consequences for its efficiency. This is perhaps most clearly seen in the largest study of efficiency in life-saving public policy in the US, carried out by Harvard University's Center for Risk Analysis.[944]

The areas investigated cover health care, as well as residential, transportation, occupational and environmental aspects of society. This analysis *only* looked at policies that had as their *primary* objective to save human lives. Thus, it doesn't analyze policy options in such areas as biodiversity or coastal oxygen depletion. But it does give us a clear measure of the efficiency within the crucial EPA areas like pollution control, including Carson's worries about pesticides, compared to other life-saving policies.

The results revealed an astounding variation in the efficiency of the various interventions. Some policies cost nothing or actually save money.

These include, for example, informing black women not to smoke during pregnancy as this will give fewer birth complications – the net savings for society is about $72 million.[945] For $182,000 a year it is possible to screen black newborns for sickle cell anemia and save 769 life-years: a cost of just $236 per life-year. By spending $253 million on heart transplants, an extra 1,600 life-years can be saved at a cost of $158,000 per life-year. Equipping all school buses with passenger safety belts would cost around $53 million, but because this would only save much less than one child a year, the cost would be $2.8 million per life-year. Regulating radionuclide emission at elemental phosphorus plants (refining mined phosphorus before it goes to other uses) would cost $2.8 million, but would only save at most one life per decade. This gives an estimated cost of $9.2 million per life-year.

The result of analyzing a total of 587 policies showed a distinct pattern, as is evident in Figure 56. Here it is quite obvious that there are tremendous differences in the price to be paid for extra life-years by means of typical interventions: the health service is quite low-priced at $19,000, and the

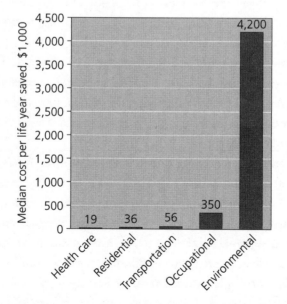

Figure 56 *Typical cost per life-year saved for policies in different areas.*[946]

environment field stands out with a staggeringly high cost of $4.2 million. This does not mean that there are no good environmental investments to be made – only that the typical investment is much worse.

The advantage of this method of accounting is that it is possible to see the overall effectiveness of the American public effort to save human life. Information exists about the actual cost of 185 programs that account for the annual spending of $21.4 billion, which saves around 592,000 life-years. But we could have done much better. Spending almost $3 million to control radionuclide emissions from phosphorus plants to save only one life per decade is a poor way of saving lives. If one really wants to save the maximum possible number of human lives, it would be a much better idea to implement the most efficient programs first and then to continue with less and less efficient programs for as long as funds are available.

The Harvard study did make such calculations and discovered that instead of saving 592,000 life-years, 1,230,000 life-years could have been saved for the same money.[947] Without further costs it would have been possible to save around 600,000 more life-years or 60,000 more human lives.[948]

As a society we use large amounts of resources to regulate both health risks and environmental risks. But if media attention to small but highly hyped risks – like Carson's poisons – makes us overfocus on some issues, we end up underfocusing on other issues that attract less attention but where we could do more good. The Harvard study clearly indicates that bad news, conflicts and blame make us pursue our goal of saving lives poorly. We spend resources badly on issues with high media profiles, when we could have done much more good elsewhere.

There is a real risk that with global warming we are moving down the same path of scary stories, outlining a conflict between fossil fuels and human survival, blaming big oil companies and the Bush administration.[949] This black-and-white confrontation easily ends up replacing a sensible dialogue on trade-offs. This becomes clear when we observe how extreme global warming is being described and put in context by some of the leading participants. Al Gore calls it a "planetary emergency" and Rob Gelbspan places the blame squarely on the oil industry being engaged in "a crime against humanity."[950]

A collection of green and development groups recently stated that development could come to an end, with the world starting to backslide: "After a decade of UN conferences designed to end poverty and save the global environment, disasters – driven or exacerbated by global warming – could spell out the end of human development for the poor majority, and perilous political and economic insecurity for the rest of the world."[951]

An EU-sponsored children's book with the telling title *What Scorching Weather* tells the story of a kid and a fireman caught in fires due to global warming. In between the action, the fireman solemnly tells the kid:

> You see, Tom, the problem is that the world is getting warmer. The climate is changing, so we're getting heat waves like this one. And storms, and floods, and all sorts of other natural disasters! The ice at the north and south poles is melting, and so are the glaciers on high mountains like the Alps. The melted water runs off into the rivers and down to the sea, so the sea level is rising. Some islands and coasts are likely to disappear under the water! At the same time, if the climate goes on getting hotter, some countries will become deserts![952]

Leading UK debater George Monbiot explains to us that we need to find out "how to stop the planet burning" and says climate change is as devastating as nuclear war.[953] UK scientist James Lovelock tells us "before this century is over billions of us will die and the few breeding pairs of people that survive will be in the Arctic where the climate remains tolerable."[954]

The EU commissioner for the Environment, Stavros Dimas, in early 2007 even claimed that we would need a "world war" on climate change.[955] "Damaged economies, refugees, political instability and loss of life are typically the results of war. But they will also be the results of unchecked climate change. It is clear that the fight against climate change is much more than a battle. It is a world war that will last for many years."

These statements all ride on the back of incessant news coverage of bad weather being caused by global warming and new science predicting ever worse futures. A *Time* special issue on global warming tells us "Be worried. Be *very* worried. Climate change isn't some vague future problem – it is already damaging the planet at an alarming pace."[956] *New Scientist* tells us that we are standing at "The edge of the abyss."[957] Perhaps taking the accolades for most outrageous description, a popular UK magazine told us that, with global warming, some experts "predict a future in which our children see rainforests burst into flame and seas boil – unless we act today."[958]

Now, some of the leading scientists are beginning to speak out against this one-sided alarm.[959] One climate scientist even wondered whether some of the dire predictions push the science too far: "Some of us are wondering if we have created a monster."[960]

Crucially, one of the UK's top climate scientists spoke out against this hysteria in late 2006.[961] Mike Hulme is director of the Tyndall Centre for Climate Change Research. He said, yes, climate change is real and humans are definitely partly responsible. But words like "catastrophic" and phrases such as "climate change is worse than we thought," that we are approaching "irreversible tipping in the Earth's climate," and that we are "at the point of no return" are simply used as "unguided weapons with which forlornly to threaten society into behavioural change."

"Why is it not just campaigners, but politicians and scientists too, who are openly confusing the language of fear, terror and disaster with the observable physical reality of climate change, actively ignoring the careful hedging which surrounds science's predictions?" Hulme finds in the desperation over the failure of Kyoto and in preparation for the emerging negotiations for a future treaty, that a stage-managing of the new language of catastrophe is taking place. Daringly, he also says catastrophe speak helps avoid cut-backs in science funding. But ultimately "We need to take a deep breath and pause. The language of catastrophe is not the language of science. It will not be visible in next year's global assessment from the world authority of the IPCC."

Framing climate change as an issue which evokes fear and personal stress becomes a self-fulfilling prophecy. By "sexing it up" we exacerbate, through psychological amplifiers, the very risks we are trying to ward off.

The careless (or conspiratorial?) translation of concern about Saddam Hussein's putative military threat into the case for WMD has had major geopolitical repercussions. We need to make sure the agents and agencies in our society which would seek to amplify climate change risks do not lead us down a similar counter-productive pathway.

Jumping on the bandwagon of catastrophe, sexing up the ramifications of global warming and exploiting the fear of disaster may be good for selling papers, captivating viewers and getting attention. But its stark and unfounded scares cut us off from having a sensible dialogue on the political and economic arguments for action here and with the many other problems facing the future.

The economics: the loss of a sensible dialogue

Global warming will definitely not be costless. As we have gone through its many issues, we have seen that it will definitely cause more heat deaths; it will see sea level rise, plausibly cause more intense hurricanes and more flooding; it will give rise to more malaria, starvation and poverty. This is an important message to convey.

Equally, doing something about global warming will not be costless. Switching fuels from coal to gas or to renewables comes at a price. Restricting transportation will make the economy less efficient; cutting back on hot showers, plane trips and cars will leave you less well off. It will also reduce the number of people being saved from cold, it will increase the number of water stressed, and will allow fewer to get rich enough to avoid malaria. This is also an important message to convey.

Doing something about global warming has both benefits and costs. How to weigh these benefits and costs correctly is clearly a dialogue we need to have. But in the current panic, the climate changes are portrayed as so severe and overwhelming that talking about the costs simply seems unreasonable and uncaring. As the argument seems to play out, we just have to aim for the benefits and not think about the costs.

But even if we don't talk about the costs, we still have to pay. Even if we don't debate our priorities, we still end up prioritizing. Even if we just accept the benefits we get, we still might have done much better.

If we are to embark on the potentially most costly global policy program ever, we might want to make sure it is a good use of our resources.

In Fred Pearce's book on *The Last Generation*, he eloquently gives us 300 pages of worst-case outcomes, designed as one long pleading for strong carbon emission cuts. In the last four pages of a fifteen-page appendix he briefly mentions that doing something (of undefined magnitude and undefined impact) will not be cheap (in the order of $8 trillions) but that this in the long run would be a blip.[962] While Fred is definitely right that combating climate change would not put us in the poorhouse, then neither would any other conceivable change in public policy (simply because spending 1–5% of GDP will not ruin us, but still we should spend our scarce resources in the best possible way). In all, it is a remarkably relaxed way to analyze the costliest public investment program ever.

Nevertheless, Fred Pearce's analysis is still much better than Al Gore's who, in his *whole* book and *whole* movie, doesn't once mention the cost of seriously addressing global warming. Yet, in his recent speech to New York University, he did explicitly say that he would eliminate payroll taxes and substitute them with pollution taxes, principally a CO_2 tax.[963] Yet he never actually says how much this would cost or how much good it would do.

If one calculates the impact of such a promise, it shows that payroll taxes (social security) in the US amounted to $841 billion in 2006.[964] With the US emitting about 6 Gt of CO_2 this means a tax of $140/t$CO_2$, and a tax on gasoline at about $1.25 per gallon.[965] In one respected model, the annual economic cost amounts to about $160 billion for the US economy in 2015. This would cut emissions to about half in 2015 and to about 25% in 2105.[966] Yet, since the US will make up an ever smaller amount of the total CO_2 emitted throughout the century, the total effect in 2100 will be a reduction of global temperature by 0.1°C.[967] Essentially, what Al Gore is suggesting is that the US carries through a Kyoto-type restriction all by itself.

There is obviously an issue of feasibility, as Clinton/Gore in 1993 tried to increase gas prices but, with a democratic congress, had to settle for a ¢4.3/gallon tax rise.[968] More importantly, it seems to me that not having a dialogue on such a significant use of resources ($160 billion per year) to achieve a relatively small climate impact (0.1°C) means that we are likely to make less-than-optimal judgments.

One of the leading British commentators, George Monbiot, has also written a book on how every facet of global warming is calamitous.[969] Climate change will simply destroy the conditions which make human life possible.[970] He concludes that climate change is the project we must put before all others.[971] He claims we need to avoid temperatures from rising more than 2°C from pre-industrial levels (i.e. less than 1.4°C more from now), which is also the official EU position. We will look at that decision below.

Much to his credit, he squarely faces that this target requires an extra-ordinary restriction in CO_2 emissions – by his estimates this will require the OECD countries to reduce their emissions by a bit more than 96% by 2030.[972] This essentially means shutting down our current fossil fuel driven economy.[973] He is vague on the total costs, but assures us, that they won't lead to an economic collapse.[974] Yet he envisions that we will basically have to reorganize our planetary energy and transport systems in 23 years.[975] It will mean the end to air travel and the beginning of an all-encompassing CO_2 rationing system much like the one Britain had during the Second World War.[976]

But of course, such upheaval can happen if we just want it enough. Monbiot tells us how General Motors and Ford after Pearl Harbor swiftly changed their entire production schedules and intensity:

> If our governments decide that climate change is an issue as urgent as the international crisis in 1941 – in my view a reasonable comparison – they could turn the economy around on a sixpence. Planning objections would be ignored, incentives and regulations would be used to make companies move as swiftly as General Motors and Ford responded to the war. Wind farms, powerlines and nuclear power stations – if this is what we want – could all be built in much less than a decade.[977]

But it might be worthwhile to point out that the war didn't come cheap, and nor will such a staggering reorganization. Again, we need a dialogue on whether the benefits (much less global warming at perhaps $10 trillion) will outweigh the costs (probably much more than $84 trillion estimated in Figure 11, p. 41). The economists tell us absolutely not.

However, Monbiot says that he will not participate in such a dialogue.[978] Why? Because "it is an amoral means of comparison." He maintains that when talking about the benefits, we cannot capture the suffering of the people harmed by Hurricane Katrina, cannot capture the value of those drowned, or indeed the value of lost ecosystems or the climate itself.

This is a weak argument. Monbiot's whole book is exactly one long discourse trying to capture the value of everything – from people to eco-systems – which he wants to save. He exactly makes the argument that since the impacts will be so phenomenally overwhelming, we should be willing to make phenomenal sacrifices. But this is a trade-off. He exactly tells us that we should throw our weight behind a generational challenge of cutting carbon emissions 96% in 23 years. Of course, that weight, that effort, that generational investment, can then not be used in dealing with the world's many other challenges, like HIV, malaria, malnutrition or clean water. Monbiot truly makes his case for a prioritization.

Part of what Monbiot seems to dislike is the idea of calculating everything into one denomination – and particularly in dollars. I can understand that. It highlights the harsh consequences of our actions, and moreover the methodology is difficult. But if we are to make comparisons across many different and disparate areas it is crucial that we maintain our objectivity, and the economic approach helps us to do so.

Instead Monbiot (as do many others) goes for the simple, rhetorical points. He mentions how it does not make sense to trade-off air travel and its impacts. "Should a steward be sacrificed every time someone in Ethiopia dies of hunger?"[979] It may have oratory shock value but he seems stubbornly intent on missing the point. Maybe stopping flying is not the best way to help Ethiopians from starving.

Since flying makes up about 3.5% of the climate impact today, and by 2050 will still only make up about 5%, even a complete halt to flying, at great cost, would do very little good for an Ethiopian.[980] As the full Kyoto Protocol would cut the effective climate impact *more* than a total stop on flying, and undoubtedly at much lower cost, Monbiot is essentially saying let us pay even more than Kyoto for even less than Kyoto's outcome.[981] As we saw in the chapter on hunger, Monbiot is focusing on saving fewer than 2 million people from hunger, when efforts tens of times cheaper could help 229 million people much faster, much better.

According to Monbiot, insisting on comparing costs and benefits means "you have spent too much time with your calculator and not enough with human beings." [982] Yet I would argue that if it means you end up helping 5,000 Ethiopians each time Monbiot helps one, it certainly seems like you care more about humans too.

Far from being amoral to compare costs and benefits, it is crucially moral to ask: how do we help the most? Can it really be moral to do anything less?

Unfortunately, the lack of a sensible dialogue is also evident in the EU climate policy. It has adopted the same stringent limit as Monbiot, requiring the global mean temperature not to rise more than 2°C above pre-industrial times.[983] Yet the first peer-reviewed study from 2007 analyzing the basis for this target is scathing. It finds that the "target is supported by rather thin arguments, based on inadequate methods, sloppy reasoning, and selective citation from a very narrow set of studies."[984] It traces back the arguments for this limit to studies with little scientific or economic merit, often dramatically misrepresenting the literature. It concludes very tautly: "the 2°C target of the EU seems unfounded."

There is a unifying theme behind the sloppy reasoning of the EU, Monbiot's singleminded focus on stopping flying or Gore's coy lack of interest in the cost and efficiency of his solution. It is a neglect of thinking about priorities. Essentially, we need to get to grips with how much we should focus on global warming compared to all the other ills of the world. This was what we talked about in chapter 2 – what should be the right CO_2 tax? It is probably about $2 and not higher than $14 per ton.[985] But this will only lead to a minor emission reduction – perhaps in the order of 5–20% of CO_2 emissions (Figure 9, p. 35). This is why the major peer-reviewed economic cost-benefit analyses show, as we also saw in chapter 2, that climate change is real, and that we should do something, but that our cuts should be rather small. In the latest review the previous research is summarized: "These studies recommend that greenhouse gas emissions be reduced below business-as-usual forecasts, but the reductions suggested have been modest."[986]

This was the state-of-the-art economics till October 2006, when a 600-page UK government report headed by economist Sir Nicholas Stern came out and created headlines everywhere.[987] The report presented how it saw the climate evidence, summed up rather nicely by the New York Times: the "report predicted apocalyptic effects from climate change, including droughts, flooding, famine, skyrocketing malaria rates and the extinction of many animal species. These will happen during the current generation if changes are not made soon."[988] Channel 4 television in the UK was even more succinct: "It's an apocalyptic vision – economic growth slashed, millions of people displaced, the poor made even poorer."[989]

The Stern Review's two main economic points are actually rather straightforward. First, Stern finds that the overall costs and risks from climate change are the equivalent of losing at least 5% of GDP now and forever, and possibly 20% now and forever.[990] The report itself stresses that this is the equivalent of the great wars and the economic depression of the twentieth century.[991] Second, strong action against global warming will cost just 1% of GDP.[992]

Virtually everyone has come away with the understanding that Stern has made a cost-benefit analysis and shown that the benefit (avoided damage from global warming) is 20% and the cost just 1%, making strong climate action a slam-dunk.[993] This has made Stern a very popular man. As the UK environment minister pointed out: "Nick Stern is now an international rock star in the climate change world."[994]

Yet, a raft of academic papers have now come out, all strongly criticizing Stern, characterizing the report as a "political document" and liberally using such terms as "substandard," "preposterous," "incompetent," "deeply flawed" and "neither balanced nor credible."[995] While there is a long list of problems with the analysis, I think it is enough to point out three issues.

1. The review's presentation of the science is massively exaggerated toward scary scenarios.[996] This is also what we find when looking at its treatment of increasing poor, choosing an extreme, out-of-range scenario, extra-high impacts and very high thresholds. "The Review fails to present an accurate picture of scientific understanding of climate change issues" and its "analysis of the prospective impacts of possible global warming is consistently biased and selective – heavily tilted towards unwarranted alarm."[997] When the review clearly has its expertise in economics, it is disturbing that so many of its alarmist climate interpretations have been able to gain so much ground.[998]

2. The damages from climate change (the benefits of action) are vastly inflated. As several peer-reviewed papers point out, "the Stern Review

does not present new data, or even a new model."[999] How can it then find conclusions that are completely outside the standard range? It turns out that the Review has counted damages several times, and somewhat arbitrarily increases the damages eight-fold or more according to new and conjectural cost categories that have never been peer reviewed.[1000] At the same time, the Review has decided to change a key parameter in all cost-benefit analyses to a value that gives huge damage.[1001] Oddly, it forgets to use this parameter for the costs below, where it would count against a strong policy response.[1002] The parameter is also vastly out of sync with our present-day behavior: it would suggest that we should today save 97.5% of our GDP for future generations.[1003] This is patently absurd – today's saving rate is about 15% in the UK.

3. The costs of action are vastly underestimated, continuing a well-known "appraisal optimism" which was also seen from the 1950s onwards in very low cost-estimates for nuclear power.[1004] It implausibly expects renewable costs to drop six-fold by 2050.[1005] At the same time Stern forgets to count any costs of action after 2050, although these costs escalate, and are important way into the twenty-third century.[1006]

If you look at Figure 57 you see the change between the published literature and Stern. In the peer-reviewed studies, damages run at about 1% of GDP and costs at about 2%. It is important to say that you can't just compare the cost of the two, because incurring the costs doesn't avoid all the damage. But the figure gives us intuition into why economic cost-benefit studies only recommend moderate CO_2 reductions. Buying avoidance of some of the 1% damage (your benefit) for 2% is a bad deal. But look at how Stern completely turn this picture around, with damage way outside what the previous literature has found, and costs much more optimistic. Moreover, Stern is not so careful as to point out that he really didn't do a cost-benefit study – clearly he should only have compared the costs to part of the damages avoided.[1007]

The most well-known climate economist, William Nordhaus, concludes that the Stern Review is "a political document."[1008] *Nature* tells us that the UK government has tried to recruit other researchers to make this study, and is supposedly angling for the same politically convenient outcome.[1009] Mike

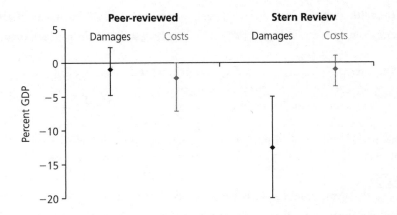

Figure 57 *Comparison of the peer-reviewed state-of-the-art and the (non-peer-reviewed) Stern Review estimates of damages and costs.*[1010] *As you can see, damages in peer-reviewed studies are not bad enough to warrant the costs of partially avoiding them. Stern swaps this argument around.*

Hulme points out "this is not the last word of scientists and economists, it's the last word of civil servants."[1011]

The Stern Review must be praised for having put the economics squarely back into the climate debate. Whether or not we like to acknowledge it, doing something about global warming will have both costs and benefits, and we need the dialogue on how much we should do. But the Stern Review does not change the fact that all peer-reviewed economic analyses show we should only reduce CO_2 emissions moderately.[1012]

The science: the loss of a sensible dialogue

The rising stakes of global warming are also closing off the dialogue in parts of the science. The IPCC has as its stated goal "to provide policy neutral information for decisionmaking."[1013] Yet its chairman Dr. R. K. Pachauri calls for immediate and very deep cuts in the CO_2 if humanity is to survive.[1014] This is clearly opting for one policy, over other policies like lower cuts, adaptation or do-nothing.

When climate scientists found serious errors in the hockey stick (the poster-picture for the 2001 IPCC report, as we talked about in pp. 68–9), this was not seen as a science issue but immediately cast as a political problem:

> When we recently established that the method behind the so-called "hockey-stick" curve of northern hemisphere temperature is flawed, this result was not so much attacked as scientifically flawed but was seen both in private conversations and public discourse as outright dangerous, because it could be instrumentalized and undermine the success of the IPCC process.[1015]

Respected – but skeptical – climate scientist Richard Lindzen from MIT points out that "Scientists who dissent from the alarmism have seen their grant funds disappear, their work derided, and themselves libeled as industry stooges, scientific hacks or worse. Consequently, lies about climate change gain credence even when they fly in the face of the science that supposedly is their basis."[1016]

The Climatic Research Unit at University of East Anglia constructs the global temperature series that has become the de facto standard for the IPCC. When a researcher asked for access to examine its underlying data and methods, Professor Phil Jones, director of CRU, said: "Why should I make the data available to you, when your aim is to try and find something wrong with it?"[1017] Given that this data set constitutes a crucial part of the background for potentially costly climate policy, we should certainly hope some researchers would spend a lot of time scrutinizing it for errors.[1018] Unfortunately, such incidences of rejection of scrutiny are not uncommon.[1019]

Science is supposed to help the ultimately political dialogue on where to spend scarce resources by telling us the extent of the problems and the likely effect of many different policies to ameliorate them. If scientists become spokespeople for specific solutions – like chairman Pachauri arguing for dramatic CO_2 cuts – they effectively become agenda-driven advocates. Misusing their standing as scientists to pursue a political agenda eventually undercuts the credibility of the scientific discipline, making us all worse off.

Over the years it has become obvious that part of – and it is important to say only part of – the IPCC has become more politicized. Take the famous statement from the 2001 report that most warming in the last 50 years is due to humans.

In April 2000, the text was supposed to read "there has been a discernible human influence on global climate."[1020] In the October 2000 draft, it was stated "it is likely that increasing concentrations of anthropogenic greenhouse gases have contributed substantially to the observed warming over the last 50 years."[1021] Yet, in the official summary, the language was further toughened up to say that "most of the observed warming over the last 50 years is likely to have been due to the increase in greenhouse gas concentrations."[1022]

When asked about the scientific background for this change by *New Scientist*, the spokesman for the UN Environment Program, Tim Higham, responded very honestly: "There was no new science, but the scientists wanted to present a clear and strong message to policy makers."[1023] When scientists – without new science – "sex up" their message, it is no longer just science. It is advancing a particular agenda, namely that their area is more important for funding, attention and rectification than it really is. Sending a stronger message to politicians is simply using science to play politics.

Likewise, some parts of the IPCC reports read more like an ecological vision statement. Climate policy is here used as a tool and justification for charting an alternative course of development that is seen as preferable.[1024] "Against the background of environmental scarcities," we have to focus on eco-efficiency, industrial ecology, eco-efficient consumption, etc.[1025] Basically, IPCC concludes that it will be necessary to decouple well-being from production.[1026]

Indeed, it will be necessary to make people understand that the performance of things cannot keep improving, for the sake of the environment. For instance, ever "higher speed in transportation [is] (efficiency gains notwithstanding) unlikely to be environmentally sustainable in the long run." But this is okay, since "it is doubtful that this trend really enhances the quality of life." Instead, the IPCC suggests that we should build cars and trains with lower top speeds, and extol the qualities of sails on ships, biomass (which "has been the renewable resource base for humankind since time immemorial") and bicycles. Likewise, it is suggested that in order to avoid demand for transport, we should obtain a regionalized economy.[1027]

Essentially, what the IPCC suggests – and openly embraces – is that we need to change individual lifestyles, and move away from consumption. We must focus on sharing resources (e.g. through co-ownership), choosing free time instead of wealth, quality instead of quantity, and "increase freedom while containing consumption." Because of climate change we have to remodel our world, and find more so-called "appropriate lifestyles."[1028]

The problem is that "the conditions of public acceptance of such options are not often present at the requisite large scale."[1029] Actually, it is often "difficult to convince local actors of the significance of climate change and the need for corrective action."[1030] The IPCC even suggests that the reason why we are unwilling to accept slower (or no) cars, and regionalized economies with bicycles but no international travel, is that we have been indoctrinated by the media, where we see TV characters as reference points for our own lives, shaping our values and identities.

Consequently, the IPCC finds that the media could also help form the path toward a more sustainable world: "Raising awareness among media professionals of the need for greenhouse gas mitigation and the role of the media in shaping lifestyles and aspirations could be an effective way to encourage a wider cultural shift."[1031]

When we think we want more goods, the IPCC reassures us it is just because we have been conditioned that way.[1032] Actually, we do not need more consumption – research shows that "there is no clear link between level of GNP and quality of life (or satisfaction) beyond certain thresholds."[1033] The argument is based on a study showing that "although consumption in the USA has doubled since 1957, it is reported that the average US citizen considers his or her happiness to have decreased since then."[1034] Yet, 1957 was the peak year of US happiness measurements in a survey that shows no trend and is notoriously difficult to compare over time.[1035] Happiness in 2004 was essentially indistinguishable from 1957.[1036] Moreover, the claimed absence of a link between income and happiness is incorrect – it is true that there is *less* more satisfaction, the richer you get, but there is still more.[1037]

When parts of the IPCC begin to tell us what sort of world we need to embrace because of global warming, they tend toward using science to further a political view. Perhaps most clearly, this was seen when the IPCC scenario makers, without any explicit criteria, ranked the four global futures (scenarios), giving the global-environmental future the top grade "good" whereas the global-economic future only gets a "fair."[1038] As scientists in a peer-reviewed article, they tell us that they prefer a society with less wealth but also with less climate change.

Considering that the difference for the world in economic terms is some $7,000 trillion (or in present-day value some $550 trillion – more than eleven times the present global GDP, as we saw in Figure 51, p. 163) such a hand-waving opinion seems rather cavalier. The average person in the third world loses out on about 70% more income in 2100 – it is not clear that he or she would quietly concur with the modelers. In order to reach a prudent judgement of scenario, we need a healthy dialogue, considering the advantages but also the disadvantages to one future over the other, looking at *both* the environment and the economy.

Stephen Schneider of Stanford University, one of the most publicly visible global warming scientists, has accurately and surprisingly honestly considered the "ethical double bind" that might occur to a scientist who is also concerned about contributing to a better world, of which we have seen several expressions above. As a scientist he focuses on truth. As a concerned citizen he must take an interest in political efficiency. Quite obviously, Schneider finds that this presents a delicate dilemma and he expresses the hope that one might be both honest and effective. However, as Schneider agonizes over this dilemma he does offer the following bit of unambiguous advice: "We need to get some broad base support, to capture the public's imagination. That, of course, entails getting loads of media coverage. So we have to offer up scary scenarios, make simplified, dramatic statements, and make little mention of any doubts we might have."[1039]

Such a strategy might be very politically effective, but it undermines the opportunity for society to make informed choices between different policy goals. Global warming is not the only issue, and having some scientists making scary scenarios and dramatic statements simply closes off the vital dialogue on the social priorities.

The politics: the loss of a sensible dialogue

The increasing rhetoric of Hulme's "fear, terror and disaster" is also affecting the political debate on global warming. It is fast becoming polarized to an extent that it incapacitates any sensible dialogue.

This is perhaps no more clear than in the growth of the phrase "climate change denier" which now has more than 41,000 hits on Google.[1040] This phrase, of course, is hard to take literally, since presumably nobody would suggest the climate is not always changing, but it is typically used as a catchall for anybody who doesn't accept the standard interpretation that mankind is squarely to blame for global warming and that we should cut CO_2 emissions dramatically.[1041]

The semantic similarity to Holocaust deniers is often explicit and certainly represents a strong symbolic undercurrent. One Australian columnist has proposed outlawing climate change denial: "David Irving is under arrest in Austria for Holocaust denial. Perhaps there is a case for making climate change denial an offence – it is a crime against humanity after all."[1042]

Mark Lynas is the author of a book revealing "the truth about our climate crisis."[1043] (Disclaimer: I first met Mark when he pied me in an Oxford bookstore as a media stunt for his then upcoming book.) He finds that climate denial is "in a similar moral category to Holocaust denial" and envisions Nuremberg-style "international criminal tribunals on those who will be partially but directly responsible for millions of deaths from starvation, famine and disease in decades ahead."[1044]

Likewise David Roberts from *Grist* (he did their long interview with Al Gore) talks about the "denial industry" and states that we should have "war crimes trials for these bastards – some sort of climate Nuremberg."[1045]

Even the top scientist of the UN Climate panel, IPCC chairman Dr. Pachauri, has ventured into the Holocaust comparison. When presented with my economic analyses of doing the most good first, he compared my way of thinking to Hitler's.[1046] "Where is the difference between Lomborg's view on humans and Hitler's? You cannot just treat people like cattle."

A correspondent for CBS *60 Minutes* didn't want to present a skeptical view on climate change: "If I do an interview with Elie Wiesel, am I required as a journalist to find a Holocaust denier? ... There becomes a point in journalism where striving for balance becomes irresponsible."[1047]

Even when the alternative view is not immediately outlawed and hitlerized, it is often ridiculed. Al Gore typically replies to critical questions: "Fifteen per cent of the population believe the Moon landing was actually staged in a movie lot in Arizona and somewhat fewer still believe the Earth is flat. I think they all get together with the global warming deniers on a Saturday night and party."[1048]

The UK environment minister, David Miliband, combines ridicule with declaring the debate to be over: "People say there should be a debate about global warming. But I tell you the debate is over; the reckoning has begun. The truth is staring us in the face. Climate change is here, in our country; it is an issue for our generation as well as future generations; and those who deny it are the flat-earthers of the 21st century."[1049]

The problem here is that the debate is closed off not with arguments but with reference to authority. If some people are so stupid as to suggest something being the intellectual equivalent of flat-earthers, or so depraved as to suggest a comparison to something as immoral as Hitler, we can just reject it out of hand. When Gore was challenged on the *Oprah Winfrey Show* that his estimates of sea-level rise are unrealistically high and his claims about malaria in Nairobi are unsupported by facts, he simply responded that many of the organizations that come out with studies questioning the effects of global warming are funded by the worst polluters.[1050]

While I appreciate the underlying moral intent to do good for humanity, the unwavering certainty that CO_2 cuts are the best way to help humanity is problematic, as we have seen throughout this book. For instance, if we cut CO_2 emissions it will mean less water stress in central Africa but it will cause even more people to be water stressed in eastern Africa (Figure 46, p. 154). Glib comparisons to flat-earthers and Apollo-deniers simply deflect considerations of these real-world impacts in Africa. A sanctimonious cry for a climate Nuremberg – while being ironic in that focusing on CO_2 cuts could likewise be said to divert attention from many other and better solutions – is simply an unwarranted cop-out from taking responsibility to debate policy options in a democracy with good arguments.

MAYBE GLOBAL WARMING IS NOT ALL ABOUT FIXING IT

With all the fervor directed at global warming, you would imagine most people would be excited at the opportunity for humanity to deal with it cheaper and smarter. But you would be wrong. It seems that only cutting CO_2 is good enough.

Over the past decades a number of alternative solutions have been suggested. Let's just look at a few of them.

Atmospheric physicist John Latham suggested in 2006 that we

could increase the reflectivity of low-lying clouds by creating more salt droplets from the ocean.[1051] This is augmenting a natural process (breaking waves are constantly throwing vast quantities of salt up into the atmosphere) and it carries little risk (since we could simply stop and the system would return to its normal state). Perhaps most importantly, it could potentially stabilize temperatures at today's levels – doing much, much better than Kyoto, at about 2% of its cost.[1052]

Yet the environmental groups seem curiously uninterested. Friends of the Earth say: "It's not something we think we should be spending money and time on." They deny that they are being dismissive: "It's not a question of being dismissive; it's a question of whether this is worth any time and effort even thinking about."[1053] The same story with Greenpeace: "Greenpeace wouldn't be interested in this sort of thing. We're looking for reductions in the use of fossil fuels rather than these technologies that in all likelihood would come to nothing." Although Latham's research has been printed up in *Nature*, it might of course not work.[1054] But shouldn't we want to check out if we could solve one of civilization's major problems at very low cost?

The same story is repeated in the experiments of fertilizing the Pacific.[1055] Essentially, most of the Pacific is a biological desert. Although it has plenty of nutrients there is virtually no plankton, because the region has very low levels of iron. The thinking was that if we fertilized the ocean with iron, it would cause algae to bloom, soaking up CO_2, and when dead they would sink to the bottom, removing the CO_2 from the atmosphere. This approach was thought to have the potential to capture CO_2 much more efficiently and at much less cost than forest regrowth, although current studies are now questioning whether these estimates are too optimistic.[1056]

Yet, the important part here is the description by a journalist of a scientific meeting describing the outcome of the first large-scale experiment. The experiment had been a failure (though mainly due to weather – many later projects went on to success and turning the patches of the Pacific green). He described the situation in the

Smithsonian: "What surprised me was the reaction of the environmental scientists present. It was almost as if there was a collective sigh of relief, as if the prospect that humanity might find an easy way out of the greenhouse problem was just too much for them to bear."[1057]

And take the episode back in March 1989, when electrochemists B. Stanley Pons and Martin Fleischmann shocked the world, announcing that they had achieved fusion at room temperature.[1058] It didn't work, but for some few months the world contemplated having cold fusion within reach – essentially giving humanity access to clean, cheap and unlimited power with no CO_2.

In April 1989 the *Los Angeles Times* interviewed a number of top environmentalists about their view on cold fusion.[1059] With the assumption that the technology would be cheap and clean, Jeremy Rifkin, who had already started the Global Greenhouse Network, nevertheless thought "It's the worst thing that could happen to our planet." Inexhaustible power, he argues, only gives man an infinite ability to exhaust the planet's resources, to destroy its fragile balance and create unimaginable human and industrial waste.[1060] UC Berkeley physicist John Holdren pointed out "clean-burning, non-polluting, hydrogen-using bulldozers still could knock down trees or build housing developments on farmland."

Stanford biologist Paul Ehrlich said that cold fusion, even if clean and cheap, would be "like giving a machine gun to an idiot child."

What sea salt, iron fertilization and cold fusion all have in common is that the opposition to them comes not from a CO_2 perspective. When the environmental movement doesn't want clean and cheap energy, when they don't want a simple solution to global warming, it seems that there are other, and possibly more important agendas out there. Possibly it is a search for other values, an argument for a decentralized society which is less resource oriented, less industrialized, less commercialized, less production oriented. Such an agenda is entirely valid, but it should not be conducted under the subterfuge of global warming. Doing so further erodes the possibility of a constructive dialogue on how to tackle the world's big challenges.

Yet, for many politicians global warming has also been seized as a subject that can lift you out of the tedious bickering of distributional politics and instead allow you to stage yourself as a statesman, concerned with the grandest issue of the planet's survival. Here you can capture the high ground as defender of the interests of humanity, distancing yourself from the everyday infighting of self-interested politics. A clear example is Al Gore's casting of global warming as not a political issue but a moral one, essentially saying there is only one right answer to the challenge – his.

In the short run, this has been a successful strategy for many politicians. It has allowed them to go after a number of related policy issues with global warming as the overarching theme, as for instance Senator Timothy Wirth (D-Colorado) put it: "We've got to ride the global warming issue. Even if the theory of global warming is wrong, we will be doing the right thing, in terms of economic policy and environmental policy."[1061]

In many ways global warming has for a long time been the perfect issue, because it allows the politician to talk about things that have grandeur and yet are close to people; it actually makes some taxes popular and yet the true costs of policies are far removed. Since the climate is constantly changing there will always be a change that can be blamed on global warming, while it has an immediacy that communicates well with voters. One on-line editor has compiled a list of more than 300 problems claimed in the popular press to be caused by global warming – from allergies, through gender inequality and maple syrup shortages, to yellow fever.[1062]

Similarly, global warming worries make some taxes popular (or at least a lot less unpopular) – a politician's wet dream. At a recent climate demonstration in London the protesters actually chanted: "What do we want? Carbon taxes! When do we want them? Now!"[1063]

And perhaps most importantly, the real costs of cutting CO_2 are postponed, preferably to the next generation of politicians. Kyoto was negotiated in 1997, but the restrictions would first hit in 2008–12. The politicians who could claim victory in 1997 would typically not be the same ones to implement the costs to abide by the restrictions starting in 2008. Likewise, the Californian equivalent to Kyoto has reaped a lot of political goodwill for Governor Schwarzenegger since he signed it in September 2006, but it will reduce emissions less than the average Kyoto restrictions, and some 14 years later, in 2020.[1064]

When the US pulled out of Kyoto, it left the remaining restrictions very weak. Nevertheless it bears repeating that it seems unlikely most governments or the public would have accepted the outcome of a full Kyoto, not least the annual transfers to Russia of more than $50 billion for hot-air quotas.[1065] Thus, in some ways Kyoto was saved by Bush, simply because it is now so toothless that it will be politically feasible to bear.

Many countries and the EU are beginning to suggest long-term CO_2 cuts, where again the honor lies with the present-day promoters and the hard work with politicians far down the line. This is perhaps most evident with Tony Blair's proposal to reduce CO_2 emissions by 60% in 2050. This of course sounds grand – which undoubtedly was the intention – but is also very far into the future. While the UK has been one of the most vocal on climate change, its reductions are principally the consequence of Thatcher's breaking of the British miners' union in the 1980s. Since 1997 the UK CO_2 emissions have *increased* by more than 3%.[1066] Thus, many in the UK were understandably skeptical about the 60% target cut and more than half the parliamentarians suggested that there should be annual goals that would suddenly bring the grand goals for 2050 to be evaluated by 2008.[1067] The government was horrified and resisted this – at present the solution seems to be five-year plans, which reasonably allows judgement to be put off.

Nevertheless, this shows that when the time comes to commit to the political rhetoric of global warming, the support suddenly withers away, because governments know that such cuts will quickly become very expensive and likely turn into political suicide.

This then is the depressingly obvious but debilitating consequence of the many years of riding global warming, accepting and even reveling in the language of "fear, terror and disaster," from politicians, media and NGOs. We have created a situation that is portrayed as ever more apocalyptic, but have lost the possibility of a sensible dialogue.

If one suggests – as I do here – that we need to take a long-term perspective and that we should increase R&D in non-carbon emitting energy technologies to $25 billion per year, most people's reaction is simply that this is nowhere enough, as we are facing an imminent environmental Armageddon. When emotions run this high, people stop listening to evidence and instead suggest solutions that are ever grander but also ever more unrealistic.

Our problem is that we have institutionalized hypocrisy. Politicians will stoke the climate scares and claim that they will cut back CO_2 in 15–40 years, when they have long left office. But we haven't seen much in terms of actual cut-backs, because these would be tremendously politically damaging. Perhaps even clearer, politicians will talk about facing the greatest threat to mankind from CO_2, but still insist on opening new airports, as the UK government has done repeatedly.[1068]

Likewise the media will push the climate scare as the ultimate good bad-news story, especially the *Guardian* and the *Independent* in the UK. Yet, at the same time, both papers carry reader travel offers to far-away destinations and ads for cars, cheap flights and energy-intensive consumer products.[1069] If these papers took the global warming threat seriously, they would stop advertising all the trappings of the "good life." The failure to do so illustrates both hypocrisy but also our strong dependence on fossil fuels.

And we as voters are not blameless. We have let the politicians and the media underscore the climate scare and gone chanting for higher carbon taxes. Yet, when these taxes are actually considered, as in late 2006 in the UK, there was an outcry, because suddenly we couldn't just be green. We would actually have to pay.[1070]

We have to begin to be honest about two things. First, climate change is not a planetary emergency that will bring down civilization. It is one, but *only* one, of many problems that we will have to deal with over the century. Second, there are no short-term solutions to this problem. In the words of two eminent climate economists: "Stopping, or even significantly slowing, climate change will require deep emission cuts everywhere. This project will take 50 years at least, but probably a century or longer. The political will to support climate policy has to span across parties, continents, and generations."[1071]

If we are to get this support across parties, continents and generations we must discard the debilitating scares and re-create a sensible dialogue about goals and means, about costs and benefits, both across the many issues and within global warming. This is what we will look at in the final chapter.

CONCLUSION: MAKING OUR TOP PRIORITIES COOL

Time for a sensible dialogue

As we started by saying: Al Gore is right, that the debate about climate change is a debate about our generational mission. Essentially, *in the next 40 years what do we want to have accomplished?*

As we have seen above, there is a lot of "fear, terror and disaster" being bandied about – a kind of choreographed screaming. We need to move to a more sensible and fact-based policy dialogue where we can hear the arguments, sensibly debate their merits and find long-term solutions. Presumably, our goal is not just to cut carbon emissions, but also to do better for people and the environment.

Yes, climate change is a problem, but it is emphatically not the end of the world. Take sea level rise. Sea levels will rise over the coming century about a foot – or about as much as they rose over the past 150 years. This is a problem, but not a catastrophe. Ask a very old person about the most important issues that took place in the twentieth century. She will likely mention the two world wars, the cold war, the internal combustion engine and perhaps the IT revolution. But it is very unlikely that she will add: "Oh, and sea levels rose." We dealt with sea levels rising in the past century, and we will do so in this century, too. It doesn't mean that it will be unproblematic, but it is unhelpful – and incorrect – to posit it as the end of civilization.

Moreover, what we have realized is that sea level rise will be a much bigger problem for countries that are poor than for countries that are wealthier. In fact, if we work hard on reducing sea level rises, it is likely that we will reduce the rise by 35% but at the same time end up making each person about 30% poorer. The upshot is that places such as Micronesia and Tuvalu will get three times *more* flooded, simply because lower incomes more than outweigh the lower sea level rise.

Thus, we cannot just talk about CO_2 when we talk about dealing with climate change – we need to bring into the dialogue considerations *both* about carbon emissions *and* about economics, for the benefit of both humans and the environment.

Yes, we should take action on climate change, but we also need to be realistic. The screamers claim that we need to act now with drastic cuts, acting with the urgency equivalent to Pearl Harbor. But really, take a look at the politics: The UK government, which is arguably the government with the most high-pitched rhetoric on the issue, makes grand gestures and at the same time expands Heathrow and other airports and major road constructions. Since the new Labour government in 1997 promised to cut emissions by a further 15% by 2010, emissions have *increased* by 3%.[1072]

Look at our past behavior. We promised to zero our emissions between 1990 and 2000 but increased them by 12%. We have promised to cut emissions in 2010 by 11% but will probably end up with 0.7%. We were supposed to start negotiations about a future commitment in Nairobi in late 2006, but no such timeline was agreed to, and a full review was postponed until 2008.[1073] It seems unlikely that even the current level of unsubstantiated screaming will drastically change our future emissions.

Many believe that dramatic political action will follow "if only people knew better and elected better politicians."[1074] But look at the facts. For the last ten years there has been a dramatic difference between the US and the EU citizenry in their awareness and concern over global warming, and likewise a dramatic difference between the Kyoto enthusiasm of the EU leadership and the Kyoto derision of the Bush administration. Yet, the developments in EU and US emissions since 1990 are very similar, as you can see in Figure 58. Actually, if anything, the EU emissions have pulled slightly ahead, at 4% since 1990 levels.[1075]

And even if the rich world manages to reign in its emissions, the vast majority of twenty-first-century emissions will come from developing countries, as is also evidenced by the dramatic increases (from low levels) in emissions from China and India.

In a surprisingly candid statement from Tony Blair at the Clinton Global Initiative, he pointed out:

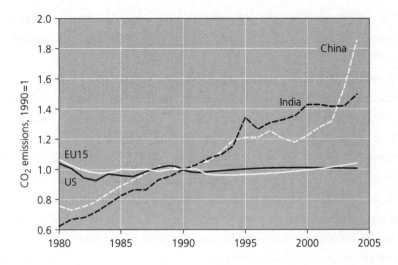

Figure 58 *Development of CO_2 emissions per person in the US, EU, China and India, 1980–2004, with 1990 as 1.*[1076]

> I think if we are going to get action on this, we have got to start from the brutal honesty about the politics of how we deal with it. The truth is no country is going to cut its growth or consumption substantially in the light of a long-term environmental problem. What countries are prepared to do is to try to work together cooperatively to deal with this problem in a way that allows us to develop the science and technology in a beneficial way.[1077]

Similarly, one of the top economic researches tell us: "Deep cuts in emissions will only be achieved if alternative energy technologies become available at reasonable prices."[1078]

We need to tone down the screaming and reclaim the sensible dialogue. **We should tax CO_2 at the economically correct level of about \$2/ton, or maximally \$14/ton.** Yet, let us not expect this will make any major difference. In the economically optimal scenario shown in Figure 11, p. 41, the tax slowly increases from about \$3 today to about \$20 by the end of the century, cutting temperature increase from 2.53°C to 2.44°C.[1079] The emissions will be reduced by 5% today and about 10% by 2100. But before we scoff at 5%, let us remember that the Kyoto Protocol, which has caused us ten years of political and economic toil, will reduce emissions by 0.4% in 2010.[1080]

However, this is not the solution. Neither such a small tax, nor Kyoto, nor the draconian proposals for future cuts will move us far toward finding better ways for the future. As we saw above, R&D in renewables and energy efficiency is at its lowest for 25 years. Instead, we need to find a way that allows us to "develop the science and technology in a beneficial way," a way that will enable us to provide alternative energy technologies at reasonable prices. It will take the better part of a century, and it will need a political will spanning parties, continents and generations. We need to be in for the long haul and find a cost-effective strategy, that doesn't splinter through over-arching ambitions or false directions.

This is why one of our generational challenges should be for **all nations to commit themselves to spending 0.05% of GDP in R&D of non-carbon emitting energy technologies**. It would cost a relatively minor $25 billion per year (seven times cheaper than Kyoto and many more times cheaper than a Kyoto II). It could embrace all nations and yet have the richer pay the larger share. It would let each country focus on its own future vision of energy needs, whether that means concentrating on renewable sources, nuclear energy, fusion, carbon storage, conservation or searching for new and more exotic opportunities.

It would create a global research momentum that could recapture the vision of delivering both a low-carbon and high-income world. It would carry a low price tag and high spin-off innovation benefits. It would also avoid ever stronger temptations to free-riding and the ever harder negotiations over ever more restrictive Kyotos. It is plausible that it will enable us to stabilize climate at a reasonable level. I believe it would be the way to bridge a century of parties, continents and generations, creating a long-run, low-cost opportunity to create the alternative energy technologies that will power the future.

To move toward this goal we need to get a sensible policy dialogue that allows us to debate global warming as the problem it is, not the catastrophe it is being sold as, and talk sensible and realistic solutions, not we-must-act-like-Pearl-Harbor drastic cuts.

This requires us to talk openly about priorities. Often there is a strong sentiment in any public discussion that we should do *anything* required to make a situation better. But clearly we don't actually do that. When we talk about schools, we know that having more teachers will likely give our kids a better education.[1081] Yet, we do not pile on more and more teachers, simply because we also have to spend money on other issues. When we talk about hospitals, we know that access to better technical equipment is likely to provide better treatment, yet we don't supply an infinite amount of resources.[1082] When we talk about the environment, we know tougher restrictions will mean better protection, but they also have higher costs.

In all of these situations, we explicitly or – most often – implicitly make a trade-off. We would like to do the best, but we accept that in the real world we can only do it well. This concept of trade-off is important to get into the global warming debate. Often, the argument is instead made that "we have the technology" to deal with global warming – and the moral implication is made that clearly we should go all the way.[1083] But it neglects the trade-offs.

Look at a similar issue with respect to traffic fatalities. Most people don't realize that traffic deaths are one of the ten leading causes of death in the world. In the US 42,600 people die in traffic accidents and 2.8 million people are injured each year.[1084] In the UK, 3,500 people die and a quarter of million people are injured.[1085] Globally, it is estimated that 1.2 million people die from traffic accidents and 50 million are injured every year.[1086] Moreover, car traffic also has a strong impact on nature – it is estimated that cars kill about 57 million birds each year just in the US.[1087]

About 2% of all deaths in the world come from traffic and about 90% of the traffic deaths occur in third world countries.[1088] The total cost is a phenomenal $512 billion a year.[1089] Due to increasing traffic, especially in the third world, and due to ever better health conditions, the World Heath Organization estimates that by 2020 traffic fatalities will be the second leading cause of death in the world, right after heart disease.[1090]

Yet, amazingly, we have the technology to make all this go away. We could literally overnight save 1.2 million humans, eliminate $500 billion worth of damage and stop hundreds of millions of birds dying every year. This would of course especially address the plight of the third world, which suffers by far the hardest from traffic deaths.

The answer is simply to lower speed limits to 5 mph.[1091] Nobody dies – probably we could avoid almost all of the 50 million injuries each year. But of course we will not do this. Why? The simple answer that almost all of us would offer is that the benefits from driving moderately fast vastly outweigh the costs. While the cost is obvious in terms of killed and maimed, the benefits are much more prosaic and dispersed, but none the less important – traffic interconnects our society, by bringing goods at competitive prices to where we live, by bringing people together to where we work, and letting us live where we like while we can visit and meet with friends and family. Thinking about a world only moving at 5 mph is a lot like a world gone medieval.

Notice, this is not meant to be flip. We really could solve one of the world's top problems if we wanted to. We know traffic deaths are almost entirely caused by man, we have the technology to reduce it to zero, yet we seem to persist in going ahead and exacerbating the problem each year, pushing traffic deaths to become the number two killer in the world by 2020.

I would suggest that the comparison with global warming is insightful. We also know that global warming is strongly caused by man and we have the technology to reduce it to zero, yet we seem to persist in going ahead and exacerbating the problem each year, causing the temperature to increase to new heights by 2020. Why? Because the benefits from moderately using fossil fuels vastly outweigh the costs. Yes, the costs are obvious in the "fear, terror and disaster" we read about in the papers every day – global warming causing sea level rise, more heat deaths or more poor.

But the benefits, though much more prosaic, are none the less important. Fossil fuels give us low-cost light, heat, food, communication and travel.[1092] Electrical air-conditioning means that people in the US no longer die in droves during heat waves.[1093] Cheaper fuels would have saved a significant number of the 150,000 people who have died in the UK since 2000 due to cold winters.[1094] Food can be grown cheaply and we can have access to fruits and vegetables year round, which probably has reduced cancer rates by at least 25%.[1095] Cars give us an opportunity to get more space and nature around our home and still keep our commute constant, whereas communication and cheap flights have given ever more people the opportunity to experience other cultures and forge friendships globally.[1096]

In the third world, access to fossil fuels is crucial. About 1.6 billion people don't have access to electricity, which seriously impedes human development.[1097] Some 2.5 billion people rely on biomass such as wood, waste and dung to cook and keep warm.[1098] Searching for wood costs many Indian women three hours each day – sometimes they have to walk more than 10 km a day – and also causes excess deforestation.[1099] About 1.3 million people – mostly women and children – die each year due to heavy indoor air pollution. Access to fossil fuels would dramatically improve lives; the cost of $1.5 billion annually would be greatly superseded by benefits of about $90 billion.[1100] For both the developed and the developing world, thinking of a world without fossil fuels in the short or medium term is a lot like a world gone medieval.

Notice, this does not mean that we should not talk about how to reduce the impact of traffic and global warming. Most countries have strict regulation on speed limits – if they didn't, fatalities would be much higher. Yet, studies also show that lowering the average speed in western Europe by just 5 kph could reduce fatalities by 25% – about 10,000 fewer killed each year.[1101] Apparently democracies around Europe are not willing to give up on the extra benefits from faster driving to save 10,000 people. This is a political priority setting, where there is more than one solution. Speed limits across Europe are 50 or 60 kph in cities. But it is not 40 or 70.[1102] We can have a discussion about increasing the speed limit a bit, allowing for faster travel, or lowering it a bit, allowing for fewer killed. But 5 kph or 250 kph are unlikely to succeed.

This is parallel to the debate we are having about global warming. We can realistically talk about $2 CO_2 tax or even $14 dollars. But suggesting $85 as Nicholas Stern did seems to be far outside the envelope.[1103] Suggesting a move from the Standard Scenario of the International Energy Agency to the Alternative Scenario (Figure 53, p. 170) is absolutely possible, although, given our past willingness to pay, unlikely. This would involve a substantial CO_2 reduction of 16% by 2030, and 15% in the OECD countries.[1104] But again, suggesting Monbiot's 96% carbon reduction for the OECD by 2030 seems a bit like suggesting 5 kph in the traffic debate. It is technically doable, but it is just very unlikely to happen.

Moreover, in the traffic case, we realize that in the short and medium term we are unlikely to move the speed limit much, and so instead we spend much of our attention on how else to reduce the fatalities. This is where air bags, seat belts, motorcycle helmets, better highway construction, speed bumps, cycle tracks, etc. show their value. They can allow us to hold a reasonable speed *while* substantially reducing death and injury. If our discussion was entirely focused on just the speed limit and polarized between 65 kph and 5 kph, we would likely forget the many easy, low-cost and substantial injury reductions we could make.

Likewise with global warming, the debate has often become so fixated on CO_2 cuts that it neglects what presumably is our primary objective – to improve the quality of life and the environment. In the battles over whether we should cut 4% or 96%, we might easily forget that in the short and medium term we can help real people much better through alternative policies. As we will see below, we can cut diseases, malnutrition, and lack of access to clean drinking water and sanitation, while improving the economy with much cheaper policies that will have much greater impact.

THE PRECAUTIONARY PRINCIPLE CUTS BOTH WAYS

Cost-benefit analyses show that only very moderate CO_2 reduction is warranted, simply because cutting CO_2 is expensive and will do little good, a long time from now.

Often people will then claim that we should do so anyway because of the so-called "precautionary principle."[1105] Although as a legal principle it really only says that lack of full scientific certainty about global warming should not be used as an excuse for doing nothing,[1106] it is typically reformulated as common-sense adages like "do no harm."[1107] While the legal principle is clearly correct, the adage approach is much more tricky.

It is normally argued that "do no harm" obviously means that we must make strong CO_2 cuts now – after all, better incur some costs now than cause harmful heat later. This is problematic in several ways. First, if strong action (say 25% cuts) is warranted, why not cut 50% or 75% – that would mean even less harmful heat. This naturally ends with only one outcome, namely 100%, which is the least harmful of all. Yet, few would defend this outcome, because the costs would be too high, and this points to the need for trade-offs. Second, talking about 'harm' from warming neglects the trade-off that costs borne now will also harm us. Essentially, spending money on cutting emission means less money for schools, hospitals and all the other good items on the social budget.

Thus, when applying the precautionary principle carefully, we have to face the trade-off between benefit of avoiding future harm versus the cost of incurring harm right now. We are then back to discussing the cost-benefit trade-off, and the precautionary principle really hasn't added any new insight.[1108]

In practice it seems the principle is mainly used to focus on preventing the harm from global warming, while ignoring the harm from emission cuts. In that way, it simply becomes a way of legitimizing an already established stance.

This is perhaps most clear in looking at the precautionary approach to traffic injuries. Clearly the intention to "do no harm" in the traffic arena means cutting speed limits to 5 kph. Just as clearly, we also need to consider the harm inflicted by having no reasonably fast interconnections in modern society. And we're back to cost-benefit trade-offs.

And in the long term, our goal should be to make a transition to a low-carbon future so inexpensive that our kids and grand-kids will want to do it. So cheap that China and India will want to join. This is why we need to focus on R&D to improve the future.

Thus, if we are going to be able to get back a sensible debate, this requires journalists – and the rest of us – to start asking better questions. Here is a list of ten questions I think we should all start asking – to reduce the amount of screaming and increase the amount of information.

Top ten questions for journalists – and the rest of us:
1. *What is the size of the problem?*
2. *Is it also good for something?*
3. *Tell me your solution.*

4. How much would that fix?
5. How much would it cost?
6. Ask other experts what their solution would be.
7. Ask other experts how much that would fix.
8. Ask other experts how much that would cost.
9. Ask economists for a cost-benefit analysis.
10. Compare these to other solutions to the world's problems.

1. Of course we need to know what the problem is. Yet, this is also where most news stories end. Say the problem is increasing temperatures from global warming, as we discussed in chapter 2. Increasing temperatures mean more heat deaths. Tell us just exactly how many people are we talking about: 365,000 extra deaths in 2050 (Figure 13, p. 45).

2. Is it all problems, or do increasing temperatures also improve something? Rarely is an issue entirely, completely and utterly negative. We need to know both sides – not to diminish the problem – but in order to assess it properly. It turns out that we will get 1.7 million fewer cold deaths. Seems like an important piece of information.

3. What is the solution? Problems are only interesting if there are solutions, and solutions are the ones we have to weigh against each other. Here we will likely be told cutting CO_2 – maybe even Kyoto.

4. How much will your solution fix? Surprisingly, many people advocate solutions whose efficiency they know little about. But if we are lucky, we will be told that, by 2050, Kyoto will save 4,000 lives in the third world but (and if this doesn't come we should tease it out) cause an extra 88,000 deaths elsewhere.

5. How much would this cost? Again, knowing a solution without the cost is like ordering in a fancy restaurant without prices on the menu – unnecessarily anxiety provoking. The best estimates for Kyoto are $180 billion.

6. This is where we should ask other experts if there are other solutions to the problem. Rarely is the solution being promoted the only one around. There are many options here, but possibly we get to know that we could

lower inner city temperatures – where 80% of humanity will be living – by simple means such as running water, cool gardens and white structures.

7. How much would that fix, we ask, somewhat skeptical? The answer is, in Los Angeles, we could lower temperatures almost immediately by 3°C – or more than is expected from global warming over the entire century.

8. And the price? It has a one-time cost of $1 billion to plant 11 million trees, re-roofing most of the 5 million homes, and painting a quarter of the roads. However, *annually* it would also lower air-conditioning costs by about $170 million and provide $360 million in smog-reduction benefits. Plus the added benefits of a greener LA.

9. We only ever hear about some costs and some benefits – after all we don't have all the time in the world. Ask an economist who has tried to sum *all* the benefits and *all* the costs. The total effect of Kyoto is clearly not from heat deaths (since it will actually be outweighed by fewer cold deaths), but it has other advantages: slightly cutting sea level rises, slightly reducing poverty toward the end of the century, etc. But at $180 billion annually, it is still a bad deal. For each dollar spent, it will do about ¢33 worth of social good. For each dollar spent greening LA we will perhaps do $2 worth of good.[1109]

10. What else could we do? The Copenhagen Consensus has estimated the price tags for some of the world's top issues (Table 2, p. 51). Benefits range from about $40 of good for each dollar spent on prevention of HIV/AIDS, $30 on malnutrition, $20 on free trade and $10 on malaria to ¢33 on Kyoto and perhaps ¢2 on grand strategies à la Monbiot.

With this information – which admittedly takes some harder questioning – we are much better placed to make good judgements when confronted with the screaming headlines of global warming or whichever problem is at the forefront of the agenda of the day.

Hopefully it will make us think harder about solutions, force people to come up with better, more cost-efficient solutions, and ultimately make us talk less about the problems where we can do little at high cost, and talk much more about the problems where we have great solutions at low cost.

In 40 years I hope we will not have to tell our kids that we went for a long series of essentially unsuccessful command-and-control Kyotos that had little or no effect on the climate, but left them poorer and less able to deal with the problems of the future. Hopefully, nor we will have to say that we monomaniacally focused on global warming, neglecting most of all the other future challenges.

In 40 years we should be able to look our kids in the eye and say we've managed the first part of the century-long effort to tackle climate change by making low-carbon energy technologies much cheaper and much more accessible. We should be able to tell our kids that our decisions have left them a world better equipped to deal with the future: richer, better fed, healthier and with a better environment.

Making best things cool

Reestablishing a sensible and fact-based dialogue on climate will mean that we can start doing the smart things first. Dealing with global warming will take a century and will need a political will spanning parties, continents and generations. We need to be in for the long haul and find a cost-effective strategy, that doesn't splinter through overarching ambitions.

We should cut CO_2, and more than Kyoto without the US will manage, but still only by 5%, moving to 10% by the end of the century.

We should also increase our R&D in low-carbon energy tenfold – 0.05% of GDP or $25 billion annually would enable us to stabilize climate at a reasonable level.

But we should also realize that how good we make the twenty-first century is not primarily about how we tackle global warming. If we take a look at Figure 59, we realize that even if we could magically make global warming go away, we could maximally improve this century by some $14.5 trillion. More realistically, global warming policies can only do about $0.6 trillion worth of good, and if we overdo it, we easily risk making the cure worse than the initial problem.

However, whichever social path we choose – focusing on the economy or on the environment, a world with higher or lower growth – we could end up making future generations much less better off, with the average person in the developing world missing out on 70% higher incomes in 2100.[1110] With both attention and money in scarce supply, what matters is that we tackle

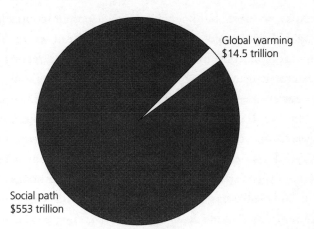

Figure 59 *The relative importance of global warming and the social choice between a globalized world focused on environment (B1) and economy (A1) measured over the twenty-first century.*[1111]

the problems with the best solutions first, doing the most good throughout the century. What matters is making sure we leave our descendants with the most opportunity.

But perhaps Figure 59 seems just a little too snug in counting everything in trillions of dollars. Let us look at the actual impacts on environment and humans, raised in the climate debate, and let us start with the developed world.

There is a great concern for polar bears. Possibly, global warming is affecting the bear population, in a worst-case scenario with as many as 15 bears dying in a population of 1,000. Yet, when we also shoot 49 bears in the same population each year, it would make sense to *first* consider tackling the rather easy policy point of ending polar bear killings (essentially revoking hunting rights and introducing police enforcement, with a price tag of much less than $0.001 trillion) before contemplating ending fossil fuel use (essentially bringing our current economy to a halt at much more than $85 trillion).

Likewise, we care about people dying in ever more prevalent heat waves due to global warming – possibly like the heat wave in August 2003 in Europe, costing 35,000 lives, with 3,500 in Paris alone. Again, caring for these victims, it seems reasonable to suggest that we should *first* look into making better medical services and air-conditioning available to these people. In the US, this has generally made the population much less vulnerable to heat deaths, whether caused by climate change or not.

We could also try to cut carbon emissions dramatically. Even if very expensive, in the very best of worlds this would save about 365,000 people by 2050. The problem is that global warming at the same time would mean many fewer people dying from cold spells; ending global warming would simultaneously mean more than 1.7 million more dead each year. So we have the choice between investing little in specific solutions that will greatly help present people dealing with heat, whether caused by global warming or not – or investing a lot in helping future people by only dealing with one kind of heat, and simultaneously killing even more.

When people in Dresden, Germany, were flooded in 2002, it was used as a spectacular example of how we need to deal with global warming. Yet, stopping global warming would probably do very little to deal with an issue which is predominantly caused by poor planning, excessive levees and lack of wetlands. Apart from environmental benefits, increasing flood areas and wetlands, better information, more stringent building policies and fewer floodplain subsidies would be able to stabilize or even reduce losses at much lower cost and much sooner. At best, global warming policies – at extremely high cost – could only stabilize losses, whereas studies from the UK indicate that minimal cost flood management can *reduce* these costs by 91%. Our *first* policy choice ought perhaps be to help more people, better, cheaper.

When Katrina hit New Orleans in 2005, there was similar outrage, suggesting that global warming was responsible and CO_2 ought to be radically cut. Yet, as with flooding, the attention seems curiously stuck on implementing a solution that will only marginally address the alleged concern. Even if we could end global warming, it would cut hurricane damage by just 10% in 2050 at overwhelming cost. Yet, if we want to curtail hurricane damage, we could do much more through social policies like zoning, regulation, taxing and public acquisition of land at risk, dropping state subsidized insurance, improving building codes and enforcement, upgrading levees and reducing environmental degradation of wetlands and beaches that act as natural sea walls against hurricanes. These policies could reduce damage by more than 50% at a tiny fraction of the climate policy cost.

One of the top hurricane damage researchers pointed out:

> Given knowledge of the significant benefits of adaptive responses one of the great puzzles of the debate over climate change is how people who express great concern about the plight of future generations expected to experience the impacts of changes in climate can be simultaneously apparently so callus about those who suffer climate impacts in today's generation. Images of poor people suffering in the aftermath of Hurricane Katrina are more often used to justify changes in energy policies than to recommend those adaptive actions that might have an appreciable impact on the lives of those who suffer the effects of today's disasters.[1112]

We have to ask why we seem so focused on cutting CO_2 when there are so many other policies that would do so much more good. I think it stems to a large extent from the ecological feeling of the inherent "wrong" in adaptation and "right" in tackling the problem head-on. Al Gore tells us that our willingness to adapt is an important part of the global warming problem – it is "a kind of laziness."[1113] Yet, if Kyoto can save 0.06 polar bear and hunting policies 49 bears, is focusing on the 0.06 really ethical? Is focusing on the best and most effective policies really just derisive laziness or just being smart?

In the metaphor of the last chapter, I think Gore's argument is similar to politicians wanting to combat traffic mortality but being stubbornly intent on only achieving the goal by reducing speed limits to 5 kph. Apart from being unrealistic, it entirely misses the enormous benefits from other policies like air bags and seat belts.

This is even more clear when discussing the problems for the developing world. Climate change will negatively impact the third world much more, and thus it is often concluded that we have a moral duty to cut carbon. But we still have to ask whether that is the best way to help.

Malaria kills more than a million each year, and more than 2 billion are infected each year, retarding both development and the economy. Since malaria is weakly connected to temperature, a worst-case analysis shows that global warming over the coming century will put about 3.2% more at risk of malaria. Thus, if we could entirely stop global warming at much more than $85 trillion, we could save perhaps a billion incidences of malaria over the century. Yet, helping people directly with mosquito nets, spraying and medicine at $3 billion annually would save more than 28 billion people. We can do amazingly much more good at a much lower price.

Global warming has been alleged to increase poverty. Yet, entirely stopping global warming might lift about 10 million people out of poverty whereas smart policies toward free trade and globalization might lift 1,000 million people out of poverty.

Commentator George Monbiot says we should stop flying in order to help the starving people in Ethiopia. But this would quite plausibly be one of the least effective ways to help them. Even if we completely brought society to a halt, we could at best avoid 28 million malnourished. Yet, through political choices of promoting economic growth – exactly the kind of policies Monbiot would thwart – we could avoid almost a billion people being malnourished.

For water, we are told that global warming will cause droughts and more people water stressed. Yet, global warming will on average mean more precipitation, and thus, on average, actually decrease the number of people with little water – in 2085 it will reduce the number of people with water stress by 1.2 billion. Or, if we stop global warming completely, we will have a future with 1.2 billion *more* people water stressed.

Again, is it laziness to point out that even dramatic climate policies can do very little about most of these issues, at very high cost, whereas other, low-cost policies can do immense amounts of good?

Over the next 40 years what do you want us to have accomplished?

This is the question that should keep ringing in our ears. Nobel laureate and expert in the Copenhagen Consensus in 2004 Thomas Schelling told me a story that has left a lasting impression. Imagine a rich Chinese in 2100. At that time, this will be your average Joe (or Xi in this case) as we saw in Figure 15, p. 53. Actually, the UN Climate Panel expects that most people in the developing world in 2100 will be much richer than the average person in the developed world today.

So, imagine an average rich Chinese, Congolese or Columbian in 2100, thinking back on 2007. He will probably be amazed to think how we cared so much about him and his problems with global warming that we were willing to spend vast sums of money to help him just a little bit, even though he is better off than we were in 2007. But probably he will also think "how odd, that they cared so much for me, who is rich, but cared so little for my grand-father and my great-grandfather, whom they could have helped so much more, at much lower cost – and who needed the help desperately."

Climate change is not the only issue out there to make our generational mission. As we talked about on pp. 50–1, the Copenhagen Consensus ranked some of the best solutions in the world. Some we have talked about above; some are entirely unrelated to climate.

HIV/AIDS kills about 3 million people and 4.3 million get infected each year, yet we have the technology entirely to avoid this. We could spend about $7 billion annually and save 3.5 million individuals each year.

Malnutrition is not just lack of calories. More than half the world's population lack essential micronutrients; this damages eyesight, lowers IQ, reduces development and restricts human productivity. At a cost of $3 billion annually we could lift out half the world's population from these deficiencies.

Free trade is hampered especially by heavy subsidies to agriculture in the EU, the US and Japan. If we scrapped these, and got the currently stalled negotiations on free trade (the Doha round) back on track, we could achieve amazing results. We could possibly achieve $2,400 billion extra, with $1,200 billion going to the developing world. This would dramatically increase nations' and individuals' ability to tackle their own problems, affecting all the other issues we have talked about here.[1114]

Finally, more than a billion people are without clean drinking water and more than 2 billion without sanitation. For just $4 billion annually we can help about 3 billion get access. This would avert a billion cases of diarrhea and save each of the affected people 200 hours each year.

With a language of "fear, terror and disaster," climate change has captured most of our attention. But I would say, we need to cool it. We want to help the world – great. But it is not a given that the best way to help is to cut CO_2. What we have seen throughout this book and summarized here is that there are many other places where we could do much more good, faster and cheaper.

An effort like Kyoto – which has spent much of the world's political will for the last decade, and which will cost $180 billion annually if concluded in full, yet yield surprisingly little benefit by the end of the century – shows the case clearly.

In Table 3 I have tried to compare the efficiency between Kyoto and a collection of smart policies – let us call them "feel good" and "do good" strategies, respectively. Of course, Kyoto could be tweaked and made better, but these are the proposals that are on the table, and in any case the differences are so huge and obvious that a better carbon cuts proposal will only marginally change the individual entries and certainly not the outcome.

Table 3 The annual cost and efficiency of doing Kyoto or of doing a collection of smart strategies, with cost in parentheses[1115]

	Feel good (e.g. Kyoto)	Do good
Polar bears	0.06 saved	49 saved
Temperature deaths	84,000 *more* deaths	Already better
Flooding	$45 million in damage reduction	$60 billion damage reduction ($5b)
Hurricanes	0.6% damage reduction	250% damage reduction ($5b)
Malaria	70 million infections avoided	28 billion avoided ($3b)
Poverty	1 million fewer	1 billion fewer
Starvation	2 million fewer	229 million fewer
Water stress	84 million *more*	Already better
HIV/AIDS		3.5 million lives saved ($7b)
Micronutrients		Avert 1 billion-plus malnourished ($3b)
Free trade		An extra $2.4 trillion annually
Drinking water and sanitation		Give 3 billion access ($4b)
Deal with climate effectively		$2/ton CO_2 tax
		R&D for low-carbon energy ($25b)
PRICE TAG	**$180 billion/year**	**$52 billion/year**

We can debate just exactly what should be in the "do good" column. And we should. When we regain the sensible, fact-driven dialogue, we should debate whether we should spend more on hurricanes, less on flooding, more on malaria and perhaps less on starvation.

Many will tend to say we should do everything in both columns. Yes, in principle we should do all good things. But until we do them all, we should focus on doing the best things first. Up until today we have done pretty badly in both columns, so let's start with the smart one.

We also have to start seriously addressing the necessity of agricultural reform, and down-to-earth but difficult subjects like wetland restoration to minimize flooding risk, the scrapping of subsidized insurance in hurricane zones, or better availability of medical care and air-conditioning in central Paris. These conversations will have a pedestrian feel compared to the exciting feel of discussing climate change and the overall conditions of the world hundreds of years from now. But they will do amazing good for real people and real nature, with realistic time-frames and plausible funding.

Over the next 40 years what should we have accomplished?

I hope we will cool our conversation, rein in the exaggerations and start focusing where we can do the most good. This does not mean doing nothing about climate change, but it does mean realizing that there are many other and many better solutions.

When people spend $5 to offset a ton of CO_2 they do some good (probably providing about $2 of benefits to the world).[1116] But the same $5 dollars donated to a different organization could have done $200 worth of social good used for HIV/AIDS prevention or $150 worth of social good on malnutrition. I would like it to be cool to have done $200 good before $2 good.

I hope we will all work to make the best solutions cool. I would like to see college drives for mosquito nets against malaria before drives for universities to adopt Kyoto. I would like to see demonstrations for improved hurricane-resistant building codes and enforcement before demonstrations against single-occupancy cars. I would like to see ardent letters to the editor about the unconscionable subsidies to industrialized agriculture, keeping third world farmers from achieving their potential, before the ardent pleas to impose high carbon taxes. I would like it to be cool to be impassioned about doing the best first for the planet.

I hope we can look the coming generations squarely in the eye and say, we didn't just do a little but fashionable good, we massively and thoroughly changed the world for the better through simple, tested and cool strategies.

We didn't just do something that made us feel good, we did something that actually did good.

NOTES

1   2001:208.

2   Blair, 2004b; Cowell, 2007.

3   "This is the biggest threat that human beings have had. This is the stuff of the Genesis myth. This is about how human beings handle knowledge." Mr Gummer thinks the governments of the industrialized world should have it at the top of their political agendas to limit their own carbon emissions. (McSmith, 2006.)

4   Arthur, 2004.

5   DW staff, 2006.

6   Prodi, 2004.

7   Buncombe, 2005.

8   Pew Center, 2006b.

9   AP, 2006a.

10   Gore & Melcher Media, 2006.

11   Gelbspan, 2004; J. D. Cox, 2005; F. Pearce, 2006a.

12   Bunting, 2006.

13   McCarthy, 2006.

14   *Time* magazine, 2006.

15   "And with sea ice vanishing, polar bears – prodigious swimmers but not inexhaustible ones – are starting to turn up drowned. 'There will be no polar ice by 2060,' says Larry Schweiger, president of the National Wildlife Federation. 'Somewhere along that path, the polar bear drops out.'" (Kluger, 2006).

16   Gore & Melcher Media, 2006:146; see also Iredale, 2005.

17   Eilperin, 2004.

18   BBC Anon., 2005.

19   2°C is now unavoidable, and "it will mean polar bears are wiped out in their Arctic homeland. The only place they can be seen is in a zoo" McCarthy, 2006.

20   J. Berner, Symon, Arris, & Heal, 2005; Hassol, 2004; Norris, Rosentrater, & Eid, 2002.

21 Very surprisingly, the World Conservation Union has the acronym IUCN. The Polar Bear Specialist Group website is at http://pbsg.npolar.no/default.htm (IUCN Species Survival Commission, 2001).

22 The IUCN actually counts 20 groups, but everyone else talks about 19 groups (IUCN Species Survival Commission, 2001:22).

23 Krauss, 2006.

24 Michaels, 2004. See springtime temperatures in Przybylak, 2000:606.

25 Monnett, Gleason, & Rotterman, 2005.

26 Amstrup et al., 2006:slide 44; Stirling, Lunn, & Iacozza, 1999:302. Stirling et al. are coming out with a new data set, but they would not share it before it was published. Stirling points out (personal communication) that sample sizes and area covered were increasing rapidly through the early eighties, which may be why population is seen as initially increasing.

27 O'Driscoll, 2006; and playing the extinction card, WWF, 2006b.

28 It was *threatened* in 1965, two years after the first red list, and has been listed *vulnerable* in 1982 and again in 1986, 1988, 1990 and 1994, then *lower risk* till 2006 where it is *vulnerable* again (Schliebe, Wiig, Derocher, & Lunn, 2006). In 1970 the Polar Bear Specialist Group voiced their "concern for polar bear survival" (IUCN Polar Bear Specialist Group, 1970).

29 Harden, 2005; WWF, 2006a.

30 Stirling et al., 1999:302, as confirmed by Amstrup et al., 2006:slide 44; Rosing-Asvid, 2006.

31 IUCN Species Survival Commission, 2001:22.

32 Taylor, 2006.

33 The Arctic Climate Impact Assessment finds it likely that disappearing ice will make polar bears take up "a terrestrial summer lifestyle similar to that of brown bears, from which they evolved" (J. Berner et al., 2005:509). They talk about the "threat" that they would become hybridized with brown and grizzly bears (ibid.) Dramatic declines seem unlikely simply because we would likely choose to sustain the polar bears through relatively low-cost feed programs.

34 "While there will be some losses in many arctic areas, movement of species into the Arctic is likely to cause the overall number of species and their productivity to increase, thus overall biodiversity measured as species richness is likely to increase along with major changes at the ecosystem level" (J. Berner et al., 2005:997).

35 J. Berner et al., 2005:998.

36 J. Berner et al., 2005:256.

37 Eilperin, 2004.

38 Based on a simple model starting in 2000 with a population of 1,000, with a reduction of 1.5% (15 bears first year), and with the full Kyoto Protocol reducing global warming by about 7% in 2100 (Wigley, 1998).

39 Which is also the conclusion of the IUCN Polar Bear Specialist Group, pointing out that "the decline was due to a combination of anthropogenic removals (defence and harvest kills) and reduced demographic rates from climate warming" such that they recommended "appropriate management action be taken without delay" (2005).

40 Motavalli, 2004.

41 "Heat waves are a major mortal risk, number one among so-called natural hazards in postindustrial societies. In France, the elderly, especially women, were most vulnerable, but excess mortality was observed even for men in the 35–44 years age group (23% excess). Strong correlations appear as well with urban living conditions, poverty, isolation, and ill health. Thus, heat wave is confirmed as the silent killer of mute victims, unveiling social inequalities in the face of risks" (Poumadere, Mays, Le Mer, & Blong, 2005:1491).

42 Kates, Colten, Laska, & Leatherman, 2006.

43 Karl & Trenberth, 1999; Mahlman, 1997.

44 In this book we will primarily discuss CO_2 since it makes up 60% of the present extra heat-trapping gasses and is expected to constitute an even larger part in the future. In 2100 CO_2 is expected to constitute anywhere from 68% of total forcing in scenario A2 to 97% in scenario B1 (IPCC, 2001a:403).

45 IPCC, 2001a:89.

46 IPCC, 2001a:208.

47 IPCC, 2001a:195–6.

48 IPCC, 2007b:2.3.1.

49 IPCC, 2001a:187.

50 Nakicenovic & IPCC WG III, 2000.

51 Developing countries emitted 10.171 Gt of global 26 Gt in 2004 (IEA, 2006c:513, 493); OECD countries 51% in 2003 (OECD, 2006d:148). Weyant estimates 29% from industrialized countries (1998:2286); IPCC emission scenarios from 23% in the Business-as-Usual A1 to 36% (Nakicenovic & IPCC WG III, 2000).

52 From atmosphere–ocean general circulation models (AOGCMs) to earth system models.

53 Shows the scenario A1B (IPCC, 2007a:14; 2007b:fig 10.3.1), described as the Business-As-Usual scenario (Dai, Wigley, Boville, Kiehl, & Buja, 2001).

54 Easterling et al., 1997; Vose, Easterling, & Gleason, 2005.

55 Alexander et al., 2006.

56 Easterling et al. 2000:419; Zhai et al. 1999; Jones et al. 1999; Heino et al. 1999.

57 See also IPCC, 2007b:3.8.2.1.

58 Michaels, Knappenberger, Balling, & Davis, 2000.

59 Easterling et al., 2000:419.

60 Plummer et al., 1999.

61 Easterling et al., 2000:419.

62 Horton, Folland, & Parker, 2001; Jones et al., 1999.

63 G. Edwards, 2006; Vergano, 2006.

64 Climate scientist Bill Chameides of the conservation group Environmental Defense (Vergano, 2006).

65 Rosenthal, 2005.

66 Lean, 2004. This line of thinking is also expressed by William Collins of the National Center for Atmospheric Research when he says: "Scientists are sure that we're changing the climate for the foreseeable future. What we're not sure about is whether or not we'll be able to live with those changes" (G. Edwards, 2006).

67 Gore & Melcher Media, 2006:75.

68 IPCC, 2007b:ch. 10 summary.

69 IPCC, 2007b:fig. 10.3.6.

70 IPCC, 2007b:fig. 10.3.8.

71 IPCC, 2007b:ch. 10 summary.

72 The model referred to in IPCC, 2007b:10.3.6.2. Weisheimer & Palmer (2005) write two to three years, and estimate their 5% extreme to increase to "around 40% or so," but the straight average of their numbers in Table 2 gives 34% and 37%, around one to three years.

73 An increase from 1.66 to 2.08 incidences per year for Chicago, from 1.64 to 2.15 for Paris (Meehl & Tebaldi, 2004:995).

74 76% reduction in 2050 (S. Vavrus, Walsh, Chapman, & Portis, 2006), referred to in IPCC, 2007b:10.3.6.2.

75 Ebi, Mills, Smith, & Grambsch, 2006; see also Basu & Samet, 2002; A. J. McMichael, Woodruff, & Hales, 2006. Both *only* talk about heat related deaths.

76 W. J. M. Martens, 1998.

77 The last 44 days lie within the 3°C optimum temperature zone.

78 Helsinki has a population of about 1.2 million, which means the figures for all of Helsinki should be 20% higher.

79 Keatinge et al., 2000:672.

80 El-Zein, Tewtel-Salem, & Nehme, 2004; Gouveia, Hajat, & Armstrong, 2003; Kan, Jia, & Chen, 2003; Laaidi, Karine, & Jean-Pierre, 2006; Nakaji et al., 2004.

81 Vandentorren et al., 2004.

82 Vandentorren et al., 2004:1519.

83 Larsen, 2003.

84 Poumadere et al., 2005.

85 Larsen, 2003.

86 Schar & Jendritzky, 2004; Trigo, Garcia-Herrera, Diaz, Trigo, & Valente, 2005.

87 Chase, Wolter, Pielke, & Rasool, 2007.

88 BBC Anon., 2006c.

89 Notice that these numbers are a factor of two to four smaller than the numbers in Table 1, simply because the BBC numbers only sample excess deaths from December to March and compare them to the rest of the year (where there are still many cold deaths).

90 Larsen, 2003.

91 Estimated in the text, using Keatinge et al., 2000:672.

92 207,000; based on a simple average of the available cold and heat deaths per million, extended for the entire population, cautiously excluding London, and using WHO's estimate for Europe's population at 878 million (WHO, 2004a:121).

93 1.48 million estimated in the same way as total heat deaths.

94 It is about 15% of the total death toll from Europe (9.56 million deaths; WHO, 2004a:121).

95 Keatinge et al., 2000:672.

96 Keatinge & Donaldson (2004:1096) and Langford & Bentham (1995) likewise estimate 9,000 fewer cold deaths.

97 W. J. M. Martens, 1998:342.

98 Davis, Knappenberger, Michaels, & Novicoff, 2003; Davis, Knappenberger, Novicoff, & Michaels, 2002.

99 Davis et al., 2002:182.

100 Davis et al., 2002.

101 UNPD, 2006b:9.

102 Anon., 2006; Arnfield, 2003.

103 Tel Aviv (Saaroni, Ben-Dor, Bitan, & Potchter, 2000), Tucson (Comrie, 2000), Baltimore and Phoenix (Brazel, Selover, Vose, & Heisler, 2000), Guadalajara, Mexico (Tereshchenko & Filonov, 2001), Shanghai (L. X. Chen, Zhu, Zhou, & Zhou, 2003), Barrow, Alaska (Hinkel, Nelson, Klene, & Bell, 2003), Korea (Chung, Choi, & Yun, 2004), Milan (Maugeri, Buffoni, Delmonte, & Fassina, 2002), Vienna (Bohm, 1998), and Stockholm (Moberg & Bergstrom, 1997).

104 Comrie, 2000:2418; DUPD, 2006; WRCC, 2007.

105 Comrie (2000:2422) estimates 2.1°C over 1969–98. With the figure of 0.071°C/year this would be 2.63°C until 2005.

106 Philandras, Metaxas, & Nastos, 1999.

107 Akbari, Pomerantz, & Taha, 2001.

108 Rosenzweig et al., 2006.

109 Streutker, 2003.

110 Hung, Uchihama, Ochi, & Yasuoka, 2006.

111 Hung et al., 2006:41.

112 Hung et al., 2006:41.

113 58.5 km², New York City (2006). In Encyclopaedia Britannica. Retrieved November 17, 2006, from Encyclopædia Britannica Online: http://search.eb.com:2048/eb/article-215659.

114 Wilby, 2004.

115 Greater London Authority, 2006.

116 We have to remember that the 2.6°C is a global average, and it is likely to be bigger on land; moreover that many of the urban heat island figures are only valid for minimum or maximum temperatures. Yet, for a city like Bangkok, the mean day temperature is 6°C higher throughout the dry season and Tokyo ranges between 3 and 12°C throughout the year, thus still at least on scale with the 2.6°C average increase. Khandekar, Murty, & Chittibabu (2005:1573) quote that Tokyo temperature over the past 150 years has increased 4°C.

117 For example: "On local and regional scales, changes in land cover can sometimes exacerbate the effect of greenhouse-gas-induced warming, or *even exert the largest impact on climatic conditions*. For example, urban 'heat islands' result from lowered evaporative cooling, increased heat storage and sensible heat flux caused by the lowered vegetation cover, increased impervious cover and complex surfaces of the cityscape" (emphasis added, Patz, Campbell-Lendrum, Holloway, & Foley, 2005:310).

118 For London, the urban heat island added effect is estimated to be 0.26°C extra and 15 more days of intense urban heat per year in 2080 (Wilby, 2004:5).

119 Greater London Authority, 2006.

120 Wilby & Perry, 2006:92.

121 Greater London Authority, 2006.

122 Synnefa, Santamouris, & Livada, 2006.

123 Greater London Authority, 2006.

124 The authors actually don't calculate the total cost, but given trees at $45, reroofing when necessary, extra cost at $25/100 m², and painting of asphalt at $29/100 m², it gives a total of $1.17 billion (Rosenfeld, Akbari, Romm, & Pomerantz, 1998).

125 See Grubb, 2004; for text see UNFCCC, 1997. A UK government minister says: "The government's view is that Kyoto is the only game in town" (Dalyell, 2004).

126 Blakely, 1998; see also Gore & Melcher Media, 2006:282–3, 288–9. Rob Gelbspan sees it as one of the few causes for optimism (Gelbspan, 2004:x). For Leggett (2001) it constitutes the culmination of his epic story.

127 Wigley, 1998:2285. The industrial nations are the so-called Annex I countries.

128 Radetzki, 1999:373.

129 Wigley, 1998:2286.

130 H. Lee, Martins, & Mensbrugghe, 1994:42, 44.

131 "A continuing rift over [global warming] will have a profound impact on the overall relationship between the United States and Europe" (Halperin, 2001).

132 Based on Wigley, 1998. He does runs for climate sensitivity of 1.5, 2.5 and 4.5°C, showing that in all cases they change about 7%. Thus, the graph here is adjusted for the IPCC middle scenario of 2.6°C.

133 Same size of result (1.33°C instead of 1.39°C in 2050) is referenced in Parry, Arnell, Hulme, Nicholls, & Livermore, 1998.

134 Anon., 2004.

135 Malakoff, 1997.

136 Malakoff, 1997.

137 Milliken, 2004.

138 "Our efforts to stabilize the climate will need, over time, to become far more ambitious than the Kyoto Protocol" (Blair, 2004a).

139 Of the world's 33.3 billion tons of CO_2 equivalent emitted, the US emits 6.9 billion tons (WRI, 2005:204–5).

140 Alcamo et al. (2002) make runs on five different climate/energy models for two different scenarios. (Because results are only given with one decimal and the changes are so minute, this probably causes a large part of the uncertainty.) On average, he finds that, with the US, temperatures are reduced 6 or 11%, and without the US 4.4 and 6.6%; standardizing these results to the 7% of Wigley (1998) with the US, means 4.6% reduction without the US, or a temperature reduction of 0.12°C.

141 BBC Anon., 2002; WRI, 2005:204–5.

142 Bohringer & Vogt, 2003:479.

143 UNFCCC, 1997:20; 2006:8.

144 Canadian Press, 2006; Reuters, 2006. According to the new environment minister, Rona Ambrose, "it is impossible, impossible, for Canada to reach its Kyoto targets" (Economist Anon., 2006). See also van Kooten, 2003.

145 EEA, 2006:9.

146 35%, (UNFCCC, 2006:12).

147 UNFCCC, 2006:12; Michael Grubb, 2004:25.

148 Bohringer & Vogt, 2003:478.

149 UNFCCC, 1997:article 17.

150 Brandt & Svendsen, 2005; Economist Anon., 2006; Ellerman & Wing, 2000; Klepper & Peterson, 2005.

151 Bohringer & Vogt, 2003:478. Notice this is substantially less than what is expected in Figure 7.

152 Bohringer & Vogt, 2003:478.

153 Bohringer & Vogt, 2003:478.

154 0.7% reduction (Bohringer & Vogt, 2003:481), about 0.8–1% (Nordhaus, 2001:1283; 2006:fig. 4).

155 Blair, 2003: "At best Kyoto will mean a reduction of 2% in emissions. That is better than emissions just continuing to rise and rise. But we know now, from further research and evidence, that to stop further damage to the climate we need a reduction in 60% reduction world-wide."

156 Bohringer & Vogt, 2003:487.

157 Based on the simplified assumptions of 1% reduction in emissions over five years (2008–12) compared to the base run, modeled on the DICE-99 model (Nordhaus & Boyer, 2000).

158 IEA, 2006c:41.

159 The lack of participation of developing countries and cost (Lisowski, 2002), reinforced by the unanimous 95–0 Senate decision (Byrd-Hagel, 1997).

160 Graham-Harrison, 2006; see also Zhang, 2000.

161 Joseph, 2006.

162 Weyant & Hill, 1999; also quoted in IPCC, 2001c:537 and Golub, Markandya, & Marcellino, 2006:522.

163 $5–10 billion (Dagoumas, Papagiannis, & Dokopoulos, 2006:37), somewhere between 0.2 and 0.4% GDP due to expectations of future commitments and depending on the ability of Russia to limit supply of permits, making them more expensive (Manne & Richels, 2004:453). If EU were to make the cuts themselves, this would still be very expensive, somewhere between 0 and 5% of national GDPs (Viguier, Babiker, & Reilly, 2003:479).

164 Craig, Vaughan, & Skinner, 1996:135.

165 Estimated at 80.1 million barrels/day at $54.57 (average 2005) (EIA, 2006c:87) against a global GDP of $47.767 billion (IMF, 2006:189).

166 In the modeling literature, this is known as the Autonomous Energy Efficiency Improvement (or AEEI) factor, often estimated at between 0.7

and 1% (Weyant, 1996:1007), criticized by Grubb, Kohler, & Anderson (2002), and shown to be possible to incorporate in a more general model by Schwoon & Tol (2006).

167 Lomborg, 2001:126; the equivalent of a 0.77% annual efficiency improvement.

168 From 13.6 mpg in 1973 to 22.4 mpg in 2004 (EIA, 2006d:17.

169 Europe used 24% less energy per square meter in 1992 than in 1973; the US used 43% less (Schipper, Haas, & Sheinbaum, 1996:184).

170 Schipper et al., 1996:187; Jaffe, Newell, & Stavins, 1999:13. In Denmark electric home appliances have become 20–45% more effective over the last ten years (NERI, 1998:238).

171 Newell, Jaffe, & Stavins, 1999.

172 The Autonomous Energy Efficiency Improvement (or AEEI) factor, often estimated at between 0.7 and 1% (Weyant, 1996:1007).

173 Lomborg, 2001:79.

174 Weyant, 1996.

175 For EU households, despite energy efficiency gains, consumption *increased* by 2% annually in the last decade (Almeida, Fonseca, Schlomann, Feilberg, & Ferreira, 2006).

176 BA, 2006.

177 A typical economist's expression is that "there is no such thing as a free lunch," i.e. costs are bound to occur somewhere along the line. That there should be profitable carbon dioxide emission reductions thus means: "In the colloquialism of economics, this analysis suggests not only that there are free lunches, but that in some restaurants you can get paid to eat!" (Lomborg, 2001:312–13).

178 AP, 2006c.

179 AP, 2006c.

180 Metcalf & Hassertt, 1997.

181 Quoted in Monbiot, 2006a:xvi.

182 "When we did the Kyoto Treaty, everybody said, even recently, oh, well, Clinton went off on a wild goose chase and those targets weren't realistic and all that sort of stuff. Dupont reduced its greenhouse gas emissions by 65 percent and saved about $1.5 billion over three years" (Clinton, 2005); see also Northrop, 2005; theclimategroup, 2006.

183 IPCC, 2001a:388; McFarland, 2005.

184 Heijnes, Brummelen, & Blok, 1999.

185 There seems to be some lack of clarity about where the cost is related and which chemicals are the more important. McFarland claims that the cuts come especially from HFCs: "Through a technology breakthrough in our

fluorochemical operations, we have reduced our global carbon-equivalent emissions by over 72%" (McFarland, 2005), whereas Paul Tebo, DuPont's Vice President for Safety, Health & Environment, is quoted as saying that the $50 million in cost is related to reductions in nitrous oxides (theclimategroup, 2006).

186 In order to achieve this, energy teams were set up across DuPont's business units and facilities worldwide. Each month, the teams calculated detailed metrics for energy used per pound of product, and the steam and electricity usage for every building. This allowed them to see how improvements could be made in the areas of efficient lighting, heating, cooling, compressed air and cogeneration (theclimategroup, 2006).

187 WRI, 2006.

188 Their global environmental manager talks about how their hold-energy-use-flat goal helped them "focus effort on energy savings activities and projects that might not have otherwise risen far enough up on our capital spending priorities to have been pursued" (McFarland, 2005). Of course, that sounds very much as if other capital spending might have had a bigger payoff.

189 Beinecke, 2005; Hawkins, 2001; Sierra Club, 2007.

190 Mendelsohn, 2004.

191 Estimating that each mom drives 8 km at the average rate of 0.916 lb/mile or 0.258 kg CO_2/km (EPA, 2000), converted at 3.7 kg CO_2 = 1 ton carbon (IPCC, 1990; Houghton, Jenkins, Ephraums, & Working Group I, 1990:364).

192 The US average conversion rate is 1,630 kWh/ton CO_2 (EIA, 1999:2; 2002:4), the EU (marginal) conversion rate higher at about 2,000 kWh/ton CO_2 as estimated for 300 TWh for 150 million tons (Almeida et al., 2006) and a stand-by phone charger average of 1.5 W/h, (Almeida et al., 2006:fig. 14). Attenborough was promised about four times that amount, but with no references (BA, 2006).

193 Postman (2006) estimates 342 lb CO_2 for a 2 min. hot shower.

194 EIA (2006f) estimates 8.87 kg CO_2 per gallon of motor gasoline, or ¢0.887 per gallon.

195 The DICE-99 model (Nordhaus, 2006b).

196 This is about $390 million per year.

197 Notice that the cost function is strongly non-linear since deeper carbon cuts get much more expensive – we will do the cheap, easy cuts first ("pick the low hanging fruit").

198 Tol, 2005.

199 $50 per ton of carbon (Tol, 2005:2071).

200 From the Environmental Assessment Institute we asked him in July 2005: "Would you still stick by the conclusion that $15/tC seems justified or

would you rather only present an upper limit of the estimate?" He answered: "I'd prefer not to present a central estimate, but if you put a gun to my head I would say $7/tC, the median estimate with a 3% pure rate of time preference." ($7/tC = $1.9/tCO$_2$.) This is comparable with D. Pearce's estimate of $1–2.5/tCO$_2$ ($4–9/tC) (2003:369).

201 Stern, 2006:287; likewise the EU consider £20 (about $25) per ton of CO$_2$ "affordable" (EU, 2001).

202 Nordhaus (2006b) with permanent $85/tCO$_2$ ($314.5/tC), discounted present (2005) value.

203 $11,678 billion (OECD, 2005:13).

204 D. Pearce (2003:377–8) estimates £45/tC, at 1 GBP = 1.93158 USD (25–11–06). This is equivalent to $23.7 per ton of CO$_2$.

205 Nordhaus, 1992; 1994; 2001; Nordhaus, 2006a; Nordhaus & Boyer, 2000; Nordhaus & Yang, 1996.

206 Nordhaus & Boyer, 2000.

207 IPCC, Bruce, Yi, Haites, & Working Group III, 1996:385.

208 IPCC et al., 1996:189; Nordhaus & Boyer, 2000:4–35.

209 IPCC et al., 1996:187.

210 Nordhaus, 2006c. Compare with Nordhaus, 2006e:25. Conceptually, this is the $150 billion annually, over the century, discounted to present day (2005) value.

211 Nordhaus, 2006c.

212 BEA, 2006a; W. D. Nordhaus, 2006c.

213 Nordhaus, 2006e:10.

214 Nordhaus, 2006c.

215 See Figure 11, difference between Free trade and Only OECD.

216 Nordhaus, 2006c.

217 £310/tC (D. Pearce, 2003:380).

218 Nordhaus, 2006c.

219 Bohringer & Loschel (2005) find that most experts expect some reduction after 2012 but most expect fairly little.

220 The council believed "that global average temperatures should not exceed 2°C above pre-industrial level" (EU, 1996b; quoted in EU, 2005b:3). Of course, the EU already in 1991 expected EU emissions to stabilize at 1990 levels in 2000 (EU, 1996a:iv).

221 See also the discussion in pp. 44–8, and Tol, 2007.

222 Nordhaus & Boyer, 2000:7–6.

223 Nordhaus, 2006c.

224 Notice that Nordhaus & Boyer mark this scenario mainly as a benchmark: "This is not presented in the belief that an environmental pope will

suddenly appear to provide infallible canons of policy that will be scrupulously followed by all. Rather, the optimal policy is provided as a benchmark for policies to determine how efficient or inefficient alternative approaches may be" (Nordhaus & Boyer, 2000:7–7).

225 Peck & Teisberg, 1992. Notice that all these statements deal with deterministic outcomes. We will talk about risk of catastrophes later.

226 D. Maddison, 1995:345.

227 Parson & Fisher-Vanden, 1997:614.

228 Tol, 2002c:372–3.

229 D. Chapman & Khanna, 2000:225.

230 Nordhaus, 1998:18.

231 Stern, 2006:298. See pp. 195–7 for a critique of Stern's update.

232 Kavuncu & Knabb, 2005:369, 383.

233 Nordhaus, 2006c.

234 Bosello, Roson, & Tol, 2006:582. Notice that cardiovascular numbers include both deaths increased from heat stress and and deaths avoided from cold stress, with deaths avoided consistently exceeding deaths increased.

235 Notice that when we talk about saved lives, it really means deaths postponed (since we don't know how to confer immortality).

236 Tol, 2002b:154–5.

237 Tol, 2002a:61.

238 Calculated on the basis of Wigley (1998).

239 Estimating the payment of $180 billion annually instead invested at 5% pa, to be used 40 years later ($1.25 trillion) to save 15,000 people.

240 30 life–years at an average cost of $62 (Hahn, 1996:236).

241 Devastation p. 13, overheating in Europe p. 12 (he talks about 30,000 dead), stone age p. 3, and Wagner p. 1 (Lovelock, 2006b).

242 Lovelock, 2006a. While Lovelock is technically correct – billions of us will die, since only very few of the 6 billion alive today will live to 2100 – clearly his statement is that most of us will die and much before time. As quoted by Lovell (2006), Lovelock specifies that "a hot earth couldn't support much over 500 million."

243 Sir Crispin talks about how Lovelock gives "a marvellous introduction to the science" (Lovelock, 2006b:xvii), and Al Gore says: "Lovelock is truly a visionary" (Dana, 2006), clearly not challenging his science though believing that the political system will prove better than feared by Lovelock.

244 Helm (2003) gives an overview of climate change policy, yet does *not* mention anything but carbon reductions and the political implications of this.

245 Goklany, 2006:322.

246 WHO, 2002:224. Note that the attribution is only approximate and often does not entirely add up. A very similar picture for 2001 is presented by Lopez, Mathers, Ezzati, Jamison, & Murray (2006), but they do not include climate change.

247 Goklany, 2006:322.

248 R. Bailey, 2006.

249 Lomborg, 2004; 2006. You can see more at www.copenhagenconsensus.com.

250 Lomborg, 2004:606.

251 But notice that this need not have been so, because the Nobels made the priority according to where we could do the most *extra* good for *extra* funds. Thus, there could have been small, obscure illnesses where payoff would have been even better.

252 Lomborg, 2004:104.

253 Lomborg, 2004:404–5.

254 Lomborg, 2004:109; 2006:26–7.

255 Lomborg, 2004:647.

256 Lund, Søndergaard, & Faber, 2004.

257 Lund, Faber, & Søndergaard, 2004.

258 Copenhagen Consensus, 2006. Kyoto is number 23, and the other proposals 37–40 of 40.

259 Historical statistics from A. Maddison (2006a; 2006b), IPCC predictions from MESSAGE A1 (Nakicenovic & IPCC WG III, 2000), and update till 2005 from BEA (2006a). The dollars are in purchasing power parity (PPP), meaning that they show what you can *actually* buy in a specific country, not what you could buy with the exchange rate.

260 Boyle et al., 2006; Pritchett & Summers, 1996. Notice that this does not mean everyone was unhappy and wretched in times of old – just that they died much sooner (Kenny, 2006).

261 Mfenyana et al., 2006.

262 Parikh, Balakrishnan, Laxmi, & Biswas, 2001.

263 K. R. Smith, 2000.

264 Armstrong, Conn, & Pinner, 1999.

265 Actually data for 1915, but clearly the number was even higher in 1900 (USCB, 1999:874).

266 Lebergott, 1993:102, 113.

267 Moore, 2006; Roos, Magoon, Gupta, Chateau, & Veugelers, 2004; van Doorslaer, Masseria, & Koolman, 2006; Westman, Hasselstrom, Johansson, & Sundquist, 2003. It even means that you have lower chance of committing suicide – if you are a man (Westman et al., 2003).

268 Johnson & Krueger, 2006. Oh, and it allows you to buy that DVD-player.

269 This is the A2 scenario, with very high population growth and low economic growth.

270 A. Maddison, 2006a.

271 Roy Morgan, 2006.

272 Pew Center, 2006a. Notice that this shows the percentages of people who have heard of global warming, so e.g. Pakistan has 56% worried. However, only 12% have heard about global warming in Pakistan, so of these 12%, 56% were worried, or 7% of the total population. The other 93% have either said they are unworried or don't know about global warming (and are therefore also unworried).

273 Chicago Council, 2006a:14, 16. Only India found "combating world hunger" slightly more important than "improving the global environment."

274 Chicago Council, 2006b:68.

275 Gore & Melcher Media, 2006:13.

276 Gore & Melcher Media, 2006:13. See also Gore: "I believe there is a hunger in the country to be part of a larger vision that changes the way we relate to the environment and the economy" (Dana, 2006).

277 Gore & Melcher Media, 2006:13, 291.

278 EIA, 2006a; 2006b; 2006e. Actually Gore had the highest growth rate: Bush (growth by 1.03% per year), Gore (1.32%), Bush Sr. (0.5%) and Reagan (1.12%), for Bush W compounded growth over the four years 2001–5, Gore 1993–2001, Bush Sr. 1989–93, Reagan 1981–89. Only under Carter did the growth rate drop, because of the first oil crisis, about 0.98% per year.

279 US aid budgets have been declining since the mid-sixties from almost 0.6% of national income to below 0.1% in 2000. They dropped from 0.154% of GNI in 1993 to 0.111% in 2001 (OECD, 2006b; 2006c). Interestingly, Bush has more than doubled aid spending, so that in 2005 it was at 0.221%, though a subtantial part is also due to the $14 billion debt relief to Iraq (OECD, 2006a).

280 Notice that this book is subject to the same restriction. We're talking about climate change, because that is what everyone is talking about, rather than malaria.

281 $1,024 in 2005 (Worldwatch Institute, 2006:85). Both Claus Töpfer of UNEP and the organizers of Global Conscience refer to the military costs (Ledgard, 2005). Other variants focus on the cost of the Iraq war or first world agricultural subsidies.

282 T. Weiss, 2006.

283 Cary, 2000.

284 Gore & Melcher Media, 2006:13.

285 Gore & Melcher Media, 2006:13.

286 See the documentation in Lomborg, 2001:133ff.

287 The same kind of approach is built in to the Asia-Pacific Partnership on Clean Development and Climate, which focuses on energy efficiency and diffusion of advanced technologies in electricity, transport and key industry sectors. Because it focuses on some of this century's biggest emitters, including China, India and the US, it is forecast to reduce global carbon emissions by 11% in 2050 (Fisher et al., 2006) – for reference, a full Kyoto would only reduce emissions by 9% in 2050. The cost, however, is unclear at the moment. It is seen as cheap and voluntary, but it is doubtful that entirely voluntary measures will achieve all of the AP6 potential. And certainly, in the long run, more smart measures will be needed.

288 Augustin et al., 2004:623.

289 A. Berger, Melice, & Loutre, 2005.

290 His quote is: "It's a complicated relationship, but the most important part of it is this: when there is more CO_2 in the atmosphere, the temperature increases because more heat from the Sun is trapped inside" (Gore & Melcher Media, 2006:67). He essentially says that it is complicated, but still the basics of global warming hold. That is true, but this graph exactly does *not* show this.

291 Temperature from Augustin et al. (2004) and Jouzel (2004), using the estimate of 9‰ per °C (Petit et al., 1999:431). CO_2 from Indermuhle et al. (1999); Petit et al. (2001); Petit et al. (1999); Siegenthaler (2005); Siegenthaler et al. (2005); Gore's numbers from Gore & Melcher Media (2006:66–7); the estimates on temperature in 2050 from IPCC (2007b:A1B in fig. 10.3.1); compare with IPCC (2001a:824) estimate of CO_2 in 2050 from SRES, in IPCC, 2001a:807.

292 H. Fischer, Wahlen, Smith, Mastroianni, & Deck (1999) estimate 600±400 years; Indermuhle, Monnin, Stauffer, Stocker, & Wahlen (2000) find 600–1,200 years; Mudelsee (2001) 1,300±1,000 years; Monnin et al. (2001) find coming out of the last glacial that CO_2 lags temperature by 800±600 years; Petit et al. (1999:433) find lags of several thousand years and Siegenthaler et al. (2005:1316) estimate 1,900 years.

293 H. Fischer et al., 1999:1713. Notice that the discrepancy at 330,000, where the temperature seems to spike some 10,000 years earlier, seems to be a scaling problem (the temperature data come from Dome C and CO_2 data from Vostok) – it disappears when Vostok temp is scaled against Vostok CO_2, as is also evident in fig. 4 in Siegenthaler et al., 2005.

294 Gildor, Tziperman, & Toggweiler, 2002; J. L. Russell, Dixon, Gnanadesikan, Toggweiler, & Stouffer, 2006; Toggweiler, Russell, & Carson, 2006.

295 Abelmann, Gersonde, Cortese, Kuhn, & Smetacek, 2006.

296 D. Weiss, Shotyk, & Kempf, 1999.

297 Wilkinson, 2005.

298 Acsadi & Nemeskeri, 1970; Botkin & Keller, 1998:91; Preston, 1995:30; Worldbank, 2006:289.

299 Prosperity has increased from about PPP\$115/person/year in most of history to more than PPP\$9,000 in 2005 (DeLong, 2007; Worldbank, 2006:289). Violence has dropped 30–fold over the past 800 years (Eisner, 2003). Democracy has gone from an outlier in the ancient world to predominant in the world's regimes (64%) (Freedom House, 2007).

300 As is independently verified by Bintanja, van de Wal, & Oerlemans (2005:126).

301 Andersen et al., 2004:148.

302 In his book he clearly shows how CO_2 will lie above 600 ppm by 2050 (Gore & Melcher Media, 2006:67), although the IPCC scenarios clearly state that the CO_2 concentration in 2050 will lie between 472 and 567 (IPCC, 2001a:807). This becomes all the more ironic, since he confidently but incorrectly states that "there is not a single part of this graph – no fact, date or number – that is controversial in any way or in dispute by anybody" (Gore & Melcher Media, 2006:67.

303 Gore & Melcher Media, 2006:67, written with an arrow pointing to the temperature graph. He makes the same gesture in the movie, showing us how temperature will increase enormously.

304 For A1B, the estimates run from 1.00°C to 1.86°C (IPCC, 2001a:824).

305 It is measured by the ratio of the two naturally occurring oxygen isotopes ^{18}O and ^{16}O (by far the more common), which varies according to temperature. When the deep sea foraminifera made their tiny calcium carbonate shells, they imprinted the ratio of the oxygen isotopes (and the temperature at which they lived), and when they later died, their shells were preserved, layer by layer, and dug up and averaged globally by Zachos et al. (2001b; see also Schmidt, 1999).

306 Based on deep-sea foraminifera (Zachos, Pagani, Sloan, Thomas, & Billups, 2001a; 2001b). They point out that a large amount of the variability from 32 million years ago until today is caused by the glaciation of Antarctica and other ice volume, but the graph is presented as by Sorokhtin, Chilingar, Khilyuk, & Gorfunkel (2007:4) and it also looks similar to that of Aguirre & Riding (2005:585; Pearson & Palmer, 2000:698).

307 Pagani, Zachos, Freeman, Tipple, & Bohaty, 2005a; 2005b; Pearson & Palmer, 2000. Data are much sparser, combined from two different sources and smoothed.

308 The somewhat problematic connection is acknowledged by Pagani et al. (2005b:602) and Pearson & Palmer (2000:699).

309 Measuring the temperature over the past 500 million years is difficult. It seems from the simple interpretation of the ratio of oxygen isotopes that temperatures have been ever higher ever further back in time, but most are reluctant to make that conclusion firmly. See the data in Shields & Veizer 2002; Veizer et al., 1999. In the model by Wallmann, he estimates the likely temperature evolution consistent with the oxygen isotope ratio (Wallmann, 2004:20). Notice, the absolute temperature is scaled somewhat lower.

310 Beerling & Royer (2002:546) find 1,000–2,000 ppm. Ekart, Cerling, Montanez, & Tabor (1999:822) find 1,000–3,000 ppm. R. A. Berner & Kothavala (2001; R. A. Berner, 2003:325; R. A. Berner & Kothavala, 2001:201) find about 10 times today (3,000 ppm) 200 million years ago, and 15–25 times (about 6,000 ppm) around 400–500 million years ago, with similar results from Wallmann (2004:14).

311 Shaviv & Veizer (2003:5) compare with the same point, but not nearly as sharply formulated (Veizer, Godderis, & François, 2000).

312 Left out is the more technical p in front of CO_2 (for partial pressure CO_2 or "pCO_2") (Rothman, 2002:4170). Notice how critics like Crowley & Berner (2001) have offered little in refutation. However, they still and somewhat inconsistently admonish that "it may be hazardous to infer that existing discrepancies between models and data cloud interpretations of future anthropogenic greenhouse gas projections."

313 Mann, Bradley, & Hughes, 1998; 1999.

314 BBC Anon., 2004.

315 IPCC, 2001a:3.

316 IPCC, 2001a:3.

317 Parker & Horton, 2005.

318 McIntyre & McKitrick (2005a) showed that this would happen with red noise data series; in a long exchange, the discussion was not on *whether* Mann's process had a tendency-toward-hockey-stick but how much so (Huybers, 2005; McIntyre & McKitrick, 2005b; 2005c; von Storch & Zorita, 2005).

319 von Storch, Zorita et al., 2004, and corroborated in D'Arrigo, Wilson, & Jacoby, 2006; Esper et al., 2005.

320 See e.g. Crok, 2005. NRC (2006) only confirmed with high confidence that present-day temperatures are higher than during any time in the past

400 years, but that less confidence could be placed in the reconstructions for 900–1600.

321 See e.g. Osborn & Briffa (2006), showing how temperatures are now going up everywhere in concert.

322 Moberg, Sonechkin, Holmgren, Datsenko, & Karlen (2005) are also the only ones to accurately track the only measured temperature, the borehole temperature from Pollack, Huang, & Shen (1998), a problem with tree rings only, as pointed out by Harris & Chapman (2005).

323 Moberg et al., 2005; and Hadley data from Brohan, Kennedy, Harris, Tett, & Jones, 2006; CRU, 2006b.

324 Hughes & Diaz, 1994.

325 Dillin, 2000; the following from EB, 2006c.

326 EB, 2006c.

327 EB, 2006c.

328 J. A. Matthews & Briffa, 2005; Paul Reiter, 2000.

329 Reiter, 2000.

330 Burroughs, 1997:109.

331 Reiter, 2000.

332 Le Roy Ladurie, 1972:68; population around 1700 estimated at 21 million, http://en.wikipedia.org/wiki/Demographics_of_France, accessed on 27–12–06.

333 Reiter, 2000.

334 Gore & Melcher Media, 2006:42–59; F. Pearce, 2005b.

335 Joerin, Stocker, & Schluchter, 2006.

336 While not entirely disappearing more than twice, they are labeled Bjørnbren I to VI (J. A. Matthews et al., 2005).

337 IPCC, 2007b:box 6.3.

338 Oerlemans, 2000.

339 EB, 2006d.

340 J. A. Matthews et al., 2005:31; notice this is only schematic.

341 Oerlemans, 2005.

342 Kaser, Hardy, Molg, Bradley, & Hyera, 2004.

343 Kaser et al., 2004:330.

344 Kaser et al., 2004:331.

345 Kaser et al., 2004.

346 Cullen et al., 2006.

347 Greenpeace, 2001. *Rolling Stones* even displays – without a hint of irony – the picture of Kilimanjaro as its first image of the "planetwide damage caused by global warming" and subtitle the picture from 1970 with "Before the warming: Kilimanjaro, 1970" (Rolling Stones, 2007).

348 Reuters, 2001.

349 Thijssen, 2001.

350 Ijumba, Mosha, & Lindsay, 2002; Richey, 2003; Soini, 2005:316; F. Vavrus, 2002.

351 Barnett, Adam, & Lettenmaier, 2005:306; Gore & Melcher Media, 2006:58.

352 Coudrain, Francou, & Kundzewicz, 2005:930.

353 T. P. Barnett et al., 2005.

354 T. P. Barnett et al., 2005:307.

355 Gore & Melcher Media, 2006:58.

356 28% more in summer (Singh, Arora, & Goel, 2006:1991–2). Notice that this is for glacier-fed rivers, whereas snowfed rivers will see a decrease (Singh & Bengtsson, 2005), and for a basin with both glacier and snow feed "reduction in melt from lower zones is counterbalanced by the increase in melt from upper zones" (Singh & Bengtsson, 2004:2382).

357 Lehmkuhl & Owen, 2005; Ruhland, Phadtare, Pant, Sangode, & Smol, 2006. At the same time there also seems to have been a lower Himalayan snow accumulation since 1840 due to the weakening of the trade winds over the Pacific (Zhao & Moore, 2006).

358 IPCC, 2007c:3.4.1; Schneeberger, Blatter, Abe-Ouchi, & Wild, 2003.

359 By 1700, France's forests had been reduced in size by more than 70% compared to 1000 CE, (UNECE, 1996:19). The US cut down about 30% of its original forest area, most of this happening in the nineteenth century (UNECE, 1996:59).

360 Fowler & Archer, 2006.

361 Fowler & Archer, 2006:4291.

362 EB, 2006a.

363 M. Lee, 2006; an attribute that Gore, however, was too modest to accept (Winfrey, 2006:slide 8).

364 McKibben, 2004.

365 IPCC, 2007b:fig 6.8; Siddall et al., 2003.

366 Woodworth, 2006:793.

367 Leuliette, Nerem, & Mitchum, 2004.

368 Parkinson, 2006:42.

369 IPCC, 2007b:table 5.5.2. Expansion of water seems unlikely to raise sea levels for most people. Economist Richard Tol frequently uses the example of a cup of coffee that does not perceptibly shrink when it cools; then he reminds people that the ocean is deep, and that a 0.1% expansion of a kilometer of water yields 1 metre of sea level rise.

370 Ekman, 1999.

371 Ekman, 1999:217.
372 IPCC, 2007b:fig 5.5.3.
373 Woodworth & Player, 2003.
374 IPCC, 2007b:question 5.1, fig. 1.
375 Oppenheimer, 2003.
376 This is consistent with IPCC, 2007b:ch. 5 and generally in the same
     range as Church & White (2006) and White, Church, & Gregory
     (2005), and compatible with the satellite measurements of Leuliette et al.
     (2004).
377 IPCC, 2007b:question 5.1, fig. 1, adjusted to 29 cm ± 15 cm, 10.6.5;
     Jevrejeva, Grinsted, Moore, & Holgate, 2006a; 2006b.
378 IPCC, 2007b:10.6.5. Notice that in the available data IPCC (2007a) has a
     midpoint of 38.5 cm.
379 IPCC, 2001a:75.
380 1996: 38–55 cm (IPCC & Houghton, 1996:364); 1992 and 1983 EPA from
     Yohe & Neumann (1997:243, 250).
381 Shute et al., 2001.
382 N. Matthews, 2000.
383 Yohe & Neumann, 1997.
384 IPCC, 2001b:396.
385 EDD, 2006a:11.
386 EDD, 2006b.
387 Gore & Melcher Media, 2006:196–209.
388 Gore & Melcher Media, 2006:196.
389 Yet, he also says: "First of all, this is not the worst case. The worst case,
     you don't want to hear! I think I'm right down the middle and in fact, the
     scientific community has validated the science in this film, and, for
     example, the six metre, six to seven metre sea level rise – that would come
     if Greenland broke up and slipped into the sea. It would come if west
     Antarctica, the portion that's propped up against the tops of islands with
     the warmer sea coming underneath it, if it went. If both went, it would be
     12 to 14 metres" (Denton, 2006).
390 IPCC, 2007b:10.6.1.
391 IPCC, 2007b:10.6.3; it is actually 8.8 cm, but the 0.8 seems to get lost
     somewhere in the sums.
392 IPCC, 2007b:10.6.4.
393 IPCC, 2007b:10.6.4.
394 IPCC, 2007b:fig. 10.6.1.
395 IPCC, 2007b:table 4.1.1.
396 IPCC, 2007b:table 4.1.1.

397 Huybrechts & de Wolde, 1999.

398 Johannessen, Khvorostovsky, Miles, & Bobylev, 2005; Zwally et al., 2005.

399 Cazenave, 2006; J. L. Chen, Wilson, & Tapley, 2006; Luthcke et al., 2006; Murray, 2006; Velicogna & Wahr, 2006.

400 Murray, 2006.

401 Velicogna & Wahr, 2006:330.

402 Howat, Joughin, & Scambos, 2007; Kerr, 2007.

403 Shepherd & Wingham (2007) estimate Greenland losing 100 Gt/year or 0.28 mm/year.

404 0.7 mm per year in a thousand years is 7 m.

405 Ridley, Huybrechts, Gregory, & Lowe, 2005.

406 Oerlemans et al., 2005:235.

407 New Scientist anon., 2006.

408 Gore, 2006c.

409 J. E. Hansen, 2006.

410 J. E. Hansen, 2006.

411 J. E. Hansen (2005:270) referencing Parizek & Alley (2004) for a doubling of CO_2. Apparently, Hansen has read it wrong, since it is actually an *additional* 0.6–6.6 cm (Parizek & Alley, 2004:1024).

412 J. E. Hansen, 2005:278.

413 Gregory & Huybrechts, 2006:1721.

414 IPCC (2007b:10.6.4.3) saying 0.2 m, using Parizek & Alley (2004:1024), who only give 21 cm at eight times the pre-industrial CO_2 level, or two to four times higher than any of the IPCC scenarios by 2100. See also Gregory & Huybrechts, 2006:1727.

415 Assuming that it starts out at the current level, almost 0, it would have to reach 140 mm/year to make an average of 70 mm/year over the century (i.e. 7 m).

416 IPCC estimates that in 2100 Greenland will contribute 0.7 mm/year (IPCC, 2007b:10.6.4.3).

417 IPCC (2007b:10.7.4.3), using Gregory & Huybrechts (2006) and Huybrechts & de Wolde (1999).

418 Chakravorty, Roumasset, & Tse, 1997; Lomborg, 2001:284ff. If it is not maintained, it seems likely that the ice sheet could regrow as found in a higher-resolution model: "This indicates that following a complete melting, the Greenland ice-sheet could regrow, provided that the greenhouse gas concentrations returned to their present day values" (Lunt, de Noblet-Ducoudre, & Charbit, 2004:693), cf. IPCC, 2007b:10.7.4.3.

419 Ridley assumes 1,160 ppm (2005:3413), compare to 549–970 ppm in 2100 (IPCC, 2001a:807). The maximal sea level rise from Greenland is estimated

at 5 mm/year for the first 300 years, then declining (IPCC, 2007b:10.7.4.3; Ridley et al., 2005:3421).

420 Chylek, Box, & Lesins, 2004.

421 Chylek, Dubey, & Lesins, 2006.

422 Vinther et al., 2006b.

423 Vinther, Andersen, Jones, Briffa, & Cappelen, 2006a; 2006b, with a 13–year running mean, 0 at average for twentieth century.

424 Zachos et al., 2001b:688.

425 Parkinson, 2006:35.

426 J. B. Anderson, Shipp, Lowe, Wellner, & Mosola (2002), Bindschadler (2006) and Huybrechts & de Wolde (1999:2172) estimate Antartica contributing almost 4 cm/century to sea level in stable mode.

427 4% from Bindschadler (2006:1584).

428 Doran et al., 2002; Turner, Colwell et al., 2005). Schneider et al. (2006) estimate that the Antarctic temperatures across the continent have increased about 0.2°C since late 1800s.

429 A decline of 0.4°C till 2006 by regression (GISS, 2006).

430 Marshall, Orr, van Lipzig, & King, 2006; Vaughan et al., 2003:266.

431 W. L. Chapman & Walsh, 2005; very similar to Humlum, Netherlands (Monaghan & Bromwich, 2006).

432 Gore & Melcher Media, 2006:182–3.

433 Right after Gore's discussion of the Larsen-B break-up, he shows us a double-spread picture of high tides washing in over Tulavu (Gore & Melcher Media, 2006:186–7.

434 Pudsey, Murray, Appleby, & Evans, 2006.

435 Pudsey et al., 2006:2375; Vaughan, Marshall, Connolley, King, & Mulvaney, 2001.

436 Greenpeace (2006c) points out that it is nonetheless "a dramatic reminder of the effects of warming in the area."

437 A. J. Cook, Fox, Vaughan, & Ferrigno, 2005; Parkinson, 2006.

438 Turner, Lachlan-Cope, Colwell, & Marshall (2005) show increasing precipitation. Wingham, Shepherd, Muir, & Marshall (2006:1629) and Zwally et al. (2005:512) show large and increasing accumulation on the peninsula. Morris & Mulvaney (2004) show that with conditions over the past 30 years, 2°C temperature increases would mean about 0.012 mm/year *lower* sea level rise. They do, however, expect that future sea level increases from increased ablation could happen, and here it would be necessary to include increased precipitation explicitly.

439 Gregory & Huybrechts, 2006:1721.

440 IPCC, 2007b:4.6.2.2; Gregory & Huybrechts, 2006:1721.

441 Notice how the policy summary of IPCC WG II states all its main findings in its only table, bluntly admitting: "Adaptation to climate change is not included in these estimations" (IPCC, 2007:1174).

442 Gore & Melcher Media, 2006:178–9.

443 Barbraud & Weimerskirch, 2001:184. Gore claims a 70% decrease, but with no reference.

444 Only winter temperatures increased in the 1970s, which should actually have been of benefit to the penguins, because it would make hatching more successful (Barbraud & Weimerskirch, 2001:185). Moreover, winter temperatures declined again in the eighties and onwards, without population increases.

445 Australian Antarctic Division, 2003.

446 Woehler & Croxall (1997:44) note that Kooyman finds colonies in the Ross Sea may be increasing. Kooyman (1993) estimates both Cape Washington and Coulman Island populations at around 20,000 fledgling chicks (or breeding pairs). In 1964 Cape Washington was only registered as having about 2,500–3,800 pairs (Wilson, 1983:5).

447 BirdLife International (2004) and Grzimek (n.d.) even list the population as stable or increasing.

448 Jenouvrier, Barbraud, & Weimerskirch, 2006, with 1.77% increase over the period.

449 Stern, 2006:133.

450 OST, 2004:12–13.

451 OST, 2004:30, 33, estimating GDP for World Markets to £800 billion today and £13,500 in 2080, or a growth rate of 3.8%, compared to a growth rate starting with 4% on additional costs or about £20 million extra per extra year.

452 The same type of over-stating of the problems was made in the 2001 IPCC report, see Lomborg, 2001:289–90.

453 Nakicenovic & IPCC WG III, 2000:169ff.

454 Remarkably, the scenario authors, without any explicit criteria, rank the four scenarios, giving B1 the top-grade "good" whereas A1 only gets a "fair." B2 gets a "medium," and it is quite honestly difficult to say whether that is better or worse than "fair" (Kram et al., 2000:369).

455 Pielke & Landsea, 1998:fig. 3.

456 Waltham, 2002:95.

457 Nicholls (2004) and Nicholls & Tol (2006), using the category smart protection, evolving in phase and with upgraded protection. Nicholls & Tol (2006) unfortunately never show the impact of increase without climate change, so these numbers taken from Nicholls (2004) are

probably too high, since they rely on less smart protection. The A1 scenario used is A1FI, which is a high-CO_2 intensive scenario, so the argument in the text is even stronger. Nicholls & Tol (2006:fig. 5) have switched B1 and B2.

458 Waltham, 2002:97.

459 Nicholls, 2004:71, this being a slightly older model than the basis for the new 2007 IPCC report.

460 Or make a twofold reduction, from 100 million to 50 million.

461 BEA, 2006a; Nicholls, 2004:72, in 2005$.

462 Notice that in all of these models there is no modeling change of behaviour from individuals; but clearly if some places were left unprotected, individuals would move, and thus the actual number of people flooded would be even smaller.

463 Nicholls & Tol, 2006:1088, although low-lying undeveloped coasts in places such as Arctic Russia, Canada and Alaska are expected to be undefended. Notice that the numbers presented are for loss of dryland, whereas up to 18% of global wetlands will be lost.

464 Micronesia (CIA, 2006).

465 Tol, 2004:5.

466 West Potomac Park is 394 acres, http://www.cr.nps.gov/history/online_books/nace/adhi2a.htm, accessed 17–12–06 (Nicholls & Tol, 2006:1086).

467 Tulavu (CIA, 2006). The White House Rose Garden is 18 acres, http://www.sites.si.edu/exhibitions/exhibits/white_house/main.htm, accessed 17–12–06.

468 Maldives (CIA, 2006).

469 "A cursory comparison of protection costs and the costs of dryland loss indicates why protection levels are so high" (Tol, 2004).

470 Blair, 2004a.

471 Greenpeace, 2006c.

472 Adapted to 29 cm from Wigley (1998).

473 NRDC, 2006.

474 FOE, 2006.

475 Greenpeace, 2006a. Greenpeace (2006b) tells us "as climate change gathers pace, devastation caused by extreme weather is becoming more common."

476 FOE, 2000.

477 Chea, 2006.

478 Pope, 2005.

479 Kennedy, 2005.

480 Gelbspan, 2005.

481 Spiegel, 2005; Trittin, 2005.

482 "Es gibt es nur eine Konsequenz daraus: Treibhausgase müssen radikal reduziert werden."

483 WMO-IWTC, 2006a; 2006b; WMO, 2006. This was concluded in December 2006, whereas the material deadline for IPCC is early/earlier 2006.

484 WMO-IWTC, 2006b.

485 Gore & Melcher Media, 2006:92.

486 Power as the integral of the cube of the maximum winds over time (Emanuel, 2005a).

487 Webster, Holland, Curry, & Chang, 2005.

488 Schmid, 2005.

489 Landsea, Harper, Hoarau, & Knaff, 2006. No satellites before 1970 (IPCC, 2007b:3.8.3).

490 Curry, Webster, & Holland, 2006; Karl, Nicholls, & Gregory, 1997.

491 Curry et al., 2006.

492 Blake, Rappaport, Jarrell, & Landsea, 2005; Klotzbach & Gray, 2006.

493 Landsea, 2005; see also reply (Emanuel, 2005b).

494 WMO-IWTC, 2006a.

495 WMO-IWTC, 2006b.

496 Webster et al.'s (2005) own data globally, translated into annual numbers, and Webster, Curry, Liu, & Holland's (2006) own data from Chan (2006). Webster et al. have a preference for relative numbers, but here I present the absolute numbers, which are arguably more relevant since that is what hit people.

497 Chan, 2006. The time series goes back to 1945, but Webster et al. (2006) accept focusing on 1960–2004.

498 Landsea et al., 2006; Webster et al., 2006.

499 Curry et al., 2006:1032: "We anticipate that it may take a decade for the observations to clarify the situation as to whether the hypothesis has predictive ability. In short, time will tell."

500 WMO–IWTC, 2006b.

501 Gore & Melcher Media, 2006:202.

502 Gore, 2006a.

503 6.465 billion in 2005 versus 2.519 billion in 1950 (UNPD, 2006a:5). Average income of $9,233 in 2005 versus $2,803 in 1950 (Worldwatch Institute, 2006:53). With increasing income, more wealth can be accumulated, making wealth grow faster than income, even as people move to coastal areas (see Pielke, 1999; Swiss Re, 1999:8).

504 Personal communication from Angelika Wirtz, Munich Re, and http://www.webcitation.org/5PhPrdxCJ.

505 Pielke & Landsea, 1998.

506 Pielke et al., 2007.

507 NOAA, 2006c.

508 NOAA, 2006c.

509 Notice that both the Great Miami and the Galveston hurricanes caused many deaths – the Galveston actually being the deadliest in US history, with 8,000 dead. Had they hit today, obviously better warning systems would have evacuated much of the city and avoided many of the deaths, but the material damage would have been equally severe.

510 Pielke & Landsea, 1998; Pielke, 2006b; Pielke et al., 2007, using PL normalization.

511 Pielke et al., 2007.

512 Pielke et al., 2007. Notice the half-decade 1900–5 is scaled up to ten years.

513 Association of British Insurers, 2005. They make a number of other statements about the effectiveness of climate change policies, but do not compare them to the effects of socio-economic factors, as we will look at below.

514 Insurance Journal, 2006b.

515 UNEP, 2006:14.

516 Unfortunately, he was not alone. A spokesperson from UNEP misrepresented their own report and said about hurricane damages, "such losses linked to global warming were seen doubling every 12 years" (Wallis, 2006). This was what AP reported. Likewise, a representative from one of the world's largest reinsurance companies, Munich Re, restated a link between the twelve-year past trends and future global warming (Insurance Journal, 2006a).

517 Pielke, 2005; Pielke, Klein, & Sarewitz, 2000; an average of the three very similar climate increases and the A1 scenario social increase.

518 With Kyoto we would see 6% lower temperatures in 2050 (Figure 7), leading to 0.6 percentage points less increase than the 10% envisioned by R. A. Pielke (2005; Pielke et al. 2000).

519 The following examples are mainly from Pielke et al. (2000).

520 E. Mills & Lecomte, 2006:16.

521 Stern, 2006:420.

522 McCallum & Heming, 2006.

523 Congleton, 2006; Travis, 2005.

524 McCallum & Heming, 2006:2113.

525 Tol, 2002a:49.

526 Sarewitz & Pielke, 2005.

527 Emanuel et al., 2006.

528 Sarewitz & Pielke, 2005.

529 J. K. Mitchell, 2003.

530 For a link between warming and flooding see Petrow, Thieken, Kreibich, Bahlburg, & Merz (2006); for the call to commit to Kyoto see "Blair, Chirac and German Chancellor Gerhard Schroeder urged final ratification of the Kyoto Protocol on climate change, recalling floods that hit central Europe last month" (Reuters, 2002).

531 Reuters, 2002; Xinhuanet, 2002.

532 Groisman et al., 2005; IPCC, 2007b:10.3.2.3, 10.3.6.1.

533 Milly, Wetherald, Dunne, & Delworth, 2002.

534 IPCC, 2007b:Q9.1. See also T. Barnett et al. (2005) for general attribution of precipitation; Bronstert (2003) and Huntington (2006) for weak or no connection between floods and climate.

535 Kundzewicz et al. (2005), contradicting the much smaller data set from Milly et al. (2002).

536 Svensson, Kundzewicz, & Maurer, 2005.

537 Small, Islam, & Vogel (2006), also confirming Lins & Slack (1999; 2005) and USGS (2005), though Groisman, Knight, & Karl (2001) find a signal also in high streamflow.

538 Mudelsee, Borngen, Tetzlaff, & Grunewald, 2003.

539 Thorndycraft, Barriendos, Benito, Rico, & Casas, 2006.

540 Demaree, 2006.

541 Demaree, 2006:895–96; Pfister, Weingartner, & Luterbacher, 2006.

542 Mudelsee, Deutsch, Borngen, & Tetzlaff, 2006.

543 Yiou, Ribereau, Naveau, Nogaj, & Brazdil, 2006.

544 J. K. Mitchell, 2003.

545 J. K. Mitchell, 2003.

546 Brazdil, Kundzewicz, & Benito, 2006; J. K. Mitchell, 2003.

547 Pielke, 1999:419ff.

548 Pinter, 2005.

549 Pielke, 1999:416.

550 GAO, 1995:37.

551 Larson, 1994.

552 Pinter & Heine, 2005.

553 Pinter, van der Ploeg, Schweigert, & Hoefer, 2006:159.

554 BEA, 2006a; 2006b; Downton, Miller, & Pielke, 2005a; 2005b; Pielke & Downton, 2000. Exponential trend lines, $y = 0.4871\exp(0.0308(x-1928))$ and $y = 172.01\exp(-0.0046(x-1928))$.

555 It is definitely an inexact way to do so, and if relatively more people are settling in floodplains it will also be a conservative measure. Yet, it is the best estimate we currently have.

556　E. Evans, Ashley, Hall, Penning-Rowsell, Saul et al., 2004:225.

557　Assuming linearity in temperatures, with A1FI temperature in 2100 at 4.49°C, B1 at 1.98°C, and Kyoto reduction at 7% of A1FI temperatures in 2100 (IPCC, 2001a:824; Wigley, 1998).

558　Pinter, 2005.

559　Pinter, 2005.

560　E.g. "green rivers" that could be agricultural fields or nature and leisure areas (DGPWWM, 2001:45).

561　E. Evans, Ashley, Hall, Penning-Rowsell, Sayers et al., 2004:217–18.

562　Using the GDP estimates for the world scenario and the relative efficiencies explained above (E. Evans, Ashley, Hall, Penning-Rowsell, Saul et al., 2004:225; E. Evans, Ashley, Hall, Penning-Rowsell, Sayers et al., 2004:217–18).

563　Changnon, 2003:286.

564　Gore & Melcher Media (2006:86–7), correct as pointed out in NOAA (2004).

565　Analysis of NOAA (2006e). There is only a record of F0, whereas even F1 is greater in 1973 and all F2 and upwards are declining as explained in the main text.

566　NOAA, n.d.

567　Only 19 of 5,435 people have died in F0 tornadoes (NOAA, 2006e).

568　AP, 2006b; Perkins, 2002; Verbout, Brooks, Leslie, & Schultz, 2006.

569　AP, 2006b.

570　NOAA, 2006b.

571　NOAA, 2006d.

572　NOAA, 2006d.

573　NOAA, 2006d, http://www.spc.noaa.gov/climo/torn/monthlytornstats.html.

574　NOAA, 2006e, for deaths; Verbout et al., 2006:89, on trend.

575　NOAA, 2006e.

576　Brooks & Doswell, 2001; Changnon, 2003:281.

577　Changnon, 2003:284.

578　Changnon, 2003:283.

579　Curran, Holle, & Lopez, 2000.

580　Adekoya & Nolte, 2005.

581　Elsom, 2001.

582　Holle, Lopez, & Navarro, 2005.

583　Williams, 2005.

584　NOAA, 2006a; USCB, 2006c; 2006d, with 11-year smoothing. Notice the numbers from NOAA only go to 2004 but would obviously change for hurricanes with Katrina in 2005.

585 Including the North Atlantic Current (EB, 2006b; Seager, 2006). In the text I'll just use the "Gulf Stream" for all of these currents. I will also use it as a short and popular understanding for the so-called thermohaline circulation, because it is primarily wind-driven, as in the Gulf Stream (Wunsch, 2002). "Thus the Gulf Stream, and hence the wind, rather than being minor features of oceanic climate are best regarded as the primary elements" (Wunsch, 2006).

586 Gore & Melcher Media, 2006:151.

587 Gore & Melcher Media, 2006:149 flap.

588 Gore & Melcher Media, 2006:150 flap.

589 Gore, 2006b:48 min.

590 Barber et al., 1999; Meissner & Clark, 2006.

591 Barber et al., 1999:347; Wiersma & Renssen, 2006.

592 =0.000035 km times 361,000,000 km^2 of ocean surface per hundred years.

593 Gore & Melcher Media, 2006:150 flap.

594 Schiermeier, 2006:258.

595 Jungclaus, Haak, Esch, Roeckner, & Marotzke, 2006.

596 Jungclaus et al., 2006.

597 F. Pearce, 2006a:185.

598 Schiermeier, 2006:258.

599 Calvin, 1998:47.

600 Stipp, 2004; Townsend & Harris, 2004.

601 Schwartz & Randall, 2003.

602 Schwartz & Randall, 2003:9.

603 Schwartz & Randall, 2003:11.

604 Schwartz & Randall, 2003:19.

605 Schwartz & Randall, 2003:15.

606 The study never actually makes this conclusion, though they several times hint at it, but both *Fortune* and especially the *Observer* say so explicitly.

607 The movie's website linked to news reports from February 2004 about "a secret report prepared by the Pentagon" that warned climate change would "lead to global catastrophe costing millions of lives." Moreover, academic papers have used the "Day after tomorrow" reference, see e.g. B. Hansen, Osterhus, Quadfasel, & Turrell, 2004.

608 Wiersma & Renssen, 2006:72.

609 Barber et al., 1999; Wiersma & Renssen, 2006:73.

610 Rough calculation from 4°C digitized global temperature map from NCEP (2006), with Europe to 40°E at 6.94°C and with Siberia defined from 60°E and north of 50°N with –5.86°C. A similar estimate for Siberia comes from

FAO (2001:ch. 27) with western Siberia −4°C, south Siberia −0.5°C, Siberian plateau −12°C and central Siberia −13.5°C, or a simple average of −7.5°C.

611 Stouffer et al. (2006:1367) use a hosing with 0.1 Sv, with 6 mm/yr from Greenland equivalent to 0.07 Sv.

612 Stouffer et al., 2006:1375.

613 R. A. Wood, Vellinga, & Thorpe, 2003:1963.

614 Stouffer et al., 2006:1382-3.

615 Notice Al Gore talks about annual temperatures and the difference between Madrid and New York, but here the difference is less than 2°C annually, and it is only during the winter that there is a 5.6°C difference (temperatures retrieved from http://data.giss.nasa.gov/gistemp/station_data/ and averaged from 1960–1991 if possible). It is in places higher up, like Copenhagen in Denmark and at comparable longitude in Ontario at Fort Albany, that the difference in temperature in the wintertime is 20°C. Compare this to Prince Rupert in British Columbia, which has temperatures almost comparable with Copenhagen.

616 The following is from Seager (2006; Seager et al., 2002), also acknowledged by R. A. Wood et al. (2003).

617 Wunsch, 2004.

618 Schellnhuber, Cramer, Nakicenovic, Wigley, & Yohe, 2006 and http://www.stabilisation2005.com.

619 Schlesinger et al., 2006. Schiermeier (2006:258) says "Michael Schlesinger … views the possibility of a thermohaline circulation shutdown as more likely and more worrying than many of his peers."

620 Stommel, 1961.

621 Wunsch, 2005.

622 Caporali et al., 2004; Gupta, Hastak, Ahmad, Lewin, & Mukhtar, 2001; Mestas & Hughes, 2004.

623 FDA, 2005: "One weak and limited study does not show that drinking green tea reduces the risk of prostate cancer, but another weak and limited study suggests that drinking green tea may reduce this risk. Based on these studies, FDA concludes that it is highly unlikely that green tea reduces the risk of prostate cancer."

624 It is slightly more complicated than that, but unfortunately not much, and this statement explains the thrust of the model.

625 They tell us six times how it is only ¢5 for $10 tax, but only once and cryptically tell us that "this carbon tax rises through time at the then prevailing interest rate that is determined by the model." You would imagine $6/gallon tax would be an interesting piece of information. The

$36 trillion is a replication of their DICE dynamic, the net economic loss after subtracting $5 trillion of environmental benefits, in 2005$.

626 Brown, 2005.
627 Wood, Collins, Gregory, Harris, & Vellinga, 2006.
628 Wood et al., 2006:51.
629 See e.g. Link & Tol, 2004.
630 Bryden, Longworth, & Cunningham, 2005; Kerr, 2005.
631 Bryden et al., 2005:657.
632 Owen, 2005.
633 Connor, 2005; Henderson, 2005; D. Smith, 2005.
634 F. Pearce, 2005c.
635 F. Pearce, 2005a; Schiermeier, 2006:259.
636 Schiermeier, 2006:258.
637 Kerr, 2006.
638 Merali, 2006.
639 Based on a Google search for "RAPID array observations Birmingham," "Rapid Climate Change Conference Birmingham" and "RAPID bryden Birmingham."
640 Randerson, 2006.
641 Visbeck, 2006.
642 It is perhaps curious that *Nature* didn't tell their readers that the Gulf Stream facts may be different, but they did report the *Guardian* story in passing – without Visbeck's important corrections (Hopkin, 2006.
643 Battersby, 2006.
644 IPCC, 2007b:question 10.2.
645 IPCC, 2007b:question 10.2.
646 McMichael et al., 2003; WHO, WMO, & UNEP, 2003.
647 Khaleque, 2006; LibDem, 2006:6; Tindale, 2005.
648 Plumb, 2003.
649 Campbell-Lendrum, Corvalán, & Prüss–Ustün, 2003.
650 Patz et al., 2005; it has almost exactly same numbers in DALYs and also shows the break-out in mortality.
651 "Climate change attributable deaths were calculated as the change in proportion of temperature-attributable deaths (i.e. heat-attributable deaths plus cold-attributable deaths) for each climate scenario compared to the baseline climate" (Campbell-Lendrum et al., 2003:142). They only have old and very limited surveys for these results – for Europe they use Kunst, Looman, & Mackenbach (1993) which only covers the Netherlands, when the European total survey is available from Keatinge et al. (2000).

652 "Relative risks for 2000 have been estimated as described above, and applied to the disease burden estimates for that year, with the exception of the effects of extreme temperatures on cardiovascular disease, for the reasons described above" (Campbell-Lendrum et al., 2003:152). However, there are no "reasons described above" anywhere.

653 Patz et al., 2005:312.

654 CRU (2006a) shows 0.361°C change from 1961–90 average in 2000; WHO et al. (2003:7) estimate 0.4°C. The estimate comes from a linear extrapolation from Bosello et al. (2006), who estimate increases of 1.03°C from today's temperature. Taking the proportional (0.35=0.361/1.03) cold and heat deaths gives the numbers here indicated. It also gives an estimate of all other illness at 193,000, which compares fairly well with WHO's 150,000.

655 Patz et al., 2005:312.

656 Estimated with assumption of local linearity in temperature response from Bosello et al. (2006).

657 Gore, 2006b:53 min.

658 Chastel, 2004; Hui, 2006.

659 Gore, 2006b:53 min.

660 Ducati, Ruffino-Netto, Basso, & Santos, 2006; R. A. Weiss & McMichael, 2004.

661 Ducati et al., 2006; Olle-Goig, 2006.

662 Olle-Goig, 2006.

663 WHO, 2004a:107. And, of course, she could have done with a better father.

664 Hui, 2006:909.

665 Hui, 2006.

666 Gore, 2006b:53 min.

667 R. A. Weiss & McMichael, 2004:S74.

668 Derraik, 2004; Gratz, Steffen, & Cocksedge, 2000.

669 300–500 million in WHO & UNICEF (2005:xvii), 515 million in Snow, Guerra, Noor, Myint, & Hay (2005); compare to almost 2 billion febrile episodes resembling malaria each year (Breman, 2001).

670 CDC, 2006, http://en.wikipedia.org/wiki/Progress_of_the_West_Nile_virus_in_the_United_States accessed 29–12–06 (NSC, 1999:16).

671 DiCaprio, 2000 (removed an extra "for example" that comes from the direct transcription).

672 Blair, 2006. Notice how this was also part of the justification for climate action from Blair's chief adviser, David King (2004).

673 Annan, 2006.

674 Shute et al., 2001.

675 CMO, 2002:33.

676 Kington, 2007.

677 Snow & Omumbo, 2006:195.

678 Breman, 2001.

679 89% (WHO & UNICEF, 2005:19), 90% (WHO & UNICEF, 2003:17).

680 Snow & Omumbo, 2006:197.

681 P. Martens et al., 1999; van Lieshout, Kovats, Livermore, & Martens, 2004), behind the claims of King (2004).

682 Arnell et al. (2002:439) interpolated from 1990 and 2025; world population at 6.6 billion (USCB, 2007).

683 Reiter et al., 2004.

684 CDC, 2006; Reiter, 2000; Swellengrebel, 1950.

685 Kuhn, Campbell-Lendrum, Armstrong, & Davies, 2003; Reiter, 2000. See also map of spread in 1900 in Hay, Guerra, Tatem, Noor, & Snow (2004).

686 Sallares, 2006.

687 Reiter, 2000:3.

688 Dobson, 1980.

689 Reiter (2000:4) estimates a 95 death rate, compared to non-marsh areas at 44 and to under-five mortality for developing world in 2005 at 83 (UNICEF, 2006:105).

690 Conroy, 1982:42.

691 Conroy, 1982:41.

692 Conroy, 1982:52; Reiter, 2005.

693 Watson, 1939:490.

694 Mégroz, 1937:353.

695 Sokolova & Snow, 2002.

696 Hulden, Hulden, & Heliovaara, 2005.

697 Romi, Sabatinelli, & Majori, 2001:915.

698 Reiter, 2000:6.

699 Kaufman & Ruveda, 2005.

700 Kuhn et al., 2003.

701 Italy offered low-priced quinine after 1900 (H. Evans, 1989).

702 E.g. in Italy (Romi et al., 2001).

703 R. T. Boyd, 1975; CDC, 2004; Reiter, 2000:9.

704 Thompson, 1969:199.

705 Thompson, 1969:199.

706 Madden, 1945:2.

707 USCB, 1999:875; Mégroz, 1937:353.

708 CDC, 2004.

709 CDC, 1999:106; Konradsen, van der Hoek, Amerasinghe, Mutero, & Boelee, 2004.

710 Brierly, 1944.

711 Kington, 2007; Romi et al., 2001.

712 Longstreth, 1999.

713 Guerra, Snow, & Hay, 2006; Hay et al., 2004; Snow et al., 2005.

714 Beard, 2006; Rosenberg, 2004; Schapira, 2006; Walker, 2000.

715 Jamison et al., 2006:3; Snow & Omumbo, 2006:205.

716 Snow & Omumbo, 2006:208.

717 Epstein, 2000; Epstein et al., 1998; Patz et al., 2005.

718 Hay, Cox et al., 2002; Hay, Rogers et al., 2002; Hay et al., 2002; Pascual, Ahumada, Chaves, Rodo, & Bouma, 2006; Patz et al., 2002; Reiter et al., 2004; Shanks, Hay, Stern, Biomndo, & Snow, 2002. Personally, I found this statement from advocates of a warming link to malaria very telling: "The absence of a historical climate signal allows no inference to be drawn about the impact of future climate change on malaria in the region" (Patz et al., 2002). So data should not tell us something about the future?

719 Snow & Omumbo, 2006:208.

720 Purcell, 2006; Shanks, 2006.

721 Arnell et al., 2002; P. Martens et al., 1999; van Lieshout et al., 2004. Arnell finds 289.5 m as average between unmitigated scenarios. We here use Arnell, since he is the only one to publish population at risk without climate, but he stays within the same framework and range of outcomes as the other referred articles.

722 Van Lieshout et al., 2004:91: "This assessment will describe potential populations at risk based on the *current* level of adaptation to malaria."

723 Worldbank, 2006:289.

724 Van Lieshout et al., 2004:97.

725 Hay, Guerra, Tatem, Atkinson, & Snow, 2005; Utzinger & Keiser, 2006:530; van Lieshout et al., 2004:96–7.

726 Rogers & Randolph, 2000.

727 Arnell et al., 2002:439.

728 289.5 m/9109.5 m.

729 289.5 m/9109.5 m * 7% (Wigley, 1998:2287).

730 Speaking of 550 ppm stabilization, (Arnell et al., 2002:440).

731 A. Mills & Shillcutt, 2004:84–5.

732 Calculated from 500 million actual annual malaria cases in 2000 and proportional from there with Arnell et al. (2002:439).

733 This is also evident in Tol, Ebie, & Yohe, forthcoming.

734 Bosello et al., 2006.

735 Based on Arnell et al. (2002:439).

736 Bosello et al., 2006:582.

737 WHO & UNICEF, 2003:20.

738 WHO & UNICEF, 2003:28.

739 WHO & UNICEF, 2003:28, 35.

740 WHO & UNICEF, 2003:35.

741 All in 2005$ (BEA, 2006a; Department of Commerce, 1982:54; 2006:D-71).

742 Worldbank, 2006:289.

743 Tol & Dowlatabadi, 2001.

744 Tol & Dowlatabadi (2001:178–9), expecting that a full Kyoto would be equivalent to a 3% annual reduction. Notice that they only model climate related mortality, whereas including non-climate related mortality – which would also respond to increased health care spending – would strongly tilt the balance in favour of not reducing greenhouse gasses (p. 180).

745 Hanley, 2006b.

746 Hanley, 2006a.

747 Gore & Melcher Media, 2006:173.

748 Reiter, 2007.

749 Reiter, 2007.

750 Njagi & Were, 2004:171.

751 Snow, Ikoku, Omumbo, & Ouma, 1999:6.2.

752 Snow et al., 1999:6.2.

753 Hay et al., 2005:88. In personal communication, Robert Snow points out that there are few or no strong data after the colonial administration. There is still malaria in Nairobi today, but it is mostly due to travel outside Nairobi.

754 Similar to the findings of Shanks, Hay, Omumbo, & Snow (2005).

755 UNDESA, 2006:5.

756 McCarthy, 2005; Pullélla, 2005.

757 Ehrlich, 1968:xi.

758 Malthus, 1798.

759 Meadows, Meadows, Randers, & Behrens, 1972.

760 Population has increased from 3 billion to 6.3 billion from 1961 to 2003, whereas net food production increased 2.7 times. For the developing world, population increased 2.4 times and net food production increased 4.1 times. (FAO, 2007).

761 IMF, 2007; Lomborg, 2001:62; USCPI, 2007.

762 G. Fischer et al., 2005; G. Fischer, Shah, & van Velthuizen, 2002; G. Fischer, Velthuizen, Shah, & Nachtergaele, 2002; Parry, Rosenzweig, & Livermore, 2005; Parry, Rosenzweig, Iglesias, Livermore, & Fischer, 2004;

Rosenzweig & Parry, 1994. As G. Fischer et al. (2005) give the only recent attempt that uses a variety of climate models, this will be the central one used here.

763 For A1 and increase from 1800 Mt to 3900 Mt, Parry et al. (2004:64).

764 G. Fischer et al., 2005:2080.

765 FAO, 2006:8; 2007.

766 Grigg (1993:50) gives estimates for 1949–79. Undernourished count as individuals with less than 20% above physical minimum (1.2 BMR); these have been adjusted to the FAO definition of 55% above physical minimum (1.55 BMR). (FAO, 2006:14; G. Fischer, Shah, Tubiello, & van Velhuizen, 2005:2080; G. Fischer, Shah, & Velthuizen, 2002:112–13; Nakicenovic & IPCC WG III, 2000; WFS, 1996:1:table 3.) Note that the climate models give different absolute results than FAO, so here only the relative results for A1 in 2080 are represented.

767 This is the HadCM3 model with a high climate sensitivity (G. Fischer et al., 2005:2071) and the A1FI which has the absolutely highest CO_2 concentration (G. Fischer, Shah, & van Velthuizen, 2002:109).

768 A2 and NCAR (G. Fischer, Shah, & van Velthuizen, 2002:109).

769 FAO, 2006:16.

770 It is important to point out that we expect lower growth rates in the future, but that is because of lower demand, not because of inherent production limits, as the A2 scenario clearly shows, enabling total cereal production of 4800 Mt (Parry et al., 2004:64).

771 G. Fischer, Shah, & van Velthuizen, 2002:109.

772 Max $3.6 trillion of $380 trillion (G. Fischer, Shah, & van Velthuizen, 2002:108; Nakicenovic & IPCC WG III, 2000).

773 In this chapter, it is assumed that the full CO_2 effects are captured. Long, Ainsworth, Leakey, Nosberger, & Ort (2006) raised doubts about this, but Tubiello et al. (in press) show that FACE studies are in line with previous studies. IPCC (2007c:5.4.1.1) also concludes "our assessment is that main crop simulation models, such as CERES, Cropsys, EPIC, SoyGrow, and main pasture models CENTURY and EPIC, are in line with recent findings – in fact a bit lower – by assuming crop yield increases of about 8–17%."

774 Parry et al., 2004:64.

775 G. Fischer, Shah, & van Velthuizen, 2002:96.

776 LCDs in A1 (G. Fischer, Shah, & van Velthuizen, 2002:98).

777 G. Fischer et al., 2005:2079.

778 G. Fischer, Shah, & van Velthuizen, 2002:112.

779 M. L. Parry et al., 2004:66.

780 M. L. Parry et al. (2004:62) and see especially the A2 and B2 versus A2s and B2s in G. Fischer, Shah, & van Velthuizen (2002:100). "The significance of any climate-change impact on the number of undernourished depends entirely on the level of economic development assumed in the SRES scenarios" (G. Fischer, Shah, & van Velthuizen, 2002:112).

781 Parry, 2004.

782 Hunger is only 26% about increased food availability but much about women's education, status and health (Sanchez, Swaminathan, Dobie, & Yuksel, 2005:22–3).

783 Left out are "wealthy societies of scenario A1" (G. Fischer, Shah, & van Velthuizen, 2002:112–13).

784 28 m * 7% (Wigley, 1998:2287).

785 Sanchez et al., 2005:189.

786 UN Millennium Project (2005:252) estimates the total extra cost of meeting the Millennium Development Goals at 0.44–0.54% of OECD GDP for 2005–15; 0.5% of OECD GDP is $165 billion (OECD, 2005:13). Sanchez et al. (2005:18) estimate the total cost of hunger reduction to be 5–8% of the total MDG cost, which is $8.25–13.2 billion. The 5–8% seems to be fairly well reflected in the cost structure given by UN Millennium Project (2005:244). The 229 million are the *extra* people saved through the extra effort over the period, the difference between expected number of hungry in 2015 without the extra effort is 749 million, and with the MDG extra spending 520 million (UN Millennium Project, 2005:259).

787 1/8 of 2 million (111,111) phased in for 2050–80 and constant till 2100, averaged over the entire century.

788 Estimating the 229 million phased in for 2005–15, constant thereafter (this is a *very* conservative estimate, since the economic growth and human wellbeing involved in avoiding 229 million people going hungry will probably quickly make these gains self-sustaining), meaning 206 million over the century: 39,000/206m = 5,282.

789 Simms, Magrath, & Reid, 2004:4.

790 Gore & Melcher Media, 2006:117.

791 Quotes from his own website (Monbiot, 2006b).

792 UNEP, 2000:362.

793 See the analysis by Lomborg (2001:149–58).

794 The total amount of precipitation on land is about 113,000 km³, and taking into account an evaporation of 72,000 km³ we are left with a net fresh water influx of 41,000 km³ each year, or the equivalent of 30 cm of water across the entire land mass. Since part of this water falls in rather remote

areas, such as the basins of the Amazon, the Congo, and the remote North American and Eurasian rivers, a more reasonable, geographically accessible estimate of water is 32,900 km^3. Moreover, a large part of this water comes within short periods of time. In Asia, typically 80% of the runoff occurs between May and October, and globally the flood runoff is estimated at about three-quarters of the total runoff. This leaves about 9,000 km^3 to be captured. Dams capture an additional 3,500 km^3 from floods, bringing the total accessible runoff to 12,500 km^3 (Postel, Daily, & Ehrlich, 1996).

795 Shiklomanov, 2000:24; World Water Council, 2000:26; same numbers as Simonovic (2002).

796 Lomborg, 2001:151.

797 WRI, 2005:208.

798 Craig et al., 1996:387.

799 Falkenmark & Widstrand, 1992:14.

800 Al-Rashed & Sherif, 2000.

801 WRI, 2005:209.

802 Sirajul et al., 2007; Oki & Kanae, 2006:1070; UNESCO, 2006:422.

803 Postel, 1998:table 1.

804 Postel, 1999:130.

805 Oron et al., 2001; Worldwatch Institute, 1993.

806 WRI, 1996:303.

807 Postel, 1999:174.

808 Worldwatch Institute, 1993:34.

809 Tsur, Dinar, Doukkali, & Roe, 2004.

810 UNESCO, 2006:45. Also "There is a enough water for everyone. The problem we face today is largely one of governance" (UNESCO, 2006:executive summary 3).

811 World Water Council, 2000:xix.

812 JMP, 2007.

813 Since the definitions and estimates vary, these lines are logistic best-fit lines, based on estimates for 1975–90 (Worldbank, 1994:26), 1970–83 (WHO, 1986), 1980–90 (Gleick, 1998:262, 264), 1990–2000 (Annan, 2000), 1990–2004 (JMP, 2007).

814 Ashton, 2002; Revenga, Brunner, Henninger, Payne, & Kassem, 2000; Serageldin, 1995; Simonovic, 2002; UNEP, 2000.

815 Equivalent to 1,700 m^3/year, 1,000 m^3/year and 500 m^3/year (Wallensteen & Swain, 1997:8).

816 Arnell, 2004.

817 E.g. Cairncross, 2003.

818 Such a shift can actually be economically advantageous, since this will make societies move toward more profitable production in industry and especially service (Barbier, 2004; J. Edwards, Yang, & Al-Hmoud, 2005).

819 Arnell, 2004.

820 1,974 million, based on an interpolation for 2007 between 1995 and 2025 for A1/B1 without climate change (Arnell, 2004:39).

821 1.368 billion people in 1995. Less than 1,000 m³/year (Arnell, 2004:41), averages of all models for A2 and B2. Using the other limits would have displayed similar qualitative characteristics.

822 This is for the A1B scenario (Nohara, Kitoh, Hosaka, & Oki, 2006:1081).

823 Arnell (2004:50) stresses that increases in runoff will generally occur during high-flow seasons, but, with a multiple of models, this is true for the Amazon, Ganges and Mekong, but not for Amu Darya, Columbia, Danube, Euphrates, Lena, Mackenzie, Nile, Ob, Syr Darya, Volga and Yenisei (Nohara et al., 2006:1085–6). Arnell (2004:50, repeated 42) also mentions that "the watersheds that apparently benefit from a reduction in water resources stress are in limited, but populous, parts of the world, and largely confined to east and southern Asia: areas that see an increase in stress are more widely distributed," as if area counts besides the number of humans for human welfare. To me, this argument seems indefensible.

824 Personal communication, data from Arnell (2004).

825 About $10 billion from a range of global studies (Toubkiss, 2006:7); compare to about $100 billion over the period given by Rijsberman (2004:521). The annuity is calculated at a 5% discount rate for $10 billion for 2007–15.

826 As there is not a complete overlap of the different populations, the total number is estimated at about 3 billion (Hutton & Haller, 2004:24).

827 Hutton & Haller, 2004:25.

828 Hutton & Haller, 2004:32. Surprisingly, perhaps, the biggest gain comes from sanitation, not water.

829 Gore & Melcher Media, 2006:119.

830 Dai, Lamb et al., 2004; Giannini, Saravanan, & Chang, 2003. Of course, all that says is that the climate system is causally connected – what we then need is to show that the Indian Ocean heightened sea temperatures are caused by global warming.

831 Hoerling, Hurrell, Eischeid, & Phillips, 2006; Lau, Shen, Kim, & Wang, 2006.

832 Lau et al., 2006:8.

833 Hoerling et al., 2006.

834 Nicholson, 2001.

835 J. M. Russell & Johnson, 2005.

836 IPCC, 2007b:6 summary.

837 Burke, Brown, & Christidis, 2006; Meehl et al., 2006; Wang, 2005.

838 Van der Schrier, Briffa, Jones, & Osborn (2006:2830) about Dai, Trenberth, & Qian (2004).

839 Van der Schrier et al., 2006.

840 Robock, Mu, Vinnikov, Trofimova, & Adamenko, 2005:4.

841 Robock et al., 2000).

842 Li, Robock, & Wild, in press.

843 E.g. Pachauri, Chairman of the IPPC, in Simms et al. (2004:1).

844 F. Pearce, 2006b.

845 F. Pearce, 2006b; Simms et al., 2004:2.

846 Stern, 2006:55; see also Simms et al., 2004:18.

847 Adam & Elliott, 2006; *Sydney Morning Herald*, 2006.

848 Coudouel, Hentschel, & Wodon, 2002; Worldbank, 2000:17; 2006:290. Over 400 socioeconomic sample surveys spanning 100 countries underlie the data (PovcalNet, 2007).

849 The other main concerns being access and availability (Coudouel et al., 2002:30).

850 G. Fischer et al., 2005:2080.

851 A2 "representative of a *worst case* scenario" (G. Fischer et al., 2005:2080).

852 The world poverty line has been assembled for 1950–77 (Berry et al. 1983:341; 1991:73), 1981–2015 (Worldbank, 2004:21; 2005:table 2.5), and data on South Asia and Sub-Saharan Africa for 1981–2001 (Worldbank, 2004:21; 2005:table 2.5), and calculations based on the model from the Stern report (E. Anderson, 2006) and spreadsheets obtained directly from Anderson, using scenario A1 and CIESIN (2002); Datt (1998); Nakicenovic & IPCC WG III (2000). The kink in the graph around 2020–25 is due to India effectively growing out of poor people, temporarily breaking the poverty reduction speed.

853 Worldbank, 2004:17.

854 E. Anderson, 2006:2.

855 Actually 219 million. Choosing the 95th percentile impact – the level of impact below which reality will be in 19 out of 20 times.

856 Based on the model from the Stern report (E. Anderson, 2006) and spreadsheets obtained directly from Anderson, using scenario A1 and CIESIN (2002); Datt (1998); Nakicenovic & IPCC WG III (2000).

857 World Bank has 79% in 2001 and predicts 59% in 2015, predicting a drop of 20% (Worldbank, 2004:22); the A1 scenario has 75% in 2002 and

expects 56% in 2015, predicting a drop of 19%, whereas A2 has 75% in 2002 but 68% in 2015, predicting a drop of only 7%.

858   1.07 million, calculated as the difference in numbers of poor per year, averaged over 100 years.

859   983 million poor averted on average. If we compare the effect of dealing with global warming within A1, it is less than half a million, making the A1 policy more than 2,000 times better.

860   Based on the dynamic discounting from Nordhaus (2006b), and with data from BEA (2006a); Nakicenovic & IPCC WG III (2000).

861   IMF, 2006:189.

862   From $381 trillion in 2100 to $227 trillion. A1 MINICAM, B1 IMAGE (Nakicenovic & IPCC WG III, 2000).

863   IPCC estimates that developed countries use 1–2% of GDP on environment. Here we assume that all, including developing countries, use the high end of this estimate throughout the twenty-first century (Lomborg, 2001:317).

864   It is important to note that all these comparisons are partial – that is, they do not take into account other, secondary effects. Of course, imposing Kyoto does not only cut the number of malaria cases (it also decreases heat deaths, increases cold deaths, increases food availability but decreases water availability, etc.). Likewise, implementing malaria policies will not just cut disease and death but will likely lead to much greater economic prosperity, because of increased productivity. In the final analysis, all of these effects (and many more, that are not quantified here) should be tallied and accounted, which is what the cost-benefit analysis does below. (Suffice to say, it shows much the same picture.)

865   We could think of this cost weighing up against Kyoto's increased water stress.

866   Sarewitz & Pielke, 2007.

867   EU, 2007c:12. Note, that promising such a goal is not the same as reaching it. In the same EU document, EU actually starts out lauding the accomplishments of its Lisbon Strategy from 2000, "aimed at making the European Union the most competitive economy in the world" (EU, 2007b). A central target here is achieving 3% of GDP for R&D. Yet, a recent LSE assessment shows that the target "will not be achieved by 2010" (CEP, 2006). Actually, while the EU average for R&D in 2000 was 1.86%, the latest figures from 2005 have *declined* to 1.84% (for EU-27; for EU-15 it went from 1.92% to 1.91%: EU, 2007a).

868   IEA, 2006c:507.

869   As estimated by Nordhaus (2006c).

870   Based on the calculations of Bohringer & Vogt (2003:478).

871 As estimated by Nordhaus (2006c).

872 IEA, 2006a:II.4; 2006c:493, 529; Marland, Andres, & Boden, 2006.

873 Sarewitz & Pielke, 2007.

874 EIA, 2006b.

875 Bohringer & Vogt, 2003:478.

876 UNFCCC, 1992:4.2a.

877 The Annex II countries (IEA, 2006a:II.4).

878 20.8% and 107.5% (IEA, 2006c).

879 Of the total energy demand (IEA, 2006c:492).

880 IEA, 2006a; 2006c; Marland et al., 2006; B. R. Mitchell, 1993; WDI, 2007.

881 IEA (2006c:193) finds that the increased need for investments by consumers should be more than offset by fewer energy investments needed by governments, but that regulation still would be needed. If indeed this logic holds, one has to ask why it hasn't happened earlier. Again, we are possibly faced with the problems of "cutting emissions and making money" – assumptions that we talked about above (Box, pp. 32–3).

882 A reduction from the standard to the alternative scenario of 17% in the developing world, compared to 15% in the OECD and 13% in the transition countries.

883 Seventy-eight climate policy experts expect a 10% reduction (Bohringer & Loschel, 2005).

884 Sarewitz & Pielke, 2007.

885 Runci, 2000:18, emphasis added.

886 Sarewitz & Pielke, 2007:11.

887 IEA, 2006b; Nemet & Kammen, 2007; Runci, 2005.

888 Neuhoff & Sellers (2006:3): "There are few reliable assessments of the investment made by industry in R&D, but recent studies by the IEA have illuminated the funding provided by IEA governments, which is thought to constitute the vast majority of global government investments."

889 IEA (2007); WDI (2007): average of individual country percentages. (The average of total investment against total GDP is similar, but highly influenced by Japan, which spends almost half of all R&D in energy efficiency.) Here using the same list of countries as Paul Runci (2005), though without the US: Canada, Denmark, France, Germany, Italy, Japan, the Netherlands, Spain, Sweden, the United Kingdom, and the US, representing about 95% of industrialized country R&D investments in 2003. Private R&D data for the US from Nemet & Kammen (2007).

890 Nemet & Kammen, 2007:749.

891 When compared to the total public R&D in renewables and conservation of about $2 billion (IEA, 2007).

892 Sarewitz & Pielke, 2007:13.

893 Neuhoff & Sellers, 2006:11.

894 Kammen & Nemet (2005) and IPCC (2001a:185) estimate pre-industrial CO_2 at 280 ppm; thus a CO_2 concentration of 560 ppm would probably cause about 2.38°C (A1T from 2000 with 575 ppm (IPCC, 2001a:808, 824)).

895 Jaffe, Fogarty, & Banks, 1998; Nemet & Kammen, 2007:752; O'Rangers, 2005.

896 Ereaut & Segnit, 2006:7.

897 Meilby, 1996:58.

898 Altheide & Michalowski, 1999; compare to Young, 2003.

899 Ereaut & Segnit, 2006:7.

900 The Actant model of Thorsen & Møller (1995).

901 Singer & Endreny, 1993:103ff.

902 Finkel, 1996.

903 IPCC, 2007b:ch. 10.

904 Cook (1998): "global warming is making the effects of the periodic weather pattern known as El Niño worse. 'We know that as a result of global warming, there is more heat in the climate system, and it is heat that drives El Niño,' the vice president explained '. . . unless we act we can expect more extreme weather in the years ahead.'" Monastersky (1998): "Global temperatures reached all-time highs during the first part of 1998, reflecting a synergy between El Niño and global warming, according to a report issued last week by Vice President Gore and the National Oceanic and Atmospheric Administration (NOAA)."

905 Dunn, 1998.

906 Ridnouer, 1998.

907 Anon., 1998b.

908 Brady, 1998.

909 Gorman, 1998.

910 Griffith, 1998.

911 Nash & Horsburgh, 1998.

912 Because of Disney's lower theme park attendance (Anon., 1998a).

913 Nash & Horsburgh, 1998.

914 Changnon, 1999.

915 Behringer, 1999; Oster, 2004.

916 Oster, 2004:217.

917 For 1520–1770 (Oster, 2004:220).

918 Miguel, 2005.

919 Von Storch & Stehr, 2006:108.

920 Von Storch & Stehr, 2006:109.

921 Gwynne, 1975.

922 R. W. Anderson & Gainor, 2006:9.

923 R. W. Anderson & Gainor, 2006:9.

924 Von Storch & Stehr, 2006:109.

925 R. W. Anderson & Gainor, 2006:8–9.

926 R. W. Anderson & Gainor, 2006:9.

927 Ponte quoted in von Storch & Stehr (2006:109).

928 R. W. Anderson & Gainor, 2006:13.

929 R. W. Anderson & Gainor, 2006:7.

930 Quoted in Bray (1991:82).

931 Quoted in Bray (1991:83).

932 Nigel Calder quoted in Bray (1991:83).

933 1975 (R. W. Anderson & Gainor, 2006:3).

934 Schwartz & Randall, 2003:11, 15.

935 Hume, 1754:464.

936 Quoted in Simon (1995b).

937 Quoted in Simon (1996:17). However, the original quote has no reference, so this may be apocryphal.

938 Anon., 1999; Carson, 1962.

939 Colborn, Dumanoski, & Myers, 1996:202.

940 Fosberg, 1963.

941 Doll & Peto, 1981; Lomborg, 2001:263; Ritter, Heath, Kaegi, Morrison, & Sieber, 1997; WCRF, 1997.

942 Lomborg, 2001:247–8.

943 Milne & Milne, 1962.

944 Graham, 1995; Tengs, 1997; Tengs et al., 1995; Tengs & Graham, 1996.

945 Tengs, 1997:Table II.

946 Typical (or median) cost of all health policies is the price, which splits all the other policies in two equal parts, where 50% are cheaper and 50% are more expensive. The advantage of the median is that it is less affected by very atypical (high) prices. Of the costs $5, $10, $70, $100, and $1000, $70 would be the median, whereas the average would be $237, highly affected by the single value of $1000. 1993$ and number of interventions for each sector is 310, 30, 87, 36, and 124 respectively (Tengs et al., 1995:371).

947 Tengs, 1997.

948 Graham, 1995; Tengs, 1997.

949 Gelbspan, 2004; Leggett, 2001; F. Pearce, 2006a:16.

950 Gelbspan, 2004; Gore & Melcher Media, 2006. Gore: "Wealthy right-wing ideologues have joined with the most cynical and irresponsible companies in the oil, coal and mining industries to contribute large sums of money to finance pseudo-scientific front groups that specialize in sowing confusion in the public's mind about global warming" (R. W. Anderson & Gainor, 2006:6).

951 Simms et al., 2004:18.

952 EU, 2005a:9.

953 Monbiot, 2006a:90.

954 Lovelock, 2006a.

955 EurActiv, 2007.

956 Cover text of Kluger, 2006.

957 New Scientist anon., 2005.

958 Pearson in *Take a Break*, quoted by Ereaut & Segnit (2006:30). Perhaps ironically, the magazine's slogan is "Take a Break Magazine – the world can wait..."

959 E. Berger, 2007.

960 E. Berger, 2007.

961 Hulme, 2006.

962 F. Pearce (2006a:307–10) talks about $8 billion for stabilization (but not mentioning at what level), but gives no explanation of how much global warming that will avoid (and how much we will still have to endure).

963 Gore, 2006b.

964 USCB, 2006b.

965 Extrapolation to 2006 from EIA (2006b).

966 Using Nordhaus (2006c), compared to business-as-usual.

967 From 2.52°C to 2.43°C.

968 CRS, 2005:CRS-6.

969 Monbiot, 2006a:3–15.

970 Monbiot, 2006a:206, dust jacket.

971 Monbiot, 2006a:15.

972 Monbiot suggests it is about 90% (2006a:16), but this is only very rounded, and from current data. With his estimates of 0.33 tC per person in 2030, OECD will have a population of about 1.288 billion, and thus an emission allowance of 425 MtC. Today OECD emits 7.1 GtC and in 2030, by the IEA standard scenario, it will emit 11.0 GtC, leading to a 94% reduction of today's emissions and 96% reductions of emissions in 2030 (IEA, 2006c:56, 493; OECD, 2005:7).

973 It means cutting emissions more than 13% each year for the next 23 years – more than 1% a month.

974 Monbiot, 2006a:52.

975 Although he does try to make it sound fun, suggesting that parents could take turns to escort "walking busses" – crocodiles of children – to school, which would cut both traffic and obesity (Monbiot, 2006a:167).

976 Monbiot, 2006a, 170–88. Monbiot even tell us that "flying across the Atlantic is as unacceptable, in terms of its impact on human well-being, as child abuse" (Heartfield, 2006). Perhaps more surprisingly, the UK environment minister even supported the idea of rationing: "If the impacts of climate change are as bad as predicted, we may need to go back to rationing" (Anon., 2007).

977 Monbiot, 2006a:98.

978 With specific reference to me (Monbiot, 2006a:49–53). He also says that he could find lots of other arguments against me, but unfortunately chose not to produce them here.

979 Monbiot, 2006a:175.

980 IPCC (1999a:SPM 4.8), and this includes best estimates for contrails.

981 Kyoto in 2050 would be 5.2% below business-as-usual CO_2 emissions (Wigley, 1998:2286).

982 Monbiot, 2006a:50.

983 EU, 1996b; 2005b.

984 Tol, 2007. It is amusing, if somewhat depressing, to realize that a previous target was circulated of not exceeding 0.1°C/decade. Although this target was frequently mentioned in the literature, "the main defense was always a reference to a previous paper. The 0.1°C/decade target can be traced to the late 1980s, but then the trace vanishes. Apocryphal evidence holds that the 0.1°C/decade target is appropriate for a plant species on the shores of a lake in North America. This study was never published, but mentioned at dinner during an early climate conference. Someone else repeated the information the next day in plenary, and an urban legend was born."

985 Tol, 2005.

986 Stern, 2006:298. This is similar to the conclusion from a meeting of all economic modelers: "Current assessments determine that the 'optimal' policy calls for a relatively modest level of control of CO_2" (Nordhaus, 1998:18).

987 E.g. Gibbon, 2006; Stern, 2006; Timmons, 2006. The UK UN councillor said worldwide attention has gone "beyond the wildest expectations" of the UK government (Hagen, 2007.

988 Timmons, 2006.

989 Gibbon, 2006.

990 Stern, 2006:vi.

991 Stern, 2006:vi.

992 Stern, 2006:vi.

993 Even Prime Minister Tony Blair: "Stern shows that if we fail to act, the cost of tackling the disruption to people and economies would cost at least 5% – and possible as much as 20% – of the world's output. In contrast, the cost of action to halt and reverse climate change would cost just 1%. Or put another way for every £1 we invest now, we can save at least £5 and possibly much more" (Blair, 2006).

994 Grice, 2006.

995 Byatt et al., 2006; Carter, de Freitas, Goklany, Holland, & Lindzen, 2006; Dasgupta, 2006; Nordhaus, 2006d; Tol, 2006; Tol & Yohe, 2006; Varian, 2006; Weitzman, 2007; Yohe, 2006.

996 Carter et al., 2006:193.

997 Carter et al., 2006:194, 189; cf. Tol & Yohe, 2006:236.

998 In a critical BBC interview, the following exchange took place, which is hard not to interpret as Stern thinking himself smarter than IPCC:
Nick Stern: "We've drawn on the basic science. We have not tried to do new scientific research. We're not scientists."
Simon Cox (BBC): "I just wonder why your figures are different if you've just drawn from the existing literature, why your figures would be different from the IPCC?"
Nick Stern: "The IPCC is a good process, but it does depend on consensus. It means that they have to be quite cautious in what they say. We were able to look at the evidence and use it in a very particular way to look at the economics of risk" (S. Cox, 2007:11 min.).

999 Byatt et al., 2006:203; Tol & Yohe, 2006:235.

1000 Byatt et al., 2006:204–5; Tol, 2006:979; Tol & Yohe, 2006:238.

1001 Tol, 2006:979; Tol & Yohe, 2006:238.

1002 They simply stop counting the cost after 2050, while the cost escalates from 2.2% to 6.4% of GDP in 2100 (Tol & Yohe, 2006:239).

1003 Dasgupta, 2006.

1004 Byatt et al., 2006:206.

1005 Mendelsohn, 2007:45.

1006 Tol & Yohe, 2006:239.

1007 Tol, 2006:979–80.

1008 Nordhaus, 2006d:5.

1009 Giles, 2006.

1010 Tol & Yohe, 2006:235.

1011 Giles, 2006.

1012   Stern, 2006:298. This is similar to the conclusion from a meeting of all economic modelers: "Current assessments determine that the 'optimal' policy calls for a relatively modest level of control of CO_2," (Nordhaus, 1998:18).

1013   IPCC, 1999b; 2004.

1014   Lean, 2005. See also his remarkable introduction to the new 2007 IPCC report: "I hope this report will shock people, governments into taking more serious action as you really can't get a more authentic and a more credible piece of scientific work" (Bhalla, 2007). Setting aside the jarring disconnect between serious science and shock value, it is clear that policy neutral does not mean scaring people senseless.

1015   Von Storch, Stehr, & Ungar, 2004. At least one prominent (unnamed) scientist wanted the Medieval Warm Period to go away, sending an e-mail to someone what he thought was a fellow believer: "We have to get rid of the Medieval Warm Period" (Deming, 2005).

1016   Lindzen, 2006.

1017   Carter et al., 2006:190.

1018   Carter et al. (2006:190) compares the temperature index having a similar role in climatology as the Consumer Price Index has in national economic research, though the CRU temperature is secret whereas the CPI is very public.

1019   Carter et al. (2006:190) mention that this has happened to von Storch as well. (Wegman, Scott, & Said, 2006:51): "Sharing of research materials, data, and results is haphazard and often grudgingly done. We were especially struck by Dr. Mann's insistence that the code he developed was his intellectual property and that he could legally hold it personally without disclosing it to peers. When code and data are not shared and methodology is not fully disclosed, peers do not have the ability to replicate the work and thus independent verification is impossible."

1020   Kerr, 2000.

1021   Preliminary version of IPCC, 2001a:SPM5.

1022   IPCC, 2001a:xi.

1023   F. Pearce, 2001.

1024   "Alternative Development Pathways" is the title in IPCC, 2001c:95.

1025   IPCC, 2001c:99.

1026   IPCC, 2001c:101.

1027   IPCC, 2001c:102.

1028   IPCC, 2001c:102.

1029   IPCC, 2001c:101.

1030   IPCC, 2001c:106–7.

1031   IPCC, 2001c:369.

1032 IPCC, 2001c:638. IPCC tells us that lifestyles are "not economically rational, but they are still culturally rational," meaning that our Western consumerism is merely another way of relating ourselves to others. This we do through consuming, but really we are partaking in "a cultural project the purpose of which is to complete the self" (quoting approvingly by McCracken).

1033 IPCC, 2001c:101.

1034 IPCC, 2001c:639, based on UNDP, 1998.

1035 A changed proportion of respondents calling themselves "very happy" could be caused by many other factors apart from happiness. Over time, tendency to reply dishonestly (faking happiness) could decline, the format of the interviews could change, etc. (see T. W. Smith, 1979, which is the original reference). Simon noticed a similar decline in the evaluation of the American "situation of the country" since the late 1950s (Simon, 1995a:6). However, here we have another question to check the answers with, namely the respondent's view of his or her own life. Here the average remained constant over time, indicating that the decline in "situation of the country" was one not of absolute decline but of decline in perception.

1036 GSS (2007) at 33.5% versus 34.7% in 1957.

1037 For a review, see Argyle (1987:91ff).

1038 B1 and A1 (Kram et al., 2000:369). B2 gets a "medium," and it is quite honestly difficult to say, whether that is better or worse than "fair."

1039 Schell, 1989.

1040 See O'Neill (2006a) for an extended discussion, and following part of his argument here.

1041 Some make a distinction between the science and the policy but many do not (see J. Bailey & English, 2006; Rising Tide, 2007).

1042 Kingston, 2005.

1043 Lynas, 2004.

1044 Lynas, 2006.

1045 Roberts, 2006a; 2006b.

1046 Dohm & From, 2004: "'If you should follow the thinking of Lomborg, then possibly what Hitler did was right' is the harsh commentary from Pachauri." [Hvis man skal følge Lomborgs tankegang, var det måske rigtigt, hvad Hitler gjorde,« lyder den barske kommentar fra Pachauri].

1047 Montopoli, 2006.

1048 Ben-Ami, 2006. This was also Gore's answer on Danish TV, when confronted with a critical question about me.

1049 BBC Anon., 2006a.

1050 Winfrey, 2006:slide 13.

1051   Blackman, 2006.
1052   £40 billion until CO_2 doubles, or about $2.4 billion annually at 3% (Blackman, 2006).
1053   Blackman, 2006.
1054   Bower, Choularton, Latham, Sahraei, & Salter, 2006; Latham, 1990.
1055   Trefil, 1996.
1056   P. W. Boyd et al., 2004.
1057   Trefil, 1996.
1058   Bishop, 1993; Hartill, 1998.
1059   Ciotti, 1989.
1060   Ciotti, 1989. Summing up, Rifkin thought that "The Age of Progress is really an illusion. Far more people – 800 million – go to bed hungry today than at any time in history." This statement is obviously incorrect as can be seen in Fig. 41.
1061   Fumento, 1993:362; Sarewitz & Pielke, 2000.
1062   Brignell, 2006.
1063   O'Neill, 2006b. Although it is rather hard to imagine this chant to feel particularly rhythmic.
1064   California Assembly, 2006. The average Kyoto restriction is 5.2% below 1990 levels in 2008–12, whereas California will reduce theirs to 1990-levels by 2020, starting with some caps in 2012.
1065   Nordhaus, 2006e:10.
1066   1997–2004 (EIA, 2006b).
1067   Forster, 2006:15.
1068   Forster, 2006:12.
1069   Forster, 2006:13.
1070   Forster, 2006:15.
1071   Tol & Yohe, 2006:245.
1072   Labour have said 20% CO_2 emission cut from 1990 in 2010 in three election manifestos (BBC Anon., 2006b); this translate into a 14.6% reduction from 1997 levels. From 1997 to 2004, CO_2 emissions increased 3.4% (EIA, 2006b).
1073   EDIE, 2006.
1074   Take for instance both Gore's "we have to find a way to communicate the direness of the situation" and Hansen's "scientists have not done a good job communicating with the public" (D. Fischer, 2006).
1075   We are here talking about relative changes in emissions. The absolute EU emissions, for many reasons of history, geography, infrastructure and environment, are about half of the US emissions per capita.
1076   EIA, 2006b.
1077   Clinton Global Initiative, 2005:15.
1078   Tol, 2007:430.

1079 Nordhaus & Boyer, 2000:7–28, 31.

1080 There are many advantages to taxes over emission caps, mainly that, with taxes, authorities have an interest in collecting them (because they fund the government), whereas with caps individual countries have much less interest in achieving such effort, because the benefits are dispersed (global) and the damages localized (to local industries.

1081 Akerhielm, 1995; Angrist & Lavy, 1999; Graddy & Stevens, 2005. Of course, this could be modified in many ways: it could be better paid teachers, more resources for books, computers, etc. It is also important that we should be saying "more teachers will at least not make schools worse, and will likely make them better" as most studies show some or no effect of extra resources, but very few show negative results.

1082 E.g. Fleitas et al., 2006; Gebhardt & Norris, 2006. On the other hand it is less clear that (after a certain limit) more doctors and bed space is the answer, since they may just make for more visits and more possibility of infections and harm (Weinberger, Oddone, & Henderson, 1996; Wennberg et al., 2004).

1083 Beinecke, 2005; Hawkins, 2001; Sierra Club, 2007.

1084 USCB, 2006a:672.

1085 UKNS, 2004:327.

1086 Lopez et al., 2006:1751; WHO, 2002:72; 2004b:3, 172.

1087 AWEA, 2007:2.

1088 WHO, 2004b:172.

1089 WHO, 2004b:5.

1090 WHO (2002:129) puts it second, whereas later (WHO, 2004b:5) it puts it third.

1091 Curiously – and with humor – 5 mph is about Monbiot's 96% reduction of 55 mph.

1092 This only looks at the marginal benefit of fossil fuels – which is the relevant one for our discussion. On a basic level, though, it is important to remember that they have fundamentally changed our lives. Before fossil fuels, we would spend hours gathering wood, contributing to deforestation and soil erosion – as billions in the third world still do (Kammen, 1995). We have electric washing machines that have cut especially women's work dramatically. The historical economist Stanley Lebergott wrote only semi-jokingly: "From 1620 to 1920 the American washing machine was a housewife" (Lebergott, 1993:112). In 1900 a housewife spent seven hours a week laundering, carrying 200 gallons of water into the house and using a scrub board. Today she spends 84 minutes, with much less strain (Robinson & Godbey, 1997:327). We have a fridge, that has given us more spare time, allowed us to avoid rotten food, and helped us to eat a more healthy diet of fruit and vegetables (Lebergott, 1995:155). By the end of the nineteenth century human labor made up 94% of all industrial work in the US. Today, it constitutes only 8% (Berry, Conkling, Ray, & Berry, 1993:131). If we think for a moment of the energy we use in terms of "servants," each with the same work power as a human being, each person in western Europe has access to 150 servants, in the US about 300, and even in India each person has 15 servants to help along (Craig et al., 1996:103).

1093 Davis et al., 2003.

1094 Steve Jones of Help the Aged said: "Many pensioners still agonise about whether or not to heat their homes in the cold weather. In the world's fourth richest country, this is simply shameful" (BBC Anon., 2006c).

1095 The World Cancer Research Fund study estimates that increasing the intake of fruit and vegetables from an average of about 250 g/day to 400 g/day would reduce the overall frequency of cancer by around 23% (WCRF, 1997:540).

1096 Schäfer, 2006.

1097 IEA, 2004:338–40.

1098 IEA, 2006c:419ff.

1099 IEA, 2006c:428; Kammen, 1995; Kelkar, 2006.

1100 Mainly from fewer deaths and less time use (IEA, 2006c:440).

1101 WHO, 2002:72; 2004b:172.

1102 http://www.europe.org/speedlimits.html.

1103 Yohe, 2006:66.

1104 IEA, 2006c:529.

1105 Boykoff & Boykoff, 2006.

1106 UNCED, 1992:15: "Where there are threats of serious or irreversible damage, lack of full scientific certainty shall not be used as a reason for postponing cost-effective measures to prevent environmental degradation."

1107 SEHN, 2007.

1108 I. M. Goklany, 2000.

1109 Estimate, since we don't seem to have a formal cost-benefit analysis on this.

1110 Going 67% up from $227 trillion to $381 trillion in 2100 with the same population.

1111 See Figure 52.

1112 Pielke, 2006.

1113 Gore, 1992:240.

1114 Depressingly, parts of the EU seem willing to counter or even run afoul the WTO in order to place carbon taxes on imports (E Smith, 2006).

1115 The costs and benefits are from the individual chapters throughout the book, the periods are somewhat different given the diverse nature of the subjects.

1116 The low-cost estimates at (EcoBusinessLinks, 2007). The average is about $17. The benefit estimates from Tol, 2005.

BIBLIOGRAPHY

Abelmann, A., Gersonde, R., Cortese, G., Kuhn, G., & Smetacek, V. (2006). Extensive phytoplankton blooms in the Atlantic sector of the glacial Southern Ocean. *Paleoceanography*, 21(1).

Acsadi, G., & Nemeskeri, J. (1970). *History of Human Life Span and Mortality*. Budapest: Akademiai Kiado.

Adam, D., & Elliott, L. (2006, October 31). Simple verdict after a complex inquiry: time is running out. *Guardian*. Retrieved 10–1–07, from http://www.guardian.co.uk/science/story/0,,1935975,00.html.

Adekoya, N., & Nolte, K. B. (2005). Struck-by-lightning deaths in the United States. *Journal of Environmental Health*, 67(9), 45–50.

Aguirre, J., & Riding, R. (2005). Dasycladalean algal biodiversity compared with global variations in temperature and sea level over the past 350 Myr. *Palaios*, 20(6), 581–8.

Akbari, H., Pomerantz, M., & Taha, H. (2001). Cool surfaces and shade trees to reduce energy use and improve air quality in urban areas. *Solar Energy*, 70(3), 295–310.

Akerhielm, K. (1995). Does class size matter. *Economics of Education Review*, 14(3), 229–41.

Al-Rashed, M. F., & Sherif, M. M. (2000). Water resources in the GCC countries: an overview. *Water Resources Management*, 14(1), 59–75.

Alcamo, J., Füssel, H. M., Kram, T., Masui, T., Onigkeit, J., Pitcher, H., et al. (2002). *Progress since Rio? Consequences of Recent Climate Policies*. Center for Environmental Systems Research, University of Kassel.

Alexander, L. V., Zhang, X., Peterson, T. C., Caesar, J., Gleason, B., Tank, A., et al. (2006). Global observed changes in daily climate extremes of temperature and precipitation. *Journal of Geophysical Research–Atmospheres*, 111(D5).

Almeida, A. de, Fonseca, P., Schlomann, B., Feilberg, N., & Ferreira, C. (2006). Residential monitoring to decrease energy use and carbon emissions in Europe. *Working Paper*. Retrieved 21–11–06, from http://mail.mtprog.com/CD_Layout/Day_2_22.06.06/1400–1545/ID170_Almeida_final.pdf.

Altheide, D. L., & Michalowski, R. S. (1999). Fear in the news: a discourse of control. *Sociological Quarterly*, 40(3), 475–503.

Amstrup, S. C., Durner, G., York, G., Regehr, E., Simac, K., & Douglas, D. (2006, July 14). polar bear: sentinel species for climate change. *Environmental Science Seminar Series*. Retrieved 7–11–06, from http://www.ametsoc.org/atmospolicy/documents/AmstrupFinal.pdf.

Andersen, K. K., Azuma, N., Barnola, J. M., Bigler, M., Biscaye, P., Caillon, N., et al. (2004). High-resolution record of northern hemisphere climate extending into the last interglacial period. *Nature*, 431(7005), 147–51.

Anderson, E. (2006). *Potential Impacts of Climate Change on $2-a-Day Poverty and Child Mortality in Sub-Saharan Africa and South Asia*. Stern Review background report. Retrieved 8–1–07, from http://www.hm-treasury.gov.uk/independent_reviews/stern_review_economics_climate_change/stern_review_supporting_documents.cfm.

Anderson, J. B., Shipp, S. S., Lowe, A. L., Wellner, J. S., & Mosola, A. B. (2002). The Antarctic ice sheet during the Last Glacial Maximum and its subsequent retreat history: a review. *Quaternary Science Reviews*, 21(1–3), 49–70.

Anderson, R. W., & Gainor, D. (2006). Fire and ice. *Business & Media Institute*. Retrieved 21–1–07, from http://www.businessandmedia.org/specialreports/2006/fireandice/FireandIce.pdf.

Angrist, J. D., & Lavy, V. (1999). Using Maimonides' rule to estimate the effect of class size on scholastic achievement. *Quarterly Journal of Economics*, 114(2), 533–75.

Annan, K. (2000, March 14). Progress made in providing safe water supply and sanitation for all during the 1990s. *Economic and Social Council*. Retrieved 7–1–07, from http://www.un.org/documents/ecosoc/cn17/2000/ecn172000–13.htm.

Annan, K. (2006, November 15). UN Secretary-General Kofi Annan's address to the Climate Change Conference, as delivered in Nairobi. *United Nations*. Retrieved 2–1–07, from http://www.un.org/News/Press/docs/2006/sgsm10739.doc.htm.

Anon. (1998a). Disney blames El Niño, ABC for stock fall. *Electronic Media*, 17(11), 22.

Anon. (1998b). Weird weather. *Junior Scholastic*, 100(15), 8.

Anon. (1999, June 14). Persons of the century. *Time*, 8.

Anon. (2004, November 6). Kyoto ratification, editorial. *Washington Post*, 22. Retrieved 18–11–06, from http://www.washingtonpost.com/wp-dyn/articles/A29459–2004Nov5.html.

Anon. (2006, October 28). Urban heat island. *New Scientist*, 58.

Anon. (2007, January 30). Britain could go back to rationing. *This Is London*. Retrieved 31–1–07, from http://www.thisislondon.co.uk/news/article–23383454-details/Britain%20could%20go%20back%20to%20rationing/article.do.

AP (2006a, 26 September). AP Interview: Schwarzenegger says global warming a top priority. Retrieved 6–11–06, from http://www.iht.com/articles/ap/2006/09/26/america/NA_GEN_US_Schwarzenegger_Global_Warming.php.

AP (2006b, December 14). Illinois sets tornado record. *Chicago Sun–Times*. Retrieved 23–12–06, from http://suntimes.com/news/metro/173367,tornado-121406.article.

AP (2006c, February 23). Japan tries some conservation the hard way: environment ministry shuts off heating in race to meet Kyoto target. *Associated Press*. Retrieved 20–11–06, from http://www.msnbc.msn.com/id/11522280/.

Argyle, M. (1987). *The Psychology of Happiness*. London: Routledge.

Armstrong, G. L., Conn, L. A., & Pinner, R. W. (1999). Trends in infectious disease mortality in the United States during the 20th century. *JAMA–Journal of the American Medical Association*, 281(1), 61–6.

Arnell, N. W. (2004). Climate change and global water resources: SRES emissions and socio-economic scenarios. *Global Environmental Change*, 14(1), 31–52, from http://www.sciencedirect.com/science/article/B6VFV–4BM8RY3–3/2/2702-a6dbe565c0ca1a92187842f3d5e8.

Arnell, N. W., Cannell, M. G. R., Hulme, M., Kovats, R. S., Mitchell, J. F. B., Nicholls, R. J., et al. (2002). The consequences of CO2 stabilisation for the impacts of climate change. *Climatic Change*, 53(4), 413–46.

Arnfield, A. J. (2003). Two decades of urban climate research: a review of turbulence, exchanges of energy and water, and the urban heat island. *International Journal of Climatology*, 23(1), 1–26.

Arthur, C. (2004, 27 May). MPs say Global warming is as big a threat to the world as terrorism. *Independent*. Retrieved 6–11–06, from http://www.perfect.co.uk/2004/05/mps-say-global-warming-is-as-big-a-threat-to-the-world-as-terrorism.

Ashton, P. J. (2002). Avoiding conflicts over Africa's water resources. *Ambio*, 31(3), 236–242.

Association of British Insurers (2005). Financial risks of climate change, summary report. *Climate Risk Management*. Retrieved 20–12–06, from http://www.abi.org.uk/Display/File/Child/552/Financial_Risks_of_Climate_Change.pdf.

Augustin, L., Barbante, C., Barnes, P. R. F., Barnola, J. M., Bigler, M., Castellano, E., et al. (2004). Eight glacial cycles from an Antarctic ice core. *Nature*, 429(6992), 623–8.

Australian Antarctic Division (2003). Where do emperor penguins breed and where do we study them? *Australian Antarctic Division*. Retrieved 15–12–06, from http://www.aad.gov.au/default.asp?casid=2879.

AWEA (2007). Facts about wind energy & birds. *American Wind Energy Association*. Retrieved 30–1–07, from http://www.awea.org/pubs/factsheets/avianfs.pdf.

BA (2006). Click for the climate. *The BA National Science Week 2006*. Retrieved

20–11–06, from http://www.the-ba.net/the-ba/Events/NSEW/AboutNSEW/NSEW_
archive/NationalScienceWeek2006/ClimateChange/ClickfortheClimate.htm.

Bailey, J., & English, O. (2006). Emptying the sceptic tank. *Corporate Watch*. Retrieved 26–1–07, from http://www.corporatewatch.org.uk/?lid=2715.

Bailey, R. (2006, November 14). Carbon reduction or poverty reduction, not both. *Reason Online*. Retrieved 29–11–06, from http://www.reason.com/news/show/116724.html.

Barber, D. C., Dyke, A., Hillaire-Marcel, C., Jennings, A. E., Andrews, J. T., Kerwin, M. W., et al. (1999). Forcing of the cold event of 8,200 years ago by catastrophic drainage of Laurentide lakes. *Nature*, 400(6742), 344–348.

Barbier, E. B. (2004). Water and economic growth. *Economic Record*, 80(248), 1–16.

Barbraud, C., & Weimerskirch, H. (2001). Emperor penguins and climate change. *Nature*, 411(6834), 183–6.

Barnett, T., Zwiers, F., Hegerl, G., Allen, M., Crowley, T., Gillett, N., et al. (2005). Detecting and attributing external influences on the climate system: a review of recent advances. *Journal of Climate*, 18(9), 1291–1314.

Barnett, T. P., Adam, J. C., & Lettenmaier, D. P. (2005). Potential impacts of a warming climate on water availability in snow-dominated regions. *Nature*, 438(7066), 303–9.

Basu, R., & Samet, J. M. (2002). Relation between elevated ambient temperature and mortality: a review of the epidemiologic evidence. *Epidemiologic Reviews*, 24(2), 190–202.

Battersby, S. (2006, April 15). Climate change: the great Atlantic shutdown. *New Scientist*, 42ff.

BBC Anon. (2002, June 5). Australia rejects Kyoto pact. Retrieved 18–11–06, from http://news.bbc.co.uk/2/hi/asia-pacific/2026446.stm.

BBC Anon. (2004, August 16). Climate legacy of "hockey stick". Retrieved 06–12–06, from http://news.bbc.co.uk/2/hi/science/nature/3569604.stm.

BBC Anon. (2005, January 30). Climate change "disaster by 2026." Retrieved 7–11–06, from http://news.bbc.co.uk/1/hi/england/oxfordshire/4218441.stm.

BBC Anon. (2006a, September 27). Miliband fears on climate change. Retrieved 26–1–07, from http://news.bbc.co.uk/2/hi/uk_news/politics/5384206.stm.

BBC Anon. (2006b, March 28). UK to miss CO2 emissions target. Retrieved 29–1–07, from http://news.bbc.co.uk/2/hi/science/nature/4849672.stm.

BBC Anon. (2006c, October 27). "Winter death toll" drops by 19%: deaths in England and Wales fell to 25,700 last winter, a decline of 19% on the previous year. Retrieved 13–11–06, from http://news.bbc.co.uk/2/hi/uk_news/6090492.stm.

BEA (2006a). Table 1.1.9. Implicit price deflators for Gross Domestic Product.

Bureau of Economic Analysis. Retrieved 22–11–06, from http://bea.gov/bea/dn/nipaweb/TableView.asp#Mid.

BEA (2006b). Table 1.1. Current-cost net stock of fixed assets and consumer durable goods. *Bureau of Economic Analysis.* Retrieved 23–12–06, from http://www.bea.gov/bea/dn/FA2004/TableView.asp#Mid.

Beard, J. (2006). DDT and human health. *Science of the Total Environment,* 355(1–3), 78–89.

Beerling, D. J., & Royer, D. L. (2002). Fossil plants as indicators of the phanerozoic global carbon cycle. *Annual Review of Earth and Planetary Sciences,* 30, 527–56.

Behringer, W. (1999). Climatic change and witch-hunting: the impact of the Little Ice Age on mentalities. *Climatic Change,* 43(1), 335–51.

Beinecke, F. (2005). The Natural Resources Defense Council. *StopGlobalWarming.* Retrieved 29–1–07, from http://www.stopglobalwarming.org/sgw_partner.asp?376.

Ben-Ami, D. (2006, September 18). Global warming: time for a heated debate. *Spiked.* Retrieved 26–1–07, from http://www.spiked-online.com/index.php?/site/article/1675/.

Berger, A., Melice, J. L., & Loutre, M. F. (2005). On the origin of the 100-kyr cycles in the astronomical forcing. *Paleoceanography,* 20(4).

Berger, E. (2007, January 22). Climate scientists feeling the heat. *Houston Chronicle.* Retrieved 23–1–07, from http://www.chron.com/disp/story.mpl/front/4487421.html.

Berner, J., Symon, C., Arris, L., & Heal, O. W., Arctic Climate Impact Assessment, National Science Foundation (U.S.), et al. (2005). *Arctic Climate Impact Assessment.* Cambridge: Cambridge University Press. Retrieved 7–11–06, from http://www.acia.uaf.edu/.

Berner, R. A. (2003). The long-term carbon cycle, fossil fuels and atmospheric composition. *Nature,* 426(6964), 323–6.

Berner, R. A., & Kothavala, Z. (2001). GEOCARB III: a revised model of atmospheric CO2 over phanerozoic time. *American Journal of Science,* 301(2), 182–204.

Berry, A., Bourguignon, F., & Morrison, C. (1983). Changes in the world distribution of income between 1950 and 1977. *Economic Journal,* 93: 331–50.

Berry, A., Bourguignon, F., & Morrison, C. (1991). Global economic inequality and its trends since 1950. In Lars Osberg (ed.), *Economic Inequality and Poverty: International Perspectives* (pp. 39–59). Armonk, NY: M. E. Shape Inc.

Berry, B. J. L., Conkling, E. C., Ray, D. M., & Berry, B. J. L. (1993). *The Global Economy: Resource Use, Locational Choice, and International Trade.* Englewood Cliffs, NJ: Prentice Hall.

Bhalla, N. (2007, January 25). U.N. climate report will shock the world – chairman.

Reuters. Retrieved 26–1–07, from http://www.alertnet.org/thenews/newsdesk/ DEL33627.htm.

Bindschadler, R. (2006). The environment and evolution of the West Antarctic ice sheet: setting the stage. *Philosophical Transactions of the Royal Society A: Mathematical, Physical and Engineering Sciences*, 364(1844), 1583–1605. http://dx.doi.org/10.1098/rsta.2006.1790.

Bintanja, R., van de Wal, R. S. W., & Oerlemans, J. (2005). Modelled atmospheric temperatures and global sea levels over the past million years. *Nature*, 437(7055), 125–8.

BirdLife International (2004). *Aptenodytes forsteri*. In IUCN, *2006 IUCN Red List of Threatened Species*. Retrieved 16–12–06, from http://www.iucnredlist.org/ search/details.php/49667/all.

Bishop, J. E. (1993). It ain't over till it's over . . . cold fusion: the controversial dream of cheap, abundant energy from room-temperature fusion refuses to die. *Popular Science*, 243(2), 47–52.

Blackman, S. (2006, November 15). Every silver lining has a cloud. *Spiked*. Retrieved 28–1–07, from http://www.spiked-online.com/index.php?/site/article/2097/.

Blair, T. (2003, February 24). "Concerted international effort" necessary to fight climate change. Retrieved 19–11–06, from http://www.pm.gov.uk/output/ Page3073.asp.

Blair, T. (2004a, September 14). PM Speech on climate change. Retrieved 18–11–06, from http://www.pm.gov.uk/output/Page6333.asp.

Blair, T. (2004b, April 27). Speech at the launch of the Climate Group. Retrieved 6–11–06, from http://www.number-10.gov.uk/output/page5716.asp.

Blair, T. (2006, October 30). PM's comments at launch of Stern Review. Retrieved 29–12–06, from http://www.number-10.gov.uk/output/Page10300.asp.

Blake, E. S., Rappaport, E. N., Jarrell, J. D., & Landsea, C. W. (2005). The deadliest, costliest, and most intense United States tropical cyclones from 1851 to 2004 (and other frequently requested hurricane facts). *National Hurricane Center*. Retrieved 18–12–06, from http://www.nhc.noaa.gov/pdf/NWS-TPC-4.pdf.

Blakely, S. (1998). Climate treaty faces cold reception in Congress. *Nation's Business*, 86(2), 8–9.

Bohm, R. (1998). Urban bias in temperature time series – a case study for the city of Vienna, Austria. *Climatic Change*, 38(1), 113–28.

Bohringer, C., & Loschel, A. (2005). Climate policy beyond Kyoto: quo vadis? A computable general equilibrium analysis based on expert judgements. *Kyklos*, 58(4), 467–93.

Bohringer, C., & Vogt, C. (2003). Economic and environmental impacts of the Kyoto Protocol. *Canadian Journal of Economics–Revue Canadienne d'Economique*, 36(2), 475–94.

Bosello, F., Roson, R., & Tol, R. S. J. (2006). Economy-wide estimates of the implications of climate change: human health. *Ecological Economics*, 58(3), 579–91.

Botkin, D. B., & Keller, E. A. (1998). *Environmental Science: Earth Is a Living Planet*. New York: John Wiley & Sons.

Bower, K., Choularton, T., Latham, J., Sahraei, J., & Salter, S. (2006). Computational assessment of a proposed technique for global warming mitigation via albedo-enhancement of marine stratocumulus clouds. *Atmospheric Research*, 82(1–2), 328–36.

Boyd, P. W., Law, C. S., Wong, C. S., Nojiri, Y., Tsuda, A., Levasseur, M., et al. (2004). The decline and fate of an iron-induced subarctic phytoplankton bloom. *Nature*, 428(6982), 549–53.

Boyd, R. T. (1975). Another look at the "fever and ague" of western Oregon. *Ethnohistory*, 22(2), 135–54.

Boykoff, J., & Boykoff, M. (2006, July 6). An inconvenient principle. *CommonDreams.org*. Retrieved 30-1-07, from An Inconvenient Principle.

Boyle, M. H., Racine, Y., Georgiades, K., Snelling, D., Hong, S. J., Omariba, W., et al. (2006). The influence of economic development level, household wealth and maternal education on child health in the developing world. *Social Science & Medicine*, 63(8), 2242–54.

Brady, S. (1998). El Niño dampens area tourist trade. *Business Journal: Serving Greater Tampa Bay*, 18(12), 1–2.

Brandt, U. S., & Svendsen, G. T. (2005). Surplus emission allowances as implicit side payments: could "hot air" have saved the Kyoto Agreement? *Climate Policy*, 4(3), 303–18.

Bray, A. J. (1991). The ice-age cometh – remembering the scare of global cooling. *Policy Review*, 58, 82–4.

Brazdil, R., Kundzewicz, Z. W., & Benito, G. (2006). Historical hydrology for studying flood risk in Europe. *Hydrological Sciences Journal–Journal des Sciences Hydrologiques*, 51(5), 739–64.

Brazel, A., Selover, N., Vose, R., & Heisler, G. (2000). The tale of two climates – Baltimore and Phoenix urban LTER sites. *Climate Research*, 15(2), 123–35.

Breman, J. G. (2001). The ears of the hippopotamus: manifestations, determinants, and estimates of the malaria burden. *American Journal of Tropical Medicine and Hygiene*, 64(1–2), 1–11.

Brierly, W. B. (1944). Malaria and socio-economic conditions in Mississippi. *Social Forces*, 23(1), 451–9.

Brignell, J. (2006, November 2). Got a problem? Blame global warming! *Spiked*. Retrieved 27-1-07, from http://www.spiked-online.com/index.php?/site/article/2045/.

Brohan, P., Kennedy, J. J., Harris, I., Tett, S. F. B., & Jones, P. D. (2006). Uncertainty estimates in regional and global observed temperature changes: a new data set from 1850. *Journal of Geophysical Research-Atmospheres*, 111(D12).

Bronstert, A. (2003). Floods and climate change: interactions and impacts. *Risk Analysis*, 23(3), 545–57.http://www.blackwell-synergy.com/doi/abs/10.1111/1539–6924.00335.

Brooks, H. E., & Doswell, C. A. (2001). Normalized damage from major tornadoes in the United States: 1890–1999. *Weather and Forecasting*, 16(1), 168–76.

Brown, P. (2005, February 2). Hotter world may freeze Britain: fifty-fifty chance that warm Gulf Stream may be halted. *Guardian*. Retrieved 27–12–06, from http://www.guardian.co.uk/climatechange/story/0,12374,1403798,00.html.

Bryden, H. L., Longworth, H. R., & Cunningham, S. A. (2005). Slowing of the Atlantic meridional overturning circulation at 25 degrees N. *Nature*, 438(7068), 655–7.

Buncombe, A. (2005, August 19). Climate change: will you listen now, America? *Independent*. Retrieved 6–11–06, from http://www.findarticles.com/p/articles/mi_qn4158/is_20050819/ai_n14918176.

Bunting, M. (2006, November 6). It's hard to explain, Tom, why we did so little to stop global warming: looking back, 40 years on, we were intoxicated with an idea of individual freedom that was little more than greedy egotism. *Guardian*. Retrieved 6–11–06, from http://www.guardian.co.uk/commentisfree/story/0,,1940384,00.html.

Burke, E. J., Brown, S. J., & Christidis, N. (2006). Modeling the recent evolution of global drought and projections for the twenty-first century with the Hadley Centre climate model. *Journal of Hydrometeorology*, 7(5), 1113–25.

Burroughs, W. J. (1997). *Does the Weather Really Matter? The Social Implications of Climate Change*. Cambridge: Cambridge University Press.

Byatt, I., Castles, I., Goklany, I. M., Henderson, D., Lawson, N., McKitrick, R., et al. (2006). The Stern Review: a dual critique, part II: economic aspects. *World Economics*, 7(4), 199–232.

Byrd-Hagel. (1997). Expressing the sense of the Senate regarding the conditions for the United States becoming a signatory to any international agreement on greenhouse gas emissions under the United Nations. *Senate, 105th Congress* (S. Res. 98). http://thomas.loc.gov/cgi-bin/query/D?c105:3:./temp/~c105nQ7itb::.

Cairncross, S. (2003). Editorial: water supply and sanitation: some misconceptions. *Tropical Medicine & International Health*, 8(3), 193–5.

California Assembly (2006, September 27). California Global Warming Solutions Act of 2006, AB 32. *California Assembly*. Retrieved 27–1–07, from http://www.leginfo.ca.gov/pub/05–06/bill/asm/ab_0001–0050/ab_32_bill_2006-0927_chaptered.pdf.

Calvin, W. H. (1998). The great climate flip-flop. *The Atlantic Monthly*, 281(1), 47–64.

Campbell-Lendrum, D. H., Corvalán, C. F., & Prüss–Ustün, A. (2003). How much disease could climate change cause? In A. J. McMichael, D. H. Campbell-Lendrum, C. F. Corvalán, K. L. Ebi, A. K. Githeko, J. D. Scheraga & A. Woodward (eds.), *Climate Change and Human Health* (pp. 133–58). Geneva: World Health Organization.

Canadian Press (2006, November 16). French minister shocked by Canada's Kyoto position. Retrieved 18–11–06, from http://www.ctv.ca/servlet/ArticleNews/story/CTVNews/20061116/french_kyoto_061116/20061116?hub=Canada.

Caporali, A., Davalli, P., Astancolle, S., D'Arca, D., Brausi, M., Bettuzzi, S., et al. (2004). The chemopreventive action of catechins in the TRAMP mouse model of prostate carcinogenesis is accompanied by clusterin over-expression. *Carcinogenesis*, 25(11), 2217–24.http://carcin.oxfordjournals.org/cgi/content/abstract/25/11/2217.

Carson, R. (1962). *Silent Spring*. Boston, MA: Houghton Mifflin.

Carter, R. M., de Freitas, C. R., Goklany, I. M., Holland, D., & Lindzen, R. S. (2006). The Stern Review: a dual critique, part I: the science. *World Economics*, 7(4), 167–98.

Cary, A. (2000). Fact or fiction? *Biography*, 4(4), 30.

Cazenave, A. (2006). How fast are the ice sheets melting? *Science*, 314(5803), 1250–2.

CDC (1999). Control of infectious diseases, 1900–1999. *JAMA – Journal of the American Medical Association*, 282(11), 1029–32. http://jama.ama-assn.org.

CDC (2004). Eradication of malaria in the United States (1947–1951). *Centers for Disease Control*. Retrieved 30–12–06, from http://0–www.cdc.gov.mill1.sjlibrary.org/malaria/history/eradication_us.htm.

CDC. (2006). 2006 West Nile virus activity in the United States (Reported to CDC as of December 11, 2006). *Centers for Disease Control*. Retrieved 29–12–06, from http://www.cdc.gov/ncidod/dvbid/westnile/surv&controlCaseCount06_detailed.htm.

CEP (2006). Boosting innovation and productivity growth in Europe: the hope and the realities of the EU's "Lisbon agenda." *Centre for Economic Performance*. Retrieved 15–3–07, from http://cep.lse.ac.uk/briefings/pa_lisbon_agenda.pdf.

Chakravorty, U., Roumasset, J., & Tse, K. P. (1997). Endogenous substitution among energy resources and global warming. *Journal of Political Economy*, 105(6), 1201–34.

Chan, J. C. L. (2006). Comment on "Changes in tropical cyclone number, duration, and intensity in a warming environment." *Science*, 311(5768).

Changnon, S. A. (1999). Impacts of 1997–98 El Niño-generated weather in the United States. *Bulletin of the American Meteorological Society*, 80(9), 1819–27.

Changnon, S. A. (2003). Shifting economic impacts from weather extremes in the

United States: a result of societal changes, not global warming. *Natural Hazards*, 29(2), 273–90.

Chapman, D., & Khanna, N. (2000). Crying no wolf: why economists don't worry about climate change, and should. *Climatic Change*, 47(3), 225–32.

Chapman, W. L., & Walsh, J. E. (2005). A synthesis of Antarctic temperatures: Department of Atmospheric Sciences at the University of Illinois. Retrieved 15–12–06, from http://arctic.atmos.uiuc.edu/.

Chase, T. N., Wolter, K., Pielke Sr., R. A., & Rasool, I. (2007). Was the 2003 European summer heat wave unusual in a global context? *Geophysical Research Letters, forthcoming*. Retrieved 13–11–06, from http://climatesci.atmos. colostate.edu/2006/11/06/was-the-2003-european-summer-heat-wave-unusual-in-a-global-context/.

Chastel, C. (2004). Emergence of new viruses in Asia: is climate change involved? *Médécine et Maladies Infectieuses*, 34(11), 499–505.

Chea, T. (2006, June 21). Sierra Club leader says global warming debate has reached "tipping point." *AP*. Retrieved 17–12–06, from http://www.free-newmexican.com/news/45354.html.

Chen, J. L., Wilson, C. R., & Tapley, B. D. (2006). Satellite gravity measurements confirm accelerated melting of Greenland ice sheet. *Science*, 313(5795), 1958–60.

Chen, L. X., Zhu, W. Q., Zhou, X. J., & Zhou, Z. J. (2003). Characteristics of the heat island effect in Shanghai and its possible mechanism. *Advances in Atmospheric Sciences*, 20(6), 991–1001.

Chicago Council (2006a, October 11). Global views 2006: comparative topline reports. *The Chicago Council on Global Affairs*. Retrieved 30–11–06, from http://www.thechicagocouncil.org/curr_pos.php.

Chicago Council (2006b, October 11). The United States and the rise of China and India: results of a 2006 multination survey of public opinion. *The Chicago Council on Global Affairs*. Retrieved 30–11–06, from http://www.thechicago-council.org/curr_pos.php.

Chung, U., Choi, J., & Yun, J. I. (2004). Urbanization effect on the observed change in mean monthly temperatures between 1951–1980 and 1971–2000 in Korea. *Climatic Change*, 66(1–2), 127–36.

Church, J. A., & White, N. J. (2006). A 20th century acceleration in global sea-level rise. *Geophysical Research Letters*, 33(1).

Chylek, P., Box, J. E., & Lesins, G. (2004). Global warming and the Greenland ice sheet. *Climatic Change*, 63(1–2), 201–21.

Chylek, P., Dubey, M. K., & Lesins, G. (2006). Greenland warming of 1920–1930 and 1995–2005. *Geophysical Research Letters*, 33(11).

CIA (2006). CIA World Fact Book. *Central Intelligence Agency, December 12*. Retrieved 17–12–06, from https://www.cia.gov/cia/publications/factbook/.

CIESIN (2002). *Country-level GDP and Downscaled Projections based on the A1, A2, B1, and B2 Marker Scenarios, 1990–2100.* Palisades, NY: Center for International Earth Science Information Network. Retrieved 3-1-07, from http://ciesin.columbia.edu/datasets/downscaled/.

Ciotti, P. (1989, April 19). Fear of fusion: what if it works? *Los Angeles Times*, A5.

Clinton, B. (2005, June 29). Former President Bill Clinton and Ted Turner discuss the future of energy policy. *American Museum of Natural History, New York.* Retrieved 20-11-06, from http://www.ppionline.org/ndol/print.cfm?contentid= 253507.

Clinton Global Initiative (2005, September 15). Special Opening Plenary Session: perspectives on the global challenges of our time. Retrieved 29-1-07, from http://attend.clintonglobalinitiative.org/pdf/transcripts/plenary/cgi_09_15_05_plenary_1.pdf.

CMO (2002). *Getting Ahead of the Curve: A Strategy for Combating Infectious Diseases (Including Other Aspects of Health Protection).* Chief Medical Officer, UK Department of Health. Retrieved 29-12-06, from http://www.dh.gov.uk/assetRoot/04/06/08/75/04060875.pdf.

Colborn, T., Dumanoski, D., & Myers, J. P. (1996). *Our Stolen Future: Are We Threatening Our Fertility, Intelligence, and Survival? A Scientific Detective Story.* New York: Dutton.

Comrie, A. C. (2000). Mapping a wind-modified urban heat island in Tucson, Arizona (with comments on integrating research and undergraduate learning). *Bulletin of the American Meteorological Society*, 81(10), 2417–31.

Congleton, R. D. (2006). The story of Katrina: New Orleans and the political economy of catastrophe. *Public Choice*, 127(1–2), 5–30.

Connor, S. (2005, December 1). Fears of big freeze as scientists detect slower Gulf Stream. *Independent.* Retrieved 27-12-06, from http://news.independent.co.uk/world/science_technology/article330454.ece.

Conroy, M. S. (1982). Malaria in late Tsarist Russia. *Bulletin of the History of Medicine*, 56(1), 41–55.

Cook, A. J., Fox, A. J., Vaughan, D. G., & Ferrigno, J. G. (2005). Retreating glacier fronts on the Antarctic Peninsula over the past half-century. *Science*, 308(5721), 541–4.

Cook, W. J. (1998). The force of El Niño. *U.S. News & World Report*, 124(24), 58.

Copenhagen Consensus (2006, October 30). A United Nations perspective. Retrieved 30-11-06, from http://www.copenhagenconsensus.com/Admin/Public/DWSDownload.aspx?File=Files%2fFiler%2fCC+UNP%2fCC06_Outcome.pdf.

Coudouel, A., Hentschel, J. S., & Wodon, Q. T. (2002). *Poverty Measurement and Analysis.* World Bank. Retrieved 10-1-07, from http://web.worldbank.org/WBSITE/EXTERNAL/TOPICS/EXTPOVERTY/EXTPRS/0,,contentMDK:20177055~pagePK:210058~piPK:216618~theSitePK:384201,00.html.

Coudrain, A., Francou, B., & Kundzewicz, Z. W. (2005). Glacier shrinkage in the Andes and consequences for water resources. *Hydrological Sciences Journal–Journal des Sciences Hydrologiques*, 50(6), 925–32.

Cowell, A. (2007, March 14). Britain drafts laws to slash carbon emissions. *New York Times*. Retrieved 15–3–07, from http://www.nytimes.com/2007/03/14/world/europe/14britain.html?em&ex=1174017600&en=c365191275dbd9f1&ei=5087%0A.

Cox, J. D. (2005). *Climate Crash: Abrupt Climate Change and What It Means for Our Future*. Washington, DC: Joseph Henry Press. http://www.loc.gov/catdir/toc/ecip057/2005002387.html.

Cox, S. (2007, January 25). The investigation. *Radio 4, BBC*. Retrieved 28–1–07, from http://www.bbc.co.uk/radio/aod/mainframe.shtml? http://www.bbc.co.uk/radio/aod/radio4_aod.shtml?radio4/theinvestigation.

Craig, J. R., Vaughan, D. J., & Skinner, B. J. (1996). *Resources of* the Earth: *Origin, Use and Environmental Impact*. Upper Saddle River, NJ: Prentice Hall.

Crok, M. (2005). Kyoto Protocol based on flawed statistics. *Naturwetenskap Techniek*, 2, 20–31.

Crowley, T. J., & Berner, R. A. (2001). Paleoclimate – CO2 and climate change. *Science*, 292(5518), 870–2.

CRS (2005). Energy tax policy. *Congressional Research Service*. Retrieved 28–1–07, from http://www.ncseonline.org/NLE/CRSreports/05apr/IB10054.pdf.

CRU (2006a). HadCRUT3 temperature: global. *Climatic Research Unit, University of East Anglia*. Retrieved 1–1–07, from http://www.cru.uea.ac.uk/cru/data/temperature/crutem3gl.txt.

CRU (2006b). HadCRUT3 temperature: northern hemisphere. *Climatic Research Unit, University of East Anglia*. Retrieved 07–12–06, from http://www.cru.uea.ac.uk/cru/data/temperature/hadcrut3nh.txt.

Cullen, N. J., Molg, T., Kaser, G., Hussein, K., Steffen, K., & Hardy, D. R. (2006). Kilimanjaro glaciers: recent areal extent from satellite data and new interpretation of observed 20th century retreat rates. *Geophysical Research Letters*, 33(16).

Curran, E. B., Holle, R. L., & Lopez, R. E. (2000). Lightning casualties and damages in the United States from 1959 to 1994. *Journal of Climate*, 13(19), 3448–64.

Curry, J. A., Webster, R. J., & Holland, G. J. (2006). Mixing politics and science in testing the hypothesis that greenhouse warming is causing a global increase in hurricane intensity. *Bulletin of the American Meteorological Society*, 87(8), 1025–37.

D'Arrigo, R., Wilson, R., & Jacoby, G. (2006). On the long-term context for late twentieth century warming. *Journal of Geophysical Research–Atmospheres*, 111(D3).

Dagoumas, A. S., Papagiannis, G. K., & Dokopoulos, P. S. (2006). An economic assessment of the Kyoto Protocol application. *Energy Policy*, 34(1), 26–39.

Dai, A. G., Lamb, P. J., Trenberth, K. E., Hulme, M., Jones, P. D., & Xie, P. P. (2004). The recent Sahel drought is real. *International Journal of Climatology*, 24(11), 1323–31.

Dai, A. G., Trenberth, K. E., & Qian, T. T. (2004). A global dataset of Palmer Drought Severity Index for 1870–2002: relationship with soil moisture and effects of surface warming. *Journal of Hydrometeorology*, 5(6), 1117–30.

Dai, A., Wigley, T. M. L., Boville, B. A., Kiehl, J. T., & Buja, L. E. (2001). Climates of the twentieth and twenty-first centuries simulated by the NCAR climate system model. *Journal of Climate*, 14(4), 485–519.

Dalyell, T. (2004). Westminster diary. *New Scientist*, 181(2439), 49.

Dana, W. (2006, July 13–27). Al Gore 3.0: the man who won the presidency in 2000 is looser and more outspoken than ever. Is his global-warming movie a warm-up for a third run at the White House? *Rolling Stone*. Retrieved 29–11–06, from http://www.rollingstone.com/news/story/10688399/al_gore_30/print.

Dasgupta, P. (2006, November 11). Comments on the Stern Review's Economics of Climate Change. Retrieved 24–1–07, from http://www.econ.cam.ac.uk/faculty/dasgupta/STERN.pdf.

Datt, G. (1998). *Computational Tools for Poverty Measurement and Analysis.* Washington, DC: International Food Policy Research Institute.

Davis, R. E., Knappenberger, P. C., Michaels, P. J., & Novicoff, W. M. (2003). Changing heat-related mortality in the United States. *Environmental Health Perspectives*, 111(14), 1712–18.

Davis, R. E., Knappenberger, P. C., Novicoff, W. M., & Michaels, P. J. (2002). Decadal changes in heat-related human mortality in the eastern United States. *Climate Research*, 22(2), 175–84.

DeLong, J. B. (2007). Estimating world GDP, one million B.C. – present. Retrieved 2–4–07, from http://econ161.berkeley.edu/tceh/2000/world_gdp/estimating_world_gdp.html.

Demaree, G. R. (2006). The catastrophic floods of February 1784 in and around Belgium – a Little Ice Age event of frost, snow, river ice . . . and floods. *Hydrological Sciences Journal–Journal des Sciences Hydrologiques*, 51(5), 878–98.

Deming, D. (2005). Global warming, the politicization of science, and Michael Crichton's "State of Fear." *Journal of Scientific Exploration*, 19(2).

Denton, A. (2006, September 11). Interview with Al Gore. *Enough Rope on Australia ABC*. Retrieved 13–1–07, from http://www.abc.net.au/tv/enoughrope/transcripts/s1734175.htm.

Department of Commerce (1982). *Survey of Current Business: August 1982.*

Department of Commerce. Retrieved 2–1–07, from http://fraser.stlouisfed.org/ publications/SCB/1982/issue/1847.

Department of Commerce (2006). *Survey of Current Business: December 2006*. Department of Commerce. Retrieved 2–1–07, from http://www.bea.gov/scb/ index.htm.

Derraik, J. G. B. (2004). Exotic mosquitoes in New Zealand: a review of species intercepted, their pathways and ports of entry. *Australian and New Zealand Journal of Public Health*, 28(5), 433–44.

DGPWWM (2001). *Room for the Rhine in the Netherlands*. Directorate-General for Public Works and Water Management. Retrieved 23–12–06, from http://www.verkeerenwaterstaat.nl/kennisplein/page_kennisplein.aspx?DossierU RI=tcm:195–17870–4&Id=205.

DiCaprio, L. (2000). Interview with Bill Clinton for ABC News' Planet Earth 2000. *Weekly Compilation of Presidential Documents*, 36(17), 907–12.

Dillin, J. (2000). Global cooling – mini-ice age. *Christian Science Monitor*, 92(191), 16.

Dobson, M. (1980). "Marsh fever" – the geography of malaria in England. *Journal of Historical Geography*, 6(4), 357–89.

Dohm, K., & From, L. (2004, April 21). FN-chef: Lomborg tænker som Hitler [UN executive: Lomborg thinks as Hitler]. *Jyllands-Posten*, A1.

Doll, R., & Peto, R. (1981). The causes of cancer: quantitative estimates of avoidable risks of cancer in the United States today. *Journal of the National Cancer Institute*, 66(6), 1191–308.

Doran, P. T., Priscu, J. C., Lyons, W. B., Walsh, J. E., Fountain, A. G., McKnight, D. M., et al. (2002). Antarctic climate cooling and terrestrial ecosystem response. *Nature*, 415(6871), 517–20.

Downton, M., Miller, J. Z. B., & Pielke, R. A. (2005a). Data: reanalysis of U.S. National Weather Service flood loss database. Retrieved 23–12–06, from http://www.flooddamagedata.org/national.html.

Downton, M., Miller, J. Z. B., & Pielke, R. A. (2005b). Reanalysis of U.S. National Weather Service flood loss database. *Natural Hazards Review*, 2(4), 157–66. Retrieved 19–12–06, from http://sciencepolicy.colorado.edu/admin/ publication_files/ resource–34–2001.03.pdf.

Ducati, R. G., Ruffino-Netto, A., Basso, L. A., & Santos, D. S. (2006). The resumption of consumption – a review on tuberculosis. *Memorias do Instituto Oswaldo Cruz*, 101(7), 697–714.

Dunn, S. (1998). Looking past El Niño. *World Watch*, 11(5), 2.

DUPD (2006). Historic components of Pima County population: 1910–2009. *Department of Urban Planning & Design*. Retrieved 13–2–07, from http:// www.tucsonaz.gov/planning/data/demographic/hcomppcp.pdf.

DW staff (2006, September 28). Merkel to target climate change as G8, EU leader. *Deutsche Welle*. Retrieved 6–11–06, from http://www.dw-world.de/dw/article/ 0,2144,2188336,00.html.

Easterling, D. R., Evans, J. L., Groisman, P. Y., Karl, T. R., Kunkel, K. E., & Ambenje, P. (2000). Observed variability and trends in extreme climate events: a brief review. *Bulletin of the American Meteorological Society*, 81(3), 417–25.

EB (2006a). Flood legend. *Encyclopædia Britannica*. Retrieved 09–12–06, from http://www.britannica.com/ebi/article–9274347.

EB (2006b). Gulf Stream. *Encyclopædia Britannica*. Retrieved 25–12–06, from http://search.eb.com.esc-proxy.lib.cbs.dk/eb/article-9038484.

EB (2006c). Holocene Epoch. *Encyclopædia Britannica*. Retrieved 07–12–06, from http://search.eb.com.esc-proxy.lib.cbs.dk/eb/article-9117456.

EB (2006d). Ice Age. *Encyclopædia Britannica*. Retrieved 07–12–06, from http://search.eb.com.esc-proxy.lib.cbs.dk/eb/article-9041958.

Ebi, K. L., Mills, D. M., Smith, J. B., & Grambsch, A. (2006). Climate change and human health impacts in the United States: an update on the results of the US National Assessment. *Environmental Health Perspectives*, 114(9), 1318–24.

EcoBusinessLinks (2007). How much does carbon offsetting cost? Price survey! *EcoBusinessLinks.com*. Retrieved 1–2–07, from http://www.ecobusinesslinks.com/ carbon_offset_wind_credits_carbon_reduction.htm.

Economist Anon. (2006). Selling hot air. *The Economist*, 360(8494), 17–19.

EDD (2006a). Miami Beach Statistical Abstract 2000–2006. *Economic Development Department*. Retrieved 10–12–06, from http://www.miamibeachfl.gov/newcity/ depts/econdev/Statistical%20Abstract%20(Long).pdf.

EDD (2006b). Tourism overview. *Economic Development Department*. Retrieved 10–12–06, from http://www.miamibeachfl.gov/newcity/depts/econdev/visitors %20Profile.asp.

EDIE (2006, November 21). Still no post-Kyoto plan as climate talks end. *EDIE Newsroom*. Retrieved 29–1–07, from http://www.edie.net/news/news_ story.asp?id=12286.

Edwards, G. (2006, April 5). Hot in here. *Rolling Stone*, 999, 27ff.

Edwards, J., Yang, B. H., & Al-Hmoud, R. B. (2005). Water availability and economic development: signs of the invisible hand? An empirical look at the Falkenmark index and macroeconomic development. *Natural Resources Journal*, 45(4), 953–78.

EEA (2006). *Greenhouse Gas Emission Trends and Projections in Europe 2006*. European Environment Agency. Retrieved 18–11–06, from http://reports.eea. europa.eu/eea_report_2006_9/en/eea_report_9_2006.pdf.

Ehrlich, P. R. (1968). *The Population Bomb*. New York: Ballantine Books.

EIA (1999). Carbon Dioxide Emissions from the Generation of Electric Power in the

United States. US Energy Information Agency Administration. Retrieved 21–11–06, from http://www.eia.doe.gov/cneaf/electricity/page/co2_report/ co2emiss99.pdf.

EIA (2002). Updated state-level greenhouse gas emission coefficients for electricity generation 1998–2000. *US Energy Information Administration*. Retrieved 21–11–06, from http://tonto.eia.doe.gov/FTPROOT/environment/e-supdoc-u.pdf.

EIA (2006a). Emissions of greenhouse gasses in the United States 2005. *US Energy Information Administration*. Retrieved 30–11–06, from http://www.eia.doe.gov/ oiaf/1605/ggrpt/pdf/057305.pdf.

EIA (2006b). International Energy Annual 2004. *US Energy Information Administration*. Retrieved 30–11–06, from http://www.eia.doe.gov/iea/.

EIA (2006c). International Energy Outlook 2006. *US Energy Information Administration*. Retrieved 20–11–06, from http://www.eia.doe.gov/oiaf/ieo/ index.html.

EIA (2006d). Monthly Energy Reivew: October 2006. *US Energy Information Administration*. Retrieved 21–11–06, from http://www.eia.doe.gov/emeu/ mer/pdf/mer.pdf.

EIA (2006e). US historical CO_2 emissions. *US Energy Information Administration*. Retrieved 30–11–06, from http://www.eia.doe.gov/oiaf/1605/ggrpt/excel/ historical_co2.xls.

EIA (2006f). Voluntary reporting of greenhouse gases program: fuel and energy source codes and emission coefficients. *US Energy Information Administration*. Retrieved 22–11–06, from http://www.eia.doe.gov/oiaf/1605/coefficients.html.

Eilperin, J. (2004). Study says polar bears could face extinction. *Washington Post*. Retrieved 7–11–06, from http://www.washingtonpost.com/wp-dyn/articles/ A35233–2004Nov8.html.

Eisner, M. (2003). Long-term historical trends in violent crime. *Crime and Justice*, 31, 83–142. Retrieved 2–4–07, from http://www.journals.uchicago.edu/ CJ/039104.pdf.

Ekart, D. D., Cerling, T. E., Montanez, I. P., & Tabor, N. J. (1999). A 400 million year carbon isotope record of pedogenic carbonate: implications for paleoatmospheric carbon dioxide. *American Journal of Science*, 299(10), 805–27.

Ekman, M. (1999). Climate changes detected through the world's longest sea level series. *Global and Planetary Change*, 21(4), 215–24.

El-Zein, A., Tewtel-Salem, M., & Nehme, G. (2004). A time-series analysis of mortality and air temperature in Greater Beirut. *Science of the Total Environment*, 330(1–3), 71–80.

Ellerman, A. D., & Wing, I. S. (2000). Supplementarity: an invitation to monopsony? *Energy Journal*, 21(4), 29–59.

Elsom, D. M. (2001). Deaths and injuries caused by lightning in the United Kingdom: analyses of two databases. *Atmospheric Research*, 56(1–4), 325–34.

Emanuel, K. (2005a). Increasing destructiveness of tropical cyclones over the past 30 years. *Nature*, 436(7051), 686–8.

Emanuel, K. (2005b). Meteorology – Emanuel replies. *Nature*, 438(7071), E13–E13.

Emanuel, K., Anthes, R., Curry, J., Elsner, J., Holland, G., Klotzbach, P., et al. (2006, July 25). Statement on the U.S. hurricane problem. Retrieved 18–12–06, from http://wind.mit.edu/~emanuel/Hurricane_threat.htm.

EPA (2000, April). Average annual emissions and fuel consumption for passenger cars and light trucks. *US Environmental Protection Agency*. Retrieved 21–11–06, from http://www.epa.gov/otaq/consumer/f00013.pdf.

Epstein, P. R. (2000). Is global warming harmful to health? *Scientific American*, 283(2), 50–7.

Epstein, P. R., Diaz, H. F., Elias, S., Grabherr, G., Graham, N. E., Martens, W. J. M., et al. (1998). Biological and physical signs of climate change: focus on mosquito-borne diseases. *Bulletin of the American Meteorological Society*, 79(3), 409–17.

Ereaut, G., & Segnit, N. (2006). Warm words: how are we telling the climate story and can we tell it better? *Institute for Public Policy Research*. Retrieved 20–1–07, from http://www.ippr.org.uk/members/download.asp?f=/ecomm/files/warm_words.pdf&a=skip.

Esper, J., Wilson, R. J. S., Frank, D. C., Moberg, A., Wanner, H., & Luterbacher, J. (2005). Climate: past ranges and future changes. *Quaternary Science Reviews*, 24(20–1), 2164–66.

EU (1996a, June 11). 1st UNFCC Communication EN. *Commission of the European Communities*. Retrieved 27–11–06, from http://ec.europa.eu/environment/climat/pdf/1st_unfcc_communication_en.pdf.

EU (1996b, June 25). Communication on community strategy on climate change. *1939th Council Meeting, Luxemburg*.

EU (2001, June). ECCP Report. *Commission of the European Communities*. Retrieved 27–11–06, from http://ec.europa.eu/environment/climat/pdf/eccp_report_0106.pdf; Press release: http://europa.eu/rapid/start/cgi/guesten.ksh?p_action.gettxt=gt&doc=IP/01/816|0|RAPID&lg=EN.

EU (2005a). *What Scorching Weather*. European Union. Retrieved 27–11–06, from http://ec.europa.eu/environment/pubs/pdf/weather/en.pdf.

EU (2005b, February 9). Winning the battle against global climate change. *Commission of the European Communities*. Retrieved 28–11–06, from http://eur-lex.europa.eu/LexUriServ/site/en/com/2005/com2005_0035en01.pdf.

EU (2007a). Gross domestic expenditure on R&D. *EUROSTAT*. Retrieved 15–3–07, from http://epp.eurostat.ec.europa.eu/portal/page?_pageid=1996,39140985&_dad=portal&_schema=PORTAL&screen=detailref&language=en&product=Yearlies_new_science_technology&root=Yearlies_new_science_technology/I/I1/ir021.

EU (2007b). Lisbon Strategy. *Europa Glossary*. Retrieved 15–3–07, from http://europa.eu/scadplus/glossary/lisbon_strategy_en.htm.

EU (2007c, March 9). Presidency conclusions of the Brussels European Council 8/9 March 2007. Retrieved 15–3–07, from http://www.consilium.europa.eu/ueDocs/cms_Data/docs/pressData/en/ec/93135.pdf.

EurActiv. (2007, January 12). EU defends leadership in "world war" on climate change. *EurActiv.com*. Retrieved 22–1–07, from http://www.euractiv.com/en/energy//article-160848.

Evans, E., Ashley, R., Hall, J., Penning-Rowsell, E., Saul, A., Sayers, P., et al. (2004). *Foresight, Future Flooding. Scientific Summary*, vol I: *Future Risks and Their Drivers*. London: Office of Science and Technology. Retrieved 14–1–07, from http://www.foresight.gov.uk/Previous_Projects/Flood_and_Coastal_Defence/Reports_and_Publications/Volume1/Thanks.htm.

Evans, E., Ashley, R., Hall, J., Penning-Rowsell, E., Sayers, P., Thorne, C., et al. (2004). *Foresight, Future Flooding. Scientific Summary*, vol II: *Managing Future Risks*. London: Office of Science and Technology. Retrieved 14–1–07, from http://www.foresight.gov.uk/Previous_Projects/Flood_and_Coastal_Defence/Reports_and_Publications/Volume2/Thanks2.htm.

Evans, H. (1989). European malaria policy in the 1920s and 1930s: the epidemiology of minutiae. *Isis*, 80(1), 40–59.

Falkenmark, M., & Widstrand, C. (1992). Population and water-resources – a delicate balance. *Population Bulletin*, 47(3), 2–36.

FAO (2001). Global forest resources assessment 2000. *UN Food and Agricultural Organization*. Retrieved 25–12–06, from http://www.fao.org/docrep/004/Y1997E/y1997e00.htm#Contents.

FAO (2006). World agriculture: toward 2030/2050 – Interim report. *UN Food and Agricultural Organization*. Retrieved 2–1–07, from http://www.fao.org/es/ESD/AT2050web.pdf.

FAO (2007). FAOSTAT database http://faostat.fao.org/default.aspx.

FDA (2005, June 30). Letter responding to health claim petition dated January 27, 2004: green tea and reduced risk of cancer health claim. *Food and Drug Administration*. Docket number 2004Q-0083. Retrieved 27–12–06, from http://www.cfsan.fda.gov/~dms/qhc-gtea.html.

Finkel, A. (1996). Comparing risks thoughtfully. *Risk: Health, Safety & Environment*, 7(325), 7(4), 325–59.

Fischer, D. (2006, December 15). Gore urges scientists to speak up. *Contra Costa Times*. Retrieved 29–1–07, from http://www.truthout.org/cgi-bin/artman/exec/view.cgi/67/24524.

Fischer, G., Shah, M., Tubiello, F. N., & van Velhuizen, H. (2005). Socio-economic and climate change impacts on agriculture: an integrated assessment,

1990–2080. *Philosophical Transactions of the Royal Society B: Biological Sciences*, 360(1463), 2067–83.

Fischer, G., Shah, M., & Velthuizen, H. van (2002). *Climate Change and Agricultural Vulnerability*. International Institute for Applied Systems Analysis for World Summit on Sustainable Development, Johannesburg 2002. Retrieved 3–1–07, from http://www.iiasa.ac.at/Research/LUC/JB-Report.pdf.

Fischer, G., Velthuizen, H. van, Shah, M., & Nachtergaele, F. (2002). *Global Agro-ecological Assessment for Agriculture in the 21st Century: Methodology and Results*. International Institute for Applied Systems Analysis and UN Food and Agriculture Organization. Retrieved 3–1–07, from http://www.iiasa.ac.at/Admin/PUB/Documents/RR–02–002.pdf.

Fischer, H., Wahlen, M., Smith, J., Mastroianni, D., & Deck, B. (1999). Ice core records of atmospheric CO_2 around the last three glacial terminations. *Science*, 283(5408), 1712–14.

Fisher, B. S., Ford, M., Jakeman, G., Gurney, A., Penm, J., Matysek, A., et al. (2006). Technological development and economic growth. *Abare Research Report 06.1*. Retrieved 29–1–07, from http://www.abareconomics.com/publications_html/climate/climate_06/06_climate.pdf.

Fleitas, I., Caspani, C. C., Borras, C., Plazas, M. C., Miranda, A. A., Brandar, M. E., et al. (2006). The quality of radiology services in five Latin American countries. *Revista Panamericana de Salud Publica–Pan American Journal of Public Health*, 20(2–3), 113–24.

FOE (2000). Climate change: the victims bear witness. *Friends of the Earth*. Retrieved 17–12–06, from http://chelus.foe.co.uk/resource/press_releases/20000911110056.html.

FOE (2006). Climate: climate change. *Friends of the Earth*. Retrieved 17–12–06, from http://www.foe.co.uk/campaigns/climate/issues/climate_change/.

Forster, A. (2006, November 30). Can we go on building roads and runways *and* save the planet? *LTT Online*. Retrieved 28–1–07, from http://www.staff.livjm.ac.uk/spsbpeis/LTT-interviewNo06.pdf.

Fosberg, F. R. (1963). Pesticides and ecology. review of *Silent Spring*. *Ecology*, 44(3), 624.

Fowler, H. J., & Archer, D. R. (2006). Conflicting signals of climatic change in the Upper Indus Basin. *Journal of Climate*, 19(17), 4276–93.

Freedom House. (2007). Freedom in the world 2007. Retrieved 3–4–07, from http://www.freedomhouse.org/template.cfm?page=15.

Fumento, M. (1993). *Science under Siege: Balancing Technology and the Environment*. New York: W. Morrow.

GAO (1995). *Midwest Flood: Information on the Performance, Effects, and Control of Levees* (Vol. GAO/RCED–95–125). US General Accounting Office. Retrieved 22–12–06, from http://www.gao.gov/cgi-bin/getrpt?RCED–95–125.

Gebhardt, J. G., & Norris, T. E. (2006). Acute stroke care at rural hospitals in Idaho: challenges in expediting stroke care. *Journal of Rural Health*, 22(1), 88–91.

Gelbspan, R. (2004). *Boiling Point: How Politicians, Big Oil and Coal, Journalists, and Activists are Fueling the Climate Crisis – and What We Can Do To Avert Disaster*. New York: Basic Books. http://www.loc.gov/catdir/toc/ecip0415/2004003223.html.

Gelbspan, R. (2005, August 30). Katrina's real name. *Boston Globe*. Retrieved 17–12–06, from http://www.boston.com/news/weather/articles/2005/08/30/katrinas_real_name/.

Giannini, A., Saravanan, R., & Chang, P. (2003). Oceanic forcing of Sahel rainfall on interannual to interdecadal time scales. *Science*, 302(5647), 1027–30.

Gibbon, G. (2006, October 30). Government pledges action. *Channel4News*. Retrieved 24–1–07, from http://www.channel4.com/news/special-reports/special-reports-storypage.jsp?id=3757.

Gildor, H., Tziperman, E., & Toggweiler, J. R. (2002). Sea ice switch mechanism and glacial–interglacial CO2 variations. *Global Biogeochemical Cycles*, 16(3).

Giles, J. (2006, November 2). How much will it cost to save the world. *Nature*, 6–7.

GISS. (2006). Amundsen–Scott temperature data, 1957–2006. *Goddard Institute for Space Studies*. Retrieved 15–12–06, from http://data.giss.nasa.gov/work/gistemp/STATIONS//tmp.700890090008.1.1/station.txt.

Gleick, P. H. (1998). *The World's Water 1998–1999: The Biennial Report on Freshwater Resources*. Washington, DC: Island Press.

Goklany, I. M. (2000). Applying the precautionary principle to global warming. *Weidenbaum Center Working Paper No. PS 158*. Retrieved 30–1–07, from http://ssrn.com/abstract=250380.

Goklany, I. M. (2006). *The Improving State of the World: Why We're Living Longer, Healthier, More Comfortable Lives on a Cleaner Planet*. Washington, DC: Cato Institute. Distributed to the trade by National Book Network.

Golub, A., Markandya, A., & Marcellino, D. (2006). Does the Kyoto Protocol cost too much and create unbreakable barriers for economic growth? *Contemporary Economic Policy*, 24(4), 520–35.

Gore, A. (1992). *Earth in the Balance: Ecology and the Human Spirit*. New York: Plume.

Gore, A. (2006a, November 19). At stake is nothing less than the survival of human civilisation. *Telegraph*. Retrieved 19–12–06, from http://www.telegraph.co.uk/news/main.jhtml;jsessionid=FAFKOMPHJAYNJQFIQMFSFFOAVCBQ0IV0?xml=/news/2006/11/19/nclim19.xml&page=1.

Gore, A. (2006b). *An Inconvenient Truth: The Movie*. Paramount DVD.

Gore, A. (2006c). The wisdom of a climate crusader/Time 100. *Time*, 78. Retrieved from http:/www.times.com/time/magazine/article/0,9171,1187255, 00.html/.

Gore, A., & Melcher Media (2006). *An Inconvenient Truth: The Planetary Emergency of Global Warming and What We Can Do about It.* Emmaus, PA: Rodale Press. http://www.loc.gov/catdir/enhancements/fy0662/2006926537-d.html.

Gorman, C. (1998). El Niño's (achoo!) allergies. *Time,* 151(11), 73.

Gouveia, N., Hajat, S., & Armstrong, B. (2003). Socioeconomic differentials in the temperature–mortality relationship in Sao Paulo, Brazil. *International Journal of Epidemiology,* 32(3), 390–7.

Graddy, K., & Stevens, M. (2005). The impact of school resources on student performance: a study of private schools in the United Kingdom. *Industrial & Labor Relations Review,* 58(3), 435–51.

Graham, J. D. (1995). Comparing opportunities to reduce health risks: toxin control, medicine, and injury prevention. *NCPA Policy Report,* 192. Retrieved 22–1–07, from http://www.ncpa.org/studies/s192/s192.html.

Graham-Harrison, E. (2006, October 30). China hopes for post-2012 Kyoto deal within 2 years. *Reuters.* Retrieved 19–11–06, from http://www.planetark.com/dailynewsstory.cfm/newsid/38721/story.htm.

Gratz, N. G., Steffen, R., & Cocksedge, W. (2000). Why aircraft disinsection? *Bulletin of the World Health Organization,* 78(8), 995–1004.

Greater London Authority (2006). *London's Urban Heat Island: A Summary for Decision Makers.* Retrieved 15–11–06, from http://www.london.gov.uk/mayor/environment/climate-change/index.jsp.

Greenpeace (2001). Kilimanjaro set to lose its ice field by 2015 due to climate change. *Greenpeace news release.* Retrieved 07–12–06, from http://www.commondreams.org/news2001/1106–02.htm.

Greenpeace (2006a). Climate change. *Greenpeace International.* Retrieved 19–12–06, from http://www.greenpeace.org/seasia/en/asia-energy-revolution/climate-change.

Greenpeace (2006b). Global warnings. *Greenpeace International.* Retrieved 17–12–06, from http://www.greenpeace.org/international/news/extreme-weather-warnings.

Greenpeace (2006c). Sea level rise. Retrieved 15–12–06, from http://www.greenpeace.org/international/campaigns/climate-change/impacts/sea_level_rise.

Gregory, J., & Huybrechts, P. (2006). Ice-sheet contributions to future sea-level change. *Philosophical Transactions of the Royal Society A: Mathematical, Physical and Engineering Sciences,* 364(1844), 1709–31. http://dx.doi.org/10.1098/rsta.2006.1796.

Grice, A. (2006, November 20). Slow talks could leave climate deal in "tatters." *Independent.* Retrieved 20–11–06, from http://news.independent.co.uk/environment/article1998840.ece.

Griffith, T. (1998). All downhill. *Boston Business Journal,* 18(3), 1–2.

Grigg, D. B. (1993). *The World Food Problem* (2nd edn). Cambridge, MA: Blackwell.

Groisman, P. Y., Knight, R. W., Easterling, D. R., Karl, T. R., Hegerl, G. C., & Razuvaev, V. A. N. (2005). Trends in intense precipitation in the climate record. *Journal of Climate*, 18(9), 1326–50.

Groisman, P. Y., Knight, R. W., & Karl, T. R. (2001). Heavy precipitation and high streamflow in the contiguous United States: trends in the twentieth century. *Bulletin of the American Meteorological Society*, 82(2), 219–46.

Grubb, M. (2004). Kyoto and the future of international climate change responses: from here to where? *International Review for Environmental Strategies*, 5(1), 15–38.

Grubb, M., Kohler, J., & Anderson, D. (2002). Induced technical change in energy and environmental modeling: analytic approaches and policy implications. *Annual Review of Energy and the Environment*, 27, 271–308.

Grzimek (n.d.). Emperor penguin. *Grzimek's Animal Life Encyclopedia*. Retrieved 16–12–06, from http://www.answers.com/topic/emperor-penguin.

GSS (2007). US General Social Survey 1972–2004. Retrieved 27–1–07, from http://sda.berkeley.edu/cgi-bin/hsda?harcsda+gss04.

Guerra, C. A., Snow, R. W., & Hay, S. I. (2006). Mapping the global extent of malaria in 2005. *Trends in Parasitology*, 22(8), 353–8.http://www.sciencedirect.com/science/article/B6W7G-4K7WJ9B-3/2/c7bc30e9ee4255e97bc8d676c0acc50c.

Gupta, S., Hastak, K., Ahmad, N., Lewin, J. S., & Mukhtar, H. (2001). Inhibition of prostate carcinogenesis in TRAMP mice by oral infusion of green tea polyphenols. *Proceedings of the National Academy of Sciences of the United States of America*, 98(18), 10350–5.

Gwynne, P. (1975, April 28). The cooling world. *Newsweek*, 64.

Hagen, J. (2007, January 19). Act on global warming now or pay later: the Stern Review. *UN Chronicle Online Edition*. Retrieved 24–1–07, from http://www.un.org/Pubs/chronicle/2007/webArticles/011907_stern.htm.

Hahn, R. W. (1996). *Risks, Costs, and Lives Saved: Getting Better Results from Regulation*. New York: Oxford University Press.

Halperin, M. H. (2001). Bush unpopular in Europe, seen as unilateralist. Commentary by Morton H. Halperin, Senior Fellow, Council on Foreign Relations. Retrieved 18–11–06, from http://pewglobal.org/reports/display.php?PageID=37.

Hanley, C. J. (2006a, November 14). Diseases appear on rise with temperatures, experts say; "may overwhelm health services." *Associated Press*. Retrieved 2–1–07, from http://nctimes.com/articles/2006/11/15//health/17_33_4411_14_06.txt.

Hanley, C. J. (2006b, December 18). Malaria cases climb in African highlands. *Associated Press*. Retrieved 2–1–07, from http://www.chron.com/disp/story.mpl/health/4408267.html.

Hansen, B., Osterhus, S., Quadfasel, D., & Turrell, W. (2004). Already the day after tomorrow? *Science*, 305(5686), 953–4.

Hansen, J. E. (2005). A slippery slope: how much global warming constitutes "dangerous anthropogenic interference"? *Climatic Change*, 68(3), 269–79.

Hansen, J. E. (2006, July 13). The threat to the planet. *New York Review of Books*. Retrieved 11–12–06, from http://www.nybooks.com/articles/9131.

Harden, B. (2005, July 7). Experts predict polar bear decline: global warming is melting their ice pack habitat. *Washington Post*, A03. Retrieved 7–11–06, from http://www.washingtonpost.com/wp-dyn/content/article/2005/07/06/AR2005070601899.html.

Harris, R. N., & Chapman, D. S. (2005). Borehole temperatures and tree rings: seasonality and estimates of extratropical northern hemispheric warming. *Journal of Geophysical Research–Earth Surface*, 110(F4).

Hartill, L. (1998). Cold fusion. *Christian Science Monitor*, 90(211), 9.

Hassol, S. J. (2004). *Impacts of a Warming Arctic: Arctic Climate Impact Assessment*. Cambridge: Cambridge University Press. Retrieved 7–11–06, from http://www.acia.uaf.edu/pages/overview.html.

Hawkins, D. (2001, July 10). Climate change technology and policy options. *Director of NRDC's Climate Center, Comments for U.S. Senate Committee on Commerce, Science, and Transportation*. Retrieved 29–1–07, from http://www.nrdc.org/globalWarming/tdh0701.asp.

Hay, S. I., Cox, J., Rogers, D. J., Randolph, S. E., Stern, D. I., Shanks, G. D., et al. (2002). Climate change and the resurgence of malaria in the East African highlands. *Nature*, 415(6874), 905–9.

Hay, S. I., Guerra, C. A., Tatem, A. J., Atkinson, P. M., & Snow, R. W. (2005). Urbanization, malaria transmission and disease burden in Africa. *Nature Reviews Microbiology*, 3(1), 81–90.

Hay, S. I., Guerra, C. A., Tatem, A. J., Noor, A. M., & Snow, R. W. (2004). The global distribution and population at risk of malaria: past, present, and future. *Lancet Infectious Diseases*, 4(6), 327–36.

Hay, S. I., Rogers, D. J., Randolph, S. E., Stern, D. L., Cox, J., Shanks, G. D., et al. (2002). Hot topic or hot air? Climate change and malaria resurgence in East African highlands. *Trends in Parasitology*, 18(12), 530–4.

Hay, S. I., Cox, I., Rogers, D. J., Randolph, S. E., Stern, D. L., Shanks, G. D., et al. (2002). Climate change – regional warming and malaria resurgence – reply. *Nature*, 420(6916), 628.

Heartfield, J. (2006, October 11). A secular version of Kingdom Come. *Spiked*. Retrieved 27–1–07, from http://www.spiked-online.com/index.php?/site/article/1839/.

Heijnes, H., Brummelen, M. van, & Blok, K. (1999). *Reduction of the Emissions of*

HFC's, PFC's and SF6 in the European Union. ECOFYS. Retrieved 20–11–06, from http://ec.europa.eu/environment/enveco/climate_change/9800043.pdf.

Heino, R., Brázdil, R., Førland, E., Tuomenvirta, H., Alexandersson, H., Beniston, M., Pfister, C., Rebetez, M., Rosenhagen, G., Rösner, S., & Wibig, J. (1999). Progress in the study of climatic extremes in Northern and Central Europe. *Climatic Change* 42(1): 183–202.

Helm, D. (2003). The assessment: climate-change policy. *Oxford Review of Economic Policy*, 19(3), 349–61.

Henderson, M. (2005, December 1). Britain faces big freeze as Gulf Stream loses strength. *The Times*. Retrieved 27–12–06, from http://www.timesonline.co.uk/article/0,,2-1898493,00.html.

Hinkel, K. M., Nelson, F. E., Klene, A. F., & Bell, J. H. (2003). The urban heat island in winter at Barrow, Alaska. *International Journal of Climatology*, 23(15), 1889–1905.

Hoerling, M., Hurrell, J., Eischeid, J., & Phillips, A. (2006). Detection and attribution of twentieth-century northern and southern African rainfall change. *Journal of Climate*, 19(16), 3989–4008.

Holle, R. L., Lopez, R. E., & Navarro, B. C. (2005). Deaths, injuries, and damages from lightning in the United States in the 1890s in comparison with the 1990s. *Journal of Applied Meteorology*, 44(10), 1563–73.

Hopkin, M. (2006, November 29). Gulf Stream weakened in "Little Ice Age." *Nature*. doi:10.1038/news061127–8.

Horton, E. B., Folland, C. K., & Parker, D. E. (2001). The changing incidence of extremes in worldwide and Central England temperatures to the end of the twentieth century. *Climatic Change*, 50(3), 267–95.

Howat, I. M., Joughin, I., & Scambos, T. A. (2007). Rapid changes in ice discharge from Greenland outlet glaciers. *Science*, 315(5818), 1559–61. http://www.sciencemag.org/cgi/content/abstract/315/5818/1559.

Hughes, M. K., & Diaz, H. F. (1994). Was there a medieval warm period, and if so, where and when? *Climatic Change*, 26(2–3), 109–42.

Hui, E. K. W. (2006). Reasons for the increase in emerging and re-emerging viral infectious diseases. *Microbes and Infection*, 8(3), 905–16.

Hulden, L., Hulden, L., & Heliovaara, K. (2005). Endemic malaria: an "indoor" disease in northern Europe. Historical data analysed. *Malaria Journal*, 4.

Hulme, M. (2006, November 4). Chaotic world of climate truth. *bbc.co.uk*. Retrieved 22–1–07, from http://news.bbc.co.uk/2/hi/science/nature/6115644.stm.

Hume, D. (1754). Of the populousness of ancient nations. In D. Hume (ed.), *Essays: Moral, Political and Literary*. Indianapolis: Liberty Classics.

Humlum, O. (n.d.). Antarctic temperature changes during the observational period:

UNIS, Department of Geology, Svalbard, Norway. Retrieved 15–12–06, from http://www.unis.no/research/geology/Geo_research/Ole/AntarcticTemperature Changes.htm.

Hung, T., Uchihama, D., Ochi, S., & Yasuoka, Y. (2006). Assessment with satellite data of the urban heat island effects in Asian mega cities. *International Journal of Applied Earth Observation and Geoinformation*, 8(1), 34–48.

Huntington, T. G. (2006). Evidence for intensification of the global water cycle: review and synthesis. *Journal of Hydrology*, 319(1–4), 83–95.

Hutton, G., & Haller, L. (2004). Evaluation of the costs and benefits of water and sanitation improvements at the global level. WHO/SDE/WSH/04.04: *World Health Organization*. Retrieved 8–1–07, from http://www.who.int/water_sanitation_health/wsh0404.pdf.

Huybers, P. (2005). Comment on "Hockey sticks, principal components, and spurious significance" by S. McIntyre and R. McKitrick. *Geophysical Research Letters*, 32(20).

Huybrechts, P., & de Wolde, J. (1999). The dynamic response of the Greenland and Antarctic ice sheets to multiple-century climatic warming. *Journal of Climate*, 12(8), 2169–88.

IEA (2004). *World Energy Outlook 2004*. IEA Publications.

IEA (2006a). *CO_2 Emissions from Fuel Combustion 1971–2004*. IEA Publications.

IEA (2006b). *Renewable Energy: RD&D Priorities*. International Energy Agency.

IEA (2006c). *World Energy Outlook 2006*. IEA Publications.

IEA (2007). IEA Energy Technology R&D Statistics Service. *International Energy Agency*. http://www.iea.org/rdd/ReportFolders/ReportFolders.aspx?CS_referer=&CS_ChosenLang=en.

Ijumba, J. N., Mosha, F. W., & Lindsay, S. W. (2002). Malaria transmission risk variations derived from different agricultural practices in an irrigated area of northern Tanzania. *Medical and Veterinary Entomology*, 16(1), 28–38.

IMF (2006). *World Economic Outlook: Financial Systems and Economic Cycles* (Vol. September). International Monetary Fund. Retrieved 20–11–06, from http://www.imf.org/external/pubs/ft/weo/2006/02/index.htm.

IMF (2007). *IMF Primary Commodity Prices*. International Monetary Fund. Retrieved 3–1–07, from http://www.imf.org/external/np/res/commod/index.asp.

Indermuhle, A., Monnin, E., Stauffer, B., Stocker, T. F., & Wahlen, M. (2000). Atmospheric CO2 concentration from 60 to 20 kyr BP from the Taylor Dome ice core, Antarctica. *Geophysical Research Letters*, 27(5), 735–8.

Indermuhle, A., Stocker, T. F., Joos, F., Fischer, H., Smith, H. J., Wahlen, M., et al. (1999). Holocene carbon-cycle dynamics based on CO_2 trapped in ice at Taylor Dome, Antarctica. *Nature*, 398(6723), 121–6.

Insurance Journal (2006a, November 15). Munich Re tells UNEP Conference

$1 trillion loss year possible. *Insurance Journal*. Retrieved 19–12–06, from http://www.insurancejournal.com/news/international/2006/11/15/74242.htm.

Insurance Journal (2006b, April 18). Sound risk management, strong investment results prove positive for P/C industry. *Insurance Journal*. Retrieved 20–12–06, from http://www.insurancejournal.com/news/national/2006/04/18/67389.htm.

IPCC (1999a). *Aviation and the Global Atmosphere*. Cambridge: Cambridge University Press. Retrieved 24–1–07, from http://www.grida.no/climate/ipcc/aviation/index.htm.

IPCC (1999b). Procedures for the preparation, review, acceptance, adoption, approval and publication of IPCC reports. *UN*. Retrieved 26–1–07, from http://www.climatescience.gov/Library/ipcc/app-a.pdf.

IPCC (2001a). *Climate Change 2001: WGI: The Scientific Basis. Contribution of Working Group I to the Third Assessment Report of the Intergovernmental Panel on Climate Change* [Houghton, J.T., Y. Ding, D.J. Griggs, M. Noguer, P.J. van der Linden, X. Dai, K. Maskell, and C.A. Johnson (eds.)]. Cambridge: Cambridge University Press. http://www.grida.no/climate/ipcc_tar/wg1/index.htm.

IPCC (2001b). *Climate Change 2001: WGII: Impacts, Adaptation and Vulnerability*. Cambridge: Cambridge University Press. http://www.grida.no/climate/ipcc_tar/wg2/index.htm.

IPCC (2001c). *Climate Change 2001: WGIII: Mitigation*. Cambridge: Cambridge University Press. http://www.grida.no/climate/ipcc_tar/wg3/index.htm.

IPCC (2004, June 22). Deputy Secretary. *UN*. Retrieved 26–1–07, from http://notesapps.unon.org/notesapps/vacs.nsf/4c8db3486491c2f543256c3f004b0401/6e11b57c7b77623243256fe300289728?OpenDocument.

IPCC (2007a). *Climate Change 2007: WGI: Summary for Policymakers*. Retrieved 13–2–07, from http://www.ipcc.ch/SPM2feb07.pdf.

IPCC (2007b). *Climate Change 2007: WGI: The Physical Science Basis*. Cambridge: Cambridge University Press.

IPCC (2007c). *Climate Change 2007: WGII: Impacts, Adaptation and Vulnerability*. Cambridge: Cambridge University Press.

IPCC, Bruce, J. P., Yi, H.-S. O., Haites, E. F., & Working Group III (1996). *Climate Change 1995: Economic and Social Dimensions of Climate Change*. Cambridge and New York: Published for the Intergovernmental Panel on Climate Change [by] Cambridge University Press.

IPCC, & Houghton, J. T. (1996). *Climate Change 1995: The Science of Climate Change*. Cambridge and New York: Cambridge University Press.

IPCC, Houghton, J. T., Jenkins, G. J., Ephraums, J. J., & Working Group I. (1990). *Climate Change: The IPCC Scientific Assessment*. Cambridge and New York: Cambridge University Press.

Iredale, W. (2005, December 18). Polar bears drown as ice shelf melts. *Sunday Times*. Retrieved 7–11–06, from http://www.timesonline.co.uk/article/0,,2087–1938132,00.html.

IUCN Polar Bear Specialist Group (1970). Press release: 2nd meeting of PBSG Morges, Switzerland, 1970. Retrieved 07–11–06, from http://pbsg.npolar.no/Meetings/Stories/01st_meeting.htm.

IUCN Polar Bear Specialist Group (2005). Resolutions from the 14th meeting of the PBSG in Seattle, USA, 2005. Retrieved 7–11–06, from http://pbsg.npolar.no/Meetings/Resolutions/14-resolutions.htm.

IUCN Species Survival Commission (2001). *Polar Bears: Proceedings of the 13th Working Meeting of the IUCN/SSC Polar Bear Specialist Group, 23–28 June 2001, Nuuk, Greenland*. Retrieved 6–11–2006, from http://pbsg.npolar.no/docs/PBSG13proc.pdf.

Jaffe, A. B., Fogarty, M. S., & Banks, B. A. (1998). Evidence from patents and patent citations on the impact of NASA and other federal labs on commercial innovation. *Journal of Industrial Economics*, 46(2), 183–205.

Jaffe, A. B., Newell, R. G., & Stavins, R. N. (1999). Energy-efficient technologies and climate change policies: issues and evidence. *Resources for the Future, Climate Issue Brief No. 19*. Retrieved 21–11–06, from http://ksghome.harvard.edu/~rstavins/Selected_Articles/RFF_Energy_Effiient_Tech_and_Climate_Change_Policies.pdf.

Jamison, D. T., Feachem, R. G., Makgoba, M. W., Bos, E. R., Baingana, F. K., Hofman, K. J., et al. (2006). *Disease and Mortality in Sub-Saharan Africa*. World Bank.

Jenouvrier, S., Barbraud, C., & Weimerskirch, H. (2006). Sea ice affects the population dynamics of Adélie penguins in Terre Adélie. *Polar Biology*, 29(5), 413–23.

Jevrejeva, S., Grinsted, A., Moore, J. C., & Holgate, S. (2006a). Data for: Nonlinear trends and multiyear cycles in sea level records. Retrieved 07–11–06, from http://www.pol.ac.uk/psmsl/author_archive/jevrejeva_etal_gsl/.

Jevrejeva, S., Grinsted, A., Moore, J. C., & Holgate, S. (2006b). Nonlinear trends and multiyear cycles in sea level records. *Journal of Geophysical Research–Oceans*, 111(C9).

JMP (2007). Joint Monitoring Programme for Water Supply & Sanitation. *WHO & UNICEF*. Retrieved 7–1–07, from http://www.wssinfo.org/en/22_wat_global.html.

Joerin, U. E., Stocker, T. F., & Schluchter, C. (2006). Multicentury glacier fluctuations in the Swiss Alps during the Holocene. *Holocene*, 16(5), 697–704.

Johannessen, O. M., Khvorostovsky, K., Miles, M. W., & Bobylev, L. P. (2005). Recent ice-sheet growth in the interior of Greenland. *Science*, 310(5750), 1013–16.

Johnson, W., & Krueger, R. F. (2006). How money buys happiness: genetic and environmental processes linking finances and life satisfaction. *Journal of Personality and Social Psychology*, 90(4), 680–91.

Johnston, I. (2006, January 17). Global warming: is it too late to save our planet? *The Scotsman*. Retrieved 5–1–07, from http://news.scotsman.com/topics.cfm?tid= 52&id=76062006.

Jones, P. D., Horton, E. B., Folland, C. K., Hulme, M., Parker, D. E., & Basnett, T. A. (1999). The use of indices to identify changes in climatic extremes. *Climatic Change*, 42(1), 131–49.

Joseph, A. (2006, November 5). "It is for the West to act." *Guardian*. Retrieved 12–11–06, from http://observer.guardian.co.uk/business/story/0,,1939743,00.html.

Jouzel, J., et al. (2004). EPICA Dome C Ice Cores Deuterium Data. *IGBP PAGES/World Data Center for Paleoclimatology*, pp. Data Contribution Series # 2004–2038. Retrieved 3–12–06, from ftp://ftp.ncdc.noaa.gov/pub/data/paleo/ icecore/antarctica/epica_domec/edc_dd.txt.

Jungclaus, J. H., Haak, H., Esch, M., Roeckner, E., & Marotzke, J. (2006). Will Greenland melting halt the thermohaline circulation? *Geophysical Research Letters*, 33(17).

Kammen, D. M. (1995). Cookstoves for the developing-world. *Scientific American*, 273(1), 72–5.

Kammen, D. M., & Nemet, G. F. (2005). Reversing the incredible shrinking energy R&D budget. *Issues in Science and Technology*, Fall, 84–8. Retrieved 20–1–07, from http://rael.berkeley.edu/files/2005/Kammen-Nemet-ShrinkingRD2005.pdf.

Kan, H. D., Jia, J., & Chen, B. H. (2003). Temperature and daily mortality in Shanghai: a time-series study. *Biomedical and Environmental Sciences*, 16(2), 133–9.

Karl, T. R., Nicholls, N., & Gregory, J. (1997). The coming climate. *Scientific American*, 276(5), 78–83.

Karl, T. R., & Trenberth, K. E. (1999). The human impact on climate. *Scientific American*, 281(6), 100–5.

Kaser, G., Hardy, D. R., Molg, T., Bradley, R. S., & Hyera, T. M. (2004). Modern glacier retreat on Kilimanjaro as evidence of climate change: observations and facts. *International Journal of Climatology*, 24(3), 329–39.

Kates, R. W., Colten, C. E., Laska, S., & Leatherman, S. P. (2006). Reconstruction of New Orleans after Hurricane Katrina: a research perspective. *Proceedings of the National Academy of Sciences of the United States of America*, 103(40), 14653–60.

Kaufman, T. S., & Ruveda, E. A. (2005). The quest for quinine: those who won the battles and those who won the war. *Angewandte Chemie–International Edition*, 44(6), 854–85.

Kavuncu, Y. O., & Knabb, S. D. (2005). Stabilizing greenhouse gas emissions: assessing the intergenerational costs and benefits of the Kyoto Protocol. *Energy Economics*, 27(3), 369–86.

Keatinge, W. R., & Donaldson, G. C. (2004). The impact of global warming on health and mortality. *Southern Medical Journal*, 97(11), 1093–9.

Keatinge, W. R., Donaldson, G. C., Cordioli, E. A., Martinelli, M., Kunst, A. E., Mackenbach, J. P., et al. (2000). Heat related mortality in warm and cold regions of Europe: observational study. *British Medical Journal*, 321(7262), 670–3.

Kelkar, G. (2006, May 8). The gender face of energy. *Presentation at CSD 14 Learning Centre, United Nations*. Retrieved 30–1–07, from http://www.un.org/esa/sustdev/csd/csd14/lc/presentation/gender2.pdf.

Kennedy, R. F. (2005, August 29). "For They That Sow the Wind Shall Reap the Whirlwind." *The Huffington Post*. Retrieved 17–12–06, from http://www.huffingtonpost.com/robert-f-kennedy-jr/for-they-that-sow-the-_b_6396.html.

Kenny, C. (2006). Were people in the past poor and miserable? *Kyklos*, 59(2), 275–306.

Kerr, R. A. (2000, April 25). U.N. to blame global warming on humans. *Science Now*, 1.

Kerr, R. A. (2005). Global climate change – the Atlantic conveyor may have slowed, but don't panic yet. *Science*, 310(5753), 1403ff.

Kerr, R. A. (2006). Global climate change – false alarm: Atlantic conveyor belt hasn't slowed down after all. *Science*, 314(5802), 1064.

Kerr, R. A. (2007, February 15). Predicting fate of glaciers proves slippery task. *ScienceNow*, 2. http://sciencenow.sciencemag.org/cgi/content/full/2007/215/2.

Khaleque, V. (2006, December 7). Bangladesh is paying a cruel price for the West's excesses. *Guardian*. Retrieved 1–1–07, from http://environment.guardian.co.uk/climatechange/story/0,,1966012,00.html.

Khandekar, M. L., Murty, T. S., & Chittibabu, P. (2005). The global warming debate: a review of the state of science. *Pure and Applied Geophysics*, 162(8–9), 1557–86.

King, D. A. (2004). Environment – climate change science: adapt, mitigate, or ignore? *Science*, 303(5655), 176–7.

Kingston, M. (2005, November 21). Himalayan lakes disaster. *The Daily Briefing*. Retrieved 26–1–07, from http://webdiary.com.au/cms/?q=node/986.

Kington, T. (2007, January 6). Climate change brings malaria back to Italy. *Guardian*. Retrieved 6–1–07, from http://www.guardian.co.uk/italy/story/0,,1983891,00.html.

Klepper, G., & Peterson, S. (2005). Trading hot-air. The influence of permit allocation rules, market power and the US withdrawal from the Kyoto Protocol. *Environmental & Resource Economics*, 32(2), 205–27.

Klotzbach, P. J., & Gray, W. M. (2006). Causes of the unusually destructive 2004 Atlantic basin hurricane season. *Bulletin of the American Meteorological Society*, 87(10), 1325ff.

Kluger, J. (2006, April 3). Polar ice caps are melting faster than ever... More and more land is being devastated by drought... Rising waters are drowning low-lying communities... By any measure, earth is at... The tipping point. *Time.* Retrieved 6–11–06, from http://www.time.com/time/magazine/article/ 0,9171,1176980,00.html.

Konradsen, F., van der Hoek, W., Amerasinghe, F. P., Mutero, C., & Boelee, E. (2004). Engineering and malaria control: learning from the past 100 years. *Acta Tropica*, 89(2), 99–108.

Kooyman, G. L. (1993). Breeding habitats of emperor penguins in the western Ross Sea. *Antarctic Science*, 5(2), 143–8.

Kram, T., Morita, T., Riahi, K., Roehrl, R. A., Van Rooijen, S., Sankovski, A., et al. (2000). Global and regional greenhouse gas emissions scenarios. *Technological Forecasting and Social Change*, 63(2–3), 335–71.

Krauss, C. (2006, May 27). Bear hunting caught in global warming debate. *New York Times.* Retrieved 7–11–06, from http://www.nytimes.com/2006/05/27/world/ americas/27bears.html?ex=1306382400&en=07809799811ff6cb&ei=5088& partner=rssnyt&emc=rss.

Kuhn, K. G., Campbell-Lendrum, D. H., Armstrong, B., & Davies, C. R. (2003). Malaria in Britain: past, present, and future. *Proceedings of the National Academy of Sciences of the United States of America*, 100(17), 9997–10,001.

Kundzewicz, Z. W., Graczyk, D., Maurer, T., Pinskwar, I., Radziejewski, M., Svensson, C., et al. (2005). Trend detection in river flow series: 1. Annual maximum flow. *Hydrological Sciences Journal–Journal des Sciences Hydrologiques*, 50(5), 797–810.

Kunst, A. E., Looman, C. W. N., & Mackenbach, J. P. (1993). Outdoor air-temperature and mortality in the Netherlands – a time-series analysis. *American Journal of Epidemiology*, 137(3), 331–41.

Laaidi, M., Karine, L., & Jean-Pierre, B. (2006). Temperature-related mortality in France, a comparison between regions with different climates from the perspective of global warming. *International Journal of Biometeorology*, V51(2), 145–53. http://dx.doi.org/10.1007/s00484–006–0045–8.

Landsea, C. W. (2005). Meteorology – hurricanes and global warming. *Nature*, 438(7071), E11–E13.

Landsea, C. W., Harper, B. A., Hoarau, K., & Knaff, J. A. (2006). Can we detect trends in extreme tropical cyclones? *Science*, 313(5786), 452–4.

Langford, I. H., & Bentham, G. (1995). The potential effects of climate-change on winter mortality in England and Wales. *International Journal of Biometeorology*, 38(3), 141–7.

Larsen, J. (2003, October 9). Record heat wave in europe takes 35,000 lives: far greater losses may lie ahead. *Earth Policy Institute*. Retrieved 13–11–06, from http://www.earth-policy.org/Updates/Update29.htm.

Larson, L. A. (1994, July). Tough lessons from recent floods – special section: America under water. *USA Today*. Retrieved 23–12–06, from http://www.findarticles.com/p/articles/mi_m1272/is_n2590_v123/ai_15594504.

Latham, J. (1990). Control of global warming. *Nature*, 347(6291), 339–40.

Lau, K. M., Shen, S. S. P., Kim, K. M., & Wang, H. (2006). A multimodel study of the twentieth-century simulations of Sahel drought from the 1970s to 1990s. *Journal of Geophysical Research–Atmospheres*, 111(D7).

Le Roy Ladurie, E. (1972). *Times of Feast, Times of Famine: A History of Climate since the Year 1000*. London: George Allen & Unwin.

Lean, G. (2004, May 2). Why Antarctica will soon be the only place to live. *Independent*. Retrieved 12–11–06, from http://www.findarticles.com/p/articles/mi_qn4159/is_20040502/ai_n12755553.

Lean, G. (2005, January 25). Global warming approaching point of no return, warns leading climate expert. *Independent*. Retrieved 26–1–07, from http://www.commondreams.org/headlines05/0123–01.htm.

Lebergott, S. (1993). *Pursuing Happiness: American Consumers in the Twentieth Century*. Princeton, NJ: Princeton University Press.

Lebergott, S. (1995). Long-term trends in the US standard of living. In J. Simon (ed.), *State of Humanity* (pp. 149–60). Oxford: Blackwell.

Ledgard, J. (2005, Spring). Bjorn Lomborg is the world's most optimistic statistician. *Strategy+Business*. Retrieved 30–11–06, from http://www.strategy-business.com/press/16635507/05108.

Lee, H., Martins, J. O., & Mensbrugghe, D. van de (1994). *The OECD Green Model: An Updated Overview*. OECD.

Lee, M. (2006). Al Gore on Oprah: follow-up. Retrieved 09–12–06, from http://marklee.typepad.com/.

Leggett, J. K. (2001). *The Carbon War: Global Warming and the End of the Oil Era*. New York: Routledge. http://www.loc.gov/catdir/enhancements/fy0651/2001018158–d.html.

Lehmkuhl, F., & Owen, L. A. (2005). Late Quaternary glaciation of Tibet and the bordering mountains: a review. *Boreas*, 34(2), 87–100.

Leuliette, E., Nerem, R., & Mitchum, G. (2004). Calibration of TOPEX/Poseidon and Jason Altimeter data to construct a continuous record of mean sea level change. *Marine Geodesy*, 27, 79–94. http://dx.doi.org/10.1080/01490410490465193.

Li, H., Robock, A., & Wild, M. (in press). Evaluation of Intergovernmental Panel on Climate Change Fourth Assessment: soil moisture simulations for the second half of the twentieth century. *Journal of Geophysical Research–Atmospheres*.

Retrieved 7–1–07, from http://climate.envsci.rutgers.edu/pdf/IPCCsm Revision5.pdf.

LibDem (2006). Consultation Paper on Climate Change. *UK Liberal Democrats.* Retrieved 1–1–07, from http://consult.libdems.org.uk/climatechange/wp-content/uploads/2006/09/climate-change-cp84.pdf.

Lindzen, R. S. (2006, April 12). Climate of fear. *Wall Street Journal.* Retrieved 26–1–07, from http://www.opinionjournal.com/extra/?id=110008220.

Link, P. M., & Tol, R. S. J. (2004). Possible economic impacts of a shutdown of the thermohaline circulation: an application of FUND. *Portuguese Economic Journal,* 3, 99–114.

Lins, H. F., & Slack, J. R. (1999). Streamflow trends in the United States. *Geophysical Research Letters,* 26(2), 227–30.

Lins, H. F., & Slack, J. R. (2005). Seasonal and regional characteristics of US streamflow trends in the United States from 1940 to 1999. *Physical Geography,* 26(6), 489–501.

Lisowski, M. (2002). The emperor's new clothes: redressing the Kyoto Protocol. *Climate Policy,* 2(2–3), 161–77.

Lomborg, B. (2001). *The Skeptical Environmentalist.* Cambridge: Cambridge University Press.

Lomborg, B. (ed.). (2004). *Global Crises, Global Solutions.* Cambridge: Cambridge University Press.

Lomborg, B. (ed.). (2006). *How To Spend $50 Billion To Make the World a Better Place.* Cambridge: Cambridge University Press.

Long, S. P., Ainsworth, E. A., Leakey, A. D. B., Nosberger, J., & Ort, D. R. (2006). Food for thought: lower-than-expected crop yield stimulation with rising CO_2 concentrations. *Science,* 312(5782), 1918–21.

Longstreth, J. (1999). Public health consequences of global climate change in the United States – Some regions may suffer disproportionately. *Environmental Health Perspectives,* 107, 169–79.

Lopez, A. D., Mathers, C. D., Ezzati, M., Jamison, D. T., & Murray, C. J. L. (2006). Global and regional burden of disease and risk factors, 2001: systematic analysis of population health data. *The Lancet,* 367(9524), 1747–57.

Lovell, J. (2006, November 28). Gaia scientist Lovelock predicts planetary wipeout. *Reuters.* Retrieved 29–11–06, from http://www.alertnet.org/thenews/newsdesk/L28841108.htm.

Lovelock, J. E. (2006a, January 16). The Earth is about to catch a morbid fever that may last as long as 100,000 years. *Independent.* Retrieved 21–11–06, from http://comment.independent.co.uk/commentators/article338830.ece.

Lovelock, J. E. (2006b). *The Revenge of Gaia: Earth's Climate in Crisis and the Fate of Humanity.* New York: Basic Books.

Lund, M., Faber, K., & Søndergaard, B. (2004, May 25). Klima: Når det regner, er det meget voldsommere [Climate: when it rains, it rains much harder]. *Politiken*, A4.

Lund, M., Søndergaard, B., & Faber, K. (2004, May 30). Globale valg: Verden set fra Uganda [Global choices: the world seen from Uganda]. *Politiken*, A5.

Lunt, D. J., de Noblet-Ducoudre, N., & Charbit, S. (2004). Effects of a melted Greenland ice sheet on climate, vegetation, and the cryosphere. *Climate Dynamics*, 23(7–8), 679–94.

Luthcke, S. B., Zwally, H. J., Abdalati, W., Rowlands, D. D., Ray, R. D., Nerem, R. S., et al. (2006). Recent Greenland ice mass loss by drainage system from satellite gravity observations. *Science*, 314(5803), 1286–89.

Lynas, M. (2004). *High Tide: The Truth about Our Climate Crisis* (1st Picador edn). New York: Picador: distributed by Holzbrinck Publishers. http://www.loc.gov/catdir/bios/hol055/2004044661.html.

Lynas, M. (2006, May 19). Climate denial ads to air on US national television. *marklynas.org*. Retrieved 26–1–07, from http://www.marklynas.org/2006/5/19/climate-denial-ads-to-air-on-us-national-television.

Madden, A. H. (1945). A brief history of medical entomology in Florida. *Florida Entomologist*, 28(1), 1–7.

Maddison, A. (2006a). *Data for the World Economy*. OECD. Retrieved 08–12–06, from http://www.ggdc.net/Maddison/.

Maddison, A. (2006b). *The World Economy*, vol. I: A Millennial Perspective; vol. II: *Historical Statistics*. Paris: Development Centre of the Organisation for Economic Co-Operation and Development.

Maddison, D. (1995). A cost-benefit-analysis of slowing climate-change. *Energy Policy*, 23(4–5), 337–46.

Mahlman, J. D. (1997). Uncertainties in projections of human-caused climate warming. *Science*, 278(5342), 1416–17. http://www.sciencemag.org.

Malakoff, D. (1997). Climate change: thirty Kyotos needed to control warming. *Science*, 278(5346), 2048. http://www.sciencemag.org.

Malthus, T. (1798). *An Essay on the Principle of Population*. Harmondsworth: Penguin.

Mann, M. E., Bradley, R. S., & Hughes, M. K. (1998). Global-scale temperature patterns and climate forcing over the past six centuries. *Nature*, 392(6678), 779–87.

Mann, M. E., Bradley, R. S., & Hughes, M. K. (1999). northern hemisphere temperatures during the past millennium: inferences, uncertainties, and limitations. *Geophysical Research Letters*, 26(6), 759–62.

Manne, A., & Richels, R. (2004). US rejection of the Kyoto Protocol: the impact on compliance costs and CO2 emissions. *Energy Policy*, 32(4), 447–54.

Marland, G., Andres, B., & Boden, T. (2006). Global, regional, and national CO_2 emissions. In *Trends: A Compendium of Data on Global Change*. Carbon Dioxide Information Analysis Center. Retrieved 18–1–07, from http://cdiac.ornl.gov/ftp/ndp030/global.1751_2003.ems.

Marshall, G. J., Orr, A., van Lipzig, N. P. M., & King, J. C. (2006). The impact of a changing Southern Hemisphere Annular Mode on Antarctic Peninsula summer temperatures. *Journal of Climate*, 19(20), 5388–5404.

Martens, P., Kovats, R. S., Nijhof, S., de Vries, P., Livermore, M. T. J., Bradley, D. J., et al. (1999). Climate change and future populations at risk of malaria. *Global Environmental Change*, 9 (Supplement 1), S89–S107. http://www.sciencedirect.com/science/article/B6VFV-3XR2V33-7/2/4b6e6b879f1eab34166820cd7d30f754.

Martens, W. J. M. (1998). Climate change, thermal stress and mortality changes. *Social Science & Medicine*, 46(3), 331–44. http://www.sciencedirect.com/science/article/B6VBF-3SX5H61-15/2/095d34ddb16539a15ab2f6814c8686b8.

Matthews, J. A., Berrisford, M. S., Dresser, P. Q., Nesje, A., Dahl, S. O., Bjune, A. E., et al. (2005). Holocene glacier history of Bjornbreen and climatic reconstruction in central Jotunheimen, Norway, based on proximal glaciofluvial stream-bank mires. *Quaternary Science Reviews*, 24(1–2), 67–90.

Matthews, J. A., & Briffa, K. R. (2005). The "Little Ice Age": re-evaluation of an evolving concept. *Geografiska Annaler Series a–Physical Geography, 87A*(1), 17–36.

Matthews, N. (2000). The attack of the killer architects. *Travel Holiday, 183*(7), 80–8.

Maugeri, M., Buffoni, L., Delmonte, B., & Fassina, A. (2002). Daily Milan temperature and pressure series (1763–1998): completing and homogenising the data. *Climatic Change*, 53(1–3), 119–49.

McCallum, E., & Heming, J. (2006). Hurricane Katrina: an environmental perspective. *Philosophical Transactions of the Royal Society A: Mathematical, Physical and Engineering Sciences*, 364(1845), 2099–2115. http://dx.doi.org/10.1098/rsta.2006.1815.

McCarthy, M. (2005, February 3). Global warming: scientists reveal timetable. *Independent*. Retrieved 3–1–07, from http://www.commondreams.org/headlines05/0203-04.htm.

McCarthy, M. (2006, February 11). Global warming: passing the "tipping point." *Independent*. Retrieved 6–11–06, from http://www.countercurrents.org/ cc-mccarthy110206.htm.

McFarland, M. (2005, June 8). Statement of Mack McFarland, Ph.D., Global Environmental Manager, DuPont Fluoroproducts, before the Committee on Science, U.S. House of Representatives. Retrieved 20–11–06, from http://www.house.gov/science/hearings/full05/june8/dupont.pdf.

McIntyre, S., & McKitrick, R. (2005a). Hockey sticks, principal components, and spurious significance. *Geophysical Research Letters*, 32(3).

McIntyre, S., & McKitrick, R. (2005b). Reply to comment by Huybers on "Hockey sticks, principal components, and spurious significance." *Geophysical Research Letters*, 32(20).

McIntyre, S., & McKitrick, R. (2005c). Reply to comment by von Storch and Zorita on "Hockey sticks, principal components, and spurious significance." *Geophysical Research Letters*, 32(20).

McKibben, B. (2004, September/October). The submerging world. *Orion*. Retrieved 03-12-06, from http://www.oriononline.org/pages/om/04-5om/McKibben.html.

McMichael, A. J., Campbell-Lendrum, D. H., Corvalán, C. F., Ebi, K. L., Githeko, A. K., Scheraga, J. D., et al. (eds.) (2003). *Climate Change and Human Health*. Geneva: World Health Organization. http://www.who.int/globalchange/publications/cchhbook/en/index.html.

McMichael, A. J., Woodruff, R. E., & Hales, S. (2006). Climate change and human health: present and future risks. *Lancet*, 367(9513), 859–69.

McSmith, A. (2006, April 3). Climate change should be the top priority for governments. *Independent*. Retrieved 6-11-06, from http://www.findarticles.com/p/articles/mi_qn4158/is_20060403/ai_n16206931.

Meadows, D. H., Meadows, D. L., Randers, J., & Behrens III, W. W. (1972). *Limits to Growth*. London: Potomac Associates Book.

Meehl, G. A., & Tebaldi, C. (2004). More intense, more frequent, and longer lasting heat waves in the 21st century. *Science*, 305(5686), 994–7.

Meehl, G. A., Washington, W. M., Santer, B. D., Collins, W. D., Arblaster, J. M., Hu, A. X., et al. (2006). Climate change projections for the twenty-first century and climate change commitment in the CCSM3. *Journal of Climate*, 19(11), 2597–2616.

Mégroz, R. L. (1937). The world-wide scourge of malaria. *Contemporary Review*, 151, 349–56.

Meilby, M. (1996). *Journalistikkens grundtrin: fra idé til artikel* [The basic steps of journalism]. Aarhus: Ajour.

Meissner, K. J., & Clark, P. U. (2006). Impact of floods versus routing events on the thermohaline circulation. *Geophysical Research Letters*, 33(15).

Mendelsohn, R. (2004). Perspective paper 1.1 on climate change. In B. Lomborg (ed.), *Global Crises, Global Solutions* (pp. 44–8). Cambridge: Cambridge University Press.

Merali, Z. (2006, November 7). No new ice age for western Europe. *New Scientist*, 13.

Mestas, J., & Hughes, C. C. W. (2004). Of mice and not men: differences between mouse and human immunology. *Journal of Immunology*, 172(5), 2731–8. http://www.jimmunol.org/cgi/content/abstract/172/5/2731.

Metcalf, G. E., & Hassertt, K. A. (1997). Measuring the energy savings from home improvement investments: evidence from monthly billing data. *National Bureau of Economic Research, Working Paper 6074.*

Mfenyana, K., Griffin, M., Yogeswaran, P., Modell, B., Modell, M., Chandia, J., et al. (2006). Socio-economic inequalities as a predictor of health in South Africa – the Yenza cross-sectional study. *SAMJ: South African Medical Journal,* 96(4), 323–30.

Michaels, P. J. (2004, November 22). Polar disasters: more predictable distortions of science. Retrieved 7–11–06, from http://www.cato.org/pub_display.php?pub_id=2888.

Michaels, P. J., Knappenberger, P. C., Balling, R. C., & Davis, R. E. (2000). Observed warming in cold anticyclones. *Climate Research,* 14(1), 1–6.

Miguel, E. (2005). Poverty and witch killing. *Review of Economic Studies,* 72(4), 1153–72.

Milliken, M. (2004, December 10). "After Kyoto" takes center stage at climate talks. *Reuters.* Retrieved 18–11–06, from http://www.climateark.org/shared/reader/welcome.aspx?linkid=37207.

Mills, A., & Shillcutt, S. (2004). Communicable diseases. In B. Lomborg (ed.), *Global Crises, Global Solutions* (pp. 62–114). Cambridge: Cambridge University Press.

Mills, E., & Lecomte, E. (2006, August). From risk to opportunity: how insurers can proactively and profitably manage climate change. *Ceres.* Retrieved 21–12–06, from http://www.ceres.org/pub/docs/Ceres_Insurance_Climate_%20Report_ 082206.pdf.

Milly, P. C. D., Wetherald, R. T., Dunne, K. A., & Delworth, T. L. (2002). Increasing risk of great floods in a changing climate. *Nature,* 415(6871), 514–17.

Milne, L., & Milne, M. (1962, September 23). There's poison all around us now. *New York Times.* Retrieved 22–1–07, from http://www.nytimes.com/books/97/10/05/reviews/carson-spring.html.

Mitchell, B. R. (1993). *International Historical Statistics: The Americas, 1750–1988.* London: Macmillan.

Mitchell, J. K. (2003). European river floods in a changing world. *Risk Analysis,* 23(3), 567–74. http://www.blackwell-synergy.com/doi/abs/10.1111/1539–6924.00337.

Moberg, A., & Bergstrom, H. (1997). Homogenization of Swedish temperature data. 3. The long temperature records from Uppsala and Stockholm. *International Journal of Climatology,* 17(7), 667–99.

Moberg, A., Sonechkin, D. M., Holmgren, K., Datsenko, N. M., & Karlen, W. (2005). Highly variable northern hemisphere temperatures reconstructed from low- and high-resolution proxy data. *Nature,* 433(7026), 613–17.

Monaghan, A. J., & Bromwich, D. H. (2006). A high spatial resolution record of near-surface temperature over WAIS during the past 5 decades. *Thirteenth Annual WAIS Workshop.* Retrieved 14–12–06, from http://igloo.gsfc.nasa.gov/wais/pastmeetings/Sched06.htm.

Monastersky, R. (1998, June 20). Global warming eggs on El Niño. *Science News,* 399.

Monbiot, G. (2006a). *Heat: How to Stop the Planet Burning.* Allen Lane, London.

Monbiot, G. (2006b, October 10). The water boom is over. *Guardian.* Retrieved 5–1–07, from http://www.monbiot.com/archives/2006/10/10/the-water-boom-is-over/.

Monnett, C., Gleason, J. S., & Rotterman, L. M. (2005, December). Potential effects of diminished sea ice on open-water swimming, mortality, and distribution of polar bears during fall in the Alaskan Beaufort Sea. Retrieved 7–11–06, from http://www.mms.gov/alaska/ess/Poster%20Presentations/MarineMammal Conference-Dec2005.pdf.

Monnin, E., Indermuhle, A., Dallenbach, A., Fluckiger, J., Stauffer, B., Stocker, T. F., et al. (2001). Atmospheric CO_2 concentrations over the last glacial termination. *Science,* 291(5501), 112–14.

Montopoli, B. (2006, March 2006). Scott Pelley and Catherine Herrick on global warming coverage. *PublicEye.* Retrieved 26–1–07, from http://www.cbsnews.com/blogs/2006/03/22/publiceye/entry1431768.shtml.

Moore, S. (2006). Peripherality, income inequality, and life expectancy: revisiting the income inequality hypothesis. *International Journal of Epidemiology, 35(3),* 623–32.

Morris, E. M., & Mulvaney, R. (2004). Recent variations in surface mass balance of the Antarctic Peninsula ice sheet. *Journal of Glaciology,* 50(169), 257–67.

Motavalli, J. (2004, November/December). Too darn hot. *E Magazine: The Environmental Magazine.*

Mudelsee, M. (2001). The phase relations among atmospheric CO_2 content, temperature and global ice volume over the past 420 ka. *Quaternary Science Reviews,* 20(4), 583–9.

Mudelsee, M., Borngen, M., Tetzlaff, G., & Grunewald, U. (2003). No upward trends in the occurrence of extreme floods in central Europe. *Nature,* 425(6954), 166–9.

Mudelsee, M., Deutsch, M., Borngen, M., & Tetzlaff, G. (2006). Trends in flood risk of the River Werra (Germany) over the past 500 years. *Hydrological Sciences Journal–Journal des Sciences Hydrologiques,* 51(5), 818–33.

Murray, T. (2006). Climate change: Greenland's ice on the scales. *Nature,* 443(7109), 277–8.

Nakaji, S., Parodi, S., Fontana, V., Umeda, T., Suzuki, K., Sakamoto, J., et al. (2004).

Seasonal changes in mortality rates from main causes of death in Japan (1970–1999). *European Journal of Epidemiology*, 19(10), 905–13.

Nakicenovic, N., & IPCC WG III (2000). *Special Report on Emissions Scenarios: A Special Report of Working Group III of the Intergovernmental Panel on Climate Change.* Cambridge and New York: Cambridge University Press. http://www.grida.no/climate/ipcc/emission/index.htm.

Nash, J. M., & Horsburgh, S. (1998, March 2). The fury of El Niño. *Time South Pacific*, 44–51.

NCEP (2006). Global surface air temperature, annual average 1982–94. *National Center for Environmental Prediction.* Retrieved 26–12–06, from http://aom.giss.nasa.gov/cp4x310.html.

Nemet, G. F., & Kammen, D. M. (2007). US energy research and development: declining investment, increasing need, and the feasibility of expansion. *Energy Policy*, 35(1), 746–55.

NERI (1998). *Natur og Miljø 1997: påvirkninger og tilstand* [Nature and environment 1997: effects and state]. National Environmental Research Institute of Denmark.

Neuhoff, K., & Sellers, R. (2006). Mainstreaming new renewable energy technologies. *Draft Paper, Faculty of Economics, University of Cambridge.* Retrieved 19–1–07, from http://www.electricitypolicy.org.uk/pubs/wp/eprg0606.pdf.

New Scientist anon. (2005, March 26). The edge of the abyss. *New Scientist*, 5.

New Scientist anon. (2006, April 2). It may be bad news, but we need to hear it. *New Scientist* 5.

Newell, R. G., Jaffe, A. B., & Stavins, R. N. (1999). The Induced Innovation Hypothesis and energy-saving technological change. *Quarterly Journal of Economics*, 114(3), 941–75. http://www.mitpressjournals.org/doi/abs/10.1162/003355399556188.

Nicholls, R. J. (2004). Coastal flooding and wetland loss in the 21st century: changes under the SRES climate and socio-economic scenarios. *Global Environmental Change–Human and Policy Dimensions*, 14(1), 69–86.

Nicholls, R. J., & Tol, R. S. J. (2006). Impacts and responses to sea-level rise: a global analysis of the SRES scenarios over the twenty-first century. *Philosophical Transactions of the Royal Society A: Mathematical Physical and Engineering Sciences*, 364(1841), 1073–95.

Nicholson, S. E. (2001). Climatic and environmental change in Africa during the last two centuries. *Climate Research*, 17(2), 123–44.

Njagi, K., & Were, E. (2004). Malaria control and prevention strategies in Kenya. In Central Bureau of Statistics (CBS) [Kenya], Ministry of Health (MOH) [Kenya] & ORC Macro (eds.), *Kenya: Demographic and Health Survey 2003*. Calverton, MD: CBS, MOH, and ORC Macro. Retrieved 28–12–06, from http://www.measuredhs.com/pubs/pdf/FR151/11Chapter11.pdf.

NOAA (2004). NOAA reports record number of tornadoes in 2004. *NOAA National Weather Service*. Retrieved 23–12–06, from http://www.noaanews.noaa.gov/stories2004/s2359.htm.

NOAA (2006a). 65-year list of severe weather fatalities. *NOAA Office of Climate, Water, and Weather Services*. Retrieved 23–12–06, from http://www.weather.gov/os/severe_weather/65yrstats.pdf.

NOAA (2006b). The enhanced Fujita scale (EF scale). *NOAA National Weather Service*. Retrieved 23–12–06, from http://www.spc.noaa.gov/efscale/.

NOAA (2006c) Hurricane history. *National Hurricane Center*. Retrieved 20–12–06, from http://www.nhc.noaa.gov/HAW2/english/history.shtml.

NOAA (2006d). Tornado climatology. *NOAA Satellite and Information Service*. Retrieved 23–12–06, from http://www.ncdc.noaa.gov/oa/climate/severeweather/tornadoes.html.

NOAA (2006e). US 1950–2005 tornado data. *NOAA National Weather Service*. Retrieved 23–12–06, from http://www.spc.noaa.gov/climo/historical.html.

NOAA (n.d.). Fujita tornado damage scale. *NOAA National Weather Service*. Retrieved 23–12–06, from http://www.crh.noaa.gov/iwx/program_areas/events/ Fscale.php.

Nohara, D., Kitoh, A., Hosaka, M., & Oki, T. (2006). Impact of climate change on river discharge projected by multimodel ensemble. *Journal of Hydrometeorology*, 7(5), 1076–89.

Nordhaus, W. D. (1992). An optimal transition path for controlling greenhouse gases. *Science*, 258(5086), 1315–19.

Nordhaus, W. D. (1994). *Managing the Global Commons: The Economics of Climate Change*. Cambridge, MA: MIT Press.

Nordhaus, W. D. (2001). Climate change – global warming economics. *Science*, 294(5545), 1283–4.

Nordhaus, W. D. (2006a). After Kyoto: alternative mechanisms to control global warming. *American Economic Review*, 96(2), 31–4.

Nordhaus, W. D. (2006b). DICE model. Retrieved 22–11–06, from http://nordhaus.econ.yale.edu/dicemodels.htm.

Nordhaus, W. D. (2006c). RICE model. Retrieved 27–11–06, from http://www.econ.yale.edu/~nordhaus/homepage/dice_section_vi.html.

Nordhaus, W. D. (2006d). The Stern Review on the economics of climate change. Retrieved 24–1–07, from http://nordhaus.econ.yale.edu/SternReviewD2.pdf.

Nordhaus, W. D. (2006e). Life after Kyoto: alternative approaches to global warming policies. *Prepared for the Annual Meetings of the American Economic Association, Boston, Massachusetts, January 5–8, 2006*. Retrieved 18–11–06, from http://nordhaus.econ.yale.edu/kyoto_long_2005.pdf.

Nordhaus, W. D. (ed.) (1998). *Economics and Policy Issues in Climate Change*. Washington, DC: Resources for the Future.

Nordhaus, W. D., & Boyer, J. (2000). *Warming the World: Economic Models of Global Warming*. Cambridge, MA: MIT Press. http://www.econ.yale.edu/~nordhaus/homepage/web%20table%20of%20contents%20102599.htm.

Nordhaus, W. D., & Yang, Z. L. (1996). A regional dynamic general-equilibrium model of alternative climate-change strategies. *American Economic Review*, 86(4), 741–65.

Norris, S., Rosentrater, L., & Eid, P. M. (2002). Polar bears at risk: a WWF status report. Retrieved 6–11–06, from http://www.wwf.org.uk/filelibrary/pdf/polar_bears_at_risk_report.pdf.

Northrop, M. (2005, February 28). Benefits of cutting emissions. *Washington Post*, A17. Retrieved 20–11–06, from http://www.washingtonpost.com/wp-dyn/articles/A58852-2005Feb27.html.

NRC (2006). Surface temperature reconstructions for the last 2,000 Years. *National Research Council*. Retrieved 06–12–06, from http://newton.nap.edu/catalog/11676.html.

NRDC (2006). Global warming basics: what it is, how it's caused, and what needs to be done to stop it. *National Resources Defense Council*. Retrieved 17–12–06, from http://www.nrdc.org/globalWarming/f101.asp.

NSC (1999). *Injury Facts, 1999 Edition*. Chicago: National Safety Council.

O'Driscoll, P. (2006, May 31). Animals scramble as the climate warms. *USA Today*, 7D.

O'Neill, B. (2006a, October 6). Global warming: the chilling effect on free speech. *Spiked*. Retrieved 26–1–07, from http://www.spiked-online.com/index.php?/site/article/1782/.

O'Neill, B. (2006b, November 7). A march of middle-class miserabilists. *Spiked*. Retrieved 27–1–07, from http://www.spiked-online.com/index.php?/site/article/2071.

O'Rangers, E. A. (2005, January). NASA spin-offs: bringing space down to earth. *AdAstra: The Magazine of the National Space Society*. Retrieved 19–1–07, from http://www.space.com/adastra/adastra_spinoffs_050127.html.

OECD (2005). *OECD in Figures*. OECD Observer.

OECD (2006a). Aid flows top USD 100 billion in 2005. *Organisation for Economic Co-operation and Development*. Retrieved 30–11–06, from http://www.oecd.org/document/40/0,2340,en_2649_34447_36418344_1_1_1_1,00.html.

OECD (2006b). Net ODA from DAC countries from 1950 to 2005. *Organisation for Economic Co-operation and Development*. Retrieved 30–11–06, from http://www.oecd.org/dataoecd/43/24/1894385.xls.

OECD (2006c). *OECD DAC Development Co-operation Report 2005. Organisation for Economic Co-operation and Development*. Retrieved 30–11–06, from www.sourceoecd.org/developmentreport.

OECD (2006d). *OECD Factbook 2006*. Paris: Organisation for Economic Co-operation and Development. Retrieved 10–11–06, from http://oberon.sourceoecd.org/ vl=16922773/cl=12/nw=1/rpsv/factbook/.

Oerlemans, J. (2000). Holocene glacier fluctuations: is the current rate of retreat exceptional? *Annals of Glaciology*, 31, 39–44.

Oerlemans, J. (2005). Extracting a climate signal from 169 glacier records. *Science*, 308(5722), 675–7.

Oerlemans, J., Bassford, R. P., Chapman, W., Dowdeswell, J. A., Glazovsky, A. F., Hagen, J. O., et al. (2005). Estimating the contribution of Arctic glaciers to sea-level change in the next 100 years. *Annals of Glaciology*, 42, 230–6.

Oki, T., & Kanae, S. (2006). Global hydrological cycles and world water resources. *Science*, 313(5790), 1068–72.

Olle-Goig, J. E. (2006). The treatment of multi-drug resistant tuberculosis – a return to the pre-antibiotic era? *Tropical Medicine & International Health*, 11(11), 1625–8.

Oppenheimer, C. (2003). Climatic, environmental and human consequences of the largest known historic eruption: Tambora volcano (Indonesia) 1815. *Progress in Physical Geography*, 27(2), 230–59.

Oron, G., Armon, R., Mandelbaum, R., Manor, Y., Campos, C., Gillerman, L., et al. (2001). Secondary wastewater disposal for crop irrigation with minimal risks. *Water Science and Technology*, 43(10), 139–46.

Osborn, T., & Briffa, K. R. (2006). The spatial extent of 20th-century warmth in the context of the past 1200 years. *Science*, 311(5762), 841–4.

OST (2004). *Future Flooding, Executive Summary*. Retrieved 16–12–06, from http://www.foresight.gov.uk/Previous_Projects/Flood_and_Coastal_Defence/ Reports_and_Publications/Executive_Summary/executive_summary.pdf.

Oster, E. (2004). Witchcraft, weather and economic growth in renaissance Europe. *Journal of Economic Perspectives*, 18(1), 215–28.

Owen, J. (2005, November 30). "Mini Ice Age" may be coming soon, sea study warns. *National Geographic News*. Retrieved 27–12–06, from http://news.nationalgeographic.com/news/2005/11/1130_051130_ice_age.html.

Pagani, M., Zachos, J. C., Freeman, K. H., Tipple, B., & Bohaty, S. (2005a). Data for atmospheric carbon dioxide concentrations during the Paleogene. Retrieved 6–12–06, from http://earth.geology.yale.edu/~mp364/data/PaleogeneCO2.xls.

Pagani, M., Zachos, J. C., Freeman, K. H., Tipple, B., & Bohaty, S. (2005b). Marked decline in atmospheric carbon dioxide concentrations during the Paleogene. *Science*, 309(5734), 600–3.

Parikh, J., Balakrishnan, K., Laxmi, V., & Biswas, H. (2001). Exposure from cooking with biofuels: pollution monitoring and analysis for rural Tamil Nadu, India. *Energy*, 26(10), 949–62.

Parizek, B. R., & Alley, R. B. (2004). Implications of increased Greenland surface melt under global-warming scenarios: ice-sheet simulations. *Quaternary Science Reviews*, 23(9–10), 1013–27.

Parker, D., & Horton, B. (2005). Uncertainties in central England temperature 1878–2003 and some improvements to the maximum and minimum series. *International Journal of Climatology*, 25(9), 1173–88.

Parkinson, C. L. (2006). Earth's Cryosphere: current state and recent changes. *Annual Review of Environment and Resources*, 31(1), 33–60 http://arjournals. annualreviews.org/doi/abs/10.1146/annurev.energy.31.041105.095552.

Parry, M. (2004). Global impacts of climate change under the SRES scenarios. *Global Environmental Change*, 14(1), 1. http://www.sciencedirect.com/science/article/ B6VFV-4BC2K5C-1/2/2efdb86d21cb7931927813e273ff0fa7.

Parry, M., Arnell, N., Hulme, M., Nicholls, R., & Livermore, M. (1998). Buenos Aires and Kyoto targets do little to reduce climate change impacts. *Global Environmental Change–Human and Policy Dimensions*, 8(4), 285–9.

Parry, M. L., Rosenzweig, C., Iglesias, A., Livermore, M., & Fischer, G. (2004). Effects of climate change on global food production under SRES emissions and socio-economic scenarios. *Global Environmental Change*, 14(1), 53–67. http://www.sciencedirect.com/science/article/B6VFV-4BDY65D-1/2/0dab1fac 37737d687be95c17d2fede5c.

Parry, M., Rosenzweig, C., & Livermore, M. (2005). Climate change, global food supply and risk of hunger. *Philosophical Transactions of the Royal Society B: Biological Sciences*, 360(1463), 2125–38. http://dx.doi.org/10.1098/ rstb.2005.1751.

Parson, E. A., & Fisher-Vanden, K. (1997). Integrated assessment models of global climate change. *Annual Review of Energy and the Environment*, 22, 589–628.

Pascual, M., Ahumada, J. A., Chaves, L. F., Rodo, X., & Bouma, M. (2006). Malaria resurgence in the East African highlands: temperature trends revisited. *Proceedings of the National Academy of Sciences of the United States of America*, 103(15), 5829–34.

Patz, J. A., Campbell-Lendrum, D., Holloway, T., & Foley, J. A. (2005). Impact of regional climate change on human health. *Nature*, 438(7066), 310–17.

Patz, J. A., Hulme, M., Rosenzweig, C., Mitchell, T. D., Goldberg, R. A., Githeko, A. K., et al. (2002). Climate change – regional warming and malaria resurgence. *Nature*, 420(6916), 627–8.

Pearce, D. (2003). The social cost of carbon and its policy implications. *Oxford Review of Economic Policy*, 19(3), 362–84.

Pearce, F. (2001). We are all guilty! It's official, people are to blame for global warming. *New Scientist*, 169(2275), 5.

Pearce, F. (2005a, December 3). Faltering currents trigger freeze fear. *New Scientist*, 6.

Pearce, F. (2005b, August 27). Global warming: the flaw in the thaw. *New Scientist*, 26.

Pearce, F. (2005c, December 24). Review 2005: climate going crazy. *New Scientist*, 16.

Pearce, F. (2006a). *The Last Generation: How Nature Will Take Her Revenge for Climate Change*. London: Eden Project Books.

Pearce, F. (2006b, November 11). The poor will pay for global warming. *New Scientist*, 8–9.

Pearson, P. N., & Palmer, M. R. (2000). Atmospheric carbon dioxide concentrations over the past 60 million years. *Nature*, 406(6797), 695–9.

Peck, S. C., & Teisberg, T. J. (1992). CETA: a model for carbon emissions trajectory assessment. *Energy Journal*, 13(1), 55–77.

Perkins, S. (2002). Tornado Alley, USA. *Science News*, 161(19), 296. Retrieved 23-12-06, from http://www.sciencenews.org/articles/20020511/bob9.asp.

Petit, J. R., et al. (2001). Vostok ice core data for 420,000 Years. *IGBP PAGES/World Data Center for Paleoclimatology*. Data Contribution Series #2001-76. Retrieved 3-12-06, from ftp://ftp.ncdc.noaa.gov/pub/data/paleo/icecore/antarctica/vostok/co2nat.txt.

Petit, J. R., Jouzel, J., Raynaud, D., Barkov, N. I., Barnola, J. M., Basile, I., et al. (1999). Climate and atmospheric history of the past 420,000 years from the Vostok ice core, Antarctica. *Nature*, 399(6735), 429–36.

Petrow, T., Thieken, A. H., Kreibich, H., Bahlburg, C. H., & Merz, B. (2006). Improvements on flood alleviation in Germany: lessons learned from the Elbe flood in August 2002. *Environmental Management*, 38(5), 717–32.

Pew Center (2006a, June 13). America's image slips, but allies share U.S. concerns over Iran, Hamas: 15-nation pew global attitudes survey. *Pew Global Attitudes Project*. Retrieved 30-11-06, from http://pewglobal.org/reports/pdf/252.pdf.

Pew Center (2006b). *Regional Initiatives*. Retrieved 6-11-06, from http://www.pewclimate.org/whats_being_done/in_the_states/regional_initiatives. cfm?preview=1.

Pfister, C., Weingartner, R., & Luterbacher, J. (2006). Hydrological winter droughts over the last 450 years in the Upper Rhine basin: a methodological approach. *Hydrological Sciences Journal–Journal des Sciences Hydrologiques*, 51(5), 966–85.

Philandras, C. M., Metaxas, D. A., & Nastos, P. T. (1999). Climate variability and urbanization in Athens. *Theoretical and Applied Climatology*, 63(1–2), 65–72.

Pielke, R. A. (1999). Nine fallacies of floods. *Climatic Change*, 42(2), 413–38.

Pielke, R. A. (2005). Misdefining "climate change": consequences for science and action. *Environmental Science and Policy*, 8(6), 548–61.

Pielke, R. A. (2006a). Climate change is serious, but we have to have a realistic response. *Guardian*. Retrieved 31-1-07, from http://www.guardian.co.uk/zurichfuturology/story/0,,1920333,00.html.

Pielke, R. A. (2006b). Disasters, death, and destruction: making sense of Recent Calamities. *Oceanography*, 19(2), 138–47.

Pielke, R. A., & Downton, M. W. (2000). Precipitation and damaging floods: trends in the United States, 1932–97. *Journal of Climate*, 13(20), 3625–37.

Pielke, R. A., Gratz, J., Landsea, C. W., Collins, D., Saunders, M. A., & Musulin, R. (2007). Normalized hurricane damages in the United States: 1900–2005. *Natural Hazards Review* (submitted). Retrieved 19–12–06, from http://science-policy.colorado.edu/publications/special/normalized_hurricane_damages.html.

Pielke, R. A., Klein, R., & Sarewitz, D. (2000). Turning the big knob: an evaluation of the use of energy policy to modulate future climate impacts. *Energy and Environment*, 11, 255–76. Retrieved 20–12–06, from http://sciencepolicy.colorado.edu/about_us/meet_us/roger_pielke/knob/text.html.

Pielke, R. A., & Landsea, C. W. (1998). Normalized hurricane damages in the United States: 1925–95. *Weather and Forecasting*, 13(3), 621–31.

Pinter, N. (2005). Environment – one step forward, two steps back on US floodplains. *Science*, 308(5719), 207–8.

Pinter, N., & Heine, R. A. (2005). Hydrodynamic and morphodynamic response to river engineering documented by fixed-discharge analysis, Lower Missouri River, USA. *Journal of Hydrology*, 302(1–4), 70–91.

Pinter, N., van der Ploeg, R. R., Schweigert, P., & Hoefer, G. (2006). Flood magnification on the River Rhine. *Hydrological Processes*, 20(1), 147–64.

Plumb, C. (2003, December 11). Climate change death toll put at 150,000. *Reuters*. Retrieved 1–1–07, from http://www.commondreams.org/headlines03/1211–13.htm.

Plummer, N., Salinger, M. J., Nicholls, N., Suppiah, R., Hennessy, K. J., Leighton, R. M., et al. (1999). Changes in climate extremes over the Australian region and New Zealand during the twentieth century. *Climatic Change*, 42(1), 183–202.

Pollack, H. N., Huang, S. P., & Shen, P. Y. (1998). Climate change record in subsurface temperatures: a global perspective. *Science*, 282(5387), 279–81.

Pope, C. (2005, October 6). Global warming after Katrina. *Sierra Club*. Retrieved 17–12–06, from http://www.sierraclub.org/carlpope/waves/.

Postel, S. L. (1998). Water for food production: will there be enough in 2025? *Bioscience*, 48(8), 629–37.

Postel, S. L. (1999). *Pillar of Sand: Can the Irrigation Miracle Last?* New York: Norton.

Postel, S. L., Daily, G. C., & Ehrlich, P. R. (1996). Human appropriation of renewable fresh water. *Science*, 271(5250), 785–8.

Postman, A. (2006, October 5). The energy diet. *New York Times*. Retrieved 21–11–06, from http://www.stopglobalwarming.org/sgw_read.asp?id=1128441052006.

Poumadere, M., Mays, C., Le Mer, S., & Blong, R. (2005). The 2003 heat wave in France: dangerous climate change here and now. *Risk Analysis, 25*(6), 1483–94. http://www.blackwellsynergy.com/doi/abs/10.1111/j.1539-6924.2005.00694.x.

PovcalNet (2007). World Bank Poverty Calculator. *World Bank*. Retrieved 10–1–07, from http://iresearch.worldbank.org/PovcalNet/jsp/index.jsp.

Preston, S. (1995). Human mortality throughout history and prehistory. In J. Simon (ed.), *The State of Humanity*. Oxford: Blackwell.

Pritchett, L., & Summers, L. H. (1996). Wealthier is healthier. *Journal of Human Resources, 31*(4), 841–68.

Prodi, R. (2004, July 15). Climate change – the real threat to global peace. Retrieved 6–11–06, from http://www.europa-eu-un.org/articles/en/article_3678_en.htm.

Przybylak, R. (2000). Temporal and spatial variation of surface air temperature over the period of instrumental observations in the Arctic. *International Journal of Climatology, 20*(6), 587–614. http://dx.doi.org/10.1002/(SICI)1097-0088(200005)20:6<587::AID-JOC480>3.0.CO;2-H.

Pudsey, C. J., Murray, J. W., Appleby, P., & Evans, J. (2006). Lee shelf history from petrographic and foraminiferal evidence, Northeast Antarctic Peninsula. *Quaternary Science Reviews, 25*(17–18), 2357–79.

Pullella, P. (2005, May 27). Global warming will increase world hunger. *Reuters*. Retrieved 3–1–07, from http://www.globalpolicy.org/socecon/envronmt/2005/0527warming.htm.

Purcell, K. (2006). Gates Foundation invests $42.6 million in malaria drug research. *HerbalGram, The Journal of the American Botanical Council, 69*(24), 252. Retrieved 30–12–06, from http://www.herbalgram.org/herbalgram/articleview.asp?a=2919&p=Y.

Radetzki, M. (1999). Taxation of greenhouse gasses: why Kyoto will not be implemented. *International Journal of Global Energy Issues, 12*(7/8), 372–6.

Randerson, J. (2006, October 27). Sea change: why global warming could leave Britain feeling the cold: no new ice age yet, but Gulf Stream is weakening; Atlantic current came to halt for 10 days in 2004. *Guardian*. Retrieved 27–12–06, from http://environment.guardian.co.uk/climatechange/story/0,,1932761,00.html.

Reiter, P. (2000). From Shakepeare to Defoe: malaria in England in the Little Ice Age. *Emerging Infectious Diseases, 6*(1), 1–10. Retrieved 07–12–06, from http://www.cdc.gov/ncidod/eid/vol6no1/reiter.htm.

Reiter, P. (2005). The IPCC and technical information. Example: impacts on human health. *UK Select Committee on Economic Affairs*. Retrieved 28–12–06, from http://www.publications.parliament.uk/pa/ld200506/ldselect/ldeconaf/12/12we21.htm.

Reiter, P. (2007, January 12). Dangers of disinformation pseudoscience. *International Herald Tribune.*

Reiter, P., Thomas, C. J., Atkinson, P. M., Hay, S. I., Randolph, S. E., Rogers, D. J., et al. (2004). Global warming and malaria: a call for accuracy. *Lancet Infectious Diseases,* 4(6), 323–4.

Reuters (2001, November 7). African mountains snow melting down – Greenpeace. Retrieved 07–12–06, from http://www.planetark.org/avantgo/ dailynewsstory.cfm? newsid=13154.

Reuters (2002, September 3). Sound of conflict blurs Earth Summit rhetoric. Retrieved 22–12–06, from http://www.planetark.org/avantgo/dailynewsstory.cfm? newsid=17557.

Reuters (2006, November 9). U.N.: Canada not pulling out of Kyoto pact. Retrieved 18–11–06, from http://edition.cnn.com/2006/WORLD/americas/11/09/ canada.kyoto.reut/.

Revenga, C., Brunner, J., Henninger, N., Payne, R., & Kassem, K. (2000). *Pilot Analysis of Global Ecosystems: Freshwater Systems.* World Resources Institute. Retrieved 7–1–07, from http://www.wri.org/biodiv/pubs_description.cfm? pid=3056.

Richey, L. A. (2003). HIV/AIDS in the shadows of reproductive health interventions. *Reproductive Health Matters,* 11(22), 30–5.

Ridley, J. K., Huybrechts, P., Gregory, J. M., & Lowe, J. A. (2005). Elimination of the Greenland ice sheet in a high CO_2 climate. *Journal of Climate,* 18(17), 3409–27.

Ridnouer, N. M. (1998). Cities bracing for "climate event of the century." *Nation's Cities Weekly,* 21(12), 14.

Rijsberman, F. (2004). Sanitation and access to clean water. In B. Lomborg (ed.), *Global Crises, Global Solutions* (pp. 498–527). Cambridge: Cambridge University Press.

Rising Tide (2007). Hall of shame. *Rising Tide.* Retrieved 26–1–07, from http://risingtide.org.uk/pages/voices/hall_shame.htm.

Ritter, L., Heath, C. J., Kaegi, E., Morrison, H., & Sieber, S. (1997). Report of a panel on the relationship between public exposure to pesticides and cancer. *Cancer,* 80, 2019–33.

Roberts, D. (2006a, May 2006). Al Revere: an interview with accidental movie star Al Gore. *Grist.* Retrieved 26–1–07, from http://www.grist.org/news/maindish/ 2006/05/09/roberts/index.html.

Roberts, D. (2006b, September 19). The denial industry. *Grist.* Retrieved 26–1–07, from http://gristmill.grist.org/print/2006/9/19/11408/1106.

Robinson, J. P., & Godbey, G. (1997). *Time for Life: The Surprising Ways Americans Use Their Time.* University Park: Pennsylvania State University Press.

Robock, A., Mu, M. Q., Vinnikov, K., Trofimova, I. V., & Adamenko, T. I. (2005).

Forty-five years of observed soil moisture in the Ukraine: no summer desiccation (yet). *Geophysical Research Letters*, 32(3).

Robock, A., Vinnikov, K. Y., Srinivasan, G., Entin, J. K., Hollinger, S. E., Speranskaya, N. A., et al. (2000). The global soil moisture data bank. *Bulletin of the American Meteorological Society*, 81(6), 1281–99.

Rogers, D. J., & Randolph, S. E. (2000). The global spread of malaria in a future, warmer world. *Science*, 289(5485), 1763–6.

Rolling Stones (2007). Extreme makeover: images of planetwide damage caused by global warming, with selected quotes from our interview with Al Gore and ten ways you can help. *Rolling Stones*. Retrieved 2–1–07, from http://www.rolling-stone.com/politics/story/10698217/extreme_makeover.

Romi, R., Sabatinelli, G., & Majori, G. (2001). Could malaria reappear in Italy? *Emerging Infectious Diseases*, 7(6), 915–19.

Roos, L. L., Magoon, J., Gupta, S., Chateau, D., & Veugelers, P. J. (2004). Socioeconomic determinants of mortality in two Canadian provinces: multilevel modelling and neighborhood context. *Social Science & Medicine*, 59(7), 1435–47.

Rosenberg, T. (2004, April 11). What the world needs now is DDT. *New York Times*. Retrieved 30–12–06, from http://query.nytimes.com/gst/fullpage.html?res= 9F0DEEDA1738F932A25757C0A9629C8B63&sec=health&spon=&pagewanted= print.

Rosenfeld, A. H., Akbari, H., Romm, J. J., & Pomerantz, M. (1998). Cool communities: strategies for heat island mitigation and smog reduction. *Energy and Buildings*, 28(1), 51–62.

Rosenthal, E. (2005, September 13). Global warming: adapting to a new reality. *International Herald Tribune*. Retrieved 12–11–06, from http://www.iht.com/ articles/2005/09/11/news/climate.php.

Rosenzweig, C., & Parry, M. L. (1994). Potential impact of climate-change on world food-supply. *Nature*, 367(6459), 133–8.

Rosenzweig, C., Solecki, W., Parshall, L., Gaffin, S., Lynn, B., Goldberg, R., et al. (2006, January 31). *Mitigating New York City's Heat Island with Urban Forestry, Living Roofs, and Light Surfaces*. Paper presented at the Sixth Symposium on the Urban Environment; AMS Forum: Managing our Physical and Natural Resources: Successes and Challenges. Retrieved 17–11–06, from http://ams.confex.com/ams/Annual2006/techprogram/paper_103341.htm.

Rosing-Asvid, A. (2006). The influence of climate variability on polar bear (*Ursus maritimus*) and ringed seal (*Pusa hispida*) population dynamics. *Canadian Journal of Zoology*, 84, 357–64. http://article.pubs.nrc-cnrc.gc.ca/ppv/ RPViewDoc?_handler_=HandleInitialGet&journal=cjz&volume=84&calyLang =eng&articleFile=z06–001.pdf.

Rothman, D. H. (2002). Atmospheric carbon dioxide levels for the last 500 million years. *Proceedings of the National Academy of Sciences of the United States of America*, 99(7), 4167–71.

Roy Morgan (2006, November 2). Protecting the environment more important than the war on terror. *Roy Morgan International*. Retrieved 30-11-06, from http://www.roymorgan.com/news/polls/2006/4100/.

Ruhland, K., Phadtare, N. R., Pant, R. K., Sangode, S. J., & Smol, J. P. (2006). Accelerated melting of Himalayan snow and ice triggers pronounced changes in a valley peatland from northern India. *Geophysical Research Letters*, 33(15).

Runci, P. (2000). *Energy R&D in the United Kingdom*. Pacific Northwest National Laboratory. Retrieved 19-1-07, from http://energytrends.pnl.gov/uk/documents/uk.pdf.

Runci, P. (2005). Energy R&D investment patterns in IEA countries: an update. *Pacific Northwest National Laboratory/Joint Global Change Research Institute Technical Paper PNWD-3581*. Retrieved 19–1–07, from http://www.glob-alchange.umd.edu/?energytrends&page=iea.

Russell, J. L., Dixon, K. W., Gnanadesikan, A., Toggweiler, J. R., & Stouffer, R. J. (2006). The once and future battles between Thor and the Midgard Serpent: the southern hemisphere Westerlies and the Antarctic circumpolar current. *Geochimica et Cosmochimica Acta*, 70(18, Supplement 1), A547. http://www.sciencedirect.com/science/article/B6V66-4KPNB29-Y9/2/3748aca8839-bca0fc5eeca951c6883bf.

Russell, J. M., & Johnson, T. C. (2005). A high-resolution geochemical record from Lake Edward, Uganda Congo and the timing and causes of tropical African drought during the late Holocene. *Quaternary Science Reviews*, 24(12–13), 1375–89.

Saaroni, H., Ben-Dor, E., Bitan, A., & Potchter, O. (2000). Spatial distribution and microscale characteristics of the urban heat island in Tel-Aviv, Israel. *Landscape and Urban Planning*, 48(1–2), 1–18.

Sallares, R. (2006). Role of environmental changes in the spread of malaria in Europe during the Holocene. *Quaternary International*, 150, 21–7.

Sanchez, P., Swaminathan, M. S., Dobie, P., & Yuksel, N. (2005). *Halving Hunger: It Can Be Done*: UN Millennium Project Task Force on Hunger. Retrieved 4–1–07, from http://www.unmillenniumproject.org/reports/tf_hunger.htm.

Sarewitz, D., & Pielke, R. A. (2000, July). Breaking the global-warming gridlock. *Atlantic Monthly*. Retrieved 29–1–07, from http://sciencepolicy.colorado.edu/admin/publication_files/resource-69-2000.18.pdf.

Sarewitz, D., & Pielke, R. A. (2005, January 17). Rising tide. *The New Republic*, 10.

Sarewitz, D., & Pielke, R. A. (2007). The steps not yet taken. In D. L. Kleinman, K. Cloud-Hansen, C. Matta & J. Handelsman (eds.), *Controversies in Science and*

Technology, vol. II. Retrieved 17–1–07, from http://sciencepolicy.colorado.edu/ prometheus/archives/climate_change/001048the_steps_not_yet_ta.html.

Schäfer, A. (2006). Long-term trends in global passenger mobility. *Bridge*, 36(4), 24–32. Retrieved 30–1–07, from http://www.nae.edu/nae/bridgecom.nsf/ weblinks/MKEZ-6WHS2U?OpenDocument.

Schapira, A. (2006). DDT: a polluted debate in malaria control. *Lancet*, 368(9553), 2111–13.

Schar, C., & Jendritzky, G. (2004). Climate change hot news from summer 2003. *Nature*, 432(7017), 559–60. http://dx.doi.org/10.1038/432559a.

Schell, J. (1989, October). *Discover*, 45–8.

Schellnhuber, H. J., Cramer, W., Nakicenovic, N., Wigley, T., & Yohe, G. (eds.) (2006). *Avoiding Dangerous Climate Change*. Cambridge: Cambridge University Press. Retrieved 26–12–06, from http://www.defra.gov.uk/environment/climatechange/ internat/dangerous-cc.htm.

Schiermeier, Q. (2006). A sea change. *Nature*, 439(7074), 256–60.

Schipper, L. J., Haas, R., & Sheinbaum, C. (1996). Recent trends in residential energy use in OECD countries and their impact on carbon dioxide emissions: a comparative analysis of the period 1973–1992. *Mitigation and Adaptation Strategies for Global Change*, 1(2), 167–96.

Schlesinger, M. E., Yin, J., Yohe, G., Andronova, N. G., Malyshev, S., & Li, B. (2006). Assessing the risk of a collapse of the Atlantic thermohaline circulation. In H. J. Schellnhuber, W. Cramer, N. Nakicenovic, T. Wigley & G. Yohe (eds.), *Avoiding Dangerous Climate Change* (pp. 37–48). Cambridge: Cambridge University Press. http://www.defra.gov.uk/environment/climatechange/internat/ dangerous-cc.htm.

Schliebe, S., Wiig, Ø., Derocher, A., & Lunn, N. (2006). Ursus maritimus. In IUCN (ed.), *2006 IUCN Red List of Threatened Species*. Retrieved 7–11–06, from http://www.iucnredlist.org/search/details.php/22823/all.

Schmid, R. E. (2005, September 15). Experts say global warming is causing stronger hurricanes. *USA Today*. Retrieved 18–12–06, from http://www.usatoday.com/ weather/climate/2005–09–15-globalwarming-hurricanes_x.htm.

Schmidt, G. A. (1999). Forward modeling of carbonate proxy data from planktonic foraminifera using oxygen isotope tracers in a global ocean model. *Paleoceanography*, 14(4), 482–97. http://pubs.giss.nasa.gov/docs/1999/ 1999_Schmidt2.pdf.

Schneeberger, C., Blatter, H., Abe-Ouchi, A., & Wild, M. (2003). Modelling changes in the mass balance of glaciers of the northern hemisphere for a transient $2 \times CO_2$ scenario. *Journal of Hydrology*, 282(1–4), 145–63.

Schneider, D. P., Steig, E. J., van Ommen, T. D., Dixon, D. A., Mayewski, P. A., Jones, J. M., et al. (2006). Antarctic temperatures over the past two centuries from ice cores. *Geophysical Research Letters*, 33(16).

Schwartz, P., & Randall, D. (2003, October). An abrupt climate change scenario and Its Implications for United States National Security. *Commissioned by the Pentagon*. Retrieved 25-12-06, from http://www.grist.org/pdf/AbruptClimate Change2003.pdf.

Schwoon, M., & Tol, R. S. J. (2006). Optimal CO2-abatement with socio-economic inertia and induced technological change. *Energy Journal*, 27(4), 25–59.

Seager, R. (2006). The source of Europe's mild climate. *American Scientist*, 94(4), 334–41.

Seager, R., Battisti, D. S., Yin, J., Gordon, N., Naik, N., Clement, A. C., et al. (2002). Is the Gulf Stream responsible for Europe's mild winters? *Quarterly Journal of the Royal Meteorological Society*, 128(586), 2563–86. Retrieved 25-12-06, from http://www.atmos.washington.edu/~david/Gulf.pdf.

SEHN (2007). Precautionary Principle: FAQs. *Science & Environmental Health Network*. Retrieved 30-1-07, from http://www.sehn.org/ppfaqs.html.

Serageldin, I. (1995). Toward sustainable management of water resources. *World Bank, Directions in Development 14,910*.

Shanks, G. D. (2006). Treatment of falciparum malaria in the age of drug-resistance. *Journal of Postgraduate Medicine*, 52(4), 277–80.

Shanks, G. D., Hay, S. I., Omumbo, J. A., & Snow, R. W. (2005). Malaria in Kenya's Western Highlands. *Emerging Infectious Diseases*, 11(9), 1425–32. http://www.cdc.gov/ncidod/EID/vol11no09/04–1131.htm.

Shanks, G. D., Hay, S. I., Stern, D. I., Biomndo, K., & Snow, R. W. (2002). Meteorologic influences on *Plasmodium falciparum* malaria in the highland tea estates of Kericho, western Kenya. *Emerging Infectious Diseases*, 8(12), 1404–8.

Shaviv, N. J., & Veizer, J. (2003). Celestial driver of Phanerozoic climate? *GSA Today*, 13(7), 4–10. http://dx.doi.org/10.1130%2F1052-5173%282003% 29013%3C0004%3ACDOPC%3E2.0.CO%3B2.

Shepherd, A., & Wingham, D. (2007). Recent sea-level contributions of the Antarctic and Greenland ice sheets. *Science*, 315(5818), 1529–32. http://www.sciencemag.org/ cgi/content/abstract/315/5818/1529.

Shields, G., & Veizer, J. (2002). Precambrian marine carbonate isotope database: Version 1.1. *Geochemistry Geophysics Geosystems*, 3.

Shiklomanov, I. A. (2000). Appraisal and assessment of world water resources. *Water International*, 25(1), 11–32.

Shute, N., Hayden, T., Petit, C. W., Sobel, R. K., Whitelaw, K., & Whitman, D. (2001, February 5). The weather turns wild. *U.S. News & World Report*, 44–50.

Siddall, M., Rohling, E. J., Almogi-Labin, A., Hemleben, C., Meischner, D., Schmelzer, I., et al. (2003). Sea-level fluctuations during the last glacial cycle. *Nature*, 423(6942), 853–8.

Siegenthaler, U. (2005). EPICA Dome C CO2 Data 650 to 390 KYrBP. *IGBP PAGES/World*

Data Center for Paleoclimatology. Data Contribution Series # 2005–77. Retrieved 3–12–06, from ftp://ftp.ncdc.noaa.gov/pub/data/paleo/icecore/antarctica/epica_domec/edc-co2–650k–390k.txt.

Siegenthaler, U., Stocker, T. F., Monnin, E., Luthi, D., Schwander, J., Stauffer, B., et al. (2005). Stable carbon cycle–climate relationship during the late Pleistocene. *Science*, 310(5752), 1313–17.

Sierra Club (2007). Smart energy solutions. *Sierra Club Website*. Retrieved 29–1–07, from http://www.sierraclub.org/energy/.

Simms, A., Magrath, J., & Reid, H. (2004). *Up In Smoke*. London: New Economics Foundation, with Working Group on Climate Change. Retrieved 3–1–07, from http://www.neweconomics.org/gen/uploads/igeebque0l3nvy455whn42vs191020 04202736.pdf.

Simon, J. L. (1995a). *The State of Humanity*. Oxford: Blackwell.

Simon, J. L. (1995b). Why do we hear prophecies of doom from every side. *Futurist*, 29(1), 19–23.

Simon, J. L. (1996). *The Ultimate Resource 2*. Princeton, NJ: Princeton University Press.

Simonovic, S. P. (2002). World water dynamics: global modeling of water resources. *Journal of Environmental Management*, 66(3), 249–67.

Singer, E., & Endreny, P. (1993). *Reporting on Risk: How the Mass Media Portray Accidents, Diseases, Disasters, and Other Hazards*. New York: Russel Sage Foundation.

Singh, P., Arora, M., & Goel, N. K. (2006). Effect of climate change on runoff of a glacierized Himalayan basin. *Hydrological Processes*, 20(9), 1979–92.

Singh, P., & Bengtsson, L. (2004). Hydrological sensitivity of a large Himalayan basin to climate change. *Hydrological Processes*, 18(13), 2363–85.

Singh, P., & Bengtsson, L. (2005). Impact of warmer climate on melt and evaporation for the rainfed, snowfed and glacierfed basins in the Himalayan region. *Journal of Hydrology*, 300(1–4), 140–54.

Sirajul, I., Taikan, O., Shinjiro, K., Naota, H., Yasushi, A., & Kei, Y. (2007). A grid-based assessment of global water scarcity including virtual water trading. *Water Resources Management*, V21(1), 19–33. http://dx.doi.org/10.1007/s11269–006–9038-y.

Small, D., Islam, S., & Vogel, R. M. (2006). Trends in precipitation and streamflow in the eastern US: paradox or perception? *Geophysical Research Letters*, 33(3).

Smith, D. (2005, December 1). Scientists forecast global cold snap. *Sydney Morning Herald*. Retrieved 27–12–06, from http://www.smh.com.au/news/science/ scientists-forecast-global-cold-snap/2005/12/01/1133311132663.html.

Smith, E. (2006, December 21). Climate tax on imports to split commissioners. *European Voice*. Retrieved 21–12–06, from http://www.europeanvoice.com/ current/article.asp?id=26995.

Smith, K. R. (2000). National burden of disease in India from indoor air pollution. *Proceedings of the National Academy of Sciences of the United States of America*, 97(24), 13,286–93.

Smith, T. W. (1979). Happiness: time trends, seasonal variantions, intersurvey differences and other mysteries. *Social Psychology Quarterly*, 42(1), 18–30.

Snow, R. W., Guerra, C. A., Noor, A. M., Myint, H. Y., & Hay, S. I. (2005). The global distribution of clinical episodes of *Plasmodium falciparum* malaria. *Nature*, 434(7030), 214–17.

Snow, R., Ikoku, A., Omumbo, J., & Ouma, J. (1999). *The Epidemiology, Politics and Control of Malaria Epidemics in Kenya: 1900–1998*. Report prepared for Roll Back Malaria, Resource Network on Epidemics, World Health Organisation. Retrieved 28–12–06, from http://www.who.int/malaria/docs/ek_report_toc1.htm#toc.

Snow, R. W., & Omumbo, J. A. (2006). Malaria. In D. T. Jamison, R. G. Feachem, M. W. Makgoba, E. R. Bos, F. K. Baingana, K. J. Hofman & K. O. Rogo (eds.), *Disease and Mortality in Sub-Saharan Africa* (pp. 195–213). World Bank.

Soini, E. (2005). Land use change patterns and livelihood dynamics on the slopes of Mt. Kilimanjaro, Tanzania. *Agricultural Systems*, 85(3), 306–23.

Sokolova, M. I., & Snow, K. R. (2002). Malaria vectors in European Russia. *European Mosquito Bulletin*, 12, 1–5.

Sorokhtin, O. G., Chilingar, G. V., Khilyuk, L., & Gorfunkel, M. V. (2007). Evolution of the Earth's global climate. *Energy Sources Part A–Recovery Utilization and Environmental Effects*, 29(1), 1–19.

Spiegel (2005, August 30). Katrina should be a lesson to US on global warming. *Spiegel*. Retrieved 18–12–06, from http://www.spiegel.de/international/0,1518,372179,00.html.

Stern, N. (2006). *Stern Review on the Economics of Climate Change*. HM Treasury, UK. Retrieved 24–11–06, from http://www.hm-treasury.gov.uk/independent_reviews/stern_review_economics_climate_change/stern_review_report.cfm.

Stipp, D. (2004, February 9). The Pentagon's weather nightmare. The climate could change radically, and fast. That would be the mother of all national security issues. *Fortune*. Retrieved 25–12–06, from http://money.cnn.com/magazines/fortune/fortune_archive/2004/02/09/360120/index.htm.

Stirling, I., Lunn, N. J., & Iacozza, J. (1999). Long-term trends in the population ecology of polar bears in western Hudson Bay in relation to climatic change. *Arctic*, 52(3), 294–306.

Stommel, H. (1961). Thermohaline convection with 2 stable regimes of flow. *Tellus*, 13(2), 224–30.

Stouffer, R. J., Yin, J., Gregory, J. M., Dixon, K. W., Spelman, M. J., Hurlin, W., et al. (2006). Investigating the causes of the response of the thermohaline circulation to past and future climate changes. *Journal of Climate*, 19(8), 1365–87.

Streutker, D. R. (2003). Satellite-measured growth of the urban heat island of Houston, Texas. *Remote Sensing of Environment*, 85(3), 282–9.

Svensson, C., Kundzewicz, Z. W., & Maurer, T. (2005). Trend detection in river flow series: 2. Flood and low-flow index series. *Hydro-logical Sciences Journal–Journal des Sciences Hydrologiques*, 50(5), 811–24.

Swellengrebel, N. H. (1950). The malaria epidemic of 1943–1946 in the Province of North-Holland. *Transactions of the Royal Society of Tropical Medicine and Hygiene*, 43(5), 445–61.

Swiss Re (1999). Natural catastrophes and man-made disasters 1998: storms, hail and ice cause billion-dollar losses. *Swiss Reinsurance Company*.

Sydney Morning Herald (2006, November 1). A clarion call: last stop before chaos. *Sydney Morning Herald*. Retrieved 10-1-07, from http://www.smh.com.au/news/environment/a-clarion-call-last-stop-before-chaos/2006/10/31/116227 8141640.html#.

Synnefa, A., Santamouris, M., & Livada, I. (2006). A study of the thermal performance of reflective coatings for the urban environment. *Solar Energy*, 80(8), 968–81.

Taylor, M. (2006, May 1). Silly to predict their demise: starling conclusion to say they will disappear within 25 years and surprise to many researchers. *Toronto Star*. Retrieved 7-11-06, from http://www.thestar.com/NASApp/cs/ContentServer?pagename=thestar/Layout/Article_PrintFriendly&c=Article&cid=1146433819696&call_pageid=970599119419.

Tengs, T. O. (1997). Dying too soon: how cost-effectiveness analysis can save lives. *NCPA Policy Report 204*. Retrieved 22-1-07, from http://www.ncpa.org/~ncpa/studies/s204/s204.html.

Tengs, T. O., Adams, M. E., Pliskin, J. S., Safran, D. G., Siegel, J. E., Weinstein, M. C., et al. (1995). 500 lifesaving interventions and their cost-effectiveness. *Risk Analysis*, 15(3), 369–90.

Tengs, T. O., & Graham, J. D. (1996). The opportunity costs of haphazard social investments in life-saving. In R. W. Hahn (ed.), *Risks, Costs, and Lives Saved: Getting Better Results from Regulation* (pp. 167–82). New York, NY: Oxford University Press.

Tereshchenko, I. E., & Filonov, A. E. (2001). Air temperature fluctuations in Guadalajara, Mexico, from 1926 to 1994 in relation to urban growth. *International Journal of Climatology*, 21(4), 483–94.

theclimategroup (2006). Dupont – corporate, science and technology. Retrieved 20-11-06, from http://www.theclimategroup.org/index.php?pid=421.

Thijssen, J. (2001). Mount Kilimanjaro expedition. *Greenpeace*. Retrieved 07-12-06, from http://archive.greenpeace.org/climate/climatecountdown/kilimanjaro.htm.

Thompson, K. (1969). Irrigation as a menace to health in California: a nineteenth century view. *Geographical Review*, 59(2), 195–214.

Thorndycraft, V. R., Barriendos, M., Benito, G., Rico, M., & Casas, A. (2006). The catastrophic floods of AD 1617 in Catalonia (northeast Spain) and their climatic context. *Hydrological Sciences Journal–Journal des Sciences Hydrologiques*, 51(5), 899–912.

Thorsen, M., & Møller, H.-G. (1995). *TV-journalistik* [TV journalism]. Copenhagen: Ajour.

Time magazine (2006). Be worried. Be very worried. *Time magazine*. Retrieved 6–11–06, from http://www.time.com/time/covers/0,16641,20060403,00.html.

Timmons, H. (2006, October 30). U.K. fears disaster in climate change. *International Herald Tribune*. Retrieved 24–1–07, from http://www.iht.com/bin/print.php ?id=3334967.

Tindale, S. (2005). Two-thirds of energy wasted by antiquated system. *Greenpeace*. Retrieved 1–1–07, from http://www.greenpeace.org.uk/climate/climate.cfm? UCIDParam=20050719112356.

Toggweiler, J. R., Russell, J. L., & Carson, S. R. (2006). Midlatitude westerlies, atmospheric CO2, and climate change during the ice ages. *Paleoceanography*, 21(2).

Tol, R. S. J. (2002a). Estimates of the damage costs of climate change. Part I: benchmark estimates. *Environmental & Resource Economics*, 21(1), 47–73.

Tol, R. S. J. (2002b). Estimates of the damage costs of climate change. Part II: dynamic estimates. *Environmental & Resource Economics*, 21(2), 135–60.

Tol, R. S. J. (2002c). Welfare specifications and optimal control of climate change: an application of fund. *Energy Economics*, 24(4), 367–76.

Tol, R. S. J. (2004). The double trade-off between adaptation and mitigation for sea level rise: an application of FUND (Vol. FNU-48): Hamburg University and Centre for Marine and Atmospheric Science, Hamburg. Retrieved 17–12–06, from http://www.uni-hamburg.de/Wiss/FB/15/Sustainability/slradaptmitigatewp.pdf.

Tol, R. S. J. (2005). The marginal damage costs of carbon dioxide emissions: an assessment of the uncertainties. *Energy Policy*, 33(16), 2064–74.

Tol, R. S. J. (2006). The Stern Review of the economics of climate change: a comment. *Energy & Environment*, 17(6), 977–81.

Tol, R. S. J. (2007). Europe's long-term climate target: a critical evaluation. *Energy Policy*, 35(1), 424–32.

Tol, R. S. J., & Dowlatabadi, H. (2001). Vector-borne diseases, development & climate change. *Integrated Assessment*, 2, 173–81. Retrieved 2–1–07, from http://www.uni-hamburg.de/Wiss/FB/15/Sustainability/iavector.pdf.

Tol, R. S. J., Ebie, K. L., & Yohe, G. W. (forthcoming). Infectious disease, development, and climate change: a scenario analysis. *Environment and Development Economics*.

Tol, R. S. J., & Yohe, G. W. (2006). A review of the Stern Review. *World Economics*, 7(4), 233–50.

Toubkiss, J. (2006). *Costing MDG Target 10 on Water Supply and Sanitation: Comparative Analysis, Obstacles and Recommendations*. World Water Council. Retrieved 8-1-07, from http://www.worldwatercouncil.org/index.php?id=32.

Townsend, M., & Harris, P. (2004, February 22). Now the Pentagon tells Bush: climate change will destroy us. *Observer*. Retrieved 25-12-06, from http://observer.guardian.co.uk/international/story/0,6903,1153513,00.html.

Travis, J. (2005). Hurricane Katrina – scientists' fears come true as hurricane floods New Orleans. *Science*, 309(5741), 1656ff.

Trefil, J. (1996, December). Phenomena, comment and notes. *Smithsonian*, 30–1.

Trigo, R. M., Garcia-Herrera, R., Diaz, J., Trigo, I. F., & Valente, M. A. (2005). How exceptional was the early August 2003 heatwave in France? *Geophysical Research Letters*, 32(10).

Trittin, J. (2005, August 29). Ein "Kyoto zwei" wird dringend gebraucht. *Frankfurter Rundschau*.

Tsur, Y., Dinar, A., Doukkali, R. M., & Roe, T. (2004). Irrigation water pricing: policy implications based on international comparison. *Environment and Development Economics*, 9, 735–55.

Tubiello, F. N., Amthor, J. S., Boote, K. J., Donatelli, M., Easterling, W., Fischer, G., et al. (in press). Crop response to elevated CO_2 and world food supply: a comment on "Food for thought . . ." by Long et al., *Science* 312: 1918–21, 2006. *European Journal of Agronomy*, in press, corrected proof. http://www.sciencedirect.com/science/article/B6T67-4MCWMJH-1/2/e1fc61a53098dfcb291f81a500fd5654.

Turner, J., Colwell, S. R., Marshall, G. J., Lachlan-Cope, T. A., Carleton, A. M., Jones, P. D., et al. (2005). Antarctic climate change during the last 50 years. *International Journal of Climatology*, 25(3), 279–94.

Turner, J., Lachlan-Cope, T., Colwell, S., & Marshall, G. J. (2005). A positive trend in western Antarctic Peninsula precipitation over the last 50 years reflecting regional and Antarctic-wide atmospheric circulation changes. In *Annals of Glaciology*, 41: 85–91.

UKNS (2004). *UK 2005 The Official Yearbook of the United Kingdom of Great Britain and Northern Ireland*. Office for National Statistics. Retrieved 30-1-07, from http://www.statistics.gov.uk/downloads/theme_compendia/UK2005/UK2005.pdf.

UN Millennium Project (2005). *Investing in Development: A Practical Plan to Achieve the Millennium Development Goals*. New York: United Nations Development Programme. Retrieved 4-1-07, from http://www.unmillenniumproject.org/reports/fullreport.htm.

UNCED (1992). Rio Declaration on Environment and Development. *United Nations*

Conference on Environment and Development. Retrieved 30–1–07, from http://www.unep.org/Documents.multilingual/Default.asp?DocumentID=78&A rticleID=1163.

UNDESA (2006). *The Millennium Development Goals Report 2006.* New York: United Nations Department of Economic and Social Affairs. Retrieved 3–1–07, from http://mdgs.un.org/unsd/mdg/Resources/Static/Products/Progress2006/MDG Report2006.pdf.

UNDP (1998). *Human Development Report 1999.* New York: United Nations Development Program.

UNECE (1996). *Long-Term Historical Changes in the Forest Resource.* United Nations Economic Commision for Europe & FAO, Timber Section, Geneva.

UNEP (2000). *Global Environment Outlook 2000.* London: Earthscan Publications.

UNEP (2006, November). Adaptation and vulnerability to climate change: the role of the finance sector. *UNEP FI Climate Change Working Group.* Retrieved 19–12–06, from http://www.unepfi.org/fileadmin/documents/CEO_briefing_ adaptation_vulnerability_2006.pdf.

UNESCO (2006). *Water – A Shared Responsibility: The United Nations World Water Development Report 2.* New York: Berghahn Books. Retrieved 7–1–07, from http://www.unesco.org/water/wwap/wwdr2/table_contents.shtml.

UNFCCC (1992). *United Nations Framework Convention on Climate Change* United Nations Framework Convention on Climate Change. Retrieved 28–1–07, from http://unfccc.int/resource/docs/convkp/conveng.pdf.

UNFCCC (1997). *The* Kyoto Protocol: United Nations Framework Convention on Climate Change. Retrieved 18–11–06, from http://unfccc.int/kyoto_protocol/ items/2830.php.

UNFCCC (2006). *National Greenhouse Gas Inventory Data for the Period 1990–2004 and Status of Reporting.* United Nations Framework Convention on Climate Change. Retrieved 18–11–06, from http://unfccc.int/resource/ docs/2006/sbi/eng/26.pdf.

UNICEF (2006). *The State of the World's Children 2007.* The United Nations Children's Fund. Retrieved 30–12–06, from http://www.unicef.org/sowc07/.

UNPD (2006a). *World Population Prospects: The 2004 Revision: Volume III: Analytical Report.* United Nations Population Division. Retrieved 19–12–06, from http://www.un.org/esa/population/publications/WPP2004/WPP2004_ Volume3.htm.

UNPD (2006b). *World Urbanization Prospects: The 2005 Revision.* United Nations Population Division. Retrieved 15–11–06, from http://www.un.org/esa/population/ publications/WUP2005/2005wup.htm.

USCB (1999). Statistical Abstract of the United States 1999. *US Bureau Census.* Retrieved 09–12–06, from http://www.census.gov/prod/www/statistical-abstract-1995_2000.html.

USCB (2006a). Statistical Abstract of the United States: 2007. *US Census Bureau*. Retrieved 30–1–07, from http://www.census.gov/prod/www/statistical- abstract.html.

USCB (2006b). Table. 464. Federal Budget Receipts by Source: 1990 to 2006. *US Census Bureau*. Retrieved 23–12–06, from http://www.census.gov/compendia/statab/tables/07s0464.xls.

USCB (2006c). US Historical Population 1780–2000. *US Census Bureau*. Retrieved 23–12–06, from http://www.census.gov/compendia/statab/tables/07s0001.xls.

USCB (2006d). US Population 1950–2005. *US Census Bureau*. Retrieved 23–12–06, from http://www.census.gov/compendia/statab/tables/07s0002.xls.

USCB (2007). Total Midyear Population for the World: 1950–2050. *US Census Bureau*. Retrieved 02–01–07, from http://www.census.gov/ipc/www/worldpop.html.

USCPI (2007). *US Consumer Price Index*. US Department of Labor. ftp://ftp.bls.gov/pub/special.requests/cpi/cpiai.txt.

USGS (2005). Streamflow trends in the United States. *US Geological Service Fact Sheet 2005–3017*. Retrieved 22–12–06, from http://pubs.usgs.gov/fs/2005/3017/.

Utzinger, J., & Keiser, J. (2006). Urbanization and tropical health – then and now. *Annals of Tropical Medicine and Parasitology*, 100(5–6), 517–33.

van der Schrier, G., Briffa, K. R., Jones, P. D., & Osborn, T. J. (2006). Summer moisture variability across Europe. *Journal of Climate*, 19(12), 2818–34.

van Doorslaer, E., Masseria, C., & Koolman, X. (2006). Inequalities in access to medical care by income in developed countries. *Canadian Medical Association Journal*, 174(2), 177–83.

van Kooten, G. C. (2003). Smoke and mirrors: the Kyoto Protocol and beyond. *Canadian Public Policy–Analyse de Politiques*, 29(4), 397–415.

van Lieshout, M., Kovats, R. S., Livermore, M. T. J., & Martens, P. (2004). Climate change and malaria: analysis of the SRES climate and socio-economic scenarios. *Global Environmental Change*, 14(1), 87–99. http://www.sciencedirect.com/science/article/B6VFV–4BM8RY3-5/2/f3f622baa4c01ddf34dd10bd6dbbd9c9.

Vandentorren, S., Suzan, F., Medina, S., Pascal, M., Maulpoix, A., Cohen, J. C., et al. (2004). Mortality in 13 French cities during the August 2003 heat wave. *American Journal of Public Health*, 94(9), 1518–20.

Varian, H. (2006, December 14). Recalculating the costs of global climate change. *New York Times*.

Vaughan, D. G., Marshall, G. J., Connolley, W. M., King, J. C., & Mulvaney, R. (2001). Climate change – devil in the detail. *Science*, 293(5536), 1777–9.

Vaughan, D. G., Marshall, G. J., Connolley, W. M., Parkinson, C., Mulvaney, R., Hodgson, D. A., et al. (2003). Recent rapid regional climate warming on the Antarctic Peninsula. *Climatic Change*, 60(3), 243–74.

Vavrus, F. (2002). Making distinctions: privatisation and the (un)educated girl on Mount Kilimanjaro, Tanzania. *International Journal of Educational Development*, 22(5), 527–47.

Vavrus, S., Walsh, J. E., Chapman, W. L., & Portis, D. (2006). The behavior of extreme cold air outbreaks under greenhouse warming. *International Journal of Climatology*, 26(9), 1133–47.

Veizer, J., Ala, D., Azmy, K., Bruckschen, P., Buhl, D., Bruhn, F., et al. (1999). Sr-87/Sr-86, delta C-13 and delta O-18 evolution of Phanerozoic seawater. *Chemical Geology*, 161(1–3), 59–88.

Veizer, J., Godderis, Y., & François, L. M. (2000). Evidence for decoupling of atmospheric CO2 and global climate during the Phanerozoic eon. *Nature*, 408(6813), 698–701.

Velicogna, I., & Wahr, J. (2006). Acceleration of Greenland ice mass loss in spring 2004. *Nature*, 443(7109), 329–31.

Verbout, S. M., Brooks, H. E., Leslie, L. M., & Schultz, D. M. (2006). Evolution of the US tornado database: 1954–2003. *Weather and Forecasting*, 21(1), 86–93.

Vergano, D. (2006, August 3). High heat: the wave of the future? *USA Today*.

Viguier, L. L., Babiker, M. H., & Reilly, J. M. (2003). The costs of the Kyoto Protocol in the European Union. *Energy Policy*, 31(5), 459–81.

Vinther, B. M., Andersen, K. K., Jones, P. D., Briffa, K. R., & Cappelen, J. (2006a). Data for: extending Greenland temperature records into the late eighteenth century. Retrieved 13–12–06, from http://www.cru.uea.ac.uk/cru/data/greenland/.

Vinther, B. M., Andersen, K. K., Jones, P. D., Briffa, K. R., & Cappelen, J. (2006b). Extending Greenland temperature records into the late eighteenth century. *Journal of Geophysical Research–Atmospheres*, 111(D11).

Visbeck, M. (2006, October 30). The Atlantic's current changes are no cause for alarm. *Guardian*. Retrieved 27–12–06, from http://environment.guardian.co.uk/climatechange/story/0,,1934904,00.html.

von Storch, H., & Stehr, N. (2006). Anthropogenic climate change: a reason for concern since the 18th century and earlier. *Geografiska Annaler Series A–Physical Geography*, 88A(2), 107–13.

von Storch, H., Stehr, N., & Ungar, S. (2004). Sustainability and the issue of climate change. Retrieved 26–1–07, from http://w3g.gkss.de/staff/storch/Media/climate.culture.041130.pdf.

von Storch, H., & Zorita, E. (2005). Comment on "Hockey sticks, principal components, and spurious significance" by S. McIntyre and R. McKitrick. *Geophysical Research Letters*, 32(20).

von Storch, H., Zorita, E., Jones, J. M., Dimitriev, Y., Gonzalez-Rouco, F., & Tett, S.

F. B. (2004). Reconstructing past climate from noisy data. *Science*, 306(5296), 679–82.

Walker, K. (2000). Cost-comparison of DDT and alternative insecticides for malaria control. *Medical and Veterinary Entomology*, 14(4), 345–54.

Wallensteen, P., & Swain, A. (1997). International freshwater resources: sources of conflicts or cooperation. *Background Document for CSD 1997*. Stockholm: Stockholm Environment Institute.

Wallis, D. (2006, November 14). Disasters losses may top $1 trillion/yr by 2040–UN. *Reuters*. Retrieved 19–12–06, from http://today.reuters.com/News/CrisesArticle. aspx?storyId=WAL445754.

Wallmann, K. (2004). Impact of atmospheric CO_2 and galactic cosmic radiation on Phanerozoic climate change and the marine delta O-18 record. *Geochemistry Geophysics Geosystems*, 5.

Wallström, M. (2001, July 2). European Climate Change Program: a successful approach to combating climate change. *ECCP Conference*. Retrieved 6–11–06, from http://europa.eu.int/rapid/pressReleasesAction.do?reference=SPEECH/01/ 322&format=HTML&aged=0&language=EN&guiLanguage=en.

Waltham, T. (2002). Sinking cities. *Geology Today*, 18(3), 95–100. http://www.blackwell-synergy.com/doi/abs/10.1046/j.1365–2451.2002.00341.x.

Wang, G. L. (2005). Agricultural drought in a future climate: results from 15 global climate models participating in the IPCC 4th assessment. *Climate Dynamics*, 25(7–8), 739–53.

Watson, M. (1939). Malaria and mosquitoes: forty years on. *Journal of the Society of Arts*, 87(4505), 482–500.

WCRF (1997). *Food, Nutrition and the Prevention of Cancer: A Global Perspective*. Washington, DC: World Cancer Research Fund & American Institute for Cancer Research.

WDI (2007). World development indicators online. *Worldbank*. http://ddp-ext. worldbank.org.esc-proxy.lib.cbs.dk/ext/DDPQQ/member.do?method=getMembers &userid=1&queryId=6.

Webster, P. J., Curry, J. A., Liu, J., & Holland, G. J. (2006). Response to comment on "Changes in tropical cyclone number, duration, and intensity in a warming environment." *Science*, 311(5768).

Webster, P. J., Holland, G. J., Curry, J. A., & Chang, H. R. (2005). Changes in tropical cyclone number, duration, and intensity in a warming environment. *Science*, 309(5742), 1844–6.

Wegman, E. J., Scott, D. W., & Said, Y. H. (2006). Ad hoc committee report on the "hockey stick" global climate reconstruction. *Committee on Energy and Commerce*. Retrieved 26–12–06, from energycommerce.house.gov/108/home/ 07142006_Wegman_Report.pdf.

Weinberger, M., Oddone, E. Z., & Henderson, W. G. (1996). Does increased access to primary care reduce hospital readmissions? *New England Journal of Medicine*, 334(22), 1441–7.

Weisheimer, A., & Palmer, T. N. (2005). Changing frequency of occurrence of extreme seasonal temperatures under global warming. *Geophysical Research Letters*, 32(20).

Weiss, D., Shotyk, W., & Kempf, O. (1999). Archives of atmospheric lead pollution. *Naturwissenschaften*, 86(6), 262–75.

Weiss, R. A., & McMichael, A. J. (2004). Social and environmental risk factors in the emergence of infectious diseases. *Nature Medicine*, 10(12), S70–S76.

Weiss, T. (2006, November 28). The $3 billion man. *Forbes*. Retrieved 1-12-06, from http://www.forbes.com/2006/11/26/leadership-branson-virgin-lead-citizen-cx_tw_1128branson_print.html.

Wennberg, J. E., Fisher, E. S., Stukel, T. A., Skinner, J. S., Sharp, S. M., & Bronner, K. K. (2004). Use of hospitals, physician visits, and hospice care during last six months of life among cohorts loyal to highly respected hospitals in the United States. *British Medical Journal*, 328(7440), 607–10A.

Westman, J., Hasselstrom, J., Johansson, S. E., & Sundquist, J. (2003). The influences of place of birth and socioeconomic factors on attempted suicide in a defined population of 4.5 million people. *Archives of General Psychiatry*, 60(4), 409–14.

Weyant, J. P. (1996). The IPCC energy assessment – commentary. *Energy Policy*, 24(10–11), 1005–8.

Weyant, J. P., & Hill, J. N. (1999). Introduction and overview. the costs of the Kyoto Protocol: a multi-model evaluation. *Energy Journal, Kyoto Special Issue*, vii–xliv.

WFS (1996). *World Food Summit: Technical Background Documents, vols. I–XV*. UN Food and Agricultural Organization. Retrieved 3-1-07, from http://www.fao.org/wfs/index_en.htm.

White, N. J., Church, J. A., & Gregory, J. M. (2005). Coastal and global averaged sea level rise for 1950 to 2000. *Geophysical Research Letters*, 32(1).

WHO (1986). *The International Drinking Water Supply and Sanitation Decade: Review of Regional and Global Data (as at 31 December 1983)*. World Health Organization.

WHO (2002). *The World Health Report 2002 – Reducing Risk, Promoting Healthy Life*. World Health Organization. Retrieved 29-11-06, from http://www.who.int/whr/2002/en/index.html.

WHO (2004a). *The World Health Report 2004 – Changing History*. World Health Organization. Retrieved 13-11-06, from http://www.who.int/whr/2004/en/.

WHO (2004b). *World Report on Road Traffic Injury Prevention*. World Health

Organization. Retrieved 30–1–07, from http://www.who.int/world-health-day/2004/infomaterials/world_report/en/.

WHO & UNICEF (2003). The Africa Malaria Report 2003. *World Health Organization.* Retrieved 29–12–06, from http://www.rollbackmalaria.org/amd2003/amr2003/pdf/amr2003.pdf.

WHO & UNICEF (2005). World malaria report 2005. *World Health Organization.* Retrieved 29–12–06, from http://www.rollbackmalaria.org/wmr2005/.

WHO, WMO & UNEP (2003). *Climate Change and Human Health – Risks and Responses, Summary.* World Health Organization.

Wiersma, A. P., & Renssen, H. (2006). Model-data comparison for the 8.2 ka BP event: confirmation of a forcing mechanism by catastrophic drainage of Laurentide Lakes. *Quaternary Science Reviews*, 25(1–2), 63–88.

Wigley, T. M. L. (1998). The Kyoto Protocol: CO2, CH4 and climate implications. *Geophysical Research Letters*, 25(13), 2285–8.

Wilby, R. (2004). Urban heat island and air quality of London, UK. Retrieved 17–11–06, from http://www.asp.ucar.edu/colloquium/2004/CH/presentations/AirQualityTutorialBackground.pdf.

Wilby, R. L., & Perry, G. L. W. (2006). Climate change, biodiversity and the urban environment: a critical review based on London, UK. *Progress in Physical Geography*, 30(1), 73–98.

Wilkinson, B. H. (2005). Humans as geologic agents: a deep-time perspective. *Geology*, 33(3), 161–4.

Williams, E. R. (2005). Lightning and climate: a review. *Atmospheric Research*, 76(1–4), 272–87.

Wilson, G. J. (1983). *Distribution and abundance of Antarctic and Sub-Antarctic Penguins: A Synthesis of Current Knowledge.* Published by SCAR and SCOR, Scott Polar Research Institute, BIOMASS Scientific Series No. 4.

Winfrey, O. (2006, December). A green "truth." *The Oprah Winfrey Show.* Retrieved 26–1–07, from http://www2.oprah.com/tows/pastshows/200612/tows_past_20061205.jhtml.

Wingham, D., Shepherd, A., Muir, A., & Marshall, G. (2006). Mass balance of the Antarctic ice sheet. *Philosophical Transactions of the Royal Society A: Mathematical, Physical and Engineering Sciences*, 364(1844), 1627–35. http://dx.doi.org/10.1098/rsta.2006.1792.

Woehler, E. J., & Croxall, J. P. (1997). The status and trends of Antarctic and sub-Antarctic seabirds. *Marine Ornithology*, 25, 43–66.

WMO (2006, December 11). Press Release: Link between climate change and tropical cyclone activity: More research necessary. *World Meteorological Organization.* Retrieved 18–12–06, from http://www.wmo.int/web/Press/PR_766_E.doc.

WMO–IWTC (2006a). Statement on tropical cyclones and climate change. *6th International Workshop on Tropical Cyclones of the World Meteorological Organization*. Retrieved 18–12–06, from http://www.wmo.ch/web/arep/press_releases/2006/iwtc_statement.pdf.

WMO–IWTC (2006b). Summary statement on tropical cyclones and climate change. *6th International Workshop on Tropical Cyclones of the World Meteorological Organization*. Retrieved 18–12–06, from http://www.wmo.ch/web/arep/press_releases/2006/iwtc_summary.pdf.

Wood, R., Collins, M., Gregory, J., Harris, G., & Vellinga, M. (2006). Toward a risk assessment for shutdown of the atlantic thermohaline circulation. In H. J. Schellnhuber, W. Cramer, N. Nakicenovic, T. Wigley & G. Yohe (eds.), *Avoiding Dangerous Climate Change* (pp. 49–54). Cambridge: Cambridge University Press. http://www.defra.gov.uk/environment/climatechange/internat/dangerous-cc.htm.

Wood, R. A., Vellinga, M., & Thorpe, R. (2003). Global warming and thermohaline circulation stability. *Philosophical Transactions of the Royal Society of London Series A: Mathematical Physical and Engineering Sciences*, 361(1810), 1961–74.

Woodworth, P. L. (2006). Some important issues to do with long-term sea level change. *Philosophical Transactions of the Royal Society A: Mathematical Physical and Engineering Sciences*, 364(1841), 787–803.

Woodworth, P. L., & Player, R. (2003). The permanent service for mean sea level: an update to the 21st century. *Journal of Coastal Research*, 19(2), 287–95.

World Water Council (2000). *World Water Vision: Making Water Everybody's Business*. London: Earthscan Publications.

Worldbank (1994). *World Development Report 1994: Infrastructure for Development*. Oxford: Oxford University Press.

Worldbank (2000). *World Development Report 2000/2001: Attacking Poverty*. The Worldbank Group. Retrieved 10–1–07, from http://web.worldbank.org/WBSITE/EXTERNAL/TOPICS/EXTPOVERTY/0,,contentMDK:20194762~pagePK:148956~piPK:216618~theSitePK:336992,00.html.

Worldbank (2004). *Global Economic Outlook 2005*. The Worldbank Group. Retrieved 10–1–07, from http://web.worldbank.org/WBSITE/EXTERNAL/EXTDEC/EXTDECPROSPECTS/GEPEXT/EXTGEP2005/0,,menuPK:538187~pagePK:64167702~piPK:64167676~theSitePK:538170,00.html.

Worldbank (2005). *World Development Indicators*. World Bank. Retrieved 10–1–07, from http://devdata.worldbank.org/wdi2005/index2.htm.

Worldbank (2006). *World Development Report 2007*. The Worldbank Group.

Worldwatch Institute (1993). *State of the World 1993*. New York: W. W. Norton.

Worldwatch Institute (2006). *Vital Signs 2006–2007*. New York: W. W. Norton.

WRCC (2007). Temperature data for Tucson, University of Arizona, Arizona

028815. Western *Regional Climate Center*. Retrieved 13-2-07, from http://www.wrcc.dri.edu/cgi-bin/cliMONtmnt.pl?az8815.

WRI (1996). *The World Resources 1996–1997*. New York: Oxford University Press.

WRI (2005). *The World Resources 2005 – The Wealth of the Poor*. Retrieved 13-11-06, from http://www.wri.org/biodiv/pubs_description.cfm?pid=4073.

WRI (2006). DuPont's Hamm-Uentrop facility: an innovative approach to implementing CHP biomass. *World Resources Institute and The Climate Group*. Retrieved 20-11-06, from http://www.theclimategroup.org/assets/DuPont%20Hamm-Uentrop%20Case%20Study_GPMDG%20EU.pdf.

Wunsch, C. (2002). What is the thermohaline circulation? *Science*, 298(5596), 1179ff.

Wunsch, C. (2004). Gulf Stream safe if wind blows and Earth turns. *Nature*, 428(6983), 601.

Wunsch, C. (2005). Thermohaline loops, Stommel box models, and the Sandstrom theorem. *Tellus Series A: Dynamic Meteorology and Oceanography*, 57(1), 84–99.

Wunsch, C. (2006). A hot topic. *The Economist*. Retrieved 26-12-06, from http://www.economist.com/displaystory.cfm?story_id=7963571.

WWF (2006a, March 18). Canada's western Hudson Bay polar bear population in decline. Climate change to blame. Retrieved 7-11-06, from http://www.panda.org/about_wwf/where_we_work/arctic/polar_bear/pbt_news_pubs/index.cfm?uNewsID=63980.

WWF (2006b, May 4). Global warming news: global warming driving polar bears to extinction. Retrieved 7-11-06, from http://www.panda.org/about_wwf/what_we_do/climate_change/news/index.cfm?uNewsID=67980.

Xinhuanet (2002, September 2). German chancellor urges all states to ratify Kyoto Protocol. Retrieved 22-12-06, from http://news.xinhuanet.com/english/2002-09/02/content_547179.htm.

Yiou, P., Ribereau, P., Naveau, P., Nogaj, M., & Brazdil, R. (2006). Statistical analysis of floods in Bohemia (Czech Republic) since 1825. *Hydrological Sciences Journal–Journal des Sciences Hydrologiques*, 51(5), 930–45.

Yohe, G. (2006). Some thoughts on the damage estimates presented in the Stern Review – an editorial. *Integrated Assessment Journal*, 6(3), 65–72.

Yohe, G., & Neumann, J. (1997). Planning for sea level rise and shore protection under climate uncertainty. *Climatic Change*, 37(1), 243–70.

Young, J. R. (2003). The role of fear in agenda setting by television news. *American Behavioral Scientist*, 46(12), 1673–95.

Zachos, J., Pagani, M., Sloan, L., Thomas, E., & Billups, K. (2001a). Data for global climate 65 Ma to present. Retrieved 5-12-06, from http://www.es.ucsc.edu/~silab/ZACPUBDATA/2001CompilationData.txt.

Zachos, J., Pagani, M., Sloan, L., Thomas, E., & Billups, K. (2001b). Trends, rhythms, and aberrations in global climate 65 Ma to present. *Science*, 292(5517), 686–93.

Zhai, P., Sun, A., Ren, F., Liu, X., Gao, B., & Zhang, Q. (1999). Changes of climate extremes in China. *Climatic Change*, 42(1):203–18.

Zhang, Z. X. (2000). Can China afford to commit itself an emissions cap? An economic and political analysis. *Energy Economics*, 22(6), 587–614.

Zhao, H. X., & Moore, G. W. K. (2006). Reduction in Himalayan snow accumulation and weakening of the trade winds over the Pacific since the 1840s. *Geophysical Research Letters*, 33(17).

Zwally, H. J., Giovinetto, M. B., Li, J., Cornejo, H. G., Beckley, M. A., Brenner, A. C., et al. (2005). Mass changes of the Greenland and Antarctic ice sheets and shelves and contributions to sea-level rise: 1992–2002. *Journal of Glaciology*, 51(175), 509–27.

INDEX